Trudeau's Tango

Trudeau's Tango

Alberta Meets
Pierre Elliott Trudeau,
1968–1972

Gutteridge
BOOKS
An Imprint of The University of Alberta Press

DARRYL RAYMAKER

Published by

The University of Alberta Press
Ring House 2
Edmonton, Alberta, Canada T6G 2E1
www.uap.ualberta.ca

Copyright © 2017 Darryl Raymaker

LIBRARY AND ARCHIVES CANADA
CATALOGUING IN PUBLICATION

Raymaker, Darryl, 1939–, author
    Trudeau's tango : Alberta meets Pierre Elliott Trudeau, 1968–1972 / Darryl Raymaker.

Includes bibliographical references and index.
Issued in print and electronic formats.
ISBN 978-1-77212-265-7 (softcover).—
ISBN 978-1-77212-319-7 (EPUB).—
ISBN 978-1-77212-320-3 (Kindle).—
ISBN 978-1-77212-321-0 (PDF)

    1. Canada—Politics and government—1963-1968. 2. Canada—Politics and government—1963-1984. 3. Alberta—Politics and government—1935-1971. 4. Federal-provincial relations—Canada—History—20th century. 5. Raymaker, Darryl, 1939–. 6. Trudeau, Pierre Elliott, 1919-2000. 7. Alberta Social Credit Party—History. I. Title.

FC625.R39 2017   971.064'4   C2016-908108-7
C2016-908109-5

First edition, first printing, 2017.
First printed and bound in Canada by Houghton Boston Printers, Saskatoon, Saskatchewan.
Editing by Joan Dixon.
Proofreading by Joanne Muzak.
Indexing by Stephen Ullstrom.

All rights reserved. No part of this publication may be reproduced, stored in a retrieval system, or transmitted in any form or by any means (electronic, mechanical, photocopying, recording, or otherwise) without prior written consent. Contact the University of Alberta Press for further details.

The University of Alberta Press supports copyright. Copyright fuels creativity, encourages diverse voices, promotes free speech, and creates a vibrant culture. Thank you for buying an authorized edition of this book and for complying with the copyright laws by not reproducing, scanning, or distributing any part of it in any form without permission. You are supporting writers and allowing University of Alberta Press to continue to publish books for every reader.

The University of Alberta Press is committed to protecting our natural environment. As part of our efforts, this book is printed on Enviro Paper: it contains 100% post-consumer recycled fibres and is acid- and chlorine-free.

The University of Alberta Press gratefully acknowledges the support received for its publishing program from the Government of Canada, the Canada Council for the Arts, and the Government of Alberta through the Alberta Media Fund.

To the memory of my wife Pat (1944–2017), for her unswerving loyalty, support, and wise counsel through our arduous but happy and fascinating fifty years of adventures as Alberta Liberals.

Contents

Acknowledgements XI

Foreword XIII
LLOYD AXWORTHY

Preface XVII
CA-NA-DA 1967

I Here Comes Mr. Trudeau

1 The Great Race Begins 3
DECEMBER 1967–MARCH 1968

2 The Coming of the Just Society 9
MARCH–APRIL 1968

3 Trudeaumania Goes West 21
APRIL–JUNE 1968

4 The Battle for Edmonton Centre 31
APRIL–JUNE 1968

5 The Battle for Alberta 37
MAY–JUNE 1968

6 Breakthrough 45
JUNE 1968

7   The Honeymoon 55
    JUNE–DECEMBER 1968

II   Oil and Other Minefields

8   In Alberta, It's About Oil, Stupid! 65
    JANUARY–APRIL 1969

9   Mr. Trudeau Lays an Egg 71
    MARCH–MAY 1969

10 Oil, Economic Nationalism, and Mean Joe Greene 79
    APRIL 1969–OCTOBER 1970

11 Hustle Grain! 91
    DECEMBER 1968–OCTOBER 1970

12 The Infernal White Paper 101
    JANUARY 1969–OCTOBER 1970

13 Fighting Inflation and the Cunning Posties 111
    APRIL 1969–SEPTEMBER 1970

III   The Arranged Marriage

14 The Evolution of the Mighty Social Credit 119
    SEPTEMBER 1968– SEPTEMBER 1969

15 A Troublesome Relationship 127
    JANUARY 1969–FEBRUARY 1970

16 The Making of a Senator 139
    FEBRUARY–OCTOBER 1970

IV   Crisis

17 Western Alienation and the Rabble-rousers 149
    DECEMBER 1968–OCTOBER 1970

18 The October Crisis 161
    AUGUST–DECEMBER 1970

V   The Second Coming

19 The Splendours of OPEC and the Saga of Home Oil 171
    OCTOBER 1970–MARCH 1971

20 The Rough Sport of Politics   179
JULY 1970–MARCH 1971

21 Blissful Times and the Beginning of the End of Tax Reform   187
NOVEMBER 1970–JULY 1971

22 As Good as It Gets   195
JULY 1971

VI The Dawning of the Lougheed Era

23 Lougheed Comes to Power   205
FEBRUARY–SEPTEMBER 1971

24 Tax Reform at Last   215
JULY–DECEMBER 1971

25 Peter Lougheed Shows His Stuff   219
JULY 1971–MARCH 1972

VII Stumbling toward the Brink

26 The Grits Falter   227
SEPTEMBER 1971–MAY 1972

27 Chickens, Eggs, and Wheat Deals   235
JANUARY 1971–JUNE 1972

28 Peter Lougheed Becomes a Star   241
DECEMBER 1971–JULY 1972

29 The Eve of the Federal Election   247
APRIL–AUGUST 1972

30 "The Land is Strong?"   255
SEPTEMBER–OCTOBER 1972

31 The Party's Over   269
OCTOBER–NOVEMBER 1972

Epilogue   281

Notes   287
Bibliography   331
Index   337

Acknowledgements

SINCE DECEMBER 1963 when I purchased my first Liberal Party membership, I have participated in the whole gamut of party activities. I've stuffed envelopes, ran as a candidate (four times), raised money, and served party organizations right up to the National Executive of the Liberal Party of Canada—all the while living and earning my living in Alberta, not exactly a Liberal Party breeding ground. Despite this hostile political environment, through it all, I learned much about Canada and the provinces, observed some history close up, and met many interesting and powerful people.

Sometime after I ran in what was to be my last campaign in 1984, I decided that I should share some of my experiences in Canadian politics and history, and so I set about writing about them. This narrative describes events of the years 1968 to 1972, the first term of the Trudeau government and an era of great political change in Canada and Alberta. It is written from my perspective as an Alberta Liberal Party activist who at that time hovered only around the edges of political power, but who nevertheless acquired a pretty good knowledge of his province and his party. Notwithstanding my party affiliation, in telling the story of the events and the personalities that dominated politics during those days, I have striven to be objective.

I have many to thank for helping me through this project. First and foremost I thank my wife, Pat, who sadly passed away before the publication of this book. Pat was, in her own right, a skillful political practitioner, and was loyally at my side every step along the way. I also thank our children Derek, Patrick, and Nicole, who over the years always strongly supported our activities despite our absences from the home front to attend to the smoke-filled rooms or the political hustings.

I also thank Peter Midgley of the University of Alberta Press, for reviewing my very raw and long manuscript, seeing something worthwhile about it, and offering me encouragement and guidance throughout the project. I owe a great debt to my first-class editor Joan Dixon, whose skill with her literary scalpel, along with her patience, tact, and humour turned my original behemoth of a manuscript into something readably efficient. I also thank journalist and author Frank Dabbs, for sharing his experiences and insights with me in both politics and publishing, and encouraging me to embark upon this project. I am also appreciative of the contribution of those who shared with me their experiences in the Liberal Party and politics over the years: Nick Taylor and the Honourable Allen Sulatycky reviewed my manuscript and offered excellent suggestions and encouragement; the Honourable Roger Kerans, Bryan Mahoney, Albert Ludwig, John Moreau, and Stan Cichon, all great Liberals, shared their anecdotes and stories and helped in any way they could. I am also indebted to Blair Williams, Charles Kelly, and David Thomson for relating to me some of their experiences and anecdotes of working in Ottawa. For their insight and knowledge of the oil and gas industry of those days and checking the accuracy of my narrative, I thank my old oilmen friends Richard Anderson and James Walasko. I also thank my dear friends Tim Crago and Ana-Marija Maroti, and countless others not only for their help, but also for their painful reminders that I should finish the book rather than just talk about it.

Foreword

LLOYD AXWORTHY, MARCH 2017

DARRYL RAYMAKER is a charter member of one the most exclusive associations in Canada—he's an Alberta Liberal.

He has used his long experience as an activist for the Liberal cause to write an intriguing tale that centres on Pierre Elliott Trudeau's first term as prime minister and the unrealized opportunity to bridge one of the classic fault lines of Canadian politics: the rift between the Liberal Party in Ottawa and Alberta's political class. In this volume, Raymaker provides an informed participant's view of the dynamics at work in Canada at a time when both the nation and Alberta were in a phase of accelerated growth and new political power alignments were being forged; a time when key decisions were being made on resource development, on Canada–US relations, on federal–provincial entanglements, and on defining the contours of the nation's emerging presence in the world.

Written by an insider, this book has a personal touch in describing the personalities and players, the intrigues and rivalries, the opportunities gained and lost, and the configuration of economic and political interests. For the political junkie, it's a rousing analysis of the flow of action and events that launched careers, made and broke reputations, and the sacrifices made by those who entered the arena of "the Blood Sport."

I was beginning my own political career as a Manitoba Liberal during the late 1960s and, contrary to Peter Lougheed's claim of exclusiveness for Albertans, we made common cause with our fellow Liberals from Alberta. This book brought back fond memories of many of the larger-than-life characters, committed partisans, and superb political operatives who toiled in the Liberal ranks of the province. Nick Taylor, Pat Mahoney, Una Maclean Evans, Mel Hurtig, Cam Millikin and so many others, gone now but not forgotten. People who made real contributions to the public wealth of their province and Canada.

But *Trudeau's Tango* is more than just a memory stick of particular people, times and places. It provides useful insights into the forces at play in that defining moment in our country's history and the consequences with which we live today. And it all begins with one of the most intriguing politicians of our time, Pierre Elliott Trudeau.

Fresh from his win at the federal Liberal Party leadership convention in Ottawa, he came west in the 1968 election campaign ready to breathe new life into western Canadian Liberalism. And the early signs were promising. Trudeaumania was as evident at the Calgary Stampede parade as it was on Spadina Avenue. Good people vied for Liberal nominations, and the election itself saw four quality members elected from Alberta. There was the making of a solid caucus base from which to grow.

Yet Raymaker reminds us that often the worst political enemies are not those in competing parties but those within our own. He describes the behind-the-scenes schemes of Senator Harry Hays, a long time Liberal power-broker, and Bud Olson to starve the provincial wing of the Liberal Party in order to shotgun a marriage with the provincial Socreds—schemes that backfired and hurt the federal Liberals.

Hu Harries, the talented former dean of business at the University of Alberta, was sore at not making cabinet so began following the rogue path of the outsider and did not participate as a team member. That was left to Pat Mahoney, a clever, outgoing lawyer from Calgary, and Allan Sulatycky, a down-to-earth man from the Rocky Mountains who understood the importance of constituency politics. But it was not a cohesive group.

Then there was the oil patch, a varied congeries of people tied to the oil business, which was primarily run from Houston. They had their friends in the media and their acolytes in the provincial Conservatives, all united by the strong belief that no Liberal from the east could do much good. Efforts by the Trudeau government to tackle economic reform by changing the tax system or solidifying national unity were greeted with scorn and hostility by those in the industry. They didn't like a government not entirely beholden to their interests. Looks familiar to a contemporary observer.

Raymaker makes an observation that is different from the conventional treatment of the early Trudeau days. Lest we forget, 1970 was the time of the FLQ and the October Crisis. Trudeau stood on the barricades, faced down the mobs, and emerged as the quintessential strong leader everywhere in Canada, including the western provinces. If there had been an election immediately post-crisis, he would have returned victorious and certainly with renewed support in Alberta. That could have been the game changer in re-aligning political forces. But Raymaker adumbrates that refusing to opportunistically take advantage of people's post-crisis emotional high was Trudeau's finest moment as a man of principle. It was also his worst moment politically, having missed an opportunity to create a truly national party with significant western representation.

The rest was downhill. Trudeau's government, caught in the crosswinds of inflation and unemployment, implemented serious cutbacks and imposed price controls. In consequence, inflation stayed high and unemployment soared. President Nixon came in with his import surcharges (*déjà vu*), causing great angst among those in the oil patch who demanded retaliation. Grain farmers were hit by tumbling prices that brought them (and their tractors) into the streets of Saskatoon. Western alienation was further fuelled by a growing sentiment in Liberal circles (strongly popularized by Mel Hurtig, a putative Liberal candidate from Edmonton) against foreign ownership of our natural resource industries; clearly anathema to oil executives.

Then there was Peter Lougheed. Alberta's new Progressive Conservative premier took no political prisoners, especially if they were Liberals. He was smart, young, and a presence in whatever room he occupied. He made common cause with other provincial premiers—especially Quebec's Robert Bourassa—who were demanding more powers for the provinces, and became the lightning rod of opposition to the Trudeau government. There was no one in Alberta able to take him on.

The Trudeau government limped into the 1972 election bedeviled by bad economic news, unrest among key provincial governments, and a tax reform package that was a whipping boy for every special interest group in the country. Their campaign was not much better. It flagged under "The Land is Strong," a lame slogan if there ever was one, making it was clear the electricity of Trudeaumania was gone.

And in Alberta, the caucus was divided and the organization weakened by the previous stratagem to bury provincial Liberals who went to Lougheed and not the federal Libs. There wasn't a caucus survivor from the Commons. The party was back in the control of Harry Hays and the senators. The chance to ride the Trudeau wave of '68 dribbled away in '72.

The book's epilogue concludes with how Trudeau's post-1972 tenure was one of fractious relations with Alberta. Any momentum to harness the province's growing wealth and importance, fully engaged in a national common cause, was lost because of the failure of the politics of resource ownership.

What began as something so promising in the election campaign of 1968 couldn't be revived. And, yet to come in the early 1980s was the National Energy Program, which deserves a treatment from Darryl Raymaker in what I hope will be an ongoing commitment to holding crucial segments of his province's history up to careful personal scrutiny.

To look back is to see history unfolding. In 2017, Canada is at another crossroads, and another Trudeau is in power. In Alberta, there is the same interest in the oil patch, the same deep conservatism of Alberta Tories, the same weakness in Liberal grassroots leadership, and the same divisions between eastern and western Canada that handicap the country.

"Plus ça change, plus c'est la même chose."

Preface

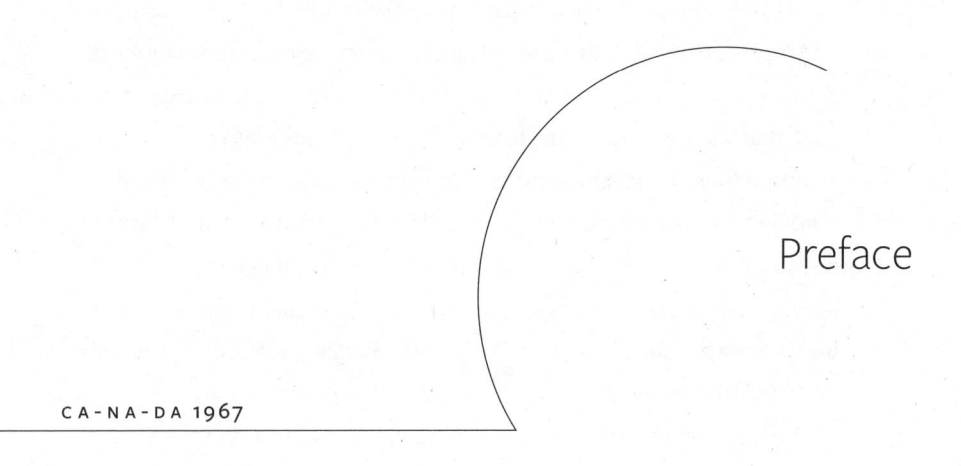

CA-NA-DA 1967

I WAS RAISED in the southwestern corner of Alberta known as the Crowsnest Pass, a mountain pass through the most eastern part of the Canadian Rockies from which the venerable and notorious Crow's Nest Pass freight rate derived its name.[1] The Crow Rate was a important factor in the evolution of western alienation toward Ottawa and central Canada, which is a major theme of this book.

Five small towns clustered within a few kilometres comprise the Alberta side of the Pass: Coleman, Blairmore, Frank (home of the Frank Slide), Bellevue and Hillcrest. Coal mining began in the region about 120 years ago and was the major industry in all these towns. Notoriously cyclical, the work was hard, the accidents many, and the fights between labour and management frequent and hard fought.

Even though the total population of the Pass seldom rose above six thousand, within that small group of hard-working people almost every European nationality was represented: from the British Isles to Ukraine and from Scandinavia to Italy, Spain, and the Balkans. Even Syrians and Lebanese settled here. As I was growing up through the 1940s and the

1950s, many residents still spoke English with strong accents. Some—particularly immigrant housewives—spoke their native languages exclusively.

My parents were children of immigrants from Belgium and Italy. Both grandfathers were connected to the coal industry. As might be expected from that background, I came from a liberal household with politics a common topic at the dinner table. However, a radical I was not. In high school I was more interested in girls and music than politics, and during my time at the University of Alberta, I worked hard enough to pass, yet have fun. My parents, like many parents in the Pass, instilled in me the importance of education and making something of oneself. To those ends I decided to become a lawyer and earned my law degree in 1963.

During a trip to Europe after graduation, I read of John F. Kennedy's victory in Theodore White's *The Making of the President, 1960*, which convinced me and countless other young people in North America that politics was a honourable and exciting calling. Surveying the political terrain upon my return, I concluded that my choice was between the Liberals and the Progressive Conservatives. Lester Pearson had just defeated John Diefenbaker to form his first minority government and the Tories[2] seemed to be on their way out. With JFK as my idol, and my natural liberal proclivities, in December 1963 I bought a membership in the Liberal Party from the senior partner of the small firm where I was completing my articles of clerkship. I cut my political teeth working in the 1965 federal campaign for the Calgary North candidate and attended my first Alberta Liberal Party convention in Calgary in January 1966.[3]

The following year I was nominated as the Liberal candidate in the Alberta general election for the Calgary riding of Queens Park. Ernest Manning's Social Credit Party, which had been riding high for years, occupied fifty-seven seats in the legislature, while the opposition Liberals held the remaining three. Peter Lougheed's Tories had no seats at all yet, but were taking their first baby steps in his first election as leader. After running a vigorous campaign with plenty of campaign workers and enough money to buy signs and pamphlets, I was defeated by a low profile ex-school teacher, Lee Leavitt, the Social Credit incumbent. He scored

The author, his wife Pat, and Trudeau chat at a Liberal Party reception during the Calgary Stampede, July 1978. Trudeau signed the photo a year later. [Courtesy of the author]

almost 5,000 votes to my paltry 1,700. In between us was Lougheed's Tory candidate, who received about 3,800 votes. It was my first attempt at public office and my first taste of defeat.

The year 1967 showcased Canada's Centennial and Expo 67 in Montreal. Accompanied by the voices of dozens of kids, jazz trumpeter Bobby Gimby's catchy and upbeat theme song "CA-NA-DA" dominated the airwaves. It conjured up a young country full of promise, vigour, and good will. The enthusiasm was contagious; my wife, Pat, and I, along with thousands of western Canadians, journeyed east to see the show firsthand.

After a few days of long queues and inflated prices in Montreal, we departed for Quebec City to attend the Canadian Bar Association annual convention. At the stately Chateau Frontenac hotel, a Calgary lawyer friend, Allan Beattie, and I listened to a panel of Quebec francophone and anglophone lawyers arguing about the two solitudes. That discussion was followed by a speech by the new federal minister of justice. Although Pierre Elliott Trudeau was well known in Quebec at the time, he was far from a household name in Alberta.

Picking up our simultaneous translation devices, Allan and I joined a crowd of perhaps four hundred lawyers in the hotel's ballroom. The nattily attired 48-year-old minister appeared youthful and lean, unlike many federal politicians who carried extra pounds and unhealthy pallor from too many late nights, scotches, and rubber-chicken dinners. He spoke English like an English-speaking Canadian—unlike any other French Canadians I had heard speak English—and he could effortlessly switch from English to French and back again. For English-speaking visitors, this was as annoying as it was impressive, because every time he spoke French, we required those awkward electronic devices to translate.

And he droned. Oh, how he droned—about constitutional reform, bilingualism, and a constitutional bill of rights guaranteeing, among other things, linguistic rights for English- and French-speaking Canadians across the country. For a couple of young lawyers not too long out of school, these topics didn't keep us at the edge of our seats; in Alberta those issues were not even on the radar screen in 1967. But Martin Sullivan, author of *Mandate '68: The Year of Pierre Elliott Trudeau*, called the speech, "one of the most lucid documents Trudeau had ever written, and it put the case concisely for making a Bill of Rights the cornerstone of Canadian constitutional change."[4]

Perhaps two-thirds through the speech, I nudged Allan and we exited the hall to wander along the escarpment toward the Citadelle and the view of the Plains of Abraham. I pondered what little I knew of Canada's history in this most historic of Canadian locations.

"I don't think he has what it takes to be the next prime minister, do you?" I asked my companion.

"Not a chance," Beattie replied.

1

Here Comes Mr. Trudeau

1

The Great Race Begins

DECEMBER 1967–MARCH 1968

THE CANADIAN BAR ASSOCIATION ADDRESS I underestimated in 1967 would prove to be an early and important step toward Trudeau's eventual dominance of the Liberal Party of Canada. Over the next few months not only would he abolish criminality in homosexual conduct between consenting adults in private, he would liberalize antiquated divorce laws. His famous quote—"There is no place for the state in the bedrooms of the nation"—remains a rallying cry for liberals almost fifty years later.[1] He was also becoming a star performer as Prime Minister Lester Pearson's point man during constitutional discussions.

Pearson, having led the party in four elections and failing in the two most recent ones to get a majority government, decided to announce his retirement in December 1967. The leadership race was on and the convention set for April 1968 in the nation's capital.

By the time of Pearson's retirement announcement, a lot of Canadians had seen Trudeau, read about his formidable intellect, and heard that he'd been a fierce opponent of Quebec separatism. Many started to believe he might have leadership potential and were urging him to enter the contest. Despite these entreaties from friends and influential Liberals, he bided his time.

In early February Pearson had Trudeau by his side during an important, nationally televised constitutional conference, which saw Trudeau defending federalism with his vision of a united Canada squaring off against nationalist Quebec premier Daniel Johnson, who wanted more powers and "special status" for Quebec. During a few telling exchanges, the "old frail fox" showed that he was no match for the bright and cool federal justice minister.[2] English-speaking Canadians watching Trudeau's domination of the debate saw "an attractive, highly intelligent federalist francophone who could…'deal with Quebec.'"[3]

That winter of 1968, I, too, sensed a leader who personified the hope and optimism of Expo 67: our very own JFK and a welcome change from those two aging and ragged gladiators, John Diefenbaker and Lester Pearson, who had been duking it out for ten years. And Trudeau was heads and shoulders more exciting than sombre Bob Stanfield, who had recently replaced Diefenbaker.

Western Canadians with long-standing grievances against central Canada also saw that Trudeau was different. Not only young and exciting, he was a potential leader from Quebec who would put Quebec in its place, just as he had done with Daniel Johnson on television. They believed that he was just what the country needed to stop the bellyaching of Quebec nationalists demanding special treatment. English Canada had forgotten neither Quebec's opposition to the war effort and conscription, nor its (recently defeated) government that demanded Quebec be *Maîtres chez nous* (masters of our own house). Furthermore, Daniel Johnson and new sovereigntist leader René Lévesque seemed as troublesome to westerners as their predecessors.

As the leadership campaign got under way in 1968, I discovered that running in the 1967 provincial election had qualified me as an ex-officio voting delegate at the federal leadership convention. My wife, Pat, had been elected as an alternate youth delegate and so we were both bound for Ottawa. During the leadership campaign, we delegates were wined and dined, flattered, cajoled, and grovelled to by the leadership hopefuls and their campaign organizers. Indeed, lavishing of attention on the Alberta rank and file by the party brass took place only during leadership campaigns and thus were rare times to be savoured.

The roster of candidates was a formidable array. At 64, Paul Martin was the oldest in the race. Elected in the riding of Windsor in 1935 he'd served in the King, St. Laurent, and Pearson cabinets as a competent minister of several portfolios. He had also run for the leadership unsuccessfully in 1948 and 1958. Because of his years on the scene, Martin had plenty of supporters throughout the country. His indefatigability at working the crowds was legendary.

In the two years leading up to his leadership run, Paul Hellyer had spent more time in Alberta than any of his competitors. Only 44, he had already been an MP for nineteen years, and his imposing stature, thinning white hair, and sombre bearing gave him a gravitas that belied his years. While serving as Pearson's minister of Defence he implemented the ambitious unification of the Canadian Armed Forces, which became his springboard to national prominence.

Minister of Trade Robert Winters was a professional engineer and big business executive, making him a favourite of the Canadian business establishment. Born and bred in Nova Scotia, Winters was first elected in 1945 and served in several senior cabinet positions. He had a toothsome smile and a hearty handshake, and was not above giving a delegate a manly hug in his quest for votes. Fiscally conservative, he had the ear of many Alberta and other western delegates, as well as that of the pro-business wing of the party.

John Turner was young—not yet 39—and handsome with penetrating blue eyes, and he'd once danced the night away with a young Princess Margaret at a formal ball. Athletic, bilingual, he was a well-connected Rhodes scholar who had lived in Vancouver, Ottawa, and Montreal. His widowed mother had been one of the first women to rise to a senior level in the federal public service, while his stepfather was a noted Canadian industrialist who became lieutenant-governor of British Columbia. Turner was elected in 1962 as MP for Montreal's riding of St. Lawrence–St. George and sat in Pearson's cabinet as minister without portfolio. His jocular locker room manner, booming voice, and delight in good scotch endeared him to a great many younger Grits,[4] particularly in the west.

Winnipeg-born Minister of Finance Mitchell Sharp, 57, was the only candidate born west of Toronto. A long-time public servant, he became deputy minister of trade and commerce. After a few years in the private sector, he returned to Ottawa in 1963 as the MP for the Eglinton riding in Toronto. Sharp was considered the leader of the pro-business wing of the caucus. On television his reserve and precise language portrayed him as a rigorous public servant. Privately, he was far more relaxed and warm. Among Sharp's supporters was young Quebec MP Jean Chretien, to whom Sharp had acted as mentor when the unilingual francophone was first elected.

Joe Greene was a lawyer from Arnprior, Ontario. His folksiness and eloquence made him one of the best orators in politics. His service with the RCAF in World War II had earned him the Distinguished Flying Cross. Elected to Parliament in 1963, two years later he became the first eastern minister of agriculture in fifty-four years. Tall and gaunt, with well-coifed greying hair, and piercing eyes, he liked to point out his physical resemblance to Abraham Lincoln. Greene was a witty and entertaining raconteur as he hustled votes in his hotel suite, where there was always a generous supply of spirits. Unfortunately, Greene lacked funds, organizers, and influential party supporters.

Allan J. MacEachen was an economics professor who had been first elected as an MP from the Cape Breton riding of Inverness–Richmond in 1953. Despite coming from a poor coal-mining family he received a blue-ribbon education at the University of Chicago and MIT. MacEachen served effectively as minister in the labour and health portfolios in the Pearson government; he deftly handled the Great Lakes shipping union turmoil and took a leading role in medicare's introduction. His support in Alberta consisted mainly of a few transplanted Cape Bretoners.

Eric Kierans' background was Irish working class but that did not stop him from becoming a brilliant businessman, a professor of business at McGill University, and president of the Montreal Stock Exchange. Kierans went into politics in 1963 as one of Jean Lesage's Liberals of the Quiet Revolution where he served stints as minister in revenue and health. Elected president of the Quebec Liberal Party in 1967, he took on the task of telling René Lévesque to either give up the idea of separation or get out. (Lévesque soon after would help found the Parti Québécois.)

Kierans' cousin, Calgary lawyer Tom Walsh, recruited two members of his firm, Gilbert (Gib) Clark[5] and Bob Young, and me to accompany Kierans through southern Alberta to seek delegate support in the smaller cities of Medicine Hat, Red Deer, and Lethbridge. In his high-pitched and staccato delivery, Kierans regaled us with tales of backroom battles with Levesque and Lesage, and candid descriptions of other politicians. He was certainly no fan of Trudeau, considering him a neophyte to politics who did not understand Quebec. Kierans' lack of federal experience made his candidacy a hard sell, given that he faced younger and more attractive opponents who already held federal cabinet posts.

Finally, there was Trudeau. New to the game of party politics, he was an unknown in most of Canada when he won his Mount Royal riding in 1965. He was one of Quebec's "three wise men," along with friends Jean Marchand and Gerard Pelletier, who were supposed to give Quebec federalists a strong voice in the Pearson government. Trudeau's main claim to fame was as a fierce opponent of the Union Nationale government, which he viewed as repressive, parochial, and standing in the way of Quebec's evolution as a modern society. He was a superbly educated lawyer and law professor having attended the University of Montreal, Harvard, L'Institut d'études politiques de Paris, and the London School of Economics. He reportedly had inherited a considerable fortune upon the premature death of his businessman French Canadian father, had grown up with a Scottish/French Canadian mother and became perfectly bilingual, well travelled, and a supporter of leftist causes. Shortly after his election he had been appointed parliamentary secretary to Prime Minister Pearson and two years later became minister of justice.

In early March, Trudeau organizers held a meeting at a downtown Calgary hotel, attended by two influential Montrealers who would play important roles in the Trudeau leadership campaign: Oxford-educated physicist and political strategist Jim Davey and Montreal lawyer Sonny Gordon. Among the locals present were Calgary businessman and philanthropist Harry Cohen, Liberal fundraiser and chartered accountant Bill Pringle, and other younger folk like me, eager to get involved.

Although we had little idea of the real Trudeau, we had heard, read, and seen enough of him on television to know that he was a different and cool cat who had a real shot at winning. Davey and Gordon described their candidate as best they could and pleaded for volunteers. Out of this meeting emerged a loose campaign committee in the Calgary region, and a few days later Trudeau appeared in a short campaign stopover at the downtown Calgary Inn as part of a one-day tour of southern Alberta. Hundreds of people—Liberals, Conservatives, and the curious with no political leanings, young and old—showed up. Calgary had never seen such excitement for a visiting politician. And scenes like this were happening all over the country. The Trudeaumania juggernaut was on the move.

2

The Coming of the Just Society

MARCH–APRIL 1968

AS THE LEADERSHIP CAMPAIGN PROGRESSED I decided to support Eric Kierans on the first ballot and Trudeau on subsequent ones, believing more than one ballot likely and that Trudeau would be the probable winner. From travelling with him through southern Alberta, I knew Kierans better and admired him for his energy, candour, and record. Although he was a long shot with only a small organization and shoestring budget, I hoped he would do well enough to serve in a future cabinet. But Trudeau's organization was aggressively lining up delegates in Quebec, Kierans' home province. Without a big share of those delegates, Kierans' chances of doing well were not good.

Pat and I had received volumes of campaign material. We met all the candidates as they passed through Calgary trying to corral delegate votes and observed them closely as they spoke at meetings or hosted us in their hotel suites. But it was Trudeau who captured our imagination. Although we did not know much about him, he was the newest and most interesting personality on the scene. Like other Canadians, we were on the hunt for our own JFK and readily signed his nomination papers.

Little did we realize as we boarded our flight to the convention that this would be a week of many tumultuous events. On Sunday, March 31, President Lyndon Johnson made the surprise announcement that he would not seek nor accept the Democratic nomination for that year's US election. The Vietnam War had brought him down. Then on Wednesday, April 3, Mitchell Sharp withdrew from the leadership race and announced his endorsement of Trudeau. This came as no surprise to me. In a campaign visit to Calgary, he had told some of us that if we could not support him, then we should consider Trudeau. Sharp's departure would not only allow Trudeau to capture most of Sharp's delegate support, but also give the business (or right) wing[1] of the party confidence that Trudeau was no closet "commie." Joining Sharp in his support of Trudeau was Sharp's political acolyte and friend Jean Chretien, already a cabinet minister and showing political savvy well beyond his 34 years.

Candidates' bands, cheerleaders, banners, and glad-handing campaign workers greeted our arrival in Ottawa and the ballyhoo would continue non-stop for the next four days amid a swirl of rallies, hospitality suites, backroom gossip, speeches, barbecues, and banquets until the wee hours of every morning. Hellyer and Winters led in the hospitality department with their well-stocked hotel-suite bars. Trudeau's watering holes, like the man himself, were more austere with only non-alcoholic beverages; however, comely young ladies clad in white and orange miniskirts and berets served his guests.

An early event of the convention was a giant reception organized by Trudeau's Quebec delegation at the Chaudière Golf Club across the Ottawa River in Aylmer, Quebec. It was Trudeaumania at full throttle. Hundreds of people, including photographers, newsmen, delegates, smitten supporters, and ordinary onlookers, had to fight through the congested and fawning crowd to catch a glimpse of the man. Such public emotion for a politician was entirely new to Canadians. After Trudeau and his entourage had awkwardly bulldozed their way to the microphone, they found the sound system not working. Since it was impossible to hear him speak above the frenzy, his exuberant supporters then carried him about the room on their shoulders, to the boisterous delight of the crowd.

Six ministers of the last Pearson cabinet were now aligned with Trudeau. No other candidate came close to having such strong support from cabinet colleagues. His Alberta support was also strong. It included book publisher and party activist Mel Hurtig, an early supporter and co-chair of his northern Alberta leadership team. Also supporting Trudeau were young Edmonton lawyer Dave McLean, Vegreville lawyer Virgil Moshansky,[2] Alberta Liberal leader-to-be Bob Russell, Jasper–Edson MLA Bill Switzer, and long-time party activist Una Maclean Evans.[3]

Winters' campaign also seemed to be on the march with a surprising number of Quebec votes. Alberta delegates supporting him included former Edmonton MP and federal minister George Prudham, Senator Harry Hays, and Calgary lawyer Ken Moore.[4]

Paul Martin's campaign, by contrast, was just limping along. One morning, he appeared in a mostly empty hotel reception room for a campaign get-acquainted session. He was no longer able to mask his advancing years and looked very tired. Suspecting that this would be one of the last times to meet this party icon, delegates came to shake his hand and pose alongside him for pictures. The delegate would then disappear into the crowd of conventioneers, inevitably replacing his Martin badge with that of his real choice. (Politics is a rough sport indeed!) Albertans supporting Martin included the son of Senator Hays, Dan Hays, Alberta provincial Liberal leader, and MLA Mike Maccagno, lawyer Peter Petrasuk of Calgary, and Senator J. Harper Prowse of Edmonton.

Hellyer was running a strong campaign behind a formidable organization headed by his long-time assistant, and now campaign manager, Bill Lee. Another of Hellyer's organizers was Senator Keith Davey from Toronto. He was a legend in the party for playing a key role in the resurrection of both the party and of Lester Pearson, after Diefenbaker's sweeping 1958 victory. However, Hellyer's stiff and dour style remained a major drawback. His Alberta delegate support included Edmonton lawyer Laurence Decore,

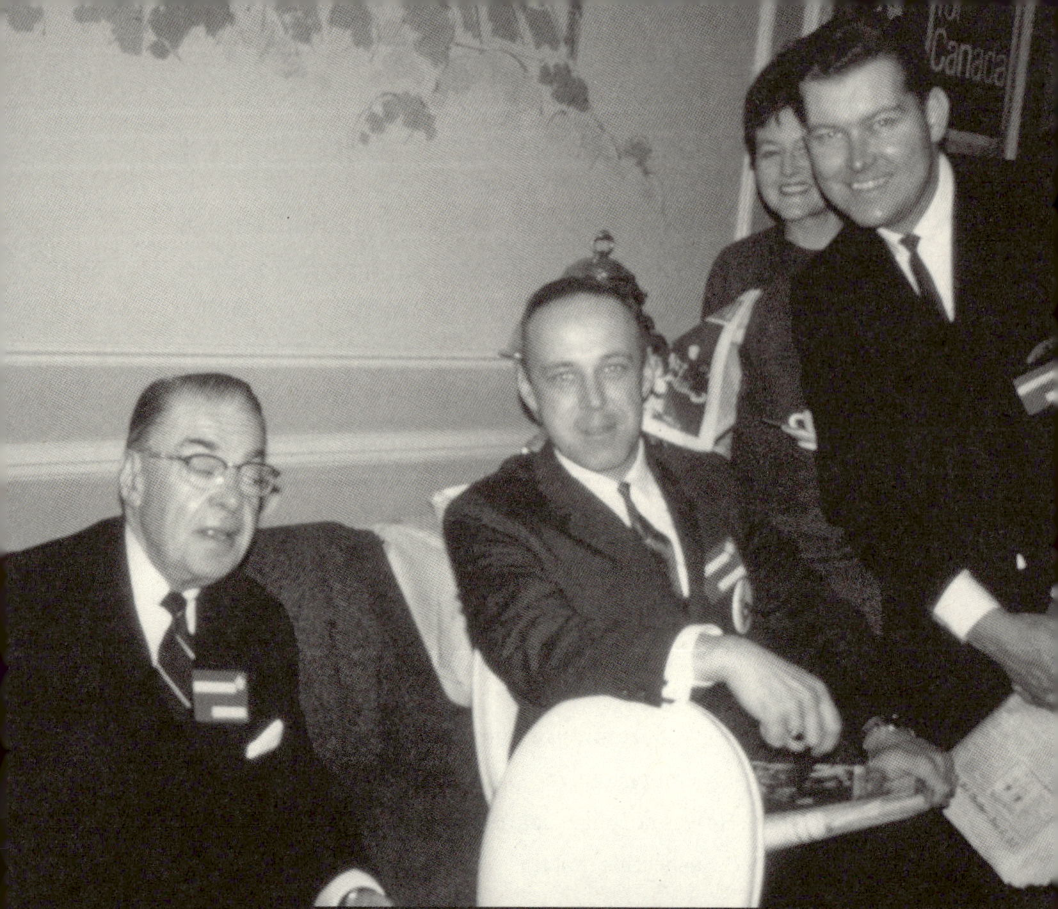
Canada

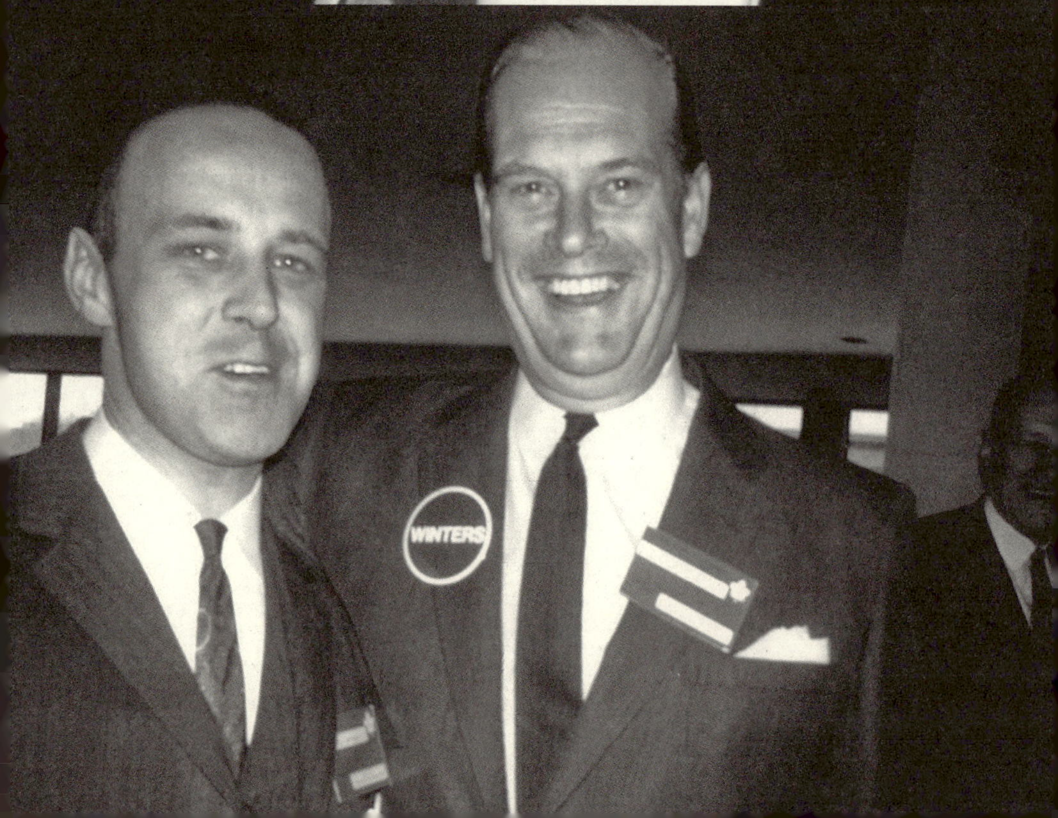
WINTERS

who would later become Edmonton mayor and leader of the Alberta Liberal Party. Other Alberta Liberals supporting Hellyer were former Alberta Liberal provincial party leader Dave Hunter, Edmonton businessman and party president Leo Lemieux, Edmonton lawyers David McDonald,[5] William Sinclair,[6] and Allan Wachowich,[7] and Calgary lawyers Jim Palmer,[8] Willis O'Leary,[9] and Brian Stevenson.[10]

John Turner had a strong following of loyal young Liberals from across the country. Wearing plastic construction hats and yellow jackets on the convention floor, many were from Turner's former home province of BC. In an afternoon policy workshop, Turner created space between him and Trudeau on the national unity issue, saying that Canadian unity could not be solved by rigidity, logic, and intellect alone, "but by the heart and gut, because that's what Canada is all about."[11] Among the Alberta delegates supporting Turner were Edmonton lawyer Roger Kerans[12] and Calgary MLA Bill Dickie.[13]

During his turn at the policy workshop, Trudeau eloquently argued for tolerance, freedom from poverty, and a charter of rights giving French-speaking Canadians throughout Canada the same rights as English-speaking Canadians had in Quebec. He also spoke of solving problems of regional disparities and, as a gesture to the conservative or business wing, said he approved of balanced budgets and means tests to determine access to social programs.[14]

Later on Thursday evening, a crowd of 8,000 congregated at the Lansdowne Park arena to give Lester Pearson and his wife, Maryon, an affectionate and rousing farewell. Pearson had not had an easy time as Liberal leader and prime minister. After the Diefenbaker sweep of 1958, the road back had been long and arduous. However, in 1962, he'd held Diefenbaker to a minority and went on to win his own minority government in 1963, which he repeated in 1965. The west, with its traditional hostility to Liberals,

< Top: Paul Martin Sr. (L) with the author at the Liberal leadership convention in Ottawa, April 1968. [Courtesy of the author]
< Bottom: The author (L) with Robert Winters at the leadership convention in Ottawa, April 1968. [Courtesy of the author]

never embraced Pearson. Besides, many westerners saw his opponent Diefenbaker— hometown Prince Albert, Saskatchewan—as one of their own.

Although Pearson served only five years as prime minister and the head of minority governments, he had compiled an impressive legislative record. His governments gave the country the Canada Pension Plan, medicare, unification of the armed forces, a new Canadian flag, and the creation of the Royal Commission on Bilingualism and Biculturalism (which led to the Official Languages Act). These accomplishments, together with his Nobel Peace Prize for his role in establishing peace during the Suez crisis, established Pearson as one of Canada's greatest prime ministers.

Pearson's final convention speech reflected on the nature of leadership with a humility and wit seldom found in political leadership. A party leader, Pearson said, "is expected, by the image maker, to be a combination of Abraham Lincoln and Batman, to perform instant miracles. Then, the poor, honest, decent chap can't live up to the image, the process of demolition begins so that another superman can be erected in the ruins."[15] The assembled Grits rewarded him with a long-standing ovation.

The next evening, Friday, April 4, just before the candidates were to make their final formal speeches to delegates, we overheard someone on the convention floor say that Martin Luther King had been shot. Charles Lynch, Southam News columnist standing only a few feet away from us, confirmed that King had indeed died. This second shock of the week cast a pall of gloom over the entire crowd. Rumours circulated of riots in American streets, closure of the border, and machine guns set up on the grounds of the White House. But as in show business, so in politics, the show went on.

Paul Martin, led up to the stage by a large bugle band, was the first to address the convention crowd. His valiant efforts to connect with his audience fell short. His ponderous speechifying, conservative attire, thick spectacles, and other signs of his generation left him no match for the new wave of leadership now demanded by the Canadian electorate.

The next speaker was Robert Winters, who was now believed to be the Trudeau's strongest challenger. A ramrod straight and robust Winters[16] was greeted by hundreds of bobbing green-and-white placards from his section on the convention floor. His call for a strong Canadian economy and a new quest for excellence was more of a boardroom presentation than a rousing war cry, but his growing support was evident.

Joe Greene followed Winters to deliver the surprise of the evening. With a hand-held microphone and without notes, Greene mesmerized the delegates with a passionate, eloquent, and often-funny ode to Canada in both French and English. Making his case for a strong united Canada, he related his World War II experience as a young English-speaking RCAF pilot befriending a young francophone pilot and sharing their homecoming dreams. (Greene's young Quebec friend did not return.) Greene's tour de force, the finest political speech I've ever heard, earned him thunderous applause.

The daunting task of following Greene fell to Paul Hellyer. His demonstrators (men in white boaters and red vests; the women in red vests, miniskirts, and high black boots) did their best to rev up the audience, marching and chanting with military precision. One of Hellyer's most prominent demonstrators, Judy LaMarsh,[17] was a formidable presence with her ample frame compressed into the team outfit. The wing-collared Senator Arthur Roebuck, despite his 90 years, was another of Hellyer's most exuberant cheerleaders. Unfortunately, Hellyer's speech had neither wit nor panache; only as an address to an economic think tank might it have sufficed.

Allan MacEachen, the favourite son of Cape Breton, followed with a pedestrian speech that failed to arouse. The most colourful part of his appearance was his pipe band. Most of the Maritime delegates he'd hoped for would cast their votes for other candidates, in particular Trudeau and Winters.

Eric Kierans was led onto the stage by a loud and exuberant university student band. His speech, although delivered in a spiritless monotone, reflected both his nationalist sentiments and sincerity. Canadians lived in a "brutal, mechanistic, material age," he cautioned, and Liberals had to "bend all our policies to preserve the gentleness that is in our society."[18]

which was as apt a reminder of the progressive component of the Liberal Party as we heard at the convention. Polite, respectful applause followed.

Next up was Trudeau. He was led to the stage by an honour guard comprised of his attractive young women volunteers dressed in his campaign colors. "Tru-deau, Tru-deau," chanted the crowd in a slow cadence—this would become the party's rallying cry whenever he spoke at a party event. The resounding, spontaneous welcome that seemed to come from every nook and corner was something of an illusion; his supporters were seated throughout the arena, not merely in the sections assigned to them. It was a brilliant strategic stroke and a seminal moment of the convention.

After the demonstration settled down, Trudeau began speaking in a sombre tone, which at first reminded me of his droning back in September in Quebec City (when I boldly predicted his bleak political future). His gunslinger days were not yet upon us. The delegates, knowing by this time that he was likely to win, listened very carefully as he spoke of some of the world's intransigent problems—war, famine, poverty, ignorance, and disease. Trudeau was the only candidate who spoke of Martin Luther King, saying, "We know that even the most favoured people suffer from external conflict and internal division," and that "the tragic events that began last night in the assassination of Martin Luther King and which have degenerated today into strife and arson, hate and murder, are a tragic reminder of that reality."[19]

He told the crowd that the hallmarks of his government would be "The triumph of logic in politics over passion, the protection of individual freedom against the collective security, and a just distribution of the national wealth." And "By building a truly just society, this beautiful, rich and energetic country of ours can become a model in which every citizen will enjoy his fundamental rights in which two great linguistic communities and people of many cultures will live in harmony, and in which every individual will find fulfillment."[20] For the most part, delegates listened in thoughtful silence until the end of his nineteen-minute speech, upon which there was a deafening outpouring of cheers that once again seemed to come from every inch of the large arena.[21]

After this, John Turner rose to the challenge with a strong and eloquent speech that once and for all established himself as a credible leadership candidate. His most resonant message: "I'm not just in this race so you will remember my name at some future date. I'm not here now for some next time. I am not bidding now for your consideration at some vague convention in 1984, when I've mellowed a bit. My time is now, and now is no time for mellow men."[22]

Although Greene and Trudeau had stolen the show, Turner's performance, together with his telegenic good looks would keep him in delegates' minds as Trudeau's natural successor for years to come.

Two other speakers who took the podium that night provide vignettes of interesting trivia. One was a largely unknown former mayor of Portage la Prairie, Presbyterian minister Lloyd Henderson, who had been the first to announce his candidacy but ended up getting no votes whatsoever. The other was a 28-year-old German immigrant who did not get enough supporting signatures to put his name on the ballot but delivered a speech attacking socialists and leftists. Ernst Zundel would make his name as a notorious anti-Semite and holocaust denier.[23]

Following the speeches, Alberta delegate and Martin-supporter Senator Earl Hastings bet me a hundred dollars that Kierans would not receive a hundred votes on the first ballot. For the first time I had money riding on the outcome. Voting day saw Pat and I in the small Kierans seating area several rows above the arena surface, and to the left of the much larger and boisterous Hellyer support. Voting began early in the afternoon. In the crowd, I spotted Alberta's only MP, Bud Olson, a long-time Social Credit MP from Medicine Hat who had crossed the floor the previous year to sit as a Liberal. Olson sported no badge of support for any of the candidates and would remain publicly uncommitted.

The voting and counting dragged on, encouraging many to retire temporarily to a bar in the arena where they could carry on their between-vote gabfest while enjoying their favourite elixirs. Shortly after three o'clock came the results of the first ballot. Trudeau was ahead with 752 votes, followed by Hellyer at 330, Winters with 293, and Martin and Turner tied

The Coming of the Just Society . 17

at 277. Greene took a surprisingly strong 169 votes, no doubt owing to his brilliant oratory the night before, while MacEachen had 165, and Kierans, 103. Senator Hastings now owed me a hundred bucks—which he promptly and honourably paid.

Who would now do what and when? Who would toss in the towel? Paul Martin soon withdrew and Kierans also bowed out, neither endorsing any other candidate. MacEachen, led by two bagpipers, joined the designated Trudeau section of the arena hoping to take his 165 votes with him.

Shortly after five o'clock came the results of the second ballot with Trudeau increasing his support to 964, followed by a surging Winters at 473, Hellyer slipping to third with 465, and Turner climbing to 347. Greene slipped to 104 and MacEachen, who had failed to notify convention officials of his withdrawal in time, received 10.

More suspense and drama followed, with Winters and Hellyer trying to come up with a deal to stop Trudeau, speaking in intimate and low voices but in full view of the crowd, with their every word heard by television viewers. The irrepressible LaMarsh made an appearance in a dramatic and memorable convention highlight. Goading Hellyer to support Winters, she said, "You know him, Paul and he knows you. You're alright with him. It's tough, but what the hell's the point of going down and letting that bastard be there! Come on Paul, you're 44, and we've still got lots of time."[24] Hellyer, despite her entreaties, stayed put, as did Turner and Greene.

The third ballot results came in after six, with Trudeau grinding along to 1,051 votes, followed now by his obvious challenger Winters with 621, then the faltering Hellyer with 377, Turner slipping to 279, and Greene last with 29. Greene joined the Trudeau section and Hellyer moved to Winters. However, Senator Keith Davey, who had been a strong Hellyer supporter and had the clout to control many of Hellyer's delegates, marched over to Trudeau's side, taking the initial steps toward what would be one of the greatest political collaborations in Canadian history. Turner was defiant; he was staying to the end.

> *Pierre Elliott Trudeau, here with Donald S. Macdonald (R), won the Liberal leadership on the fourth ballot.* [*John McNeill, Canadian Press,* Globe and Mail]

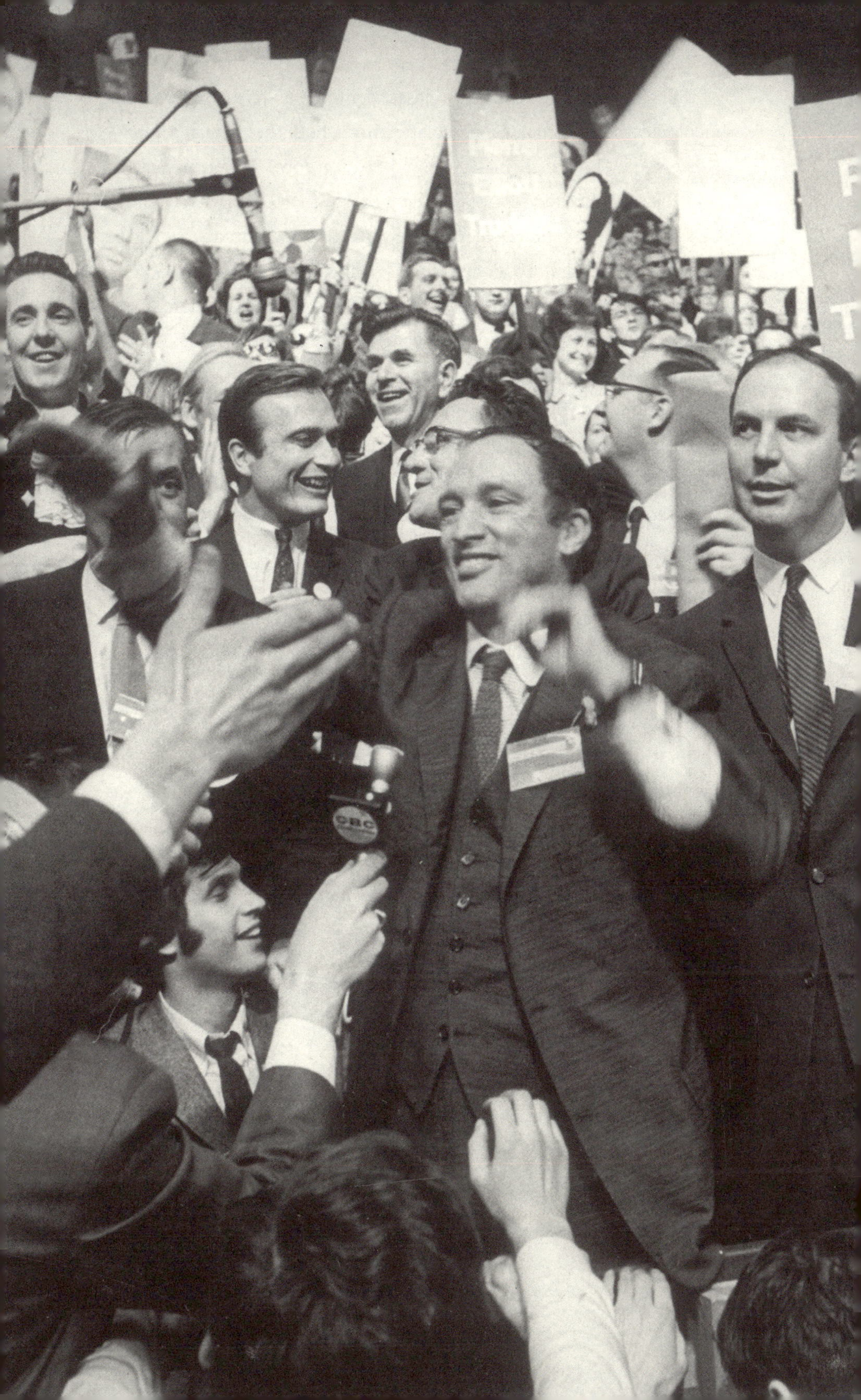
CBC

The party was now ready for a classic right-versus-left showdown: the ideological contest that had percolated throughout the campaign and convention. About eight in the evening, Senator John Nichol once again took the podium to announce the results of the fourth and what would likely be the final ballot. Delegates knew that the magic number would be less than 1,200. Nichol got only as far as saying, "Pierre Trudeau 1,203," when the arena erupted. Trudeau signs emerged from everywhere. The party had completed its work; Trudeau would be its next leader. (Winters finished the day with 954 and Turner with 195.)

Pat and I made our way back to our hotel, driven by prominent Calgarian and Liberal Harold Millican.[25] With us was long-time editor and publisher of the Lethbridge *Herald*, Cleo Mowers. Mowers was a rare born-and-bred Albertan and Liberal who had steadfastly maintained his liberal principles despite living in southern Alberta, one of the most conservative parts of the country. Mowers mused out loud about the uncertain course on which the party had now set itself, marvelled at the party's courage in electing such an unconventional leader and wondered what the United States would make of it all.

Pat and I capped our great adventure at the crammed Trudeau victory celebration in the penthouse of Ottawa's Skyline Hotel. What a week! Lyndon Johnson stepped down. King was assassinated. And Trudeau was elected Liberal leader at the greatest leadership convention Canadian politics had ever seen. Now it was time to go back to the real world in Calgary, and see how all of this would play out.

3

Trudeaumania Goes West

APRIL–JUNE 1968

THE LIBERAL PARTY OF CANADA that Trudeau now led was a federation of provincial and territorial Liberal party organizations comprising the National Liberal Federation. Each provincial or territorial organization included all Liberal members from that province or territory. In Alberta the provincial Liberal party organization was called the Liberal Association of Alberta until 1970, when the name changed to the Liberal Party in Alberta.[1]

Within this Liberal Party in Alberta, a separate arm handled provincial political activities—with its own party leader, budget, riding associations, and campaign organization. Another arm handled federal Liberal activities, but its leader was the national leader of the Liberal Party of Canada, Trudeau. In 1968 only the constitution, some basic office infrastructure for getting out communications (and when affordable, a provincial organizer) were common to these two separate components of the party.[2]

In the spring of 1968, political realists in Alberta knew that it would be difficult for the Liberals to win seats in the province. In the fourteen federal elections between 1921 and 1965, the federal Liberals were able to garner 30 percent or more of the popular vote only four times—in 1930, 1940, 1949, and 1953. Their best year for winning seats was 1940 when they picked up 7 of 17, a showing that was more about supporting the war effort than the federal Liberal Party.

In the five federal elections between 1957 and 1965, the federal Liberals in Alberta had only managed to win two seats: the northern riding of Athabaska in 1957 and Calgary South in 1963. They were shut out in the elections of 1958, 1962, and 1965. In those same five federal elections, they scored a high of 27.9 percent of the popular vote (1957) and a low of 13.7 percent (1958).

Edmonton had been a little more generous than Calgary to the federal Liberals. In every election up to and including the federal election in 1953, Edmonton produced at least one Liberal seat. After that the Grits were shut out in Alberta's capital up to and including the election of 1965. In Calgary during that same period, the federal Liberals only won seats in 1940, when they picked up two, and in 1963 when popular Calgary mayor Harry Hays won Calgary South.[3]

Alberta provincial election results had also painted a bleak picture for Liberal hopefuls. Starting from 1905 when Alberta became a province, the provincial Liberal Party's string of four victories allowed it to form the government until 1921 before losing to the United Farmers of Alberta.

From that time forward it was tough slogging. In the twelve general elections from 1921 to 1967, the Alberta Liberals won more than 10 seats only three times. Winning 5 seats in 1935 was the most seats the party would win through to and including 1967, with one exception. In 1955 with a preferential ballot voting system, 15 members were elected under the inspired leadership of J. Harper Prowse, a silver-tongued lawyer and World War II veteran. A short time later, Premier Manning's government scrapped the preferential ballot system without public hearings or debate. In 1958 Prowse decided to leave provincial politics and run (unsuccessfully) for the Edmonton mayor's chair.

Prowse was succeeded as provincial Liberal leader by J.W. Grant MacEwan. In the subsequent election of 1959, MacEwan's Liberals lost all but one seat. Illustrative of the difficulty Liberals faced in Alberta was

MacEwan, who ran as a Liberal in the riding of Calgary North. He finished third behind both the winning Social Credit and the second-place Tory candidates, receiving only 19 percent of the votes cast. The names that finished ahead of him have since faded into history. MacEwan, on the other hand, was already a distinguished professor who held several university degrees, a prolific writer of books and articles on western history and agriculture, and a Calgary alderman and MLA. He went on to become mayor of Calgary and receive scads of other honours, including having a university named after him. But in 1959 he could not get elected as a Liberal.

The provincial party's share of the popular vote through twelve provincial elections between 1921 and 1967 averaged only 19.11 percent, and in 1959, 1963, and 1967, the party's share ranged from 10.8 percent to 19.8 percent. The small consolation in these dreary provincial election results? With the exception of 1944, the Liberals had always won some seats and formed the opposition no less than seven times.

This was the sad state of the Liberal Party in Alberta at the time of Trudeau's ascension to power in the spring of 1968. Many of the reasons for this wreckage were complex and long-standing. There were old grievances about farm policies, freight rates, eastern economic domination, memories of the Great Depression, drought, taxes, eastern banks, resource ownership, and a host of others, some real and some imagined.[4]

But now, Alberta Liberals had hope. Like the spirit of Expo 67, the Trudeau fever spread out across the land from the arena in Lansdowne Park. Trudeau was a man for his time—new, youthful, superbly confident, tough, and equally articulate in both official languages. And for many western Canadians who had seen him with Daniel Johnson on television, boy, was he going to stick it to Quebec! Excitement followed him everywhere and always; crowds pressed around him like packed sardines. This was Trudeaumania: we Liberals in the west were as excited by Trudeau's coming to power as our Liberal cohorts everywhere. Even long-time supporters of the New Democratic Party (NDP), Progressive Conservatives (PC), and the Alberta Social Credit Party (Socred), which had ruled Alberta since 1935, were having a good look at him.

There were grumblers—mostly men—who found the whole spectacle ridiculous. Many of them saw Trudeau as effete and a dilettante or worse. Had he not spent most of his adult life in school? And when he wasn't at school, he was travelling—or living with his mother at home! And why had he not served in the war, when he was clearly of age? What about those rumours of a twenty-something Trudeau riding around Montreal on a motorcycle wearing a German army helmet? Was there any truth to the allegations that he was a communist? Hadn't he travelled to Moscow and China during the Cold War and hadn't he tried to row a boat to Castro's Cuba from the Florida coast?[5] Sceptics notwithstanding, Trudeaumania in the spring of 1968 presented the Liberals with ideal conditions for an election. Trudeau, sworn in as prime minister on April 20, asked Governor General Roland Michener to disssolve parliament three days later, and called the election for Tuesday, June 25.

New blood was already flowing into the party by reason of his dramatic leadership victory and obvious charisma. The Liberal riding nomination meetings quickly became the new engine of involvement. They were usually held in school auditoriums or community halls with the rules allowing each candidate's organization to recruit new members right up to the time of the meeting. The excitement of party members at these events was at such a fever pitch that they became mini-national conventions with signs, noisy cheerleaders, and the rest of the hoopla.

The euphoria of Trudeaumania also encouraged many prominent Albertans who had never before given a thought to running for public office to seriously consider the prospect. The Calgary South nomination meeting reflected the new spirit and confidence of Alberta Liberals. The riding had been formed through redistribution just before the 1953 general election. Tories had won the first four elections by whopping margins. However, in 1963 it went Liberal in a close contest that saw ex-Calgary mayor Harry Hays[6] win by 1,859 votes over his Tory opponent. Hays, a successful rancher, auctioneer, and businessman, was then appointed minister of agriculture by Prime Minister Pearson. Two years later, however, Hays' career was cut short when he lost by only 115 votes to Tory Ray Ballard.

Senator Harry Hays (L) wearing his traditional Hays Breakfast garb with Governor General Roland Michener. [*Onions Collection, City of Calgary Archives, CalA 2011-006-12176*]

In 1966 Pearson appointed Hays to the Senate whereupon he began to play an effective role as federal Liberal Party fundraiser and power broker.

The Calgary South contest pitted two highly qualified candidates against each other. One was lifelong Calgarian Bill Dickie, a 42-year-old lawyer, car dealer, and former Calgary alderman. He was also a two-time Liberal MLA for the provincial riding of Calgary Glenmore, one of three sitting Liberals.

Dickie's opponent was Patrick (Pat) Mahoney, 39, a big, burly man with a booming voice. Coming from a family of very modest means, suffering

Trudeaumania Goes West   25

polio that left him with a significant limp requiring a cane, Mahoney by dint of hard work became a self-made man. After receiving his law degree from the University of Alberta, he joined the business empire of construction magnate and former NHL hockey star Mervyn "Red" Dutton, where he worked his way up the management ladder. Despite his youth, Mahoney was reputed to have already made a fortune. He had also been president and general manager of the Calgary Stampeders football club, president of the Canadian Football League (CFL) Western Conference, and president of the Alberta Roadbuilders' Association, all of which upped his profile. Although he was short on political experience, he was long on confidence and had a wide network.[7] Up to then Mahoney had spent almost no time working for the Liberal Party[8] and had not even attended the recent leadership convention. It was only upon watching Trudeau's nomination speech on TV that he began to think of entering politics and running as a Liberal in the next federal election.[9]

The night of the nomination meeting I was part of a thousand-strong noisy crowd of Liberal enthusiasts packed into the Viscount Bennett High School to witness the Mahoney–Dickie battle. Mahoney's chief organizers were lawyers Ken Moore and Jim Palmer, who had adapted to a new era of hard-nosed politics by organizing a large group of high school students to demonstrate and vote en masse for Mahoney, taking full advantage of the riding's constitution, which allowed voting members as young as 16.

Dickie, the odds-on favourite because of his proven electoral success, seemed to be knocked off balance by the show of support for Mahoney. Normally a competent speaker, he faltered in a speech that seemed superficial and flat. Mahoney, by contrast, spoke with confidence and seemed to deal with issues with greater depth and understanding. Mahoney emerged the winner. Dickie was left embittered by the defeat, believing that many Liberals had betrayed him despite his good works on their behalf.[10]

A few days later I attended the nomination meeting in Calgary Centre, another raucous and energetic affair attended by several hundred. Nick Taylor emerged the winner against three opponents. Taylor at the time

(L to R) Pat Mahoney, his wife Mary, and Trudeau in Calgary, April 1969.
[Onions Collection, City of Calgary Archives, CalA 2011-006-0921]

was a 40-year-old geologist and former trustee with the Calgary Catholic School Board who already had a long history with the party.[11]

Even in small, staunchly conservative Lethbridge in Alberta's deep south, the Liberal Party was making waves. Several candidates did battle at a meeting at the civic centre attended by well over a thousand people. One of them was Don Peacock, a born-and-bred Albertan who had lived in Lethbridge as a youth, and a veteran journalist who had just written an excellent book on Trudeau's campaign and victory.[12] He also had strong Liberal credentials in Ottawa as a former special assistant to Harry Hays and Joe Greene, and Prime Minister Pearson.[13]

Peacock's opponents included agriculturist-turned-lawyer John Boras and the Lethbridge mayor, Frank Sherring. Boras had grown up on a farm in the region, had served with the RCAF in World War II and had been a loyal Liberal since his days at the University of Alberta. After four ballots, the party nominated Boras.

The excitement and hard fought contests were repeated in Edmonton and even some rural ridings, where there remained considerable hostility toward Liberals. Excellent candidates were coming forward everywhere. In Edmonton–Strathcona, the Liberals nominated 46-year-old Albertan Hu Harries, businessman, rancher, and dean of the University of Alberta Faculty of Commerce. He had served on Edmonton city council during the 1950s. Harries won against a very popular William Sinclair, who had been the Liberal candidate in the riding in 1965.

In Edmonton West, lawyer Tevie Miller took on the challenge of unseating the Rhodes scholar, World War II hero, and former Commons speaker, Tory Marcel Lambert. Miller, a community activist and lawyer, had political pedigree and name recognition going for him. (Miller's father, Abe, also a prominent Edmonton lawyer, had been a city alderman and Liberal MLA.)

The Liberals stood a great chance in the unlikely and awkward riding of Rocky Mountain. The riding followed the eastern slopes and foothills of the Rocky Mountains northward from the US border for 885 kilometres and included dozens of small towns. It was also the site of an internecine battle between two Tories: one was the incumbent Tory MP, who was now forced to run as an independent Conservative because he had been defeated by a challenger at the nomination meeting. With two Tories fighting it out on the ballot, the door opened wide for the young Liberal candidate, Allen Sulatycky.[14]

The Saskatchewan-born Sulatycky was a Whitecourt lawyer who had made a good showing by placing second in a federal by-election November 1967 in the Jasper–Edson riding (now part of the riding of Rocky Mountain). The sheer size of the constituency required some creative thinking as to the logistics of the voting in the nomination process. The riding executive settled upon a travelling ballot box with votes held on consecutive weekends in the towns of Whitecourt, Banff, Blairmore, and Jasper. According to one of his scrutineers, Sulatycky won by only a margin of two votes.[15]

Mike Maccagno, former mayor of Lac La Biche, leader of the Alberta provincial Liberal Party and a four-time Liberal MLA for the riding of Lac La Biche easily became the Grit standard bearer in the northeastern Alberta riding of Athabasca. Maccagno, the first Italian-born Canadian ever to lead a provincial political party, was a popular businessman running in a federal riding that had elected Liberals five times.

Even in the Tory ranching country of Crowfoot, a riding that covered a wide swath of east-central Alberta, the Liberals were trying to mount a serious challenge. Facing the intimidating cowboy presence of popular Tory incumbent Jack Horner was Liberal Noel Sharp, an Alberta schoolteacher and son of the recent Trudeau kingmaker and cabinet minister, Mitchell Sharp.

In Calgary North, Ukraine-born lawyer and engineer Peter Petrasuk, 42, took the Liberal nomination. The multilingual Petrasuk had a rapidly growing clientele and was involved in many civic activities.

In Medicine Hat the Liberals nominated H. A. (Bud) Olson, local area rancher and the riding's MP. Olson had first been elected for the riding in 1957 when he ran under the Social Credit banner. (He went down to defeat in the 1958 Diefenbaker sweep but returned as a Social Credit candidate to win the elections of 1962, 1963, and 1965.) Although he had a solid record of political success, none of it had yet come as a Liberal. In September 1967 with his Social Credit federal party dying, Olson crossed the floor to become the lone Alberta Liberal sitting in the Commons. His battle to retain the seat would not be easy, given the notoriously conservative nature of the riding.

As the dust settled on the nomination meetings, the Grit candidates were as strong as the party had ever fielded in Alberta. They also included popular Liberal lawyer Rod Knaut for the riding of Battle River, lawyer

Pat Shewchuk in Edmonton East, physician Don Branigan in Peace River, teacher Paul Chalifoux in Pembina, farmer Doug Irwin in Red Deer, mayor of St. Paul, Jules Van Brabant in Vegreville, and farmer Rene Beguin in Wetaskiwin.

But the mother of all Liberal nomination meetings in the lead up to the 1968 federal election was in Edmonton Centre.

4

APRIL—JUNE 1968

The Battle for Edmonton Centre

THE MOST SPECTACULAR Liberal nomination battle in Alberta in 1968 was for the downtown riding of Edmonton Centre with the undisputed star the city's colourful but tainted mayor, Bill Hawrelak.

Born in farming country northeast of Edmonton to a hard-working pioneer immigrant Ukrainian family, Hawrelak came of age during the Great Depression. He drifted into politics, working for a time with the Social Credit movement during its infancy just before it took power in 1935. Helping on the family farm while trying to get ahead, Hawrelak finally settled in Edmonton in 1945. He proved to be an ambitious and smart businessman who was also a tireless volunteer. Shrewdly capitalizing on his east European and Ukrainian roots (shared by many Edmontonians) he earned success in both business and politics, and in 1951 at the age of 37 he was elected mayor.[1]

Hawrelak believed that a successful mayor in an important western city would be a shoo-in to the federal cabinet; Prime Minister St. Laurent promised him so in advance of the 1957 election.[2] At the time the Liberal Party's Ottawa establishment was more than happy to have him as a star candidate and St. Laurent dispatched powerful federal ministers Jack Pickersgill and

Edmonton mayor William Hawrelak (L) with Prime Minister Louis St. Laurent in St. Paul, Alberta, 1957. [Provincial Archives of Alberta A13836]

James Sinclair[3] with fellow Ukrainian Canadian John Decore[4] (Liberal MP for Vegreville) to convince Hawrelak.

However, while getting set to run, Hawrelak got into an unseemly political dust-up with supporters of the federal minister of mines and technical surveys, George Prudham. Prudham, an Edmonton businessman, had first been elected in Edmonton West in 1949, and although well respected, he was dull and uncharismatic and of little help to other Liberal candidates in Alberta. However, when word got out that Hawrelak was seeking the Liberal nomination in Prudham's riding, many Edmonton Liberals vowed to fight the ambitious upstart. Hawrelak then decided instead to seek the Liberal nomination in the riding of Edmonton East where his Ukrainian and eastern European ethnic support was stronger, and he did not have to battle with the Edmonton Liberal establishment.

Although winning Edmonton East for the Liberals seemed a safe bet initially, Hawrelak's chances faded with the rising popularity of the new Tory federal leader from Saskatchewan, John Diefenbaker. Diefenbaker's inspired 1957 campaign boosted Tory support everywhere. Canadians began to see him as a dynamic new leader for a new era; and westerners saw him as one of their own. When the dust settled on election day June 9, 1957, the Tories had 112 seats to the Grits' 106. Diefenbaker was the new prime minister and Hawrelak remained Edmonton's mayor. He lost to the Social Credit candidate and fellow Ukrainian Canadian Ambrose Holowach by 284 votes, with the surging Tory candidate as spoiler.

Less than five months after his federal defeat, Hawrelak was re-elected mayor, capturing 65 percent of the popular vote. Whether he was wheedling money out of senior governments, creating city parks, or promoting major projects, Hawrelak was regarded as a very capable mayor for the first few years. In 1959, however, his luck changed. His business ventures included real estate investment and development—hazardous pursuits for municipal politicians. Some real estate dealings ran afoul of conflict of interest laws, and he was forced to resign as mayor in September 1959.

Undaunted, Hawrelak re-entered city politics and was re-elected mayor in 1963 and 1964. But his real estate dealings soon came back to haunt him. In March 1965 a judge of the Alberta Supreme Court took umbrage at a land sale from Hawrelak's company to the city that was completed after he was returned to office.

Believing he was unfairly ousted from office the second time, the brazen Hawrelak once again returned to the campaign trail in 1966. Hawrelak's major antagonist on city council was fellow Liberal Ed Leger, one of the great muckraking politicians in Edmonton history. Leger's efforts took their toll. This time the people of Edmonton decided the time had come for Hawrelak to take time off, and he lost by almost 10,000 votes to Tory lawyer and city alderman Vince Dantzer.

Hawrelak again turned to federal politics. Although not a voting delegate to the leadership convention, his political aide Nick Mosychuk,[5] a lawyer of shady repute, was and had voted for Trudeau. Five weeks after

Trudeau's leadership victory, Hawrelak announced that he intended to seek the Liberal nomination in Edmonton Centre, where five people were already in the race. He acknowledged that the real battle would be for the nomination but said confidently, "I'm convinced beyond a shadow of a doubt that if I get the nomination, I'll win the seat." He also noted that although support from Liberal Party officials was "lukewarm," his supporters were more important and that he could "be of special service to Edmonton" in seeking federal help to deal with pollution, transportation, and urban renewal.[6]

Some Liberal candidates said they would not appear at the podium with him. Other Liberal supporters said they would withhold campaign contributions.[7] Worse yet, many thousands of Edmontonians, who already resented him as a crude upstart and opportunist, now saw him as a crook. Waspish elements in the city and the party regarded his eastern European roots warily. And even some who admired him believed he needed more time "in the laundry." But Hawrelak's large and loyal following felt that he was the best mayor the city ever had and that his problems arose out of discrimination and nasty politics.

Five days before the contest, organizers realized that this was no run-of-the-mill nomination meeting. The candidates were recruiting such unprecedented numbers of new Liberals that a much larger site than a community hall would be needed and so the venue shifted to the 5,200-seat Edmonton Gardens hockey arena. The day before the nomination meeting Alberta Liberal campaign chairman Senator Earl Hastings told reporter Guy Demarino that "the Liberal Party might withhold support for Mr. Hawrelak as a candidate" because of reports that his nomination "would cause grave division in the Alberta Liberal Party." A meeting was then held to discuss the Hawrelak problem and confront the ex-mayor. Present were Hastings, vice-chairman of the Liberal campaign Roger Kerans (law partner of new mayor Vince Dantzer), Alberta Liberal Party president Leo Lemieux (friend of Alderman Ed Leger, Hawrelak's chief accuser on Edmonton city council), and the very angry Hawrelak. Hastings told Hawrelak that the Liberals under Trudeau were a new party and that since Hawrelak would not represent anything new, the time had come for the Liberal Party to move on.

Hawrelak's reaction was defiant: he "would stand or fall with the people" and he would "sooner have the people on my side than one or two members of the Liberal executive," and neither Hastings nor anyone else "should have any say or dictate to the will of the people."[8]

The nomination meeting had Hawrelak aligned against candidates Russell Dzenick, Bob Russell (later to become leader of the Alberta Liberal Party), Jim Whitford, former Edmonton alderman Gordon McClary, and Don Gray, an automotive sales executive who had launched his campaign a mere nine days before.

The meeting produced the now routine bedlam of bobbing signs, chants, and cheers, but also accusations of dirty tricks, loud arguments, and shoving matches among supporters and opponents of the former mayor. Among the 2,500 people in the arena, 1,661 registered members cast votes in the first ballot with Hawrelak taking the lead with 712 votes. Gray came in second garnering 425, followed by four candidates sharing 525 votes among them (after one candidate bowed out). Before the second ballot began, the four finishers behind Gray all withdrew and swung their support to him, turning the next vote into a fight between Hawrelak and Gray. The result of that second ballot had Gray with 820 votes, a mere 98 more than Hawrelak, who finished with 722. The Stop Hawrelak movement had succeeded; Gray would be the official Liberal standard bearer in Edmonton Centre.

An *Edmonton Journal* reporter wrote, "officials at the Gardens did not hide their joy at the final result. Nobody looked more relieved than chairman David McLean[9] when he told a cheering audience that they had 'chosen well.'"[10]

As expected, Bill Hawrelak did not just slink away and lick his wounds. He requested a recount and complained that many of his supporters were refused ballots and some were even refused entry. Hawrelak then wrote a letter to Prime Minister Trudeau outlining his grievances and accused the Alberta Liberal campaign committee of acting in its own selfish interests, threatening and intimidating him, and treating hundreds of Liberals with contempt. He added ominously, "Personally I am a Liberal, have been one all my life[11] and am a proud supporter of you as our leader. However, in testing public opinion as scientifically as possible it is clear to me that in order to give you Parliamentary support of Edmonton Centre, I should consider the possibility of running as Independent Liberal and win the seat for you and the Liberal Party. You may be sure of my undivided loyalty and support."[12] The bitter Edmonton Centre contest had left Hawrelak in no mood to support either Don Gray or the Liberals and he invited his supporters to join his protest by voting for him [Hawrelak] on election day.[13]

Hawrelak, a man of incredible confidence and optimism, no doubt believed that he had a good chance of winning. But at least he could get some satisfaction if he could stop Gray. A victory for the Tory candidate—Polish-born former Edmonton Eskimo football player Steve Paproski—would be a far more palatable outcome to Hawrelak than any victory for the Liberals. The dramatic contest between Hawrelak and the Liberal Party was not about to end with the nomination of Gray. It would carry on right up to election day.

5

The Battle for Alberta

MAY—JUNE 1968

THERE HAD BEEN EXCITING watershed federal elections in Alberta in the past. Barely two months after coming to power in Alberta in 1935, Social Credit marked its debut in national politics by winning 15 of 17 Alberta federal seats. In 1958 Diefenbaker's federal Tories went from winning 3 seats the year before to a clean sweep of 17. With all this interest in Trudeau, long-suffering Alberta Grits asked, could HE be the game changer for the federal Liberals to storm into prominence in Alberta in 1968?

An area captain in my home riding of Calgary North, I had a front row seat witnessing the campaign there and following what was happening elsewhere in the province. The Liberal campaign organizations were giving their very best; money was flowing into their coffers. Candidates' supporters were at the doors identifying voters; coffee parties and forums were well attended; and Liberal signs throughout the province exhorted *Go Trudeau/Taylor* in Calgary Centre, *Go Trudeau/Gray* in Edmonton Centre, *Go Trudeau/Mahoney* in Calgary South, *Vote for the Trudeau team*. From the national advertising campaign to slugging it out at the doors in individual ridings, the campaign was all about Trudeau. He had the coattails; he was the product the party was trying to sell.

Winning Alberta or any of its federal seats was not a priority with the Liberal campaign strategists in Ottawa. Up for grabs in Alberta was a meagre 19 seats. The four western provinces together had 68 seats. Ontario alone had 88 seats and Quebec had 74. Thus when it came to deciding how a hot commodity like Trudeau would divide his time on the campaign trail, the west was sure to be short-changed in favour of Ontario or Quebec. To make matters worse, the Grits had not done well in the west for a long time. Therefore, not surprisingly, the 1968 campaign would see the prime minister visiting Alberta only three times and divide his time primarily between Calgary and Edmonton.[1]

During a western campaign swing, Trudeau and his entourage made his first visit ever to Edmonton, arriving to a tumultuous reception on a brilliant sunny day in May. Five thousand mostly screaming and giggling young people turned out to greet him on the steps of the city hall as he received the traditional cane and top hat (symbols of the city's annual Klondike Days) from mayor Vince Dantzer. The event was described as a "giant love in for Pierre" and "the biggest and most frantic episode of its kind." A security detail of two Mounties and six city policemen was hard pressed to get him through the crowd. Photos of Trudeau's dramatic appearance in downtown Edmonton graced the front pages of Alberta's daily newspapers.[2]

The trip was not solely political campaigning; Trudeau was receiving an honourary doctorate from the University of Alberta in the lofty company of fellow recipient, United Nations Secretary-General U Thant. Trudeau's acceptance speech—his most important policy speech since being elected leader—showcased his characteristic eloquence and bluntness. He said that the greatest threat to Canada would come from the two-thirds of the peoples in the world who were falling behind in their search for a decent standard of living. He quoted Chateaubriand, "Try to convince the poor man, once he has learned to read and ceased to believe, once he has become as well informed as yourself, try to convince him that he must submit to

Trudeau addresses a crowd in front of Edmonton city hall early in the federal campaign, May 1968. [*Edmonton Journal/Provincial Archives of Alberta J 218.3*]

every sort of privation while his neighbour possesses a thousand times what he needs; in the last resort you will have to kill him."[3] Upon concluding his remarks Trudeau was rewarded with an enthusiastic standing ovation.[4]

Trudeau, in his first campaign appearance in Alberta could not have done any better for his troops. Although all his Alberta candidates were given a major boost from his presence and quality performance, his effort was most effectively felt in Edmonton.

Meanwhile the Grit cause in Alberta was being ably assisted by the performance of the opposition leader—the decent, but boring, 54-year-old Robert Stanfield. In September 1967, Stanfield had become leader of the national Tories after having completed an eleven-year stint as a popular moderate premier of Nova Scotia, the province where his family had made its fortune manufacturing men's underwear. But Stanfield's public image was plodding and awkward; given the telegenic demands of the McLuhan age, he was no match for Trudeau.

The one major issue dividing the two leaders was national unity. Two days after Trudeau's triumphant visit to Edmonton, Stanfield introduced banker Marcel Faribault, a Tory candidate in a Montreal riding, as his new Quebec lieutenant. Faribault, a rotund balding man, had recently been a policy and constitutional advisor to Quebec Premier Daniel Johnson, a man who many outside Quebec believed was an enemy of Canada.

Faribault was a leading proponent of a *deux nations* policy for Quebec and the rest of Canada. The policy had already been adopted at a Tory policy conference but was proving a very tough sell to the Canadian people. In the years ahead the *deux nations* concept would appear in various disguises, such as *special status* and *distinct society*, but meaning the same thing—that Quebecers would feel more at home in Canada if Quebec had more of the powers exercised by the federal government.[5]

Stanfield and Faribault's *deux nations* policy played right into Trudeau's hands. He reminded Canadians that Faribault's boss, Premier Johnson wanted Quebec to have its own powers in international affairs. Any such powers, Trudeau argued, would doom Canada and lead to its disintegration. On the campaign trail he deftly attacked both the NDP and the Tories: "In Quebec they are talking about two nations and about special status, and in the rest of the country they are talking about one nation and no special status...They think the Canadian people are going to be fooled by this type of line. You have to tell the same thing in all parts of the country, and that is what the Canadian people want."[6] *Deux nations* became the main issue of the campaign, with Trudeau keeping Stanfield constantly on the defensive.

To a great many anglophone Canadians in Alberta and elsewhere, Trudeau's attacks on Faribault and Stanfield for dividing Canada were also seen as putting Quebec in its place. Trudeau played it to great political

Nick Taylor campaigns with his Taylor Maids, 1968. [Courtesy of Nick Taylor]

advantage campaigning in the northern Alberta town of Grand Centre, saying, "Quebecers don't know what they are missing and should travel more to see what is happening in the rest of Canada," and he was applauded when he said, "There is one government that speaks for all Canadians, and it is the federal government."[7]

The Alberta Liberal candidates kept working hard. During a picnic held for his campaign workers, Calgary Centre candidate Nick Taylor showed personal true grit volunteering as target in a knife-throwing display. Nick

The Battle for Alberta   41

survived the ooohs and aaaahs to see his perfect photo op in the newspaper the next day. Some of the Liberals' more extreme opponents were scarier than the expert knife-thrower, however. Doug Irwin, the Liberal candidate in Red Deer, reported an anonymous threat he received to withdraw from the campaign. A short time later, gunshots were fired through his car windows.[8]

The Alberta oil industry establishment declared its hand June 14 when Carl Nickle announced his support of the Stanfield PCs. He worried the Liberals would enact the Carter Commission report on tax reform, which would hurt the oil industry. He also condemned medicare as "a poorly conceived, costly project" and lauded Stanfield for his sensible position on national unity as opposed to Trudeau's inflaming confrontational approach with Quebec.[9] Given that Nickle had served as a Tory MP for Calgary South between 1951 and 1957, his statement came as no surprise but it was still an ominous sign for Alberta Liberals.

Son of Alberta oil entrepreneur Sam Nickle,[10] Carl had founded the industry newsletter *Nickle's Daily Oil Bulletin* in his early twenties. With the Leduc oil discovery in 1947, the *Bulletin*'s importance and circulation grew dramatically around the world, thus helping make Nickle a powerful industry advocate and spokesman. Not only did he serve on the board of several oil and gas companies, he was also well connected to the Southam News organization, which owned the *Edmonton Journal*, *Calgary Herald*, *Medicine Hat News*, and 50 percent interest in Nickle's oil industry publishing business. When he spoke—even in his standard subdued monotone—those who owed their jobs and businesses to the oil industry listened.[11]

As the Liberal campaign approached the final stage, resentment grew that southern Alberta had not received a fair share of the Party's best asset. The prime minister had campaigned twice in northern Alberta but had been completely missing in the south. *Herald* columnist Don Sellar wrote that the Albert Liberals had waged an excellent campaign and he believed Pat Mahoney would win Calgary South. However, he noted that southern Alberta Liberals were asking, "Where are you, Pierre Trudeau, now that we need you?" Trudeau was expected for only four hours of campaign time in Calgary in a forthcoming visit.[12]

The election only eight days away, Trudeau began his only campaign visit to Calgary and southern Alberta late at night. An enthusiastic crowd of 4,000 turned up at the Calgary airport to give him a warm and noisy welcome. Although the event was marred by the collapse of the sound system and a several hour wait for his arrival on a chilly evening, his audience seemed more than satisfied simply to greet him with all of their ballyhoo.[13]

The next morning, in a white Stetson, Trudeau addressed an estimated 4,000 at the Calgary Stampede grounds. He continued to attack the Tories on their *deux nations* policy and spoke of the need for a strong federal government to unite the country. He also appealed to traditional Alberta and oil patch conservatism saying there were many areas where the government should not step in to help, and that his government would not promise handouts to all groups who asked for them. He added, "Whatever we do must be done with Canadian taxes, and since no one wants taxes to be increased, we will make no promises." Police officers could hardly hold back the crowds that surged around him and his audience cheered almost every sentence.[14]

With the exception of the microphone glitch at the airport, Trudeau's campaign visit to Calgary was a great success. However, coming as it did with only one week to go before the vote and the public appearances taking place late in the evening and in the morning when most of the city was at work, the timing was far from perfect.

In Edmonton as the election neared, former-mayor Hawrelak was doing his best to thwart his Liberal opponent by trying to confuse the electors of Edmonton Centre. His campaign ran an advertisement in the *Edmonton Journal*, claiming he was "FOR TRUDEAU—FOR EDMONTON CENTRE" and "PERSONALLY ENDORSED BY TRUDEAU'S CAMPAIGN MANAGER." In much finer print the ad read: "Mr. John Ewasew, Q.C. Campaign Manager for the Prime Minister, in his own constituency of Mount Royal, personally endorses Independent Liberal candidate Bill Hawrelak for Edmonton Centre."[15] When questioned, Ewasew told an *Edmonton Journal* reporter that he had only offered Hawrelak his best wishes and luck.[16]

As the campaign edged toward its climax, the Grits appeared to be in contention in ridings in Calgary, Edmonton, and Medicine Hat. In Athabasca, a riding that had elected Liberals numerous times, Mike Maccagno ran a great campaign. In Rocky Mountain, Allen Sulatycky's chances looked good because the two Tories in the race were battling each other.

Trudeau had received terrific national press. Dramatic headlines, flattering pictures and positive news stories helped the Liberal cause at every turn and local media treated Liberal campaigns and candidates fairly, even generously. The *Herald*'s Don Sellar likened the rise of the federal Liberals in Alberta to the rise of Lougheed in the previous provincial election, and boldly predicted that the Grits would win 2 seats in Calgary and between 7 and 9 in the province.[17]

Now everything was in the hands of the voters…almost. The prime minister had one more trick up his sleeve to help his party. On the eve of the election, Monday June 24 in Montreal, Trudeau was watching the St. Jean Baptiste parade from a reviewing stand, when several rowdy Quebec nationalists and separatists began pelting bottles and eggs. While Premier Johnson and Mayor Drapeau ran for cover, and security men attempted to get Trudeau out of harm's way, he courageously shook himself loose, and continued to watch the parade. More than a hundred were injured including forty-three policemen, and nearly three hundred demonstrators were arrested.

The next day—election day—newspapers and television news raved about Trudeau's bravery. Media coverage of the confrontation and Trudeau's courage in the face of danger saturated the country. The *Calgary Herald* printed a photo of Trudeau shaking his fist alongside a news report headlined, "Angry Trudeau Stands Up to Bottle-Hurling Rioters."[18]

To English-speaking Canadians everywhere, the incident confirmed not only Trudeau's personal courage but also that he would put Quebec in its place—a perfect election eve gift to his candidates in Alberta.

6

Breakthrough

JUNE 1968

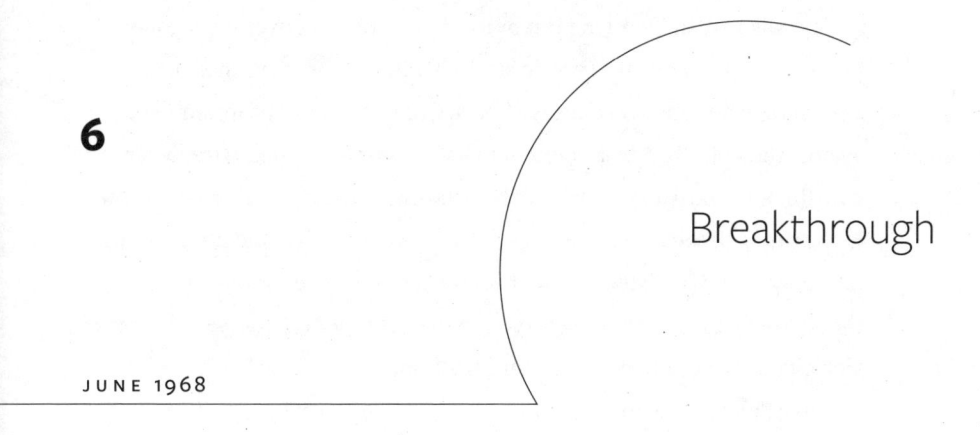

SO, ON ELECTION NIGHT would Trudeaumania end up as the right stuff for Alberta voters? Would the federal Liberals finally get on the political scoreboard and be a new force in Alberta politics? Or was it all just hot air?

Indeed, there was a breakthrough of significant proportions with the Grits capturing 4 seats—their best Alberta showing since 1953. Pat Mahoney narrowly won Calgary South, Hu Harries won convincingly in Edmonton–Strathcona, Bud Olson squeaked through in Medicine Hat, and Allen Sulatycky defeated the split Tories in Rocky Mountain.

Harries took Edmonton–Strathcona with the most substantial Liberal victory in Alberta, defeating his PC opponent by 5,846 votes. In the 1965 election, the riding's Liberal candidate had lost by 4,573 votes, so Harries had completely turned the tables.

In Calgary South, Mahoney beat his PC opponent Ray Ballard by the skimpy margin of 756 votes out of more than 40,000 cast.[1] Ballard had narrowly vanquished Harry Hays less than three years earlier by a mere 115 votes. It was clear that Mahoney would have his job cut out for him.

Mahoney had done well in the wealthier neighbourhoods while his Tory opponent did better in the less affluent.

Bud Olson won Medicine Hat by a narrow 206 votes over his second-place Tory opponent. This was in stark contrast to the more than 6,000-vote margin he had racked up as a Social Credit standard bearer in 1965 against the same Tory opponent in 1968. This time the Social Credit candidate finished third and well out of the running. Given Olson's recognition in the riding because of his string of victories as a Socred, the Liberals probably would not have won with any other candidate running. However, the narrowness of Olson's victory as a Liberal in 1968 compared to his prior victories as a Socred pointed to hard work ahead.

Allen Sulatycky won the riding of Rocky Mountain with 1,563 more votes than his closest Tory rival. Sulatycky's win also warranted a sober assessment. Since his two warring Conservative opponents combined votes added up to 2,000 votes more than he received, his victory looked like a lucky break for the Liberals. However, Sulatycky, too, had to cope with two marginal independent Liberal candidates who snared almost 700 votes between them. In any case, Sulatycky, Mahoney, and Olson would have plenty of work ahead to keep their seats.

Among the Liberal losses, the riding of Edmonton Centre was a heartbreaker. Tory Steve Paproski defeated Liberal Don Gray[2] by 12,062 votes to 11,811—a razor thin margin of 251 votes. The indefatigable tainted ex-mayor Hawrelak[3] running as an Independent Liberal garnered 7,912 votes for a strong third place. Being the spoiler for the Liberals, he exacted sweet revenge.

In addition to the ridings the Liberals actually won, they also made great headway in increasing their share of the popular vote. In Calgary Centre, Nick Taylor had put up a great fight against the former defence minister Douglas Harkness, falling short by only 301 votes—out of a total of almost 34,000 votes cast. In Calgary North, Eldon Woolliams kept the seat in Tory hands by handily defeating Peter Petrasuk by a margin of 3,523

> *Hu Harries campaigns in 1968.* [Edmonton Journal/Provincial Archives of Alberta J 219]

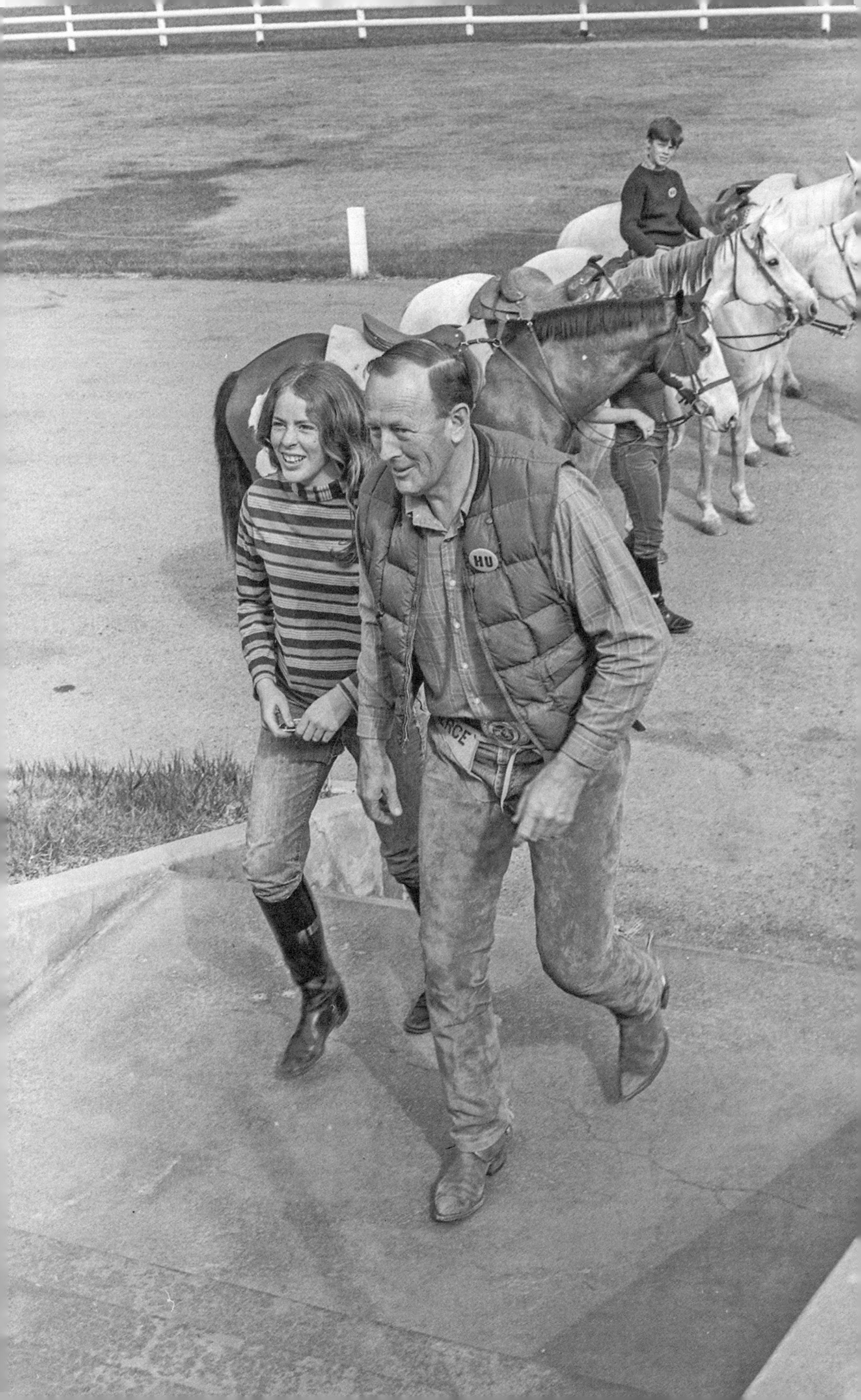
HU

votes. But in the previous election of 1965, the Liberals had finished almost 8,000 votes behind the Tories.

Tevie Miller's spirited campaign gave Tory incumbent Marcel Lambert a good run for his money in Edmonton West and slashed the former Commons speaker's margin of victory from over 12,000 votes to 2,306. In Edmonton East, although Liberal Pat Shewchuk lost to long-time Tory MP Bill Skoreyko by about 3,000 votes, he increased the Grit tally by more than 6,500 votes from the previous election. In the riding of Athabasca, Liberal Mike Maccagno lost to his Tory opponent Paul Yewchuk by 1,230 votes, whereas the Tories had won the previous election with a margin of 5,000 votes.

In Lethbridge, although Liberal John Boras lost by more than 3,700 votes, he came in second while receiving more than 3,300 votes than were cast for the Grits in 1965 when they had finished third. In Palliser, a partially rural riding abutting Calgary, Grit candidate John Ayer lost by more than 7,700 votes but still pulled off second place receiving a respectable 9,147 of the ballots.

Liberals had improved their numbers everywhere in the province. In Battle River, despite having been swamped by the Tories by a four-to-one margin, they received 1,200 more votes than in the previous election and improved their standing to second place from third. In the new redistributed riding of Crowfoot in east-central Alberta, Tory MP Jack Horner defeated Liberal Noel Sharp by almost 12,000 votes. Nonetheless, Sharp garnered 3,000 more votes than the Liberal candidate had received in 1965 while finishing second in a riding where for years Liberals had placed third behind both the Tories and the Socreds.

Only in the riding of Peace River did the Liberals do worse than second place, finishing third behind the NDP by only 210 votes. However, even there they increased their popular vote from 13 to 21.7 percent.

In all, the Liberals won four seats, placed second in fourteen ridings and third in only one, while capturing 35.7 percent of the popular vote. In 1965, they had won no seats, placed second in seven ridings, third place in eight, and fourth place in two, while garnering a mere 22.4 percent of the popular vote.

Trudeaumania in Alberta was real; the boss had worked his magic. In the nation, Trudeau led the Grits to a majority government winning 154 seats and 45.4 percent of the popular vote. The second place finishers were the Tories with 72 seats and 31.4 percent of the vote, followed by the NDP with 22 seats and 17 percent. The Créditistes (the Quebec version of Social Credit) won 14 ridings in Quebec. One lone Independent was also elected. The Liberals won 63 seats in Ontario, 56 in Quebec, 16 in British Columbia, 5 in each of New Brunswick and Manitoba, 4 in Alberta, 2 in Saskatchewan, 1 in each of Newfoundland, Nova Scotia, and the Territories, and none in Prince Edward Island.

The results tallied, speculation now turned to the cabinet. Who would Trudeau choose as his Alberta representation in the cabinet? Would it be one member or two? The day after the election, columnist Don Sellar posed a question that was on the minds of many Liberals: "Had Mr. Trudeau devoted a few more campaign hours to his Liberal country cousins in southern Alberta, how many more Grits would be joining the government caucus now?" As to the makeup of cabinet, Sellar speculated that Olson was eligible because he was seen as an excellent agriculture critic with ministerial potential, and that Harries could very well get the nod as a northern Alberta representative. He concluded, "the onus is on the Trudeau government to show it can pay more than lip service to its surging Alberta Liberal wing," and that the Alberta Liberals' hard work that moved the party forward "must be rewarded somehow. It's only just."[4]

In Calgary, Mahoney's supporters hoped he would be chosen. Not only was he smart and successful, his people had run a great campaign. Senator Hays, rapidly becoming one of the Liberal Party's heavyweights, was a Mahoney supporter but he was also a good friend of Olson's—since they both came from agriculture backgrounds and had both supported the Social Credit Party for many years. Hays was said to have been influential in Olson's 1967 defection to the Liberals.

Disquieting reports about Mahoney's arrogance and impatience threatened to destine him to the backbenches.[5] Observers who thought that Olson would be a good appointment to the cabinet included James Bentley, president of the Canadian Federation of Agriculture, Tory MP Patrick Nowlan, who considered Olson one of the five best debaters in the House, and columnist Douglas Fisher, a former NDP MP who remarked that Olson was one of the five most effective MPs overall.[6]

Harries told the press that he was not making any bets on being appointed since he had only met Trudeau once, and two days after the election, he was scheduled to fly to Pakistan for a month to consult with its government on natural gas policy.[7]

The *Calgary Herald* and *Edmonton Journal* both welcomed the majority government and gave Trudeau most of the credit. Both lambasted Stanfield for recruiting Faribault as his Quebec lieutenant, and saw the Conservative campaign as mismanaged and uninspiring. The *Herald* noted the unprecedented Trudeau-inspired participation of young people and saw Canada as having "the necessary kind of virility and vitality to respond to vigorous and imaginative leadership." It attributed Liberal gains in Alberta to Trudeau's attractive personality and to Stanfield's failure to endorse Premier Manning's conservative philosophy. The *Journal* said the west now deserved stronger representation in the cabinet and a fair share of appointments of parliamentary assistants to ministers.[8]

Trudeau's post-election cabinet was sworn in at Rideau Hall July 6th, 1968. Among the appointed several would have a significant role in the political affairs of Alberta and the west in the years ahead: Joe Greene (Ontario), Minister of Energy, Mines and Resources; Edgar Benson (Ontario) Minister of Finance; Jean Chretien (Quebec), Minister of Indian Affairs and Northern Development; Jean-Luc Pepin (Quebec), Minister of Industry, Trade and Commerce; John Turner (Ontario), Minister of Justice and Attorney General; Bryce Mackasey (Quebec), Minister of Labour; Leo Cadieux (Quebec), Minister of National Defence; Eric Kierans (Quebec), Postmaster General; Paul Hellyer (Ontario), Minister of Transport; Charles (Bud) Drury (Quebec), president of the Treasury Board; James Richardson (Manitoba), minister without portfolio; Otto Lang (Saskatchewan) minister without portfolio, and Donald Macdonald

(Ontario), president of the Privy Council. From Alberta came only Bud Olson, the new Minister of Agriculture.

Ontario led the way with eleven portfolios, Quebec received ten, three went to British Columbia, and one each to Alberta, Saskatchewan, Manitoba, Nova Scotia, New Brunswick, and Newfoundland.

Trudeau's new cabinet was well received in Alberta. The province had not yet begun to complain at being lumped in with "the Prairies" which had received three appointments—three more than they had in the last Pearson cabinet. Besides Olson, the other Prairie ministers were former University of Saskatchewan law school dean Otto Lang, and scion of the famous Winnipeg investment family, James Richardson.

The *Calgary Herald* lauded Trudeau for appointing the experienced Olson saying Trudeau had shown "skill and imagination" in making excellent cabinet choices.[9] The *Edmonton Journal*'s views on the new cabinet were not so positive, complaining that the cabinet did not have the new look that Canadians had hoped for. However, the newspaper approved Olson's appointment because he was in a good position to help solve the current problem of unsold western Canadian wheat in storage.[10] The surplus wheat problem would become one of the Trudeau government's most protracted and difficult problems in its first term in office.

The *Journal* and Edmontonians could have complained more about the exclusion of Harries. His election victory in Edmonton–Strathcona had by far the largest margin of any of the Liberal wins in the province and he was as qualified as any elected MP to be in the cabinet. He had been the dean of the faculty of Business Administration at the University of Alberta, ran his own international economic consulting business, was chairman of the board of Canadian Phoenix Pipe and Steel, had several university degrees including one in agriculture, and was in the ranching business. And Edmonton was a city traditionally kinder to federal Grits than Medicine Hat.

Fellow MP Allen Sulatycky viewed Harries' exclusion from the cabinet a mystery and Trudeau's first major mistake in his government's approach to relations with Alberta and the west. Sulatycky said of Harries, "he seemed a natural choice. No other western MP had his scope of knowledge of the issues important to the west. He was in his element whether in a Bassano barn or a Bay Street boardroom. Had he been given a chance I think he had the potential to become a dominant figure in western Canada for many years."[11]

In Olson's riding of Medicine Hat in the six previous elections, the Liberals had managed second place only twice—in 1953 and 1957—when they finished behind the Socreds. They placed third four times. In the last four elections prior to the 1968 election, the Liberal popular vote in the riding averaged a paltry 14.5 percent. In the 1949, 1953, and 1957 campaigns, Liberals had done reasonably well with an average voter support of 38 percent, but those numbers reflected the popularity of the Liberal candidate, the colourful mayor Harry Veiner.[12] By contrast, in Harries' riding of Edmonton–Strathcona in the four prior elections the Liberal popular vote had averaged a much healthier 26 percent. These statistics showed that unless Olson had the drawing power to bring his Social Credit support with him as a Liberal, Strathcona was a more promising riding for the Liberals to win than Medicine Hat.

Albertans could have been miffed at having only one of their numbers appointed to the cabinet since their province now had a population more than twice that of either Saskatchewan or Manitoba and was richer in resources. Albertans also could have made the point—to be stressed a few years later by Peter Lougheed—that it was time to scrap the idea of the Prairies being a single region for federal convenience because there were actually significant differences between the provinces—in population, culture, and economics. But the province was not yet in the mood for such muscle flexing.

The new minister of agriculture, Bud Olson, was born in 1925 in Iddesleigh, a remote hamlet in the far southeast corner of the province. He was a farmer and rancher, and owner of a general store, presenting as a modest, "aw shucks" man of the Prairies. Although only 42, he had a stooped appearance and gave the impression of a man many years older. Although his public speaking style was precise, it came off plodding and

(L to R) Bud Olson, Trudeau, Hu Harries (behind), and Allen Sulatycky at an Edmonton campaign appearance. [Courtesy of Allen Sulatycky]

dull. Most Alberta Liberals, except those living near his Medicine Hat riding or those who served with him in Ottawa, knew little of him, and many—because of his Social Credit background—looked upon him with some distrust.

Olson appeared to have had a good relationship with long-time Social Credit premier Ernest Manning, who'd attended his rallies in Medicine Hat when he ran for the federal Social Credit Party. Although Olson was rumoured to have switched parties to the Grits in 1967 due to his dislike of Manning's theory of polarizing federal politics, by then it was obvious that Social Credit was a spent force in Alberta federally and that if he was to have a future as an Ottawa MP, it would have to be with either the PCs or the Liberals.

Breakthrough 53

Although he was now a five-time winner in his riding, Olson had only won once as a Liberal and by a very narrow margin. His choice as the only Liberal minister from Alberta in the new government was a fragile foundation upon which future party success could be built. If the howling winds of Trudeaumania were to subside in the next election—even just a little— Olson's seat could very well be lost.

Whatever the reasons— his parliamentary experience, his floor crossing before Trudeau became leader, or Trudeau's belief that Olson could bring some prairie farmer support—Olson's appointment reflected that Trudeau had opted for the past over the present. At this point in its history, however, Alberta was no longer just a ranching and farming outpost in the west. The province was now dominated by two fast-growing major cities, each closing in on 500,000 in population, the economies of which were fuelled by the rapidly expanding oil and gas business, and a thriving construction industry. Alberta was marching into the modern age. The recent 1967 electoral success of the cool and urbane Peter Lougheed's Tories as the official opposition in the Alberta legislature was a clear portent of the future.

7

The Honeymoon

JUNE–DECEMBER 1968

THE ALBERTA FEDERAL LIBERAL PARTY was now strong, with a burgeoning membership, four MPs in a majority government, and one of them a cabinet minister. The success of 1968 brought new life to the federal party organization all over the country. Post-election riding association events such as fundraisers, policy meetings, federal minister visits, picnics, and other social activities were well attended. Members prepared resolutions for conventions and annual meetings and fought for executive positions. When the Alberta Liberal Party announced early in September that its annual convention would be held in November, it also disclosed that membership had jumped from 4,000 to 16,000 during the year.[1]

Several Liberal candidates who had lost in the June election were eager to get back into the arena. Peter Petrasuk, defeated in Calgary North, contested a seat on Calgary city council in a ward within the riding of his federal bid and handily defeated his Tory opponent by carrying all 24 polls. Not content with his law practice, business interests, and an aldermanic seat, Petrasuk announced he would now seek the presidency of the Alberta Liberal Party. Mike Maccagno, who had resigned the leadership when he ran for his federal seat, was now expected to be appointed to the Senate. Several Liberals were considering their prospects as his replacement.[2]

Minister of Finance Edgar Benson brought down his first budget. Modest corporate and personal tax increases, acceleration of corporate tax payments, and a deficit of $675 million were among the highlights—none of which impressed the Alberta business community.[3] But critics placed most of the blame on the previous government and its minister of finance, Mitchell Sharp.[4]

In Calgary in November, I was among 350 delegates who showed up at the party's annual convention to hear thought-provoking ideas, debate federal and provincial policy resolutions, and elect a new executive. The genial national president of the Liberal Federation of Canada from Toronto, Senator Dick Stanbury, told the delegates that the Party must marshal the public enthusiasm Trudeau had generated, and implement the concept of "participatory democracy"[5] in their policy-making process, with the riding associations taking the lead in encouraging the Party's grassroots and other Canadians to permanently engage in making policy. Stanbury decried political patronage, telling the delegates that Liberals had a chance to make their community and country better places "not just for you and your friends, but for all the people of your community."[6]

At a plenary session, a delegate from Red Deer (and spouse of prominent, eccentric lawyer John Robinson) agreed that Trudeau's "Just Society" should have no room for patronage. She said that the standing joke in Ottawa was that many Liberals in western Canada did not want Liberal MPs actually elected, because they would then have to change "the rotten patronage system upon which so many of our Liberal workers thrive." She pointed out that out of 34 Senate appointments made by Pearson, 32 were defeated Liberal candidates and claimed that Liberal candidates were "running for office with no particular desire or intention of getting elected, but with the certain knowledge that this leads the way to a political reward."[7]

Indeed, plenty of Liberal members supported the party for private or professional advancement. Many would run campaigns with little money or effort to earn an opportunity for a judicial or Senate appointment, or a coveted order-in-council appointment to one of the many federal boards or commissions. But the Liberals were, and are, no different from any other ruling political party in a provincial or federal government. Many Liberal, Conservative, and NDP lawyers work for their party to help secure federal prosecutions and other legal work to put food on the table. Many do so to become judges or senators. Architects and engineers of all political stripes pursue federal contracts and projects; Liberals are/were not the only patronage seekers.

There was also more to the patronage issue than just money or cushy jobs. Party members doing a large share of the grunt work at the local level wanted a say in who got what, rather than leaving it to the party brass in Ottawa who did not know or care about what was happening on the home front. Party money-raiser Senator Harry Hays, who was about to begin his role as the chief fundraiser in Alberta and thereby become the most important dispenser of patronage in the province, hardly ever set foot in a local party gathering.

Alberta Liberals actively working for the federal Liberals at the local level were largely invisible to, or ignored by, the party establishment in Ottawa and Toronto. Illustrative of this state of affairs was a story Liberal Senator Keith Davey[8] relates in his memoir, *The Rainmaker*. He wrote about a business trip to Calgary in 1966 when his vehicle collided with another car causing minor damage. After he returned to Ottawa, he received a letter from a lawyer threatening to sue him for a million dollars. Davey immediately visited Bay Street lawyer and party fundraiser Senator John Aird for advice. Aird told him not to worry, that he would get him the best lawyer in Calgary. The next day, the Calgary lawyer called Davey to tell him that the matter was settled and to forget about the incident. "You can imagine how grateful I was, even more so when he refused to discuss any fee. The lawyer? His name was Peter Lougheed."[9]

If there was one thing the Liberal Party had in teeming abundance in Alberta and elsewhere, it was lawyers, but when needing the name of an

(L to R) Premier Harry Strom, Harold Cardinal, and Jean Chretien, December 1970.
[Edmonton Journal/Provincial Archives of Alberta J547]

Alberta lawyer, these Liberal Party heavyweights from Toronto and Ottawa could only think of Peter Lougheed, the Tory leader.[10]

Another featured speaker at one of the convention sessions was the Cree president of the Indian Association of Alberta, 23-year-old Harold Cardinal.[11] Cardinal, who had grown up on a reserve on Lesser Slave Lake, told the delegates that he could never support the Liberal Party because of federal government paternalism and oppressive "mandarins" who were trying to turn the Indian into a "nice little brown white man." Despite his hard-hitting statements, he was treated to enthusiastic applause.[12] A few days later Cardinal would meet Minister of Indian Affairs and Northern Development Jean Chretien, who was in Alberta to meet Indigenous leaders. Thus began prolonged public confrontations and negotiations over a new Indian policy.

The convention elected a new party executive headed up by Peter Petrasuk[13] who easily captured the presidency. Petrasuk had brought a lot of new people into the Liberal Party and to politics generally, including me. One of Petrasuk's early volunteers running errands in the mid-1960s was

Ralph Klein,[14] then in his mid-twenties. Klein in those days was a congenial fellow who liked political shoptalk, drinking, and smoking other people's cigarettes.

As the Party attempted to harness the burgeoning energy at the local level, the government began dealing with its legislative program and the tough issues of the day. For example, the civil war in Nigeria and starving people in the breakaway region of Biafra had the government taking plenty of heat, particularly, when grilled by a reporter, Trudeau responded, "Where's Biafra?" It was the first of a series of flip comments that gave him a reputation for callousness. The dilemma was that by helping Biafra, Canada could appear to be supporting a secessionist movement—not a good position given the increasing noise coming from Quebec.[15]

By the end of the year, Alberta's oil and gas industry was demanding government attention. The Independent Petroleum Association of Canada (IPAC), an organization comprised of smaller Canadian oil and gas explorers and producers, urged Minister of Energy Joe Greene to make Canada self-sufficient in crude oil by November 1, 1972. They also wanted a continental oil policy with the United States whereby the Canadian share of production would be proportionate to its proven continental reserves. Since Alberta was easily the major oil producer in Canada, the province had much to gain if IPAC's proposals were adopted.[16]

Bud Olson seemed to be doing well in his new portfolio; Southam News reporter Bob Hill described him as one of the Trudeau team's ablest performers.[17] But his new farm bills were under sharp attack by Alberta Tory MP Jack Horner, who represented the Crowfoot riding, next door to Olson's Medicine Hat riding. Western farmers viewed Horner as their most effective parliamentary spokesman and champion on farm issues. According to Allen Sulatycky, this rattled Olson to no end and led Olson to take a visceral dislike of Horner, which at times made necessary legislative political compromises more difficult.[18] Opposition MPs were also demanding special help for grain farmers, due to crop losses from weather conditions and a decline in demand for Canadian wheat worldwide.

In late fall during Question Period, ex-prime minister John Diefenbaker and Calgary North MP Eldon Woolliams[19] attacked Olson with reports that 200,000 bushels of damp wheat could be lost if drying facilities were not found immediately. Olson accused opposition MPs of seeking publicity and damaging Canada's reputation for selling good grain. Covering all of his political bases he complimented the efforts of the elevator companies, the Canadian Wheat Board, the Board of Grain Commissioners, the provincial agriculture departments, and most importantly "the resourcefulness, ingenuity and capability of the individual farmer."[20]

Pat Mahoney finally made the political news, too, when he was appointed vice-chairman of the House Transport Committee. He also championed the cause of the Company of Young Canadians (CYC) to help youth unemployment and catalyze social change[21] and fought for increased funding for Canada's Olympic team.[22] The 1968 Grey Cup game played on November 30 gave him a great national photo op, given that he was still president of the Calgary Stampeders, one of the contenders. (Circumstances could have been better; his team lost to the Ottawa Rough Riders.)

Mahoney continued to make the news by setting up acting Minister of Energy Jean-Luc Pepin during Question Period, allowing Pepin to announce the appointment of a three-person task force to review the impact of petroleum development in the north, as well as improve liaison with the industry. Mahoney's move was lauded by both oil industry and Alberta government spokesmen.[23]

Before the end of the year, rumours had Mahoney's political future in Ottawa looking very good. His friendship with Senator Hays and the new Alberta minister Bud Olson was paying dividends. Edmonton–Strathcona MP Hu Harries was not doing as well. Some thought that Hays had not wanted Harries in cabinet because he wouldn't have the same influence on the self-confident Harries as he would on Olson. Harries' exclusion from cabinet soon left him embittered and not inclined to participate in the Liberal caucus or cooperate with the government. His appearances in the House of Commons became infrequent and even some of his political allies in Edmonton and Ottawa found his intellectual arrogance and aloofness very annoying.[24]

The year wound down in the Commons with Trudeau heading south to scuba dive in the Caribbean and prepare for his first Commonwealth conference in London. As MPs journeyed home for Christmas, Canadians and Albertans seemed content with their federal government. Given their hard work and success over the past year, MPs had every right to enjoy a holiday break. Yes, it had been a very good start. But the honeymoon was over.

II

Oil and Other Minefields

8

In Alberta, It's About Oil, Stupid!

JANUARY–APRIL 1969

AS THE NEW YEAR DAWNED, oil (or "crude oil"[1] in all of its facets) quickly became a source of conflict between the Trudeau government and the Alberta oil and gas industry.

By 1969 the industry's impact on Alberta's economic and population growth was profound. Calgary's population stood at nearly 400,000, almost a four-fold increase since 1941.[2] Most of that growth came directly from the expansion of the oil and gas industry.[3] The city housed 90 percent of the executive offices of all oil and gas companies operating in Canada, more than a thousand corporate head offices (which placed the city third in the country, behind only Toronto and Montreal) and about five hundred branch offices.[4] Employment estimates in industries and businesses feeding off the oil and gas business—such as construction, manufacturing, transportation, and the service sector—were as high as one-half of the city's total employment.[5]

The industry also impacted the city of Edmonton, 295 kilometres north of Calgary. Alberta's capital city had a larger population, a similar growth rate, and was the city closest to most of the productive oil fields.[6] It provided much of the muscle, tools, technical equipment, oil field services, storage capacity, and materials to find and produce hydrocarbons. Even in Alberta's smaller cities (such as Grande Prairie, Medicine Hat, and Red Deer) and dozens of towns scattered throughout the province, the oil industry was a huge job provider.[7] My former economics professor at the University of Alberta, the eminent Eric Hansen, estimated that in the late 1960s and early 1970s, some 700,000 Albertans (out of a total population of 1.6 million) were affected directly or indirectly by the oil and gas industry.[8] Exploration wells, pipelines, surveying, seismograph work, and a host of other activities required skilled and unskilled labour, manufacturers, suppliers, and the whole gamut of ancillary industries essential to searching for and producing the elusive black gold.

The future of the industry in Alberta never looked better. Conventional oil production was forecast to triple by 1980. Plants designed to extract the bitumen from the oil sands in northern Alberta to produce oil (sometimes called synthetic crude oil), were being built and many more were in the planning stage. Syncrude Canada wanted to build a plant that produced 80,000 barrels a day; Shell Canada was planning one for 100,000 barrels; and the Japanese reportedly wanted one for 300,000 barrels.[9]

The Alberta oil industry, like the oil industry the world over, was at the time "a man's game," a game played by oilmen. The oilmen's self-image was of rough and tough risk takers and hinterland explorers, self-sufficient hunters and generous providers. In 1969 women in the industry worked almost exclusively in clerical and accounting jobs. The posh downtown Calgary Petroleum Club[10] and the Ranchmen's Club did not allow women to become members, or even to be on the premises except at certain times of day in restricted areas or for special occasions.[11]

The first stirrings of trouble in early 1969 stemmed from the new oil discovery in Alaska's Prudhoe Bay, one of the largest oil fields ever discovered in the US. Some Alberta politicians and oilmen had begun to fret publicly that the current US market for Canadian oil[12] could be displaced.[13] To guard against such a catastrophe, the oilmen and politicians demanded more Canadian crude oil be exported into the United States, and more be sold throughout the Canadian domestic market.[14]

Not being able to sell Canadian oil into the whole Canadian market was a sensitive issue. The 1961 national oil policy of Tory PM Diefenbaker provided that only Canadian oil (almost all of it produced in Alberta) would be sold into the Canadian market from BC to the Ottawa Valley line (a demarcation line cut along the Ottawa Valley and then south through Ontario, west of the Quebec border, to the St. Lawrence River). The remaining market area of Quebec and the Maritimes would be served by cheaper imported oil from Venezuela and the Middle East.[15]

In the 1960s importing oil into eastern Canada at the same time as exporting Canadian oil to the United States made sense. Around 700,000 barrels of Canadian oil per day were exported to the US at a price of $2.60 a barrel. The same amount of foreign oil was imported into eastern Canada at a price of $2.20. This was not only good for the federal government's balance of payments, but prices were kept down at the pump for eastern Canadian consumers. At the same time western producers enjoyed top prices on oil exported to the US, and a market in Canada west of the Ottawa Valley protected from cheaper imported oil.[16] However, oilmen saw this only as a roadblock to increased Canadian production and sales.

By 1969 smaller independent Canadian oil companies were discovering increasing supplies of oil. As a result, many of them demanded the construction of an oil pipeline to Montreal so they could sell their oil into eastern Canadian markets to replace the imported oil. However, the major international oil companies such as Imperial Oil, Shell, Gulf, Chevron, British Petroleum, and Texaco—representing about 80 percent of Canada's industry—were at best neutral to a pipeline because they owned oil everywhere in the world that could be sold in the Quebec and Maritime market.[17]

Canadian oil was exported and sold to the US west of the Rockies without quotas. However, exports of Canadian oil east of the Rockies were subject to a 1967 US–Canada agreement that set quota limits to protect the US domestic industry. The quota agreement (secret until tabled in Parliament February 28, 1969) had set the limit at 280,000 barrels per day for 1968 and authorized annual increases for 1969 through 1971 of up to 26,000 barrels per day.[18]

The oilmen wanted the quotas on exports removed. As they saw it, demand for their oil was limited because of two major obstacles: the Ottawa Valley line restrictions and the US–Canada quota agreement. The oilmen wanted to sell all the oil they produced—and they were able to produce a lot of it. Although oil production in 1968 averaged only about 700,000 barrels a day, many believed that volume could be easily increased to a million barrels by early 1969; some industry officials even thought 1,600,000 barrels within a month.[19]

In Ottawa, there was considerable support among western politicians. Edmonton Liberal Senator J. Harper Prowse called for a new natural resources policy that addressed the production and marketing of Canadian oil. He said that not only was the development of Alberta's huge oil sands deposits jeopardized because of limited markets, they were now in even greater peril because of the Alaskan oil discovery. Prowse also reminded his fellow senators that oil provided one-third of all provincial revenues in Alberta and was as important to Albertans as cultural and linguistic rights were to Quebec.[20]

A possible solution was a continental oil policy with the US and Canada working together to provide free access to all North American oil production in a comprehensive North American market. Alberta Tory MPs quickly embraced this idea. Calgary North MP Woolliams told the prime minister that Canada needed a tough negotiating team so that Canada would get its fair share of the market. Edmonton Centre Tory MP Steve Paproski also called for a continental oil policy while asking, "How can we have a continental oil policy when we have difficulty selling our own oil in eastern Canada?" Trudeau responded that Canada's oil exports would be a subject discussed with President Nixon at their first meeting scheduled for later in the month.[21] Meanwhile in the Alberta legislature, Peter Lougheed and his small band of Tories began to badger the Strom government into talking

Otto Lang is interviewed by CFQC television reporter Greg Barnsley during the 1968 campaign. [CFQC Photographers Collection, Saskatoon Public Library QC-4468-16]

to Ottawa about marketing more Alberta oil in advance of the Nixon–Trudeau talks.[22]

Otto Lang, Liberal MP from Saskatoon–Humboldt, minister without portfolio and acting for Energy (in place of an ailing Joe Greene) addressed a Calgary meeting of the Canadian Petroleum Association (CPA). A Rhodes scholar and former dean of the University of Saskatchewan law school,[23] Lang informed the seasoned oilmen that they should expect no special treatment from the federal government, but instead a "rational" consideration of their problems. He told them that his job was not to be their "mouthpiece" but rather to understand and present their reasonable claims to the government and, when necessary, to the people of Canada.

He also described his visit to Calgary as "untimely" given that it was on the eve of the Nixon–Trudeau meetings where oil would be on the agenda.[24]

The *Calgary Herald's* Jim Armstrong wrote that Lang's audience found his speech humourless, non-informative, and that he had "never seen such a disappointing reaction to a speech before." He then said that oil executives had little confidence in the federal government protecting their interests and that the government had never understood their problems.[25] As the chief business columnist writing exclusively on oil and gas, Armstrong was widely read and expressed the opinions of many prominent oilmen.

In the Alberta legislature, Premier Strom tabled a brief that he intended for Trudeau, which called for a reduction of Canada's dependence on foreign oil and an all-new North American oil policy directing the maximum use of Canadian oil in domestic markets and maximum growth of exports to the United States. Strom added that Trudeau "is not fully conversant" with the industry and Lougheed commented that the recent remarks of Otto Lang in Calgary were "disturbing."[26]

On March 24 in Washington, DC, Trudeau and Nixon had their initial meeting to discuss a range of subjects including the economy, defence, communications, foreign policy, wheat pricing, and energy issues.[27] The tone of the meeting was said to be upbeat and friendly. Alberta oilmen could take comfort from reports that the two leaders had discussed both the issues of Canadian exports to the United States and the Alaskan discovery's impact on the Canadian industry. Further talks between officials were to work toward resolving outstanding oil and energy issues.[28] A statement at the conference's close acknowledged that Canada and the US shared an interest in expanding the cross-border movement of energy, and seemed to make some progress toward resolving the concerns of the Alberta government and the oilmen.[29]

This was the state of the relationship between the oilmen and the government on the eve of Trudeau's Calgary visit. He would have to tread very carefully to preserve or build upon the support he had received in the election. Because, in Alberta, it was about oil, stupid![30]

9

Mr. Trudeau Lays an Egg

MARCH–MAY 1969

ACCOMPANYING THE ERA of Vietnam and rock and roll were raucous civil demonstrations, sit-ins, teach-ins, love-ins, long-haired bearded hippies, and marijuana. Young people in Canada and the world vented about what was wrong with contemporary society and whatever they saw as injustice.

In 1966, in an effort to channel these rebellious social forces into something positive, the federal government had formed the Company of Young Canadians (CYC). Patterned on the US Peace Corps, the CYC was staffed and directed by young people who worked in communities across the country trying to guide and help those caught up in this new social turmoil. The CYC was active in civil rights and anti-poverty advocacy, helped organize food co-ops and drop-in centres for young people, and tried to address the problems of drug and alcohol use and addiction. Some CYC workers also dressed like hippies and demanded government address social problems.[1]

Contemporary Canadian society had never seen anything like the hippie movement and in Alberta, the most conservative of provinces, many people were convinced that Canadian society was going to hell. One of the least

Alberta Chief Justice J.V.H. Milvain. [*Legal Archives Society of Alberta 47 G 40*]

amused was J.V.H. (Val) Milvain, Chief Justice of the Alberta Supreme Court Trial Division. Raised in a conservative British household on a southwestern Alberta ranch, Milvain was the son of a homesteader who had helped introduce the genteel sport of polo to the west.[2] He had been a vigorous supporter of the Conservative Party and conservative traditions, running unsuccessfully as a Tory candidate in the 1935 provincial election that saw William Aberhart and his Social Credit movement steamroll into power.[3] Milvain's 1959 appointment to the bench came courtesy of Diefenbaker.[4]

Milvain was an articulate and well-mannered gentleman, but deeply intolerant of what he measured to be disorderly behaviour, as demonstrated in his speech to the Kiwanis Club during its Respect for Law week. He warned his audience that unless the majority of people stood behind the law, "we will be destroyed by the noisy clamorers after what they call civil rights. The clamorer after civil rights wants the freedom to break your head with his stick, but it is your duty not to go on freedom marches, camp outside legislatures or preach insurrection." He also told his listeners, "when police brutality is played up by the news media, it is playing into the hands of those who want to disrupt law and order," and called demonstrators "bearded bastards," receiving a standing ovation.[5] By current standards of judicial conduct, Milvain's speech was outrageous, signalling extreme bias and intolerance; however in 1969, the incident passed without criticism.[6]

Against this backdrop of conservative Alberta society, the social upheavals at play in its communities, and the primacy of oil in so many of its citizens' lives, Trudeau was to address a major Liberal Party fundraising dinner at the Stampede Corral hockey arena on April 12.[7]

Although his schedule had been meticulously planned by the Prime Minister's Office (PMO) and Alberta party brass, a group of social activists invited him to meet beforehand for a "Poor Man's Banquet" on the pedestrian mall in the heart of the city's downtown core. To emphasize the difference between its event and the elitist Liberal Party dinner, the group also invited the public and, through the media, reminded them to bring their own lunch.

The group that had planned the banquet was a one-month-old community action group called NOW, an acronym for No Other Way, created by the Calgary office of the federally funded CYC.[8] NOW had set up a soapbox and public address system for Trudeau to speak and respond to questions, and told the press if Trudeau refused to meet with them, they intended to march the several blocks to the arena hosting the Liberal dinner and demand an audience.[9]

MP Pat Mahoney tried to head off any embarrassing confrontation by showing up to claim that NOW's invitation had been received only two days before, so there had been too little time to fit the event into the busy schedule. Amid the thousand or so mostly young demonstrators with their placards, boos, and catcalls, a NOW volunteer jumped on the soapbox waving a double-registered mail invitation, which he said had been acknowledged by the PMO more than three weeks earlier. The crowd, now visibly angry, began their march to the arena.

Trudeau arrived outside of the Stampede Corral at seven that evening and was immediately surrounded by well-rehearsed demonstrators shouting, "We want Trudeau! We want Trudeau!" Looking tanned from a week of heli-skiing in BC, he was wearing a white cowboy hat, light sports jacket, and western tie, as well as a long string of hippie beads given to him by a demonstrator. Trudeau listened for a few moments to some jeers and demands for action, then grabbed a bullhorn. Cool and calm, he patiently answered the questions that emerged above the din. He said that Canadians had to be realistic and try to solve problems with available resources. On low-income housing, he said that the constitution prevented the federal government from building homes; this was up to the provinces or the cities. For its part, he said, the federal government was meeting its responsibility by giving "hundreds of millions" to the provinces to build homes.

Trudeau also took some heat about attending the expensive $50-a-plate dinner. He responded by telling them that in order to run a political party he would rather collect money from the party faithful than hit up a corporation for a $500,000 contribution. Trudeau appeared to enjoy the encounter. He stood his ground while escaping projectiles, including a tomato, parts of which allegedly landed on his jacket. The crowd appeared to be satisfied with the exchange and began to disperse thus allowing him and his entourage to enter the arena only about twenty minutes behind schedule.[10]

I had helped organize the event so my wife and I joined another thousand or so guests to greet Trudeau as he entered one of the biggest political fundraising dinners ever held in the province up to that time. Some ticket holders were Liberal partisans who just wanted to see, hear, and cheer along their party leader and prime minister. But at least half of the attendees were connected to the oil industry and wanted to hear about oil markets in the United States and Canada, a pipeline to Montreal, a continental oil policy, and the talks with Nixon over energy. Some wanted to know about the growing problem of world grain markets and prairie wheat surpluses, and perhaps a handful wanted to hear about Canada's changing contribution to NATO. Early scuttlebutt about the content of his speech suggested that Trudeau might give a speech exclusively about Canadian oil policy.[11]

It was not to be. The subject of Trudeau's talk was NATO and Canada's defence policy.[12] He lectured the crowd that they should understand Canada's defence policy because it ate up one-sixth of the federal budget. To the hawks in the audience, he offered a little solace by telling them, "We are not neutralists and we are not pacifists, but we must leave our military options open to our priorities." He would not allow the NATO military alliance to determine Canadian foreign policy and, until a new defence policy was presented to Parliament, he was not prepared to say what forces would be put into or drawn out of NATO.[13]

Press reaction was brutal. Joyce Fairbairn[14] writing for the *Albertan* said that there were many disappointed attendees because Trudeau had not dealt with the regional oil and agriculture issues.[15] Managing editor of the *Albertan* Don Peacock,[16] who had worked for Lester Pearson and Harry Hays in Ottawa (and had lost the Liberal nomination for the Lethbridge riding in 1968), wrote of the typical reaction: "Now you know why we think they don't understand us down there in Ottawa." He said even the "party brass and near brass" called the speech "a turkey" and "a bomb" and the dinner organization was "strictly from bleaksville, if not beautiful downtown Hicksville," and finally, "Once more the Liberal Party of Alberta covered itself in that inglory to which its adherents have become so accustomed."[17]

Albertan business reporter Tom Kennedy quoted an obviously upset Pat Mahoney saying that "oilmen with a little luck, might learn of Trudeau's intentions [about the oil industry] from another speech given, perhaps in a Maritime city." Mahoney continued, "I am disappointed because he knew we wanted to hear about these developments...and where else should one talk about oil but in Calgary."

When Trudeau was asked why he had avoided a discussion of oil, Kennedy described his response: "Trudeau, fanning himself with his newly presented white hat, retorted, 'Aren't Calgarians interested in foreign policy?'" When pressed, Trudeau said he knew that oil was on the minds of many at the dinner, but added, "I like to disappoint people sometimes," and followed up with an absolving gesture of an expansive sweep of his arms and joined a police escort to a waiting car.[18]

The most incisive analysis of the Trudeau speech came from the popular curmudgeon Fred Kennedy (no relation of Tom) who wrote in a column titled "Mr. Trudeau Lays an Egg."

> *By way of Mr. Trudeau's visit, they [Alberta Liberals] hoped to accomplish two things. Being as financially flat as beer on a plate, they hoped to recoup their coffers and at the same time, obtain a fuller measure of support for the party in both city and country. They succeeded in the first and very possibly failed in the other, and all because their august leader "would not play ball."*
>
> *It will take the local Grits a long time to recover from this one. What should have been a really big day, ended in a dismal flop.*[19]

The evening was not a complete flop. The Party picked up some pretty good coin, and, after all, that was the reason for the dinner. The NOW event, although unplanned and chaotic with everyone stumbling around trying to make the best of it, went rather well. Trudeau, calm and courageous under fire, even engaged some of the mob in intelligent discussion. However, many thousands of conservative-oriented Calgarians and Albertans would have preferred to see the PM somehow give Chief Justice

Milvain's "bearded bastards" a swift kick. Anything less could be seen as pandering to the riff-raff and just not good politics.

The evening's ruckus was tailor-made for local politics. Calgary mayor and prominent Tory Jack Leslie called for the disbandment of the CYC. Days later during a meeting with Trudeau in Ottawa, Leslie claimed the demonstration was a result of "agitators...aided and abetted by the CYC group" that had moved into NOW. He then apologized to Trudeau for the tomato. Not taking the bait, Trudeau told Leslie that there was no need to apologize as the tomato had hit a member of the press, "and as far as I am concerned they were throwing it at the press."[20]

The Leslie attack on the CYC prompted Mahoney to display his small-l liberal credentials by defending a "basically good" organization. Later he said that "organized protest demonstrations have proved an effective method for the politically impotent to catch the attention of the political establishment."[21] The CYC was becoming respectable; among the newly appointed council members that fall was 28-year-old Lloyd Axworthy, who would later serve as minister of employment and immigration, minister of transport, and minister of foreign affairs.[22]

In the end, the disappointing fundraising dinner would have some very long-term repercussions for the Liberals in Alberta.[23]

10

APRIL 1969–OCTOBER 1970

Oil, Economic Nationalism, and Mean Joe Greene

FOR TRUDEAU and his small band of Alberta Liberal MPs who had only a tenuous grip on the affections of Alberta voters, the Calgary fundraiser speech was a sign of perilous times ahead. Federal and provincial politicians in the province traditionally fell all over themselves to make the oilmen happy. But in Calgary, Trudeau showed he was not cut from that cloth.

The oilmen were not used to being treated this way. If they did not yet run federal and provincial politics in Alberta, they were not far from doing so. Their economic clout not only allowed them to dominate the provincial economy, but also gave them enormous influence over the province's political and media direction—and they were not shy about using it.

The oilmen's political and economic messages, then as now, began in executive offices and boardrooms of the oil patch.[1] They filtered down through corporate communications to the desks of geologists, engineers, geophysicists, accountants, file clerks, and secretaries, and to business reporters and editorial writers. Company shareholders were bombarded with these messages at annual meetings, as were delegates to industry conferences and meetings. The messages then spilled into the businesses that rely on the oil industry for their daily bread, and out into the hinterland where the roughnecks, labourers, drillers, truckers, merchants, and motel and restaurant operators earn their keep through the daily influx of customers connected to the oil business. Most politicians got the messages clearly and quickly, given that it was their business to receive them. And so, in very short order, a kind of groupthink set in with most everyone singing from the same songbook.

Conflicts between the oil industry and Trudeau's government became more serious as 1969 wore on. During the first quarter of 1969, oil exports to the United States east of the Rocky Mountains reached 350,000 barrels a day, more than 50,000 barrels a day over the quotas set by the 1967 Canada–US agreement. The US now demanded quota compliance. Even more galling to Alberta oilmen, the US asked Canada's own National Energy Board (NEB)[2] to tell Canadian producers to cut back or face more rigid export controls.[3]

The *Calgary Herald* called the quotas "disgraceful," saying that it was ridiculous that Canada did not open eastern Canadian markets to Canadian oil. It reiterated a familiar theme: "What if people in Eastern Canada do have to pay a little more for oil products? Western Canada from the beginning of time has been paying more for its farm machinery, for its automobiles and other goods made in Eastern Canada than it would have been paying if U.S. goods could have been allowed in without high protective tariffs. No wonder there is disgruntlement in Western Canada when protection is a one-way street."[4]

Speaking in Montreal, Calgary oil man Jack Pierce, CEO of publicly traded Ranger Oil, warned, "There is probably no oil consuming area in the world more vulnerable to being shut off from its prime energy source than Eastern Canada, especially Montreal."[5]

Voluble Tory MP Eldon Woolliams viewed the US oil quota decision and the current decline of Canadian wheat exports as acts of economic reprisals by the US for Canada's anti-NATO posture. He said he thought the US "feels that Mr. Trudeau leans toward the Communist bloc—for some

Eldon Woolliams (L) greets Tory leader Robert Stanfield at the airport.
[*Glenbow Archives NA 2564-5169*]

unknown reason—and they may be wrong on that deduction and we give the image of not wanting to go along with them collectively in the defence of the Western world."[6]

Pressure on the government over US quotes and a bigger domestic market for Canadian oil continued. In mid-June a group of high profile oil company executives together with the CPA and IPAC pressed on with a submission to the Trudeau cabinet, calling for increased oil exports, a feasibility study for a pipeline to Montreal, and negotiations for a continental oil policy. Trudeau told the press that he and his colleagues listened and asked many questions of the "very able business men" who represented an industry "important to Canada."[7]

Among the "able business men" were IPAC president Carl Nickle, R.A. (Bobby) Brown Jr.,[8] and Jack Gallagher.[9] Nickle was the veteran Tory oilman and publisher and partner with Southam News. Brown was then CEO of Home Oil, the largest independent oil company in Canada, as well as the principal bankroller of the National Public Affairs Research Foundation, which had on its payroll vehement Trudeau critic, Ernest Manning, and his son Preston.[10] Smilin' Jack Gallagher was one of the founders and driving forces behind Dome Petroleum, which was becoming one of the largest oil and gas producers in Canada.

Since there was a growing sense in Alberta's oil and gas community that Trudeau knew little (and cared even less) about its major industry, in July a group of oilmen and Alberta bureaucrats organized an orientation helicopter tour of Alberta's oil patch so Trudeau could see projects and facilities firsthand. He and Alberta Liberal MPs were accompanied and briefed by Alberta government officials (including George Govier, chair of the Alberta Petroleum and Natural Gas Conservation Board), and executives from major companies such as Mobil Oil Canada, Pembina Pipe Line, Shell Canada, and others. The press did not accompany the tour because organizers thought it could be a distraction to the serious business of educating the prime minister.[11] Thus Trudeau lost that opportunity to publicly show his interest in the industry. Over the years he did learn a great deal about oil and gas and could talk about it in detail and with ease.[12]

But despite these industry aggravations, in the spring, Otto Lang told the Commons that the NEB was forecasting a relaxation of US import quotas because its demand was increasing so fast, its own domestic oil production would soon not keep up.[13] He also wrote a strong letter to the Nixon task force urging the US to open its markets, making it clear that US access to Canadian natural gas would hinge on this.[14]

(L to R) Pat Mahoney, Trudeau, and George Govier on a tour of the Alberta oil industry in July 1969. [Courtesy of the Estate of George Wheeler Govier]

The Alberta natural gas industry was booming. Alberta was producing 88 percent of all Canadian natural gas currently sold to Canadians. Between 1960 and 1970, gas production would treble and exports increased seven-fold.[15] The president of the American Gas Association said that potential new Alberta gas supplies were coming at a good time, given that US gas demand was rising but US reserves were not.[16]

These were also happy times for people who owned oil stocks. The *Financial Times* reported that the Toronto Stock Exchange's western oil index moved from 84.85 in 1966 to 310.73 in 1969. The sixteen stocks comprising the Toronto Stock Exchange Oil index were being sold at 40 times current earnings compared to 10 to 20 times earnings for other non-oil and gas stocks.[17]

Nonetheless, the oilmen remained unimpressed with Ottawa. Oil columnist Jim Armstrong, lamenting Ottawa's silence while waiting for the US task force review, wrote, "we do not know whether it wishes greater export markets, or whether it really does not care about the health of the Western petroleum industry... The problem appears to be that age-old one where the petroleum industry is largely western and those in charge of national policies are predominately eastern."[18]

Despite all of this, 1969 was a very good year for the oilmen. Drilling activity was up for the year by about 10 percent over 1968.[19] In January 1970, crude oil production in Alberta averaged over a million barrels a day (up from 725,000 barrels one year earlier.)[20] In his February speech from the throne, Strom referred to the close ties between Alberta and Ottawa in the export negotiations between Canada and the US and to a report predicting that the demand for Canadian oil would soar to 2.1 million barrels a day by 1978, more than double the demand in 1968, and that it could go as high as 3.3 million barrels a day.[21]

The US task force study on oil policy was finally made public in February. It recommended the negotiation of a Canada–US continental energy system, more imports of Canadian oil and natural gas, but also for the time being set a quota for all imported Canadian oil at 615,000 barrels a day.[22] The study noted that by 1980, the US was expected to consume 3 million of the 4.5 million barrels Canada was forecast to produce (as compared to the 1.4 million it was expected to produce in 1970).[23]

Minister of Energy Joe Greene (now back on the job after his illness) behaved like a stalwart ally of the oil industry. He noted that with total exports to the United States (including those not subject to the quota) in the 700,000 to 800,000 barrels a day range, to cut back to the task force's recommended 615,000 barrels a day would be "economically unrealistic," and that exports should meet the demands made by US refiners.[24] In fact, quota compliance was entirely voluntary and not policed or penalized. Thus, as long as US refineries east of the Rockies wanted more oil from Canada, the oil was going to flow south—and it did, in spite of quotas. Everybody in Ottawa now seemed onside with the oilmen on the export issue. Even Trudeau said if oil or other resources were unlikely to be used domestically, "why not sell them for good hard cash?"[25]

But not all Canadians were sanguine about increasing oil exports. Many were concerned about the security of supply of Canada's own oil and gas. Economic nationalists had begun to fret publicly about Canada's economic sovereignty and the dangers presented by foreign control of Canadian corporations—particularly by US firms.[26] By 1970 American interests already controlled 60 percent of the Canadian oil and gas industry, 50 percent of the mining industry, almost 100 percent of the automobile industry, 80 percent of the chemical industry and electrical appliance manufacturing, and a healthy portion of other industries.[27]

The first strong signal that Canada's economic nationalists had the ear of the Trudeau government came in early March 1970 when the federal government blocked a planned sale of a one-quarter interest in the Canadian uranium producer Denison Mines to a US-controlled company.

Denison, controlled by Canadian multi-millionaire Stephen Roman, was going through a period of weak international uranium markets that threatened closure of its northern Ontario mine. Roman arranged for Hudson's Bay Oil and Gas Co. (known as "H-bog") to buy 25 percent of Denison stock to help stave off the crisis. H-bog, however, was 65.7 percent owned by Continental Oil of Delaware and so the federal government concluded the deal was not in the national interest. To scuttle the transaction, Greene announced new foreign ownership regulations for the Canadian uranium industry restricting foreign ownership of uranium-producing companies to not more than 33 percent, and with no single foreign investor to hold more than 10 percent. Roman speculated that his Slovakian background could have had something to do with the decision: "Maybe I should have been born a French Canadian."[28]

The oilmen worried that the Denison decision was the thin edge of the wedge that would stifle foreign investment in the Canadian oil industry. *Albertan* columnist Fred Kennedy was critical of the decision and captured local sentiment when he wrote that American money had financed the development of the oil and gas industry, "which transformed Alberta from a diet of jack rabbit stew and gopher pie, to prime ribs of beef."[29]

At the time of the Denison controversy,[30] it was well known that Herb Gray, minister without portfolio, was working on a new comprehensive foreign ownership policy.[31] The oilmen now worried that the Denison decision, Gray's new policy, and concern over new federal tax reform proposals was creating investor uncertainty that would reduce capital flow into Canada and a decline in the nation's standard of living.[32]

Joe Greene addressed these new developments in a belligerent speech to the Petroleum Association of America in Denver in May 1970. Scrapping his usual folksy eloquence, Greene's message was aimed at the Nixon administration and the oil and gas industry. He said the Nixon quota restrictions were "a wrench of arbitrary import controls" designed "to squeeze Canada into a continental oil policy," and that there was little chance of any continental energy agreement being reached until the quotas were lifted. Invoking Trudeau's analogy of Canada as a mouse sleeping with the friendly US elephant,[33] Greene said the quotas were like "the elephant rolling over on top of the Canadian mouse, a physical condition which is not only uncomfortable, but a difficult posture for the mouse from which to begin long term energy discussions."

About the recent Denison case, Greene warned that his government was in the process of reviewing foreign ownership in all—not just strategic—industries. "Canadians," he said, "are now determined that the time has come to take stock and to assure that a substantial portion of the future growth remains in Canadian hands," and that Canada "must retain freedom to apply Canadian solutions to Canadian problems."

Cutting ever closer to the US bone, Greene said that Canadians were no longer pursuing equality with the US in material possessions but were focusing instead on the differences between the two cultures because of American involvement in Cambodia and Vietnam, lawlessness on American streets and university campuses, racism, and "the crumbling of the American dream." He also said that Canada was determined to protect its Canadian identity against the threat posed by the US mass media: "We do not believe that pandering to tastes and intellects of the least common denominator, with no attempt at using the media for the uplifting of the

Energy Minister Joe Greene in full oratorical flight at the Liberal leadership convention in April 1968. [*Canadian Press/Chuck Mitchell*]

intellect or the enrichment of the human spirit is the use Canadians will want to make of these powerful forces in the years ahead."[34] The two-hour carefully crafted statement showed Canada's determination to limit US ownership in the Canadian economy, and protect its culture against US encroachment.

The oilmen and their friends quickly fought back. Woolliams accused the government of "deliberately trying to antagonize" Canada's good customers.[35] Dalton Camp, the ex-president of the federal Tories who'd engineered the fall of Diefenbaker as leader, called the speech, "rude, banal, and embarrassingly trivial."[36] IPAC president Gene Roark warned that the Trudeau government was "dangerously close" to destroying western and northern Canada's development, and that its actions had badly shaken the whole mineral industry, and had already resulted in a flight of capital and an exploration slowdown.[37]

Jack Pierce, speaking at his Ranger Oil's annual meeting, said that Greene's speech was dictated by the minister's personal political motivations, and was destructive to the oil industry, the national economy, and the country. Pierce said that he was appalled at Greene's being offended at Nixon's imposition of quotas when all Nixon was saying was "Whoops, let's hold on a little until we sort out this whole oil marketing relationship between Canada and the United States."[38]

Foreign ownership was a hot topic of discussion at June's federal Liberal Party western conference in Edmonton. Although some younger delegates, led by Mel Hurtig, expressed anti-foreign ownership sentiment, federal Minister of Public Works Arthur Laing from BC urged them to recognize that development in northern and western Canada would be financed by foreign capital. He said, "We've always looked outside for that two dollars, and when we've gotten it, we've always been able to turn it into five."[39] Although opinions at the conference about Canada's new nationalism were divided, the delegates did urge the federal government to allow marketing of western Canadian oil east of the Ottawa Valley.[40]

In a later speech to geologists, Greene softened, saying that even though Canada disliked US quotas, it would continue to pursue an energy deal that would benefit both countries. But he stuck to his guns on foreign ownership, saying that Canada would continue increasing national ownership in resource industries and that could involve a nationally owned Canadian corporation as well as government participation.[41]

Despite Canada's new economic nationalism, demands from US refineries for Canadian oil continued to soar. By the summer of 1970 Canadian oil exports to the US east of the Rockies were running at between 20,000 and 40,000 barrels per day above Nixon's new quotas and showed no signs of slowing down.[42]

In mid-July came more disquieting news for the oilmen from a whole new direction. Montreal-based company Caloil was caught selling gasoline made from imported oil from the Caribbean into markets west of the Ottawa Valley line. This was a clear breach of the 1961 national oil policy. Although compliance with this policy was only voluntary, up until then there had been only minor violations. IPAC demanded that Greene put an immediate stop to these sales, following which the NEB tightened import regulations.[43] But the courts soon ruled the new regulations unconstitutional, causing another fit of panic among the oilmen who feared the disappearance of their captive market.[44]

Although Alberta's minister of mines and minerals, A.R. Patrick, assured Albertans that the Trudeau government was trying to get the ruling changed, Lougheed's sabre rattling was more appreciated by the oilmen. He urged Premier Strom to pressure the feds to appeal the court decision or change the regulations. Lougheed had by then shown himself to be tougher than Strom or his ministers on many occasions. He was becoming the most effective provincial political spokesperson for the oil industry.[45]

The (federal) Exchequer Court soon determined that the new regulations preventing anyone from selling imported petroleum products west of the Ottawa Valley were constitutional,[46] and Greene commented, "the national oil policy is alive and thriving and doing well for Canada."[47] But the Caloil story had caused quite a scare in Alberta and highlighted the absurdity that Canada still imported refined petroleum products.

By the summer of 1970, the federal government was giving the Canadian oil business in Canada more attention. Federal ministers Jean-Luc Pepin, Jean Chretien, and Joe Greene took trips with oilmen and government officials to the Arctic and then announced guidelines for a pipeline from Prudhoe Bay to Chicago, following the Mackenzie River Valley, to allow Canadian resources to enter the pipelines at any point.[48] Alberta oilmen viewed the announcement as positive.[49]

After almost a year of deliberations the government also finally adopted a NEB decision approving the biggest single increase in natural gas exports to the United States, including substantial increases for export into the Pacific northwest, the mid-west, and California.[50] Although many oilmen approved, the economic nationalists and Alberta government did not. Edmonton Liberal Mel Hurtig said he would demand a 30 percent export tax be imposed on natural gas at November's Liberal policy convention and accused the government of dealing away its trump card without getting any concessions in return.[51]

Minister of Alberta Mines Russell Patrick chided the NEB for not approving even more gas exports. Revenues from exploration activity were expected to be down dramatically with no major oil discovery in more than five years, and that the only thing keeping exploration humming had been the search for gas.[52]

Almost simultaneously with the announcement of the natural gas exports came the US government's proposal to remove natural gas liquids from its crude oil import quotas. This extended the quota limitation (east of the Rockies) by 40,000 barrels a day of imported Canadian oil.[53]

By early October the oilmen could take comfort that Greene had settled down; economic nationalism was subdued; oil exports, oil quotas and natural gas exports were all rising; the imported foreign gasoline issue had been squelched, and a huge northern pipeline development seemed to be moving forward. But more battles lay ahead.

11

Hustle Grain!

DECEMBER 1968–OCTOBER 1970

JUST AS THE PRIME MINISTER was about to begin his early jousting with the oilmen and the US about markets, quotas, and pipelines, he began a battle with the western farmer. At a Liberal fundraiser in Winnipeg someone asked, "Mr. Prime Minister, I would like to know how and when you are going to sell the western Canadian farmers' wheat?" He replied, in his trademark Socratic style, "Well," he said, "why should I sell the Canadian farmers' wheat?" followed by a lengthy and confusing answer.[1] Just as his ill-conceived choice of subjects in Calgary determined his future relationship with the oil industry, so, too, would this non-answer determine Trudeau's future rocky relationship with the western Canadian farmer.

Problems in the wheat-producing provinces had been simmering for some months. Grain delivery backlogs caused by a lack of rail and wharf capacity left millions of bushels of grain in storage. Worse, international bumper crops had produced a huge world surplus that led to a price war among wheat exporting countries that were parties to the International Grains Agreement (IGA).[2] Canada was faced with vast amounts of unsold wheat causing farm incomes to drop. Angry farmers were looking for help and the government seemed slow to respond.[3]

Marketing of Canadian grain had for some years been handled by the Canadian Wheat Board (CWB)[4] on behalf, and for the protection, of the farmer. The CWB mandate was to receive and sell all Canadian wheat produced, at world prices, and to distribute the net earnings to the farmers.[5] The huge long-term contracts with China and the Soviet Union ended in 1968 and the CWB, the government of Canada, and Minister of Agriculture Bud Olson found themselves at the centre of the storm.

To find solutions and plan future farm policy, the government set up a five-member federal task force and ran a conference for all sectors of the agricultural industry. Instead of solutions, it produced plenty of criticism,[6] prompting Olson to tell the delegates to stop griping and instead give him advice.[7] Olson also accused the Saskatoon National Farmers' Union (NFU), which had been demonstrating about the marketing crisis, of being better at political demonstrations than coming up with constructive policy ideas.[8]

The Canadian Federation of Agriculture came up with a proposal calling for payment of a cash subsidy to help farmers through the crisis. Olson turned it down, saying that it did not do anything to solve the basic problem of grain marketing, in which Canada should be investing money to solve.[9]

Olson also ran into trouble from another important component of the agriculture industry, courtesy of his cabinet colleague, Minister of Consumer Affairs Ron Basford. Responding to public complaints about high prices, Basford vowed to lead a consumer boycott against beef. This prompted the Canadian Cattlemen's Association to send a wire to Olson, a cattle rancher himself, asking him to tell Basford "that over the period in which producers have received a 30 percent increase in their return, he as an MP has voted himself (with our money) a salary increase of over 100 per cent." The wire also pointed out that beef producers were receiving only 25 percent more for their beef than in 1952.[10]

Meanwhile Olson's testy colleague Hu Harries predicted that if the railroads did not move grain faster and the grain marketers did not improve their selling skills, "we'll see high-yielding low-grade wheat from Pakistan being sold in the Fraser Valley." He claimed it was cheaper to move wheat from Pakistan to Vancouver than from the Prairies, and took a shot at the railroads for using the same grain boxcars they had used at the turn of the century.[11]

In July the *Financial Times* forecast that Canada would record 850 million bushels unsold for the crop year ending July 31, 1969 and the next year did not look any more promising.[12] Statistics revealed that wheat production acreage was down by almost 16 percent, different grains were now being sown on what were once wheat fields, and more lands were lying summer fallow. All of this reflected that not enough wheat was being sold and what was sold realized too low a price.[13]

Interviewed on CTV's *Question Period*, Olson spoke about the western farmers' "deep feeling of isolation from the rest of the country" and "feeling that the government is far more concerned with what happens in Ontario and Quebec—and always has been—than with the West." About his chances of being re-elected, he said that the government had to make some tough decisions and that he "didn't expect to be popular while the government was doing that."[14]

The deteriorating situation on the farms sent the PM to the Prairies to have a firsthand look by helicopter of small farming communities in Manitoba, Saskatchewan, and Alberta and some cities. Dave Thomson from Redcliff, Alberta, and head of the PMO's western regional desk, organized the tour because, "The PM's like most easterners. He thinks of the prairies as a field of waving wheat with some oil in the far corner."[15]

In the meantime, angry farmers were shouting mixed messages about their dilemma. Some wanted Canada to cut wheat prices so that Canadian wheat could compete better internationally. Others wanted subsidies paid to farmers equal to the difference between the actual selling price and the IGA minimum price. Some wanted a two-price system with higher domestic prices offsetting the lower international prices, while others advocated growing different grains for which there were better markets.

Farmers drive their tractors to a demonstration against Trudeau, Saskatoon, July 1969.
[*Creative Professional Photographers' Collection, Saskatoon Public Library CP-5717-2*]

Offering neither respite nor solace to the western wheat farmer, Trudeau said in Thompson, Manitoba, that farmers must adjust production to the pressures of world demand and that his government could not control other nations that cut prices. Instead, he said bluntly that the west would have to grow less wheat.[16]

In Regina on the following day, the trip turned ugly. A hundred revved-up, horn-blowing tractors and 500 noisy demonstrators turned out in front of the Hotel Saskatchewan where the PM had been staying. A rabble-rousing speaker from the militant Saskatchewan Farmers Union asked the crowd if they should "go in and get him?" Insulting placards read, "Our PET is a pig," "Hustle Grain, Not Women," "More Action, Less Bull," and other crude messages. Speaking from the back of a truck, Trudeau had to endure boos, catcalls, insults, and wheat thrown at him. But he calmly held his ground, telling the crowd that although he understood their problems, "I'm not going to try to pacify you or satisfy you by stating that we are going to give $200,000,000 to the farmers," and reminded them there were many problems in Canada besides theirs. Although his courage and forthrightness earned him some applause, it was a hostile reception.[17]

The next day a huge but better-behaved crowd greeted Trudeau outside the Bessborough Hotel in Saskatoon. Using a bullhorn, he thanked them for their respect and made a point of contrasting it to the rude Regina reception. "If you want to see me again, don't bring signs saying, Trudeau is a pig. I didn't get into politics to be insulted." He gave assurances that some financial help should be available for the farm economy.[18] But later in Humboldt, he asked a gathering of municipal reeves how he could explain to a Maritime fisherman without assets who earned only $2,000 a year that the government was going to give a farmer who owned a farm and assets worth $100,000, a $2,000 maximum acreage payment, as was recently proposed by the Saskatchewan Wheat Pool. Trudeau said, "They'd say, are you crackers?"[19]

The trip was viewed by most of the press as a political flop,[20] though the usually hostile *Calgary Herald* came to Trudeau's defence, calling the Regina demonstration "a black disgrace to Western Canada" and giving Trudeau "full marks for courage on this western trip."[21] It spawned a withering public attack from within the Alberta Liberal Party. Shortly after the tour ended, Mel Hurtig wrote a column claiming that the tour showed that Trudeau had not been informed about western issues by his western ministers, his western MPs, his western regional desk, and his three provincial Liberal parties on the Prairies. Hurtig also accused the western Liberal parties of being dominated by a small minority of high-income backroom politicians, businessmen, and lawyers, all of whom had a vested interest in controlling their ridings and who worked "against the type of 'participatory democracy' the PM had pledged to bring about." He saw Trudeau's

Mel Hurtig in the early 1970s. [*Canadian Press*]

inability to democratize the structure of the Liberal Party as "his single most significant failure" and that Canadians everywhere "hate like hell to watch the nation fractionalized by men who are unable to see beyond their own noses and their own selfish political ambitions." He said, "government to these people means leave us and our luxuries alone, and make sure the patronage and subsidies don't stop."[22]

Hurtig, no ordinary Liberal but a co-chair of Trudeau's leadership campaign and a member of the national party's policy committee, exemplified the new idealistic generation drawn to the party by what Trudeau seemed to represent.

In midsummer 1969, the 180,000 western Canadian wheat farmers still faced a dismal situation. Record wheat production packed storage facilities and another good crop expected would increase the stockpile to 1.3 billion bushels—sufficient to fill all demand for three years. Wheat prices were at an eight-year low. Farm incomes had nosedived and agricultural businesses were going belly up across the Prairies.[23]

Some respite came from a small federal subsidy to the farmer for wheat sold into the domestic market. In addition, the government quadrupled international food aid in the form of Canadian wheat or flour and reduced interest charged to importing nations. But it was not enough to satisfy the farmers.[24]

Many experts believed that because of enhanced wheat production in some wheat-importing nations, the future for Canada's long-range wheat exports was bleak. Their recommendations included reduction of Canada's wheat production, job-retraining programs for western farmers, and government help to establish more light industries in wheat-producing centres so ex-farmers could find work.[25] Some desperate farmers were now bootlegging wheat to beef producers and other consumers in a domestic black market.[26]

To improve the Canada's wheat marketing performance, minister without portfolio Otto Lang was given the responsibility for the Wheat Board, and for working with Minister of Trade Pepin to market more Canadian wheat abroad. In January Lang happily announced that export sales for the current crop year ending July 1970 would be 375 million bushels—100 million bushels more than the previous crop year.[27] And even better, he told a London conference of an upward pattern developing in world prices that would soon return to the minimums of the International Grains Agreement.[28]

Finally, Lang and Bud Olson announced in February a new one-year program LIFT (Lower Inventories for Tomorrow) that would pay farmers incentives of $140 million to cut production by at least 75 percent and to convert wheat-producing land into summer fallow, or forage crops production. The more summer fallow converted, the more the farmers could sell of their stored wheat. The limit of financial compensation was $10,000 per farm. The program's goal was to take 22 million acres of wheat land—roughly equal to the acres seeded the previous year—out of production. Although the formulation of the plan was Lang's responsibility, Olson's department would administer it.[29]

Spokesmen for the wheat pools approved the program[30] as did Premier Strom and Tory Opposition Leader Peter Lougheed.[31] The chairman of the Canada Grains Council credited Lang for having done a pretty good job given the critical situation, and doubted that anyone else could have done better.[32]

The LIFT program however did not solve the problem of the wheat glut and the low prices that came with it. Furthermore, the program's duration was only one year, and the compensation payable to the farmer was low. It was also the first time in the memory of Canadian farmers that the country adopted the bizarre notion of paying the farmer not to grow wheat. As a result, Olson and Lang continued to take criticism.[33]

The western farmer's champion and Olson nemesis, Tory MP Jack Horner, said LIFT did not stand for "Lower Inventories for Tomorrow," but rather "Lower Income for Tomorrow," and claimed that it was concocted by academics for eastern Canadian farmers to keep western farmers out of production. He also warned that the program would make every western grain grower cheat and be more separatist minded.[34] Inside the Liberal federal caucus, Saskatchewan Liberal Senator Hazen Argue said LIFT was based on "a foolish, undemocratic and unreal notion that bureaucrats and grain company presidents, meeting in secret, know more about what's good for farmers than farmers do themselves."[35]

Because of the poor markets and the inadequacy of the LIFT program, Strom's government was thinking of getting into grain marketing for the first time.[36] From Red Deer in central Alberta south to the US border, many Alberta farmers were selling out and moving to the city. Some economists were predicting that as a result of the crisis, half of Alberta's rural population could disappear within ten years. Saskatchewan was in worse shape.[37]

In early May in Ottawa all major wheat exporters—Canada, Australia, US, Argentina, and the European Common Market—agreed to bring wheat production under control.[38] The fact that European Common Market nations, the big offender in terms of price cutting and subsidies, agreed was regarded as a breakthrough.

The news got better when the federal department of agriculture forecast sales of all grain higher than predicted.[39] In July came news that western farmers had reduced wheat plantings by more than half from the previous year per the LIFT program.[40] Plantings were up for most other grain crops including barley, flax, and rapeseed, and there was a record acreage of land in summer fallow. Export demand had also increased dramatically for wheat and barley. Wheat sales were becoming more robust,[41] and Senator Harry Hays told an agriculture conference that the following year would likely see all Canadian grain disposed of, with hardly any reserves left.[42] Lang confirmed that Canadian grain exports would reach record volumes in the current crop year and speculated that wheat exports could bounce back close to the record set seven years before (almost 60 percent greater than the previous year).[43]

Although the LIFT program had provided much-needed relief for the prairie farmer after two long years, most farmers did not give the government any credit for the improvement. Crowfoot MP Jack Horner presciently noted, "Just because the Liberals are making great grain sales doesn't mean they will be worshipped and loved by Western Canada."[44] The wheat producers and those dependent on them across the Prairies had experienced too much worry and suffering. For related agri-industries it was a period of economic devastation. Trudeau's initial response was viewed as weak and non-committal and lacking in both compassion and understanding, and a solution too long in the making. As much as it was a disaster for the farmer, it was an equal disaster to the fortunes of the Liberal Party on the Prairies.

12

The Infernal White Paper

JANUARY 1969–OCTOBER 1970

AS THE TRUDEAU GOVERNMENT'S oil and wheat wars were just getting underway, Pat Mahoney put fear in the hearts of even the most hardened of Alberta's captains of industry by announcing possibilities of major tax changes—including a capital gains tax—for the spring budget.[1] Since Alberta was blessed with a plethora of family farms and businesses, small and large companies, and of course, at the top of the food chain, the oilmen, there would be no Alberta welcoming ceremony for a capital gains tax. Albertans and most Canadians were pretty much alike in this respect: they only welcomed tax reform when it brought tax reductions.

The idea that the Liberals were about to impose tax reform that would destroy businesses and cause Canada "to cease to be a country of free men and women"[2] was first raised by Tory Palliser MP Stan Schumacher. Although the Drumheller lawyer was a pleasant fellow, he was very good at slash-and-burn rhetoric and his speech to his riding association was one of the first salvos in what would turn out to be a vicious political battle against tax reform.

Two months later Minister of Finance Edgar Benson announced the overhaul of the Canadian tax system based on the 1967 Carter Royal Commission report on taxation. Established by the Diefenbaker government and chaired by Toronto chartered accountant Kenneth Carter, it had concluded that since the Canadian tax system was inefficient, with the poor paying more than their fair share of taxes, fairness should be the main objective and that taxes should be levied on increases in economic power, however acquired, whether from salary, capital gains, cash, or in kind. In Carter's words, the basis of tax reform should be "A buck is a buck."[3]

From the start Benson promised broad public input and consultations through a series of steps that included an initial document called a white paper setting forth the government's tax reform proposals, followed by public hearings and submissions, which hopefully would improve the proposals.[4] Tax reform legislation would then be prepared and presented to Parliament. This manner of introducing legislation was supposed to be a practical application of participatory democracy, a concept touted by the Trudeau government and the Liberal Party of Canada.[5] During its first term, the Trudeau government would release several such white papers on foreign policy, social security, defence, and Indian affairs.

On November 7, Benson released the white paper on tax reform. The proposals included a capital gains tax, personal exemption increases, tax reductions for low-income earners, some tax increases for middle-income earners, and reductions in maximum tax rates for upper-income earners.[6] It also proposed closing tax loopholes respecting expense accounts, dividend stripping, and the funnelling of income into foreign tax havens.[7] The intent of the proposals, said Benson, was not to generate more revenues but to make the tax system more equitable and to remedy disparities between the workingman and the professional. He made clear that the government would consider changing some provisions if recommendations were reasonable.[8]

The first Alberta reactions were mild. Premier Strom said that the white paper was better than expected and that Albertans were pleased to see that it had not been too rough on the oil and mining industries. Peter

Edgar Benson delivers his budget as minister of finance, June 1969.
[Canadian Press/Chuck Mitchell]

Lougheed's reaction was only mildly stronger, saying that the proposals were not as harsh to Albertans as the Carter Report. However, he cautioned that the capital gains tax was not a "favorable development" for economic growth given Alberta's dependency on foreign investment.[9] Spokesmen for the oil industry were initially uncharacteristically quiet.

A preview of what was to come came from the bombastic Tory MP Eldon Woolliams. In the Commons he warned that the proposals would destroy small businesses and farmers, keep the rich privileged, and allow the government to take private property, all of which would lead to severe unemployment. Covering the whole political spectrum he called the white paper both a "Red Manifesto" and "fascist,"[10] charges he would repeat in the months ahead.

Recently elected Calgary mayor Rod Sykes complained about the white paper's proposed higher tax rates for small business, called the capital gains tax confiscatory, and forecast that the proposed reforms would hit middle-income earners the hardest.[11] At the time Sykes was a popular politician and formidable campaigner who had just trounced incumbent mayor Jack Leslie, a strong Tory. Sykes had articulated a concern for the underprivileged and the poor, which led many Liberals like myself to consider him a friend of the party, and inspired us to work hard for his election. When Benson brought his white paper tour to Edmonton and Calgary to discuss the proposals with business and government representatives, one highlight was a Liberal Party fundraising dinner at the exclusive Glencoe Club. Among the 125 people in attendance were business executives, legal and accounting professionals, assorted Liberals, Calgary South MP Pat Mahoney, and Mayor Rod Sykes, who was my guest for the evening.

Following Benson's brief introductory remarks, the largely sceptical audience spent two hours peppering him and his aide Michael Gillen[12] with questions about the white paper. At one point Benson, trying to point out what he thought was a popular federal policy, rhetorically asked the audience, "Would the people ask the government to take away medicare?" In response, several in the crowd piped up, "Yes!" In another exchange, Benson asked, "You tell me what wasteful expenditures we have?" to which a voice from the audience bellowed, "CYC [Company of Young Canadians]." Sykes, to my chagrin, also blasted Benson on both the proposed capital gains tax and the effects of the proposals on middle-income earners.

Through it all, the genial pipe-smoking Benson kept his cool and answered questions as best and as politely as he could. But much of the tone of the meeting was hostile, which surprised and visibly upset the Liberals including Calgary's lone Liberal MP Mahoney. We were angry with Sykes, who many of us, including former mayor and now Liberal Senator Harry Hays, had supported. Sykes,[13] a friend of the party? Alas, we were misinformed.[14]

Western hostility toward Benson's white paper grew. IPAC charged that the proposed capital gains tax and changes in the treatment of depletion allowances would impair their industry's ability to raise investment dollars.[15] Saskatchewan Liberal premier Ross Thatcher—with the backing of all of the western premiers except for Ed Schreyer of Manitoba—railed against the white paper at a conference, saying that it would promote unemployment and hurt the economy of the west.[16]

Meanwhile, Pat Mahoney, a member of the Commons tax committee, stoutly defended Benson's plans. He said Ottawa would not abandon the goal of creating a "just" tax system and that middle-class Canadians would have to bear the burden of tax measures because there was "no reservoir of vastly rich Canadians left to be taxed." However, even Mahoney had some complaints. With characteristic bluntness he said the proposal to tax Canadians on paper profits every five years could turn out to be "an administrative abortion" that Ottawa could find impossible to carry out.[17] Nevertheless, Mahoney's hard work and vigorous defence of the government led to Trudeau appointing him parliamentary secretary to Minister of Finance Edgar Benson.[18]

The public attacks against the white paper intensified. At a meeting of the Western Stock Growers Association early in the new year, an Alberta delegate told Bud Olson to "go back to Ottawa and tell Benson if he created this piece of irresponsible legislation it will cause him to fall on his face— along with many taxpaying ranchers."[19]

Widely read columnist Jim Armstrong delivered a preview of the attacks about to be unleashed by the oil industry. He wrote that local oilmen worried that the proposed changes could choke off investment capital into the oil business causing Alberta's economic stagnation. Many oilmen worried that oil industry professionals would lose initiative to become successful and would no longer be willing to put up with the pressure and time away from home that their work required. Armstrong even said oilmen were seriously considering moving their Canadian operations south to the US.[20]

The attacks continued through the winter. The chairman of Calgary city council gas subcommittee and a well-known Tory, alderman Jack Davis, said the Benson proposals could lead to a gas rate hike of 10 to 20 percent.[21] Peter Lougheed got on the anti-white-paper bandwagon in the legislature, saying that the white paper would cause "an economic and social upheaval of society" and would stop Alberta's economic growth. He accused Premier Strom of being "timid, weak and cautious" toward the proposals and said it was his duty as leader of the opposition to appear at the Commons finance committee hearings on the white paper, regardless of the position of the Strom government.[22]

Saskatchewan Liberal premier Ross Thatcher told a meeting of oil industry executives that his government would continue to vigorously oppose the white paper and warned, "if the White Paper is bulldozed through, I doubt if there will be a Liberal federal member left in the four Western provinces after the next election." His audience responded with wild applause.[23]

Trudeau himself struck back saying the government would not "be bullied or blackmailed" by hysterical charges. He called the accusation that his government had already made up its mind on the white paper "a persistent myth" and repeated that Canadians could suggest improvements to the proposals. He went on to explain that the white paper process was a new and unique government concept to Canada, and that Canadians had a lot to learn as to how to make it work.[24]

Lougheed, smelling the blood of a wounded Social Credit Party, demanded an Alberta all-party united front to fight for a complete revision of the white paper's "socialistic" proposals.[25] He referred to a "compelling" book he had just read entitled *The Benson Iceberg: A Critical Analysis of the White Paper on Tax Reform in Canada* by Izzy Asper.[26] Asper was critical of the contents of the white paper, but very much liked the process. He said that if the government listened, it should be able to revise the proposals to satisfy valid criticisms by responsible Canadians, and thereby establish the value of this attempt at participatory democracy. He cautioned that everyone should "make certain that notwithstanding what changes are required to make the tax reform acceptable, the white paper method is not destroyed in the process."[27]

It was clear that the white paper process was giving the government's opponents political target practice undermining both the policy proposals and the government itself. For Liberals in Alberta it was much worse. Three of its four Liberal MPs were spending most of their time in Ottawa attending to their work in Parliament and therefore could not defend the government at home. Alberta's other MP Hu Harries was increasingly alienated from both his colleagues and the government, so of no help. And unelected party regulars could never win fighting for tax reform in an arena dominated by a right-wing culture driven by a powerful and conservative oil industry, and aided and abetted by a dominant federal PC political and media establishment hostile to the Trudeau government.

One of those unelected Alberta Liberals who did try was politician-oilman Nick Taylor. Then in his early forties, Taylor was a dedicated and lifelong Liberal. He had narrowly lost Calgary Centre in 1968 to Tory Douglas Harkness and, less than two years later, was already nominated to again contest the riding. In a speech to a business group in Calgary, Taylor bravely defended the white paper, predicting that it would result in a major portion of Canada's wealth being returned to Canadian ownership and allow more Canadians to participate in their economy. Taylor called the claim that the white paper would kill enterprise a lie perpetrated by executives who were lobbying for personal tax deductions for entertainment and promotion that were not available to other Canadians. He accused corporate executives of opposing the white paper because it would force them to return more corporate earnings to shareholders. Not content with sticking it to the corporate elite, Taylor also took a shot at the media, observing that "the press seems to think defending the paper [white paper] would be telling a dirty story in public."[28]

Taylor was an Alberta rarity—a loyal Liberal who was president of six oil and mining companies. Coming from a hardscrabble farm in southeastern Alberta, he had already made millions by the time he was 40. But in the political climate of the spring of 1970 with the wheat market devastation, the attacks on the white paper, the persistent anti-government attacks from local Tory opposition MPs, and the continued griping of the oilmen, Taylor's chances of becoming an MP in the next federal election were bleak.

In late June the Alberta government released a hundred-page brief describing all that was wrong with the white paper. The brief rejected all of the proposals, and took particular exception to a capital gains tax.[29] Provincial Treasurer Anders Aalborg warned that if the white paper was not revised, Alberta could lose $3 billion in investment and $1 billion in resource revenue over the next ten years.[30]

In August Benson announced that as a result of submissions he would make major changes in the white paper to help Canada's mining industry and remove some uncertainty said to be delaying Syncrude's Alberta oil sands development. This time it was the turn of the NDP to howl foul. Its spokesman, Ontario NDP MP Max Saltsman, called the amendments "shameful and cowardly."[31] And despite the concessions, Alberta's treasurer maintained that the existing tax laws were better for the mining industry and the oil industry.[32]

The government was under attack from all sides. Even the Liberal-dominated Senate finance committee rejected most reforms dealing with corporate taxation, warning that they could have a "disastrous" effect on economic growth. This negative report did not come as a surprise, given that many senators enjoyed positions on corporate boards of directors. (One Ottawa wag commented that the Senate's corporate "directorships are showing—all 189 of them."[33]) For its part, the Commons finance committee approved proposals for tax concessions to poorer Canadians, partial taxation of capital gains, and tax reform geared to economic growth. The report stressed that effective tax reform must win taxpayer acceptance and that the preservation of an economic climate favourable to growth must be a central consideration for Canadian tax policy.[34]

Benson magnanimously received both Senate and Commons finance committee reports as useful. The white paper on taxation was put on the back burner to await the draft legislation.[35] The battle had gone on for the better part of the year and left the Trudeau government badly mauled.

13

Fighting Inflation and the Cunning Posties

APRIL 1969–SEPTEMBER 1970

ALREADY PRESSED over oil and wheat markets, and the white paper on taxation, the government saw another issue—inflation—rise to the top of its agenda. In April Trudeau began jawboning about the need to curb government spending: if more services were demanded, cuts would have to be made in other areas because government could not do it all; furthermore he said, his government intended to balance the budget.[1]

Not everyone believed him. The *Calgary Herald* saw Trudeau's cuts as merely passing expenditures onto the provinces and recommended that he abandon medicare and "trim some of the fat and frills" elsewhere.[2] It also accused the government of wasting millions on projects such as the Ottawa cultural centre, parliamentary junkets abroad, Montreal projects, and commissions and inquiries.[3]

In early June Benson introduced the first federal surplus budget in thirteen years. Alas, no champagne corks popped in Alberta. Instead, howls of derision came from every corner of the business community accusing the government of squelching a $100 million construction boom and stopping urban renewal in its tracks. What caused the fuss was a budget provision calling for a two-year deferral of capital cost allowances (depreciation of buildings for income tax purposes) on future commercial buildings in cities with populations of more than 50,000 in Alberta, Ontario, and British Columbia. Benson explained that the deferral was an attempt to control the inflation spiral caused by booming construction activity in those provinces.

The Tory Calgary mayor Jack Leslie called the deferral "a tax on prosperity and initiative" while another local Tory and future member of Lougheed's cabinet, Chamber of Commerce president Fred Peacock, called it "unfair and discriminatory." Harry Strom called Benson's plans "rank discrimination" against the three provinces concerned.[4]

Unfortunately for Liberals in Alberta, the first federal surplus budget that should have been popular in such a conservative province was instead interpreted by many as a deliberate blow to Alberta prosperity and therefore just another example of eastern Canadian discrimination. Despite the griping in the three provinces where the deferrals applied, not a single project was cancelled or delayed. Builders said openly that the penalty was not severe enough to have a significant effect on overall costs.[5] Nonetheless, the attacks against the budget continued in Alberta for months.[6]

During the summer of 1969, inflation continued its upward trend. In the previous year, the cost of living had risen by 5 percent, bank interest rates by 2 percent and house prices by 30 to 60 percent,[7] depending on where you lived.[8] Although the government had promoted an annual guideline that sought to limit wage increases to 7 to 8 percent, that guideline was being ignored in wage settlements.[9] Rents were rising and everybody saw higher prices at the stores.[10]

So the government got tougher. Recently appointed Prices and Incomes Commission (PIC) Chairman John Young launched a cross-Canada campaign against inflation, promoting voluntary price, wage, and profit restraints. He warned that the alternative was compulsory government intervention.[11] At the same time, Trudeau announced a freeze on federal spending and a dramatic reduction in the size of the civil service.[12]

Some Alberta reaction to Young's anti-inflation plan was positive. Lougheed called on the Strom government to support the policy, reminding Albertans that their provincial government was the biggest government per capita spender in the country. In the past year its expenditures had increased by 10 percent and government employment was up by 9 percent.[13]

Addressing a national conference of top Canadian business leaders organized by Dr. Young in Ottawa, Trudeau said, "Inflation is not like Dr. Strangelove's bomb. There is no way we can stop worrying and love it." And, "We have no alternative. To end the injustices and turmoil caused by inflation, we must end inflation itself." Those in attendance promised to hold 1970 price increases below cost increases, provided wage and salary increases were restrained as well.[14]

By the end of February, it looked like inflation was easing. The Bank of Canada reported that short-term interest rates were moving downward from the record high recorded at the beginning of the year and that further declines were expected.[15] But federal policies to combat inflation remained in place. In Benson's March 1970 budget, another surplus was projected for 1970/71 and for the first time since 1913, there were no tax changes.[16] The controversial deferral of new construction capital cost allowances, however, was extended for one year despite opposition from business leaders and the Alberta government.[17]

Statistics released in mid-March showed the fight against inflation was taking casualties. The Canadian unemployment rate reached a six-year high at 6.5 percent. But the government continued to hold the line;[18] it now demanded that wage settlements be not more than 6.5 percent in 1970 and 5 percent in 1971.[19] With wage contracts affecting nearly 700,000 workers about to expire, and with many of those workers falling within federal jurisdiction, fireworks were expected with possible strikes at the airlines, railways, and the post office.

The Canadian Post Office now became a principal battleground in the fight against inflation. Canadian postal workers, or "posties," were represented by the Council of Postal Unions. The Council comprised three different unions each looking for a new contract: the 3,000 strong Postal Supervisors union; the 10,000 workers of the Postmasters union; and the 27,000-member Letter Carriers and Clerks union. The federal Treasury Board was now the chief government negotiator in the collective bargaining process. The posties were demanding wage increases of 9 percent while the Treasury Board was sticking to its guns and not offering more than 6 percent.[20] The Trudeau government had already had dustups with the postal unions including strike action over attempts to make the Post Office more efficient;[21] their relationship was about to get much worse.

In mid-May, to pressure the government, Montreal's 5,500 postal workers began a twenty-four hour strike. It was followed by work slowdowns in Ontario and Alberta.[22] The Montreal union local president predicted that Canada was about to experience the worst strike in its history.[23]

On May 20, the Council of Postal Unions' members voted for strike action,[24] following which the unions began a series of rotating twenty-four hour strikes. For the posties this was the perfect weapon because they would only lose a few days rather than many weeks of pay for a longer strike. Other unions such as the Canadian Union of Public Employees (CUPE) came to the aid with financial help. A CUPE spokesman said, "The postal workers are fighting for all of us. If the government holds them to a 6 percent increase they will hold us to the same."[25]

The disrupting rotating strikes taking place throughout the country angered Canadians waiting for pension and family allowance cheques, account payments, and business communications. Their anger was directed at both sides: the postal workers who did not seem to give a damn about the people and the government because they did not seem to have the guts to deal with the problem.[26] Most Albertans had little sympathy for strikers or the right to strike at the best of times, and there was even less support for a government that would tolerate a strike of workers in what they considered an essential public service.[27]

As summer approached, the rotating strikes and the tough negotiations continued. Trudeau stuck to maintaining the wage guidelines[28] and warned that the poor people in Canada stood to get "screwed" by powerful labour unions if the unions demanded more than their fair share of the economic output.[29] The twenty-four hour strikes persisted.

After eleven months of negotiations the Postmasters and Postal Supervisors unions each signed new three-year wage deals giving them wage increases of just over 18 percent—very close to the 6 percent guideline. But the more militant 27,000 letter carriers continued their strikes.[30]

With the rotating strikes into their third month, Postmaster General Eric Kierans blasted both the Treasury Board and the unions, telling them to settle the dispute. Other members of the Liberal caucus and cabinet were also critical of the Treasury Board. The *Globe and Mail* opined, "This country and these (postal) workers have suffered enough from this Liberal farce of liberal labor relations."[31] The *Calgary Herald* urged Kierans to immediately close down the postal system and called the rotating strikes "cunning but irresponsible union harassment."[32]

While the postal dispute inched toward settlement, inflation continued to wane. By June consumer price increases were the lowest in more than two years.[33] The national unemployment rate was approaching 7 percent, the highest since 1961, while industrial production sank to its lowest level since November 1969. Some economists now feared the economy was at a standstill.[34] On July 28 PIC chairman John Young finally announced that inflation had been temporarily checked but warned that it could easily revive.[35]

Although Alberta was not nearly as impacted as other parts of the country, neither was it completely insulated by the economic slowdown. For July, the provincial unemployment rate was 4.1 percent compared to 2.3 percent for the same time in the previous year.[36] City Planning department statistics showed that by August, building permits were down by 25 percent, new apartment construction starts were down by two-thirds, and office construction was down by 90 percent compared to a year earlier.[37]

In early September after negotiations for the better part of the year and rotating strikes for almost four months, the government and the 27,000 postal workers made their deal. The posties received an annual pay increase of about 7 percent, not as much as they wanted but beating the guideline.[38] Their persistence and brilliant strategy of the rotating strikes with little cost to themselves not only got them a better deal in the end, it earned them grudging respect. The *Albertan*'s shrewd columnist Fred Kennedy wrote that the government "was the first to cry 'uncle,' [so] the posties won the battle."[39]

The government seemed to have won the battle against inflation, but the victory took a heavy toll. In Alberta much of the public was already angry with the Trudeau government for bilingualism, medicare, the wheat-marketing crisis, the white paper on taxation, and its oil policy. Now there was the pain of recession and the nasty rotating postal strikes arising out of a labour dispute that the unions had won.

III

The Arranged Marriage

14

The Evolution of the Mighty Social Credit

SEPTEMBER 1968–SEPTEMBER 1969

BY SEPTEMBER 1968 the Social Credit Party had held power in Alberta for thirty-three unbroken years. For nearly all that time it had been held in high esteem by the business community, the media, and Alberta voters. It had also been a consistent political foe of Alberta provincial and federal Liberals.

The Social Credit Party had been the creation of two men: William Aberhart and Ernest Manning. Aberhart was an Ontario farm boy who became a schoolteacher before he moved his family to Calgary. By 1915 he was the authoritarian, temperamental, workaholic principal of Crescent Heights High School. He was also a devout Christian on his way to becoming an evangelical Christian lay preacher,[1] organizing the Calgary Prophetic Bible Institute so he could teach students his version of Baptist fundamentalism.[2]

Manning was a Saskatchewan farm boy who'd left school in Grade 8 to work on the family farm. The two men's paths would cross after Aberhart started preaching on Sundays on Calgary radio station CFCN. After hearing one of Aberhart's sermons in 1927, Manning was soon on his way to Calgary to meet him.[3] Manning moved into the Aberhart home, became the Institute's first graduate in 1930, and soon began preaching the gospel under Aberhart's tutelage. Manning also married a fellow student who had been the pianist for Aberhart's religious services since she was fifteen and Aberhart gave the bride away.[4]

By the early 1930s the Great Depression had struck agriculture-dependent Alberta hard: a prolonged drought had ravaged farmlands, family incomes declined drastically, unemployment soared to 25 percent, and banks were calling in farmers' loans. Aberhart saw the social turmoil around him and believed that as a Christian he had a moral duty to do something about it. Thus he began his personal search for solutions to the people's misery.[5]

Aberhart was particularly influenced by the writings of British amateur economist Major C.H. Douglas, who claimed that the solution to the economic crisis was to issue "social credit" so people had sufficient money to buy all goods and services produced. Douglas also argued that the depression was due to a conspiracy of bankers and moneylenders, who were lining their own pockets and controlling the destiny of mankind.[6] Douglas also had an affinity for fascism; his theories met the approval of some fascists, including British fascist leader Sir Oswald Mosely.[7] By 1932, Aberhart's audience had grown to 350,000 as he began including Douglas' Social Credit theories in his sermons. In 1933, he co-wrote and distributed several leaflets promoting his ideas and began delivering public lectures that called for the government to pay each citizen of Alberta a monthly credit of $25 to buy clothing, food, and shelter. His sermons and speeches also promoted the equality of sexes, free education and health care, and the abolition of money, banks, and life insurance. This marked the beginning of the Social Credit movement in Alberta.[8]

In 1935, after Aberhart failed to convince other political parties to adopt his ideas, he and his supporters began to nominate candidates to contest the provincial election. One of those candidates was Ernest Manning. During the campaign Aberhart promised to protect Albertans from bank foreclosures and to fight for lower interest rates and taxes, wage and price controls, women's rights, and universal health care. He ran the campaign out of his Prophetic Bible Institute and adopted the hymn, "Oh God, Our Help in Ages Past, Our Hope for Years to Come" as the Social Credit campaign song. On the stump he called the bankers and their friends, the "fifty big shots," the "high-mucky-mucks," and the "sons of Satan."[9]

On voting day, August 22, 1935, Social Credit won 54 percent of the popular vote and 56 out of 63 seats in the legislature. The opposition was held to a meagre 5 Liberals and 2 Conservatives.[10] This victory also marked the beginning of the 26-year-old Manning's career in government. His patron Aberhart appointed him provincial secretary, minister of trade and industry, and to the lofty post of deputy premier.

With his province nearly bankrupt, Aberhart enacted legislation to help the poor, take power away from the banks, and muzzle the press. As a result of constitutional challenges by Mackenzie King's federal Liberal government, much of this legislation was struck down. The $25-a-month promise was changed to issuing everybody a new form of currency called prosperity certificates, which became known as "funny money" when the idea failed.

In 1940, as Alberta's economic crisis receded with the easing of the depression and the coming of World War II, Aberhart was rewarded with another win at the polls. However, he did not live out his second mandate, dying at the age of 64 in 1943. He was succeeded by his protégé, Ernest Manning, who became premier, party leader, and Aberhart's replacement preaching the Sunday radio sermons.[11] As prosperity increased, the Manning government's messages changed: anti-socialist pronouncements now replaced conspiracy and economic theories to help bring the business community and the major Alberta daily newspapers onside.

In 1947 came the major oil discovery in Leduc by Imperial Oil. Although there had been some successful oil field activity in the Turner Valley area of southern Alberta going back to 1914, the Leduc discovery made that look like small change. Alberta would no longer be a "have-not" province and agriculture would no longer be its primary resource.[12]

One of the issues that dogged the Social Credit movement was the pervading anti-Semitism found among many of its members and in the philosophical writings of Douglas. Norman Jaques, who represented the Wetaskiwin riding as a Social Credit MP through three elections from 1935 until 1949, was a well-known anti-Semite who read excerpts from the "Protocols of the Learned Elders of Zion"[13] into the parliamentary record. And by no means was Jaques alone amongst Social Credit Party members.[14] However, Manning, to his credit, shortly after becoming premier, made it clear that he had no time for such attitudes.[15]

Shortly after Leduc, Manning purged or silenced most of the remnants of the Douglas-ites and most of the anti-Semites.[16] His Social Credit now meant the promotion of individual liberty, private property, equal opportunity, and a strong economy. In lock step with Western sentiments during the Cold War, he also railed against communists who were out to sink capitalism and democracy[17] and whose views, he believed, were entrenched in the news media and universities.[18]

As Leduc brought many foreign and US oil companies looking for Alberta crude oil, Manning welcomed them, believing the government role in oil was to ensure that Albertans received a fair share of the profits, and that the industry operate in Albertans' best interests. The oil industry became a cash cow that allowed the government to spend generously in health care, education, government services, and infrastructure, without tax increases or government borrowing. But Manning stood firm against federal universal programs; in the late 1960s he vigorously opposed the federal medicare program as too costly and socialistic.[19]

The new prosperity allowed the invincible Manning Social Credit Party to win most elections by lopsided margins through to the 1960s. With the 1967 general election, things began to change. Although Social Credit captured 55 out of 65 seats, it did so with less than 45 percent of the vote. More importantly, a dynamic and urbane Peter Lougheed led his Tories in capturing 25 percent of the popular vote and 6 seats—enough to become the opposition party in the Alberta legislature. As a result of Lougheed's success many Albertans began to think that—just maybe—this could be the end for the bible-thumping Social Credit Party.

The situation was far worse for the federal Socred organization. Social Credit had been a potent federal party in Alberta since its inception in 1935. As late as the 1957 federal election, the party took 11 out of 17 Alberta seats and 37.8 percent of the popular vote. Less than one year later, the Socreds won no seats and saw its popular vote tumble to 21.6 percent. John Diefenbaker's Tories swept all 17 Alberta ridings and 208 across Canada—up to that time the largest majority government in Canadian history in terms of seats.[20] This was the beginning of the end for the federal Socreds in Alberta and Canada.

Manning, the major influence within the federal party, tried to revive its fortunes in 1961 by recruiting long-time party activist Robert Thompson[21] from Innisfail to be the federal party leader. However, in the 1962 federal election, only two Alberta Social Credit candidates won their ridings—Thompson in Red Deer and Bud Olson in Medicine Hat—and only a total of four won in western Canada. Social Credit as a federal force shifted to Quebec where under the deputy leader, populist Douglas-ite Real Caouette, the Socreds won 26 seats. Thompson and Manning, who had little understanding of Quebec, encouraged the departure of Caouette (and his 26 MPs) from the federal Social Credit caucus in 1963. Caouette and his members then formed their own party, Ralliement créditiste du Québec.[22]

Although Thompson and Olson would each win their Alberta seats in the 1965 federal election, they both soon jumped ship. In the 1968 general election Thompson took Red Deer for the Tories while Olson did the same for the Liberals in Medicine Hat. The defections ended the Social Credit movement as a federal force in English-speaking Canada and Alberta.

By 1968, with the rise of Lougheed and the demise of the federal Socreds, the Social Credit Party in Alberta was faced with a serious challenge to its provincial dominance. Politicos on the federal scene, both Liberals and Progressive Conservatives, began to see an emerging carcass of the Social Credit Party in Alberta as an enticing political prize.

As he wound down his career as premier and party leader, Manning began to promote his theory of a new political realignment for Canada. In his 1967 book *Political Realignment: A Challenge to Thoughtful Canadians*, he advanced the idea that the federal Progressive Conservative Party should become the party of "social conservatism," promoting free enterprise and conservative values and stand in opposition to left wingers, socialists, and liberals.[23]

In September 1968 after twenty-five years as premier and thirty-three years in the legislature, the 60-year-old Manning announced he was stepping down.[24] Upon his retirement he was expected to write policy for the National Public Affairs Research Foundation, which was already engaged in studying his political realignment philosophy,[25] with his son Preston.[26] The Foundation was financed by a group of wealthy businessmen headed by prominent Calgary oil baron Bobby Brown Jr. of Home Oil.[27] Once an astute businessman, by 1968 Brown was a burned-out, albeit jovial and wealthy alcoholic. The Bible-thumping, teetotalling Manning cashing Brown's cheques was supreme irony.[28]

Given the importance of oil to Alberta, Manning had over the years become friendly with oilmen, another one of whom was US oilman John Howard Pew, the head of Sun Oil Company. In his book *The Good Steward*, Brian Brennan described Manning's long-standing relationship with the fabulously wealthy Pew, a devout evangelical Presbyterian who was interested in the Fort McMurray oil sands. Sun Oil became an early investor and the basis of the present-day major oil sands player Suncor Energy. The Pew and Manning families became fast friends, even holidaying together. Unbeknownst to the Alberta public, Pew also helped finance Manning's *Back to the Bible Hour* radio program to the tune of $10,000 a year for ten years.[29] Pew's politics were of the far right, also, with family money supporting extreme causes such as the John Birch Society and the American Liberty League.[30]

No sooner would Trudeau unpack at Sussex Drive, did Manning slam the PM's first major initiative—the proposed Official Languages Act—questioning the act's constitutionality, arguing that bilingualism could be better achieved by cooperation of all levels of government rather than by statute, and warning that giving English and French legal status would build up resentments at a time when everyone should be working to strengthen national unity. Manning also predicted that official bilingualism would ensure the Canadian public service's domination by French-speaking Canadians.[31]

Harry Strom succeeded Manning as premier and leader of the Social Credit Party December 12, 1968.[32] Two months later Manning, whose party had once been an avowed enemy of banks, himself joined the "fifty big shots," and "high mucky-mucks," by accepting an appointment to the board of directors of the Canadian Imperial Bank of Commerce.[33]

Freed from his duties as premier, Manning could also focus on federal politics with Trudeau firmly in his crosshairs. In a May 1969 interview, Manning accused the federal government of neglecting the oil industry, demanded that it quickly restrict foreign oil imports, and accused it of having too few politicians and civil servants who knew how vital the petroleum industry was to Canada's economy. About the recent US demands for cuts to Canadian oil exports, Manning said he was "pretty browned off" and "holy smoke"—colourful words for the pious Manning![34] Manning described Trudeau as "the worst political leader in years," and declared that the Official Languages Act was "creating problems between ethnic and religious groups that didn't exist before." He also accused the Trudeau government of showing "no interest and understanding whatsoever in considering the diverse problems of Western Canada."[35] At the Vancouver Board of Trade he warned that parts of Canada were heading toward joining the United States, because the federal government treated the cultural and linguistic aspirations of Quebec as more important than the economic aspirations of other parts of the country.[36] The now-retired Manning had become, and would remain, one of the Trudeau government's most implacable Alberta foes.

15

A Troublesome Relationship

JANUARY 1969–FEBRUARY 1970

BUOYED BY THE DEPARTURE of the popular Manning from provincial politics and Trudeau's recent majority victory, the Alberta Liberal Party was showing signs of life in January 1969. The leadership convention to choose Mike Maccagno's successor was to begin April 25 and a number of candidates were interested in the job. Mel Hurtig had taken over as the party's policy chair and had forty people drafting new party policy. The membership numbers remained strong from the 1968 federal success.[1] But the party was choosing yet another leader—the sixth in eleven years—and its disappointing last-place finish in the 1967 provincial election and losing official opposition status were sobering realities.

The convention held at Edmonton's Macdonald Hotel produced three serious candidates, all in their late thirties: Calgarian Jack Lowery, Dr. Don Branigan, from the northwestern town of Manning, and Bob Russell, of St. Albert, near Edmonton.

Lowery was an ordained United Church minister who had moved with his family from Toronto to Hardisty, where he took over a ministry, then to

Calgary, where he ministered at the downtown Central United Church. He was also a public relations manager with ATCO industries, a large Calgary manufacturing company. In the late 1960s, Lowery had become a member of the Calgary North federal Liberal riding executive, and vigorously supported Paul Martin in the 1968 federal leadership campaign. A polished speaker, as might be expected for a minister, he was supported by seasoned party veterans, including his campaign manager Sharon Carstairs,[2] then living in Calgary.

Branigan was a cheerful physician from humble beginnings in rural Saskatchewan. While practicing medicine in Manning[3] he'd also gained political experience as mayor and finished third as the Liberal candidate in the riding of Peace River in the 1968 federal election.

Russell was employed in the sales and public relations fields. He had a youthful exuberance and considerable political experience. He had served as executive director of the Alberta Liberal Party, lost the provincial leadership in 1966 by only 33 votes, and placed a close second in the 1967 provincial election in St. Albert.[4]

Voting turned out to be the most exciting part of the convention, with Lowery finally winning over Branigan by 15 votes after three ballots. The battle ended with some divisions. Branigan[5] responded by graciously urging the delegates to throw their full support behind Lowery. Russell, smarting from his second straight defeat as leadership candidate, initially held up Branigan's arm after the results of the final ballot. However, he soon relented, promising to work for Lowery in the next election. In his victory address Lowery promised to devote his full time to the leadership and work in every constituency in the province to ensure a Liberal victory. He called the convention "a turning point" for the party and said he would make party policy "the reflection of people who work for the party."[6]

Under the leadership of policy chair Mel Hurtig, the convention approved several progressive resolutions including ones calling for Alberta to join the federal medicare program without Albertans having to pay premiums, the Sunday commercial sale of liquor in bars and restaurants, and the removal of marijuana offences from the Criminal Code.[7]

Alberta Liberal Party president Peter Petrasuk, Trudeau, and Jack Lowery, Alberta Liberal Party leader, at a party fundraiser in Calgary, April 1969.
[*Onions Collection, City of Calgary Archives, Cal A 2011-006-0946*]

Hurtig, who had strongly supported Trudeau in the 1968 leadership race, was now a rising star in the Liberal Party. The young Edmonton bookseller and publisher-to-be, had a large following of young people, and was always good copy for the media.

With more than 750 registered delegates and strong campaigns from the candidates, the convention was the most well attended Liberal leadership contest ever held in Alberta up to that point.[8] The closeness of the race and convention floor excitement had captured the interest of the public and the media. Despite some inevitable acrimony among supporters of the various candidates, Lowery was not a man to hold grudges and most delegates left the convention with a sense of optimism.

No one, however, believed the road to success would be easy. Opposition Leader Peter Lougheed was looking very good. Born and raised in Calgary, he was a grandson of the Alberta pioneer and prominent Conservative lawyer-businessman-politician Sir James Lougheed.[9] At the University of Alberta Lougheed had been student council president and he had played pro football with the Edmonton Eskimos. After receiving an MBA from Harvard University, he worked a few years as a corporate lawyer with the Mannix group of construction and resource companies, and started his own law firm. Although not wealthy (most of the family money had disappeared during the Great Depression), he had a pleasant smile, square jaw, tall attractive wife, wholesome-looking kids, and could deliver a decent speech. Furthermore, his tentacles already reached into the very innards of the Alberta corporate and oil establishment.[10]

In addition to Lougheed's head start in the legislature, Lowery had to face the challenging task of party fundraising. The provincial Liberals had not held power in more than forty-seven years, had been in a near moribund state for many of those years, and finished dead last in the latest provincial election. A potential contributor would have little incentive to support it financially.

This was in marked contrast to the federal Liberal Party in Alberta. Since the federal Liberals had held power in the country twenty-eight out of the last thirty-four years, Alberta corporations and individuals were happy to contribute to its coffers. The challenge for the provincial Liberals was to get Alberta federal Liberals to share some of their loot. Jack Lowery had to worry about money on two fronts—money by which to run the party and money by which to live. On both counts he was not likely to have an easy time.

Liberal Party fundraising in Alberta was done at three levels. At the top level funds were raised for the Liberal Party of Canada, under the jurisdiction of the Liberal Federation's Treasury Committee whose members were appointed with the PM's approval. Beginning in 1970 Alberta's member was Senator Harry Hays.[11] His mandate was to raise money in Alberta by soliciting contributions from large corporations and wealthy individuals.

Almost all the money he collected went to the Liberal Federation. These monies helped pay a stipend for the national leader and the expenses of a national office, campaigns of national party candidates that were vital to the party's electoral success, national party organizers, and a national campaign (such as advertising and travel). If there were any surplus funds, small sums would be used to help fund Alberta federal Liberal campaigns of candidates that the committee thought had a chance of winning, or lastly, to sustain federal and provincial party organizations within the province where the money was raised.[12]

The second level of fundraising was the exclusive jurisdiction of the provincial Liberal Party. It had the responsibility to solicit contributions to pay expenses incurred for provincial party purposes such as the salary and expenses of the provincial leader and party organizers, office and communications expenses of the provincial party, and the costs of a provincial political campaign.

The third level of fundraising was handled by the federal and provincial party riding associations. A federal or provincial riding association could raise money to pay the expenses of their respective campaigns. The effectiveness on this level depended mostly on the riding's candidate or the riding association. Candidates who had plenty of contacts could do well, as could ridings with an enthusiastic membership.

As Alberta's member on the Treasury Committee, Hays took his authority from the national leader—the prime minister—and had his own list of wealthy corporations and individuals from which to raise funds. Hays took no responsibility to collect money for the provincial Liberal Party, which was expected to stay away from the senator's list of contributors and find its own sources. The reality for the provincial party was that it could raise very little money because of its historical lack of success at the polls. Now, with Lougheed as the obvious frontrunner to challenge Social Credit, raising money became even more difficult for the provincial Liberals.

Calgary was just behind Toronto and Montreal as a federal Liberal cash cow, and Alberta just behind Ontario and Quebec. This success can be attributed to the prosperity of the oil and gas industry, and the number of public companies—particularly oil companies—whose head offices were in Calgary. But this money was not going to the provincial party. Somehow the provincial Liberals had to find fundraising space alongside the still strong and governing Social Credit Party and Lougheed's charging Tories.

Despite the lively leadership convention, 1969 was not a good year for Alberta provincial Liberals. By year end the 3 seats won in May 1967 had evaporated. They had already lost Mike Maccagno's Lac La Biche seat to Social Credit in a by-election in August 1968. Then Bill Switzer,[13] a folksy pharmacist and the first mayor of Hinton, died suddenly while Liberal MLA for Edson. The Lougheed Tories took that seat in an October by-election with the Liberals coming in fourth and last place. In late November the last sitting Liberal MLA, Bill Dickie, member for Calgary Glenmore who lost the federal Liberal nomination to Pat Mahoney in 1968, crossed the floor and joined his old friend Lougheed in the PC caucus. With Dickie's departure, the provincial Liberals were no longer in the legislature.

Back in February 1969 Lougheed's Tories had picked up Manning's old Edmonton riding of Strathcona East when Tory Bill Yurko won the by-election to replace Manning after he retired. So as 1969 drew to a close, the Tories with 9 seats were flying high.

Although Lougheed was a good politician and media performer, he was not a one-man band. His party organization was bringing in money and manpower, gaining credibility and prominence, and his whole caucus exuded youth, competence, and vigour. His MLAs were performing well in the legislature, peppering the government with questions and introducing their own bills. They were out-hustling and out-debating the tired-looking Socreds.

As Lowery and his party faded, the relationship between Premier Strom and Prime Minister Trudeau seemed to be glowing. Although opposite personalities—Trudeau, cerebral, charismatic, competitive, interested in lofty subjects like the constitution, and Strom, a bumbling, and soft-spoken nice guy interested in farm issues and oil revenues—they seemed to hit it off.

There was no better illustration of the warm Strom–Trudeau relationship than medicare. The federal government had established the national medicare program in 1967 with Ottawa offering to pay 50 percent of the costs of any province, provided its plan met certain conditions. In Alberta, medicare faced powerful opponents in the media, the business community, and the Social Credit government. Manning had opposed medicare because enrolment was compulsory, and he viewed the program as unaffordable. The *Calgary Herald* reflected what many Albertans were thinking when it called the plan "monstrous" and a "welfare scheme."[14]

But a few months after Harry Strom became premier, Alberta became the sixth province opting into the program. According to Strom, Alberta was joining "because there is no possible chance for us to get federal assistance for the Alberta Health Plan as things now stand."[15]

The Strom government's decision to join medicare signalled a new era of harmony in Alberta–Ottawa relations—so long as Strom was able to survive in office. Not only had he prevailed against the opposition of most of his caucus and party, but also that of his revered predecessor Ernest Manning. Although protest gatherings brought out only a handful of people, many Albertans remained dead set against medicare.[16]

Columnist Don Sellar described the relationship between Trudeau and Strom as one of "genuine mutual respect."[17] Strom was showing political courage in being on good terms with Trudeau because most Albertans were blaming the problems of the oil business and poor wheat markets on Trudeau while others still harboured lingering resentments against medicare and the Official Languages Act. Manning's ongoing hostility to the Trudeau government was also a problem; not only did Strom lack Manning's stature in the party, neither did he possess his predecessor's gospel preaching oratorical skills—and his first test at the polls as premier was only a year or so away.

This was the backdrop to the helping hand that Jack Lowery (complicit with Alberta Liberal MPs and others) was about to extend to Strom's Social Credit. It brought about a battle royal within the Liberal Party in Alberta to which all of us loyal Grits would have ringside seats.

Pat Mahoney gave the first public hint about what was about to happen while speaking to a Liberal conference in Calgary in December. Mahoney said that the Alberta federal Liberal Party had failed politically in Alberta because it did a "lousy job" developing modern mass party appeal at election time, and that it had been dominated for too long by people who had a "vested interest in losing."

> *Nothing made these nabobs happier than a Liberal government in Ottawa as long as this could be achieved without the embarrassment of MPs elected from the province. In this condition of good fortune the nabobs enjoyed the prestige of being the federal presence in Alberta while avoiding the burden of accountability to the voters.*[18]

Mahoney explained that the federal Liberals currently had to seek a consensus on national policies even though those policies could "be downright repulsive" in some parts of the country. A provincial Liberal Party should have the right to oppose federal policies, he suggested, and federal and provincial parties should be able to separate. Such a separation, said Mahoney, would allow the provincial party to meet its obligation to act in Alberta's best interests "without being duly concerned about Ottawa."

Mahoney then noted that most Albertans regarded Social Credit "as having done and as continuing to do a good job managing the province," and given that the provincial Liberal Party had no seats in the legislature, it now had a chance "unobstructed by any established interests" to restructure itself so that it would be more relevant to Albertan and Canadian voters.[19]

Despite being a political novice and having joined the Liberals less than two years before, Mahoney was now giving the Party two major pieces of existential advice. First, since the Alberta federal Liberal Party and the Alberta provincial Liberal Party did not represent the same interests, they each should go their own independent way. Second, the provincial party should consider doing a deal with Social Credit.

By this time MPs Mahoney, Olson, and Sulatycky, together with Senator Hays, all believed that the Alberta provincial Liberal Party was dragging down the federal Liberals' chances of retaining their Alberta foothold. Olson had believed for some time that the federal Liberals could even recruit some younger Social Credit talent such as Ray Speaker and Bob Clark.[20]

Three weeks later Alberta Liberal leader Jack Lowery confirmed that he'd had discussions with Premier Strom about the provincial Liberals forming an alliance with Social Credit. He explained that this was one of the alternatives open to his party, which currently held no seats and "was ten years away from being an effective political force."[21]

Alluding to Manning's replacement by the more moderate Strom, Lowery noted there had been dramatic changes within Social Credit, particularly in the areas of education and social legislation, which were now more consistent with Liberal positions. He also said that the proposals discussed (one of which was to field as many as thirty joint Social Credit-Liberal candidates in thirty ridings in the next provincial election) were getting mixed reactions from the party members.[22]

Strom also acknowledged the discussions took place but said that although Social Credit had not initiated them and was not interested in deals or mergers, it would welcome Liberal Party members or members of any other party who wished to join and work with it.[23]

Edmonton–Strathcona MP Hu Harries called the idea of a coalition "bloody nonsense" and a "selfish, stupid reaction" to the Alberta Liberal Party losing the provincial by-election in Edson when it ran a poor fourth. He predicted that Alberta Liberals would not support Lowery's proposal and said that his early retirement as leader would benefit the Party.[24] The relationship between Harries and Mahoney was already strained due to Mahoney's belief that while he was working like a dog on behalf of the government, Harries was doing little or nothing.[25]

Mel Hurtig quickly resigned his position as the provincial party's policy chair declaring, "I will have no part of any preposterous moves of second-rate political minds," and predicting that Lowery would have to resign. He blasted Lowery for representing the conservative wing of the party and accused him of bargaining for a Social Credit cabinet seat. Hurtig believed that not all had been lost, however, because if Lowery and company departed, it could give rise to a new truly (small-l) liberal alternative.

Hurtig's view was shared by Don Peacock who wrote in the *Albertan* that "liberally minded Liberals" welcomed the collapse of the provincial structure because it would allow for the development of a truly liberal party "instead of an organization too often dominated by persons—notably lawyers—with more interest in political patronage plums from the Liberal government in Ottawa than in sound policies for Alberta."[26]

But Calgary mayor Rod Sykes, a strong admirer of Social Credit and Ernest Manning, believed there were no ideological or policy differences between the two parties, so supported the proposed alliance. Recent Tory convert Bill Dickie predicted a polarization of former Liberal supporters with the left wing gravitating to Grant Notley's NDP and the others lining up behind Lougheed.[27]

Columnist Fred Kennedy, as usual, got to the heart of the issue, writing that the proposal made sense if Liberals were behind the move to engineer a deal whereby they would support Social Credit in a provincial election, in return for Social Credit support for the federal Liberals in a federal election. He noted that if Lowery pulled off the alliance, the worst that could happen to him would be a seat in the Senate.[28]

On January 7 Jack Lowery announced that negotiations had failed: Social Credit was not interested in the joint candidate proposal and his invitation to Strom to make a counter-proposal was rebuffed. The potential alliance as envisioned by Lowery was now dead.[29]

The attacks on Lowery had merely been the opening skirmishes of a major party bloodletting. Failed leadership candidate Bob Russell demanded Lowery's resignation. Red Deer Liberal John Robinson began working to convert February's annual meeting into a leadership convention. With such visceral anger toward the Lowery initiative—especially from northern Alberta and Edmonton members—the convention promised to be a donnybrook.[30]

Bud Olson had been a long-time Social Credit MP before he crossed the floor and still had many old Social Credit friends. He reportedly had meetings with Strom and Social Credit officials to discuss Lowery's initiative.[31] Pat Mahoney was said to have supported Social Credit up until he became a Liberal less than two years earlier. As an unabashed admirer of Ernest Manning, Senator Harry Hays had also supported Social Credit[32] and was even rumoured to have raised money for the party.[33] The undisputed bosses of the federal Liberal establishment in Alberta—Olson, Mahoney, and Hays—were all supportive of Lowery's moves. Although Allen Sulatycky, Liberal MP for Rocky Mountain, kept mostly silent during the turmoil and had no Social Credit pedigree, he too was supportive of distancing the federal Liberal Party from the provincial Liberal Party.[34] Thus, most of the federal Liberal caucus of MPs and senators, and the provincial leader, now stood accused of selling out the provincial Liberals to save the skins of the Alberta Liberal MPs in the next federal election.

Hu Harries' outspoken opposition to the Lowery proposal confirmed his testy relationship with the powerful Hays and his fellow Alberta MPs Mahoney and Olson. He was said to have "slit his throat in Ottawa" because of his vocal opposition to any deal with Social Credit.[35] Sulatycky viewed Harries' actions the result of his disappointment at not being in cabinet and his visceral disrespect for Olson, who Harries considered an intellectual and political lightweight.[36]

In short, less than two years after its breakthrough into federal power, the Alberta Liberals—federal and provincial—were immersed in acrimony. Even Alberta's tiny federal Liberal representation in Ottawa was divided.

Neither Olson nor Mahoney seemed concerned about Lowery's bed of nails. They held closed-door meetings in Calgary on January 21 to discuss Mahoney's pet project of a western federal Liberal caucus organization to give the west more clout in Ottawa. Edmonton MP Hu Harries gave that idea short shrift: "It reminds me of the guy with a small business who is having problems and decides that the solution is to go out and get a bigger business." Harries said that the problem in Alberta was that the north and south portions of the province did not seem to get together on anything.[37]

A little over a month after being rebuffed by Strom and just two weeks before he would have to face the wrath of the delegates at the Alberta Liberal Party convention in Red Deer, Lowery threw in the towel. The provincial party was again leaderless—the fifth time in seven years. Lowery said, "Until the party clarifies its goals, it does not require a full-time leader and I am not in the position to be a part-time one." He said that the time had come for the party to regroup and redefine itself, a process, he predicted, that could take five to ten years.[38]

Peter Lougheed reacted to Lowery's exit by expressing the hope that Liberal supporters would back his own programs. He predicted that the next election would see a two-way fight between the Tories and the Socreds.[39]

The *Albertan*'s Fred Kennedy mused that Manning's election call in May 1967 (a little over a year before Trudeau's victory) probably prevented the provincial party from benefitting from the Trudeau charisma. He sensed that the federal party looked down on its provincial counterpart for reasons he could not fathom, and opined that western Liberal MPs had not done much for the Prairies. Kennedy forecast a bleak future: "For provincial Liberals still loyal to the party, the fight for survival will be all uphill. Like the Indians, they will have to get used to being tabbed as second-class citizens in the political way of life. And don't shed any tears for former leader Jack Lowery. He's really a very lucky man."[40]

But even as the Alberta Liberals were suffering in the early part of 1970, an omen prophesized trouble for Social Credit. The house that Aberhart built, the Calgary Prophetic Bible Institute, the Social Credit birthplace and shrine, was about to become a rock and roll club. In the loft where Manning's wife had once played the organ, there would soon be gyrating go-go girls. The young club co-owner Dave Horodezky[41] philosophized that the modern age dictated religion be sold in a more attractive package. He said, "Religion has to include soul today—and that's what the kids find in their music."[42]

16

The Making of a Senator

FEBRUARY–OCTOBER 1970

AFTER THE INFIGHTING over Lowery's failed initiative and resignation, the provincial party executive showed no enthusiasm for another leadership contest at their annual convention and instead designated president Peter Petrasuk as provincial party spokesman.[1]

Just before the convention was to begin, a small group of Liberals from Calgary and Edmonton announced they would present resolutions to split the Alberta Liberal Party into separate legal entities—a provincial party and a federal party—each with an independent organization. Group spokesman John Hutton said since Alberta's Liberal Party was dominated by people whose interests were federally oriented, splitting the party in two would allow the federal Liberals and provincial Liberals to operate more freely and effectively.[2]

The rancour over Social Credit was still felt throughout the party. At the annual meeting of the Calgary Centre federal Liberal riding association, Jack King was challenged in his bid to be re-elected a director while simultaneously serving as president of a Social Credit provincial riding association.[3] During the acrimonious debate, Nick Taylor, the nominee for the next election, tried to calm the crowd and pleaded for party unity: "I want as many people as we can get in the association so we can win the next election. We have to bring in support." King was elected to the riding association's board.[4]

The February convention was aptly themed, "Why the party?" The winter weather outside matched the gloom inside the hall. Bud Olson, who was to give a speech at the opening session, was delayed and bumped from the program. Lowery, as expected, was not one of the hundred in attendance.

Angst and anger were the dominant moods of the sessions. Petrasuk warned the delegates that splitting the party would "destroy everything." Prominent Edmonton delegate Mike MacDonald said, "We're a bloody disappointing party. I'm tired of hearing that Liberals were a party of change, when in many respects we're nothing but a bunch of Tories." Another delegate shouted that the turnout was "disgraceful."[5]

The recently resigned policy chair Mel Hurtig accused the party of putting special interests and manipulation of power ahead of the problems of the people, and predicted that until the party found a truly liberal leader and "until we get rid of the patronage system and make the party a democratic structure we're not going to go anywhere."[6] He forecast that Lougheed had a good chance of becoming premier and that Social Credit would disappear forever if it were defeated.[7] Hurtig promised to report what had happened to the provincial party to Trudeau himself and would recommend that Olson be "severely reprimanded for his part in the incredible fiasco."[8]

At the plenary session, the 300 delegates voted to reject the motion to split the party, despite support by both Mahoney and Sulatycky. Olson, disappointing both Sulatycky and Mahoney, surprisingly opposed the motion, calling it "nonsense."[9] He said he could find no conflict with people being active in federal, or provincial or municipal politics all at the same time.[10] As a final rejection of Lowery's Social Credit misadventure, the convention passed a resolution opposing all coalitions with other political parties.[11]

A frustrated Mahoney described the convention as "self psychoanalysis, group therapy and self condemnation."[12]

The convention approved the formation of an action group to look into the many problems facing the party, but there was no move to find a new leader. Even when Bob Russell, the twice-defeated leadership candidate, offered himself up as an interim leader, the party declined.

Despite the catastrophe on his watch, Petrasuk was re-elected to another two-year term as president. He was joined by Edmonton alderman Una Maclean Evans as vice-president and Sharon Carstairs as treasurer.

All this turmoil was reported in the local press. The Liberals' party organizations in Alberta looked weak, confused, divided, and incompetent. The provincial Liberal Party was now leaderless and broke, and quite irrelevant to the future of the province. The federal Liberal MPs Olson, Mahoney, Harries, and Sulatycky were divided.

Given the magnitude of this political disaster, what were Alberta Liberals going to do in the looming provincial election? Would they join forces with a traditional political foe with which they shared no common history, philosophy, culture, or world view and whose values were not secular but steeped in evangelical Christian teachings? Historically, Social Credit had a murky association with anti-Semitism and fiercely opposed federal institutions. Recently, it had opposed important policy initiatives such as medicare and official bilingualism that were fundamental to all Liberals, provincial or federal.

Social Credit still had among its ranks many enemies of both the Liberal Party and liberalism. Backbencher Carl Muller, MLA from Pembina, accused Trudeau of being more interested in skiing, skin diving, and Barbara Streisand than he was in overhauling western agriculture.[13] William Tomyn, MLA for Edmonton Norwood, said that the tax reform proposals represented the federal government's "needless desire to get its greedy hands into every Canadian's pocketbook with its vicious controlling of every aspect of a person's life."[14] He labelled the tax reform proposals "a snare to trap and plunge the entire nation into socialistic materialism and totalitarian statism."[15]

It did not seem likely that many Social Credit supporters would vote for the federal Liberal Party, especially with Trudeau as the leader. Trudeau was a French Canadian intellectual, a globetrotter, a free thinker, and a suspected socialist, whose policies were anathema to most Socreds, none more so than party icon and ex-premier Ernest Manning.

Trudeau's progressive principles were, however, supported by the majority of Alberta Liberals. They loved his style and charisma; he was their JFK. Without a credible provincial Liberal Party to vote for in the next provincial election, their closest natural home was not Social Credit but perhaps with the more progressive option, Lougheed's provincial Tories.

Liberal voters and supporters were unlikely to be influenced by Olson or Mahoney, regarded by many as political parvenus. Following the uproar over Social Credit, many now saw them as devious manipulators. Furthermore, Mahoney's hectoring ways and impatience in dealing with questions from the party rank and file and the public didn't generate support. Harries' brusque and condescending manner was also driving Liberal voters and regulars away.

Olson's enigmatic personality was another handicap in selling a Liberal–Social Credit alliance to Alberta Liberals. As Roger Kerans noted, Olson came across as "shy and hesitant, a person who had learned the candidate's kind of heartiness but had great difficulty with other relationships."[16] Described as kindly and as shrewd as a good poker player,[17] his appearance, mannerisms, and lacklustre oratory still portrayed him to be the farmer and rancher that he was, out of sync with the new urbane era of Trudeau or Lougheed.

While helpful and genial, Allen Sulatycky did not have the influence of Mahoney or Olson with the Liberal leadership in Ottawa, nor a high profile outside of his riding. Sulatycky's friendly relationships with Harries and Tory agriculture critic Jack Horner made Olson distrust Sulatycky.[18]

The rebellion in the Liberal rank and file and the departure of Lowery did give Social Credit a shot of adrenalin. In early May, Premier Strom convened a thinker's conference of almost 500 Social Credit supporters at

Edmonton's Macdonald Hotel to discuss the issues of the day. Ex-Alberta Liberal leader Lowery and a handful of his supporters attended.[19] Also present was the precocious and supremely self-confident son of Ernest Manning, Preston. Just starting out in politics, Preston Manning did not let his tender age of 27 stand in the way of rendering weighty opinions. At a Social Credit nominating meeting in Edmonton a few days later, he named sixteen Socreds who he thought represented the future of the party.[20]

The Social Credit–federal Liberal mating game again made the news with the astonishing announcement that long-time Alberta minister of highways and telephones Gordon Taylor, had resigned from the Strom cabinet to become assistant deputy minister of transport with the federal government. Taylor was a right-wing former small-town teacher and Aberhart Socred who had represented a largely rural riding and had never lived outside Alberta. Taylor's job offer was another federal Liberal proposition for Social Credit support in the next federal election.[21] A day after his arrival in Ottawa to start his new job, however, Taylor resigned citing his constituents' tearful pleas for him to remain with the Alberta government, whereupon Strom magnanimously accepted him back into cabinet.[22]

The same month, Trudeau was reportedly thinking about prominent politicians from other political persuasions for the Senate. The spin advanced was that it would be in the interests of creating not only a stronger Senate but also a Senate in which there would be countervailing forces to the government-controlled House of Commons. One name bandied about? Trudeau's chief Alberta nemesis, Ernest Manning.[23]

On October 7, Prime Minister Trudeau announced Manning as the first Social Credit senator in Canadian history. Manning responded, "The opportunity accorded me by the prime minister to represent in the Senate for the first time a political philosophy responsible for the successful government of Alberta and British Columbia is an honour and a new challenge." Manning also noted that his appointment was not a retirement from active politics or his business interests, and that the Senate was an appropriate forum for his social conservative philosophy. He promised to continue to advocate "a new partnership between the private and public

Ernest Manning, 1960s. [Edmonton Journal/Provincial Archives of Alberta J 855.1]

sectors of society," as well as "the constructive political realignment necessary to ensure a secure and meaningful future for this nation and its people." Manning was still Manning.

Senator and team player Earl Hastings called Manning's appointment "ideal," a "personal tribute to his years of public service," and a step toward improving the Senate. Lougheed, no doubt thankful that Manning was moving on to federal matters, commended Trudeau for the non-partisan appointment of such an "experienced spokesman." Pat Mahoney remarked that Manning's appointment showed that Trudeau had a great interest in western Canada. Mahoney believed Alberta Liberals in general were pleased, although there might be "one or two disappointed senatorial candidates in northern Alberta" as a result of the Manning appointment."[24]

Indeed, very displeased was the long-time Lac La Biche MLA Mike Maccagno, who had won his seat in four consecutive provincial elections. During his thirteen years as lonely provincial Liberal Party workhorse, Maccagno had the thankless task of opposing Manning and his Social Credit regime, one of only a sprinkling of Liberal voices in the legislature. In fact, Maccagno's 1959 victory was the only Liberal seat won. He became interim leader of the provincial Liberals the first time in 1964 when he succeeded Dave Hunter, who had been defeated in the previous general election. In 1966 Maccagno once again stepped into the breach by becoming provincial Liberal leader after the surprise resignation of Adrian Berry, who led the Party for a few short months. Being Liberal leader was a role Maccagno had not coveted; he assumed the job only to help the party out of a bind. In May 1968 Maccagno resigned his seat in the legislature and party leadership to run in the federal election that he subsequently lost. Having lost the election and then passed over for the Senate, he was instead appointed to the National Parole Board.

In Alberta most of us Liberals did not cheer the Manning appointment. He had been an opponent of both federal and provincial Liberals since 1935 and campaigned against them in all electoral contests. He was also one of Alberta's most ferocious opponents of the Trudeau government's major initiatives. How could this arch-enemy receive this great honour, with its taxpayer-funded offices, salary, and pension? The fact that Manning would have this cushy pulpit to continue his attack for the next thirteen years was mind-boggling.

IV

Crisis

17

Western Alienation and the Rabble-rousers

DECEMBER 1968–OCTOBER 1970

WESTERN ALIENATION is as common to Alberta as oil, except it has been around longer. In boom times or busts, it is always there and it has been there from the beginning. Part of it is economics. Tariffs protecting Ontario manufacturing and freight rates discriminating against the west were on the alienation agenda since the province's earliest days. Most westerners envisioned Toronto and Montreal as the centres of the Canadian commercial and cultural universe, and Ottawa as the city that made it happen: the destiny of the west was manipulated in that golden triangle without input from the people most affected. In their minds they were being stage-managed by well-heeled and arrogant snobs from Toronto's Bay Street and Montreal's St. James Street, aided and abetted by the mandarins and politicians on Ottawa's Wellington Street, who were particularly prone to giving Quebec special treatment. And many had concluded long ago that they were also stuffing their own pockets with the fruits of westerners' labour.[1]

Many disaffected westerners were convinced the choreographer of this state of affairs was the party that by 1969 had governed for twenty-nine of the previous thirty-four years. Unhappily for Alberta Liberals, this jaundiced view was nurtured daily by most of the province's political and economic leaders and print media.

French-speaking Canadians had similar complaints, seeing themselves as long-time victims of economic and cultural discrimination by the anglophone-dominated power centres.[2] This frustration was exploited by political leadership within Quebec, resulting in rising revolutionary foment: in the 1960s the Front de libération du Québec (FLQ) was behind 160 violent incidents that killed eight people and injured many more.[3] A growing number of concerned Canadians feared that this cauldron of resentment could lead to unpredictable and tragic consequences and perhaps even to the breakup of the country.

The Trudeau government believed that a partial answer to growing Quebec hostility could be found in the reports from the Royal Commission on Bilingualism and Biculturalism (B and B Commission) that had been set in motion by the Pearson government in 1963. The Commission's mandate was to

> *inquire into and report upon the existing state of bilingualism and biculturalism in Canada and to recommend what steps should be taken to develop the Canadian confederation on the basis of an equal partnership between the two founding races, taking into account the contribution made by the other ethnic groups to the cultural enrichment of Canada and the measures that should be taken to safeguard that contribution.*[4]

Among its conclusions were that francophones were less able to participate in the Canadian job market, and were not being adequately served in their own language by federal government agencies. It made many recommendations, all promoting the ideals of equal status for both French and English languages.[5]

Since Trudeau believed that implementing the B and B recommendations could help redress many concerns of francophones, he introduced the Official Languages bill in October 1968. Its main provisions declared English and French the official languages of Canada with equal status, that all federal government publications be in both official languages, that all citizens had the right to communicate with the government in either official language, that federal services be provided in the minority official language in any district where the minority made up 10 percent or more of the population, and that services be offered in both official languages to travelers within Canada on its air and rail lines, immigration and customs offices, courts and federal agencies. An Official Languages Commissioner would oversee the program.[6]

Many English-speaking people across Canada, Albertans prominent among them, were outraged at the federal government "shoving French down our throats."[7] Some feared that their sons and daughters would be ineligible to work for the federal government because they could not speak French. Others thought that official French would dilute the prominence of English throughout the country. Disgruntled anglophones wondered, wasn't Trudeau supposed to put Quebec in its place? Many Canadians preferred their children learn a second language other than French or English. For example, the Ukrainian Canadian committee, representing 500,000 Ukrainian Canadians, argued that the Official Languages bill would "adversely and prejudicially affect the rights of Canadians of other than English or French descent who do not speak both English and French, nor intend to."[8]

Thanks to the introduction of the Official Languages bill, western alienation in Alberta was once again heating up. Such was the mood in early 1969 as Trudeau prepared for his initial first minister's conference, with the whole constitution on the table for discussion: Confederation objectives, language rights, and the division of powers.

Trudeau led off, urging constitutional change with the adoption of a charter of human rights, and outlining his position on the Official Languages bill.[9] Premier Strom's said Alberta would cooperate in making French Canadians feel more at home in Confederation but he opposed legally entrenched language rights. He also presented Alberta's long shopping list for greater provincial powers and concessions.[10] (Unhappily for Strom at that very moment, Lougheed's Tories were winning a by-election in Manning's old seat of Strathcona East in Edmonton.)

Going into the conference Trudeau still had plenty of Alberta support. On the opening day he received a telegram (organized by Mel Hurtig) from 9,000 Albertans from twenty-five communities calling Strom's objection to the Official Languages bill "an irresponsible repudiation."[11] The meetings ended with the premiers agreeing to speed up the constitutional review process and to study and deal with the issue of official languages. Trudeau was happy with the progress made.[12]

Not all Albertans were as happy. Parker Kent,[13] a *Calgary Herald* editor-columnist wrote, "I don't care what kind of constitution you have. If the people running things are clueless and irresponsible, no set of rules and regulations will prevent them from messing things up. That is what happened in our country."[14] He also warned that the Official Languages Act would ensure the federal public service and armed forces would become dominated by French Canadians and attacked both the idea and cost of bilingual labeling.[15] He also called the bill a major step toward "universal, compulsory bilingualism, positively the wrong approach toward encouragement of national unity."[16] The *Calgary Herald* called French-speaking schools a "luxury" and that Ottawa's haste and inflexibility in bringing in bilingualism aroused resentment in those parts of Canada where French was not spoken.[17]

Pat Mahoney vowed the federal government would carry out the recommendations of the B and B report, and declared that whoever opposed the Liberal position on the issue could choose another party.[18] This kind of talk was vintage Mahoney—hectoring and uncompromising. His tough defence of federal policy would soon lead to charges that he was not representing Alberta in Ottawa, but rather representing Ottawa in Alberta.

Letters to the editor expressed the outrage of many Albertans. One claimed, "The official language is the official language of Canada by right of conquest" and that he expected Trudeau would replace all money and stamps with new ones having "the figurehead of De Gaulle imprinted on them with the slogan *Vive Quebec Libre* underneath." Another wrote that the Trudeau government would abandon our allies in NATO because of costs but "the sky is the limit when the French fact is to be pushed in any part of the world."[19] An editorial in the *Calgary Herald* also criticized the government's disuse of the term "Dominion Day" for July 1, suggesting this and a number of other moves were designed "to remove all trace of connection between Canada and its Mother Country, Great Britain," and write off the "brave pioneers of British stock who settled this great country."[20]

But bilingualism was moving along—even in Calgary. When sixty parents petitioned the Calgary Separate School Board for a bilingual class, the board said that it would establish two bilingual schools to fit the concepts of the B and B Commission.[21] On July 7, 1969 the Official Languages Act was unanimously approved in the House,[22] leaving in its wake disgruntled Canadians, many from the west. A cranky oil industry and irate farmers who could not sell their wheat made for an opportune time for western rabble-rousers to politically tap into alienation sentiment.

Even some Liberals were angry. Saskatchewan Liberal Senator Hazen Argue said the faltering farm economy had given people on the Prairies a "feeling of alienation, of being overlooked, of being made second-class citizens, of being ridiculed, of being sneered at often by people in high places."[23] Independent Liberal Senator Donald Cameron called the situation on the Prairies worse than in 1929 and that the sense of injustice among westerners was the result of Trudeau policies. He predicted that if there were an election within the next six months, no Liberals would be elected from the Prairie provinces.[24]

Trudeau himself sometimes threw a little gasoline on the fire. At a student Liberal meeting in Ottawa, responding to why the government had not given more money to the western farmers, he said, "I don't think these people are poor," and "Why not give it to the small grocer in my riding who is being forced out of business by the supermarket?"[25]

The complaints against the federal government now included the recently released white paper on taxation. All of this emboldened a flamboyant Calgary criminal lawyer and former provincial Tory leader, Milt

Milt Harradence with his idol John Diefenbaker. [*Legal Archives Society of Alberta 115-G-21 (7)*]

Harradence, and a group of Calgary businessmen and friends to enter the western alienation debate.

Harradence[26] was a high profile, revolver-packing, headline-seeking criminal lawyer (and former skilled RCAF pilot[27]) who had grown up in Prince Albert, Saskatchewan, where he'd fallen under the spell of its finest criminal lawyer, John Diefenbaker. He became a Progressive Conservative, the party of his idol Diefenbaker and of his good friend and first cousin, MP Jack Horner. After settling in Calgary Harradence unsuccessfully led the Alberta PCs in the 1963 election against Premier Manning. The PCs picked up no seats and he resigned from the leadership soon after.

In February 1970 Harradence announced the formation of the New West Task Force, comprising Calgary businessmen and ordinary citizens who wanted economic consultants to study the feasibility of an independent western Canada. Harradence cited examples of the government's mistreatment of the west, including its "callous disregard" of the farm problems, its paying off Expo 67's $200 million dollar deficit while ignoring the west's priorities, its opposition to a western oil pipeline to Montreal, its unfair economic policies that supported eastern manufacturing to the west's disadvantage, its oppressive white paper on taxation that was bringing in a capital gains tax, and its failure to add western parliamentary seats to ensure proper representation.[28]

MP Hu Harries said that he had been asked to head the task force study and had only turned it down "reluctantly." He said that his own consulting firm had done a similar study for the four western provinces two years earlier and had concluded that an independent west could dramatically reduce personal income taxes on its residents and bring a significant gain in economic activity to the region. He also observed that although he opposed western separatism, he believed such studies could stir Ottawa into doing more for the west.[29]

Pat Mahoney agreed Harradence's task force idea was designed to wring more from the federal government.[30] Mel Hurtig said he suspected conservative Calgary oilmen who were "much more interested in making money than in the welfare of the citizens" were behind the study, and demanded Harradence tell the public where the money for the task force was coming from.[31]

Harradence fought on. Speaking to a crowd of 250 enthusiastic realtors about western Canada going it alone, he said, "If there is no other solution, no other alternative to guaranteeing our heritage for our children, then I will support it with all my resources and all the energy I can command." He said the federal government had treated westerners as "patsies ever since Confederation," and that "we have gone down to Ottawa with our begging cups for the last time." Speculating about the New West's defence policy, he said western Canada's soldiers would be treated with dignity, with the US supplying the hardware and Canada supplying the men.[32]

Not taking the separatist talk seriously, however, was columnist Fred Kennedy, who wrote that Harradence and his supporters were wasting both their time and money "because the West will never separate from the rest of Canada any more than will Quebec."[33] National columnist Charles Lynch, who travelled often in the west and Alberta, accused separatist-inclined westerners of merely emulating Quebec and warned, "If westerners keep escalating their cries of separatism they are going to become as tedious as Quebec separatists became years ago. And that would seem to be a terrible waste of time for a part of the country that has become, in the last ten years, the most vibrant and exciting region of Canada."[34]

But by March complaints about Confederation were getting louder. Oilmen continued to complain about the feds keeping them out of the eastern oil market fearing Quebec's anger at paying one or two cents more for gasoline. Western Canadians ranted about a pampered Quebec, the $9 million cost of the B and B Commission and the $50 million the feds put up to assist minority language education throughout Canada. Farmers continued to blame Ottawa for the poor wheat markets, and seethed over Trudeau's insensitivity to their plight.

Meanwhile, Milt Harradence's phone was ringing off the hook with calls of support and speaking requests. Bill Knights, a Calgary radio talk show host, said two-thirds of his callers were in favour of considering western separatism, and that this was "the strongest response I've ever had in five or six years on radio." Federal Tories throughout the province were also busy feeding at the separatist trough. Former Socred and now Tory MP Robert Thompson said that the sentiment in Red Deer was "a cold deliberate attitude" that only needed a leader in order to pose an immediate threat to Canadian unity. Conservative House Leader G.W. (Ged) Baldwin from Peace River saw "a deep sense of alienation," which could be quickly converted by "an irresponsible but clever demagogue." And the always rabble-rousing Woolliams said, "There are separatists. They write to me. They say 'Let's separate.' And they're not all little guys."

However, Calgary's mayor Rod Sykes, married to a French Canadian from Montreal, called western separatism "a completely phony issue" created by people who had "a large economic stake in Western Canada" and who were "displeased with political developments on a national scale." He characterized what was happening as serious attempts by certain groups to "club the federal government into action that suits them."[35]

Help for Harradence's task force came from a most unlikely assistant spokesman: Brian Stevenson, a young lawyer raised in Ottawa but new Alberta resident who became the organization chair for the crumbling Alberta provincial Liberal Party. Stevenson lamented the west's feeble representation in Ottawa and pointed out "Our MPs—vigorously though they try to represent us—are virtually bound and gagged politically."[36]

As to process, if the task force concluded that the west could be economically viable on its own, a referendum would be held. Then, Stevenson said, if the vote favoured independence, the west "would send a team of negotiators to establish an independent nation in orderly fashion."[37] Harradence commented boldly, "We dread this as an end result but won't shrink from it."

Even though most of Harradence's actions and statements were farcical, Trudeau was getting the message. Speaking in Winnipeg, Trudeau acknowledged that in the past agriculture had been neglected by the federal government, but said his government was now changing that. A constructive attitude had more impact than "vague threats of well-publicized alarmists," he said, and "there is no better way to make sure the interests of a region are known and acted upon than to send hard-working members of Parliament to Ottawa."[38]

Harradence returned to the battlefield in April in Joe Clark's hometown of High River, south of Calgary. Speaking at an anti-tax rally before a crowd of 900, many of them ranchers and farmers, Harradence was repeatedly interrupted by applause as he attacked Trudeau's policies and exhorted his audience to get ready for independence. The white paper on taxation, he said, had not been written by "that flunky Benson" but by Trudeau "who has his cabinet cow-tied, tongue-tied and bulldogged," and who was "out to sap the vitality of the middle class and destroy the capitalist system."[39]

But despite all the bellyaching, the spring of 1970 saw the economies of Alberta cities humming along. Many office-building projects were recently

Jack Horner, Alberta Tory-turned-Liberal MP. [Milton Historical Society 4548]

completed or in progress in Calgary, and leasing executives were still predicting a shortage of first-class office space in the downtown area by 1971.[40]

Tory MP Jack Horner continued his attacks on Trudeau, telling the Women's Conservative Association in Calgary that Trudeau had a "callous disregard for people" and whose idea of participatory democracy ended with Trudeau, Marchand, and Pelletier making all of the decisions. He called Bud Olson "nothing more than a servant," and said, "I tell people in his constituency that he's trying to sell the prime minister to them rather than selling them to the prime minister." Horner also accused Louis Gagnon, recently appointed as Information Canada's first director, of having a record of association with the Communist Party.[41]

Before their politicking days were over, both Jack Horner and Milt Harradence would become federal Liberals.[42]

All this western alienation ballyhoo continued at a reduced noise level through the summer of 1970 and Harradence's task force never delivered a report. In any event, western alienation would soon be banished—at least temporarily—from the newspapers, television sets, and meeting halls across the west by one of the most dramatic events in the history of the country—the October Crisis.

18

The October Crisis

AUGUST–DECEMBER 1970

BY THE FALL OF 1970 it looked as though the Trudeau Grits would have to work very hard to get re-elected. The white paper on tax reform was being attacked from all sides, the farmers were still hurting over the wheat market crisis, and people were still grumbling about postal strikes. The situation certainly looked bad for the lonely Alberta Grit MPs. The provincial Liberal Party had gone up in smoke, the Alberta federal Liberal caucus was divided, and despite a healthier industry, the oilmen continued their griping about oil policy, and western alienation was alive and kicking. Topping it all off was the unrelenting opposition of the major print media, the provincial and federal Tories, and the Social Credit government.

But despite the Liberals' woes, the plodding Tory leader Stanfield still held up poorly against the swashbuckling prime minister. As a result, certainly in eastern and central Canada, the Trudeau Liberals kept their lead over the Tories. In the west, however, they were on the ropes.

On October 5, British trade commissioner James Cross was kidnapped at gunpoint from his Montreal home. The Liberation cell of a notorious separatist terrorist group known as the Front de libération du Québec

(FLQ) claimed credit.[1] Beginning in 1963 the FLQ had been setting off bombs and attacking public and business facilities in the Montreal area; bold bank robberies had financed its operations.[2]

What was to become known as the October Crisis quickly gathered momentum. The day following the kidnapping, Prime Minister Trudeau said the federal and Quebec governments would jointly handle FLQ demands and deadlines. The kidnappers demanded $500,000 in gold, the release of twenty-three "political prisoners," the FLQ manifesto broadcast and published, public identification of FLQ informers, an aircraft to take the kidnappers to a safe haven in Cuba or Algeria, and the rehiring of Montreal mail truck drivers who had lost their jobs because of a government decision.[3]

Trudeau rejected the kidnappers' demands, saying the minority would not be allowed to impose its view on the majority by violence.[4] Dozens of people were rounded up for questioning in raids looking for the perpetrators. The kidnappers then gave assurances that Cross would not be killed over money but demanded that no more suspected separatists be brought in for questioning.[5]

On October 10 events worsened. Quebec Labour Minister and Vice-Premier Pierre Laporte was abducted at gunpoint. The kidnapping was again the work of the FLQ but of another cell—the Chenier cell. The Laporte kidnappers demanded the government meet the original demands of the Cross kidnappers or both Laporte and Cross would be executed.[6] Meanwhile, to protect politicians and other prominent persons in Ottawa and Montreal, RCMP security in Ottawa was joined by several hundred troops of the Canadian Armed Forces.[7]

On October 13 came one of the most famous and dramatic exchanges between a prime minister and the press in Canadian history. A confident-looking Trudeau emerged from his car on Parliament Hill to be confronted by CBC television reporter Tim Ralfe who questioned the security measures taken. Trudeau responded, "Yes, well there are a lot of bleeding hearts around who just don't like to see people with helmets and guns. All I can say is, go on and bleed, but it is more important to keep law and order in the society than to be worried about weak-kneed people who don't like the looks of..."

Ralfe then interjected, "At any cost? How far would you go with that? How far would you extend that?"

Trudeau: "Well, just watch me."[8] Most westerners loved Trudeau's retort; it remains one of his most popular lines in Alberta.

On October 16 Trudeau got much tougher. With negotiations going nowhere, he invoked the War Emergencies Measures Act, the first time it had been used during a time of peace. As a result, a state of "apprehended insurrection" now existed in Quebec and the FLQ became an unlawful association. Any member or supporter of the FLQ could be imprisoned; anyone arrested could be held without bail for ninety days; and anyone allowing the FLQ to hold meetings could be fined or imprisoned or both.[9]

Military and police personnel rounded up hundreds of Quebec separatists and suspected FLQ supporters. They included university professors, actors, poets, entertainers, writers, union leaders, and politicians. Firearms, pamphlets, and other political materials were seized, and the distribution of all political literature was banned.[10] Trudeau said the measures were necessary to stop people "seeking the destruction of the social order through clandestine and violent means."[11]

Trudeau met with stiff resistance from Opposition Leader Robert Stanfield and NDP leader Tommy Douglas. Stanfield called the government's response excessive while Douglas termed it "a smokescreen to destroy the liberties and freedom of Canadians," and "the black Friday for civil liberties in Canada."[12]

In a twenty-minute televised speech to the nation, Trudeau gave probably the most effective address of his political career. His hair neatly combed, white rose in the lapel of a well-cut suit and displaying a sombre demeanour, he explained the state of the negotiations, the dangers and challenges the country was facing, and the type of people who had committed the crimes.[13] For the second time in three days Trudeau was the most popular man in the country and probably the most popular Canadian prime minister of all time. Albertans and millions of Canadians coast to coast regarded this speech as his finest hour. The Alberta daily press throughout the crisis remained squarely on the government's side.[14]

All the provincial premiers supported the War Measures Act. Alberta Premier Strom said that the federal government should take whatever steps necessary to ensure the preservation of law and order.[15] Alberta Opposition Leader Peter Lougheed gave his full support.[16] Medicine Hat mayor and long-time Liberal Harry Veiner offered to contribute $2,000 toward the ransom.[17]

During the day following the invocation of the War Measures Act, the Quebec Provincial Police made 341 arrests in 1,627 raids. But the next day—Sunday October 18—the Chenier cell announced that Laporte had been executed. His strangled body was found in the trunk of a car near a suburban airport south of Montreal.[18]

In Alberta, Attorney General Edgar Gerhart said the perpetrators were "mad dogs and should be treated as such." Edmonton mayor Ivor Dent said Canada was dealing with vicious people, and the killing was "reprehensible out of all proportion.[19] In a telephone survey conducted on October 18, when 200 Calgarians were asked, "In view of the murder of Pierre Laporte, do you think the government's proclamation of the War Measures Act was justified," 172 said yes and another 20 gave qualified approval.[20] Lougheed urged Albertans to "rally around the federal authorities to ensure there is unity in this nation," and Dr. Roger Motut, a spokesman for the Alberta French-Canadian Association, said the FLQ had little support from the people of Quebec and after the killing would have even less.[21] Calgary's school boards ordered flags at schools flown at half-mast. In the city's Catholic schools, special masses were held for Laporte.[22]

Pat Mahoney stoutly defended the War Measures Act and warned that prospects for further terrorism by the FLQ were "regrettably high." He also noted that the economic situation in Quebec was partly responsible, given that unemployment in that province was at 7 percent versus the national average of 4.7 percent, and that nearly all of the unemployed there were French Canadian and half under the age of 25.[23]

The October Crisis quickly squelched almost any trace of Albertans' complaints about federal actions normally found in media coverage and commentary. Gone was most of the recent carping about oil, grain, and languages. Gone too—albeit temporarily—were the rabble-rousers of western alienation; Harradence's task force disappeared permanently. Alberta public opinion had rarely been more unconditionally Canadian than in those dark days of October 1970.

But the odd vocal critic still emerged. One month to the day of the Cross kidnapping, with the government in the thick of the crisis, the ex-premier made one of his first public statements as Senator Manning. At a northern development conference in Edmonton, he blasted the Trudeau government for unpredictability in oil and gas policy, for not consulting with the industry, and for its shaky oil negotiations with the US. He also railed against the Trudeau government's preoccupation with ecology and conservation, calling it a "fetish" that had been carried to "irrational extremes."[24]

On November 5 Trudeau was interviewed on the CBC television program *Encounter,* saying he would not call an election because of the crisis: "We were elected two and a bit years ago to govern the country. We governed it through this crisis and we are going to continue to govern after this crisis is over." He gave kudos to the people of Quebec and the rest of Canada for showing "remarkable maturity," realizing "you can't come to grips with terrorism without special measures."[25]

Had Trudeau been an opportunist, this was his moment to call an election. His popularity had reached its zenith throughout the country, even in the west. His majority would likely have been overwhelming and truly national in scope. Squandering this opportunity on principle meant throwing away what was to be his last good chance for strong representation from the west.

By the first week of November the crisis was winding down. Although weapons, dynamite, and thousands of rounds of ammunition had been seized, almost all of the detainees under the War Measures Act were soon released, and most of the troops were leaving the streets of Montreal and

Ottawa.[26] The Liberation cell holding Cross disclosed he was safe.[27] Police picked up three suspects in the Laporte case and the rest would be brought to justice before the end of the year.[28]

A public opinion poll of 1,650 respondents across Canada released on November 15 found that 80 percent of Canadians supported Trudeau's decision to implement the War Measures Act while only 10 percent thought that it had infringed on their personal liberties. Approval ratings rose for those premiers and party leaders who'd supported Trudeau (Bourassa, Robarts, and Caouette) and dropped for politicians who'd opposed or expressed reservations about Trudeau's actions (Stanfield and Douglas).[29]

Ernest Manning addressed the October Crisis six weeks after it began in his maiden Senate speech. Although he commended Trudeau for invoking the War Measures Act, he said that Canada had invited revolutionary violence because its borders were open to people who were advocates of such tactics. Manning went on to blame radio and television, such as the CBC, which "fell all over themselves to provide a national forum for advocates of violent dissent to send their message to millions of Canadians."[30] He called for the reinstatement of capital punishment for those who commit murder while advocating violent revolution.[31] One month later speaking at an Edmonton Social Credit nomination meeting, Manning called Tory actions in Ottawa during the October Crisis as "little short of a national disgrace," but at the same time accused the government of being spineless in allowing revolutionaries to come into Canada.[32]

After two months, a fit but thinner Cross was freed. As pre-arranged, a Canadian Forces plane flew his kidnappers and their accomplices to Cuba. The *Herald* editorial capturing the mood of Albertans said that Canada had set an example: "Weaker men urged governmental yielding to the outrageous demands from the kidnappers. But the men in the real positions of responsibility were equal to meeting the challenge."[33] On December 28 three prime suspects in Laporte's kidnapping were found in a tunnel under a farmhouse outside Montreal and brought to justice.

In a year-end interview, Premier Strom said that he completely supported the federal government's response to the Quebec crisis, and in his view so did 95 percent of Alberta's citizens. Strom also said that although he supported bilingualism, he still saw French language signage in Alberta's national parks as a waste of time and money: "If French-speaking tourists can get this far by following signs in English only, they don't need French signs in our parks."[34] There was still obviously work ahead for the federal government to get the province onside, and still fertile ground for western alienation to rear its head again.

Trudeau's handling of the October Crisis was a political tour de force. It had brought out the best of his charisma, intuition, and character, and his public actions remain the Canadian gold standard in political crisis management. The Liberals were in a commanding position to retain power.

V

The Second Coming

19

OCTOBER 1970–MARCH 1971

The Splendours of OPEC and the Saga of Home Oil

AS THE KIDNAPPING CRISIS UNFOLDED in Quebec, the oil and gas industry was steaming along in Alberta; even the oilmen's relationship with Ottawa had taken a turn for the better. US demand for oil was rising and Alberta wells were pumping—so much so that the oilmen believed that the US import quotas would be gone by year-end. In November 1970 total demand for Alberta oil averaged 1.13 million barrels a day and was expected to rise further. US refinery demand for Alberta crude east of the Rockies was also brisk and expected to top 515,000 barrels a day by January.[1] By comparison, two years earlier, average Alberta production of oil was 700,000 barrels a day, while authorized exports to the US east of the Rockies was merely 280,000 barrels.

Joe Greene was now enjoying some popularity among the oilmen. At an industry meeting in Calgary, Greene paid tribute to the ten members of the National Advisory Committee on Petroleum (NACOP) that had been set up to advise him on industry issues. The members included several captains of the Alberta oil industry, such as Kelly Gibson, chairman of Pacific Petroleum; F.A. McKinnon, president of BP Oil and Gas; Al Ross, president of IPAC;

and Arne Nielsen, president of Mobil Oil Canada. Greene attacked critics who questioned the capacity of some committee members to give objective advice because they worked for foreign-controlled firms, and called such criticism "McCarthyism of the lowest order."[2] According to Arne Nielsen's memoir, *We Gambled Everything,* Greene was willing to listen to the industry and far less concerned about foreign ownership than about security of supply.[3]

Long-term stability and prosperity for the industry seemed close at hand. In late November US and Canadian officials agreed that Canada would "eventually" have full access to the US market, provided they could agree on a method of building a reservoir of Canadian oil that would meet US needs in the event of a crisis.[4] Both IPAC and the CPA saw the lifting of the quotas sufficient incentive to finance future oil reserves.[5]

Another positive development was that international oil prices were rising. Carl Nickle said that meant Canadians could expect similar price increases for Canadian oil; oil supply and demand was such that "if the Arab oil countries sneeze, North America and Western Europe will catch their death of cold."[6] Those international price increases were the handiwork of the Organization of Petroleum Exporting Countries (OPEC) cartel,[7] which was about to become one of the seminal forces in Alberta's astonishing prosperity in the years ahead. The OPEC-driven price increases of late 1970 and early 1971 were the first major adjustments to the international price of oil in thirteen years.

Following OPEC's lead, the oilmen quickly began applying pressure for higher oil prices for Canadian oil, which then stood at about $2.25 a barrel, considered a bargain-basement price. They argued that Canadian prices east of the Ottawa Valley line should not be isolated from the outside forces that had now driven prices upwards for imported oil in Quebec and the Maritimes.[8]

The first general oil price increase in western Canada in more than eight years began in December with Alberta-based oil companies increasing prices an average of 25 cents a barrel.[9] The province and the producers both projected major increases in revenues even at current production levels.[10]

For the oilmen, these were the best of times. January refinery orders hit a record level with further records expected through the winter. Preliminary figures showed that 1970 was a far better year for the oilmen than 1969 with double-digit increases in sales revenue and production; it was also the first year that Alberta liquids production averaged more than a million barrels a day (1,127,000).[11] And the future looked rosier than ever—the TD Bank forecast a 30 percent rise in petroleum product demand, a 115 percent increase in oil exports, and a 70 percent rise in total Canadian oil production by 1975.[12]

Perhaps giddy from all the good oil news and Trudeau's soaring popularity following the October Crisis, Pat Mahoney took the oilmen to task. Addressing the Petroleum Tax Society in Calgary early in the new year, he claimed that oil companies, while sparing no expense to improve their competitive positions, "totally" failed to present themselves credibly to the taxpayer. Mahoney said Canadians were bothered not only by the degree of foreign ownership of the oil industry, but also by a lack of transparency in the industry's pricing practices. He added that people believed gasoline was the "prime villain in air pollution," and that the industry's business practices often showed a "reckless and callous disregard for ecological damage."[13]

Mahoney's attack, albeit courageous and forthright, was rash. The oilmen did not like being lectured to—particularly by Ottawa. Mahoney, a key spokesman for the minister of finance, was now from Ottawa in their eyes. They had come to believe that this pugnacious fellow with a penchant for searing critical rhetoric went to Ottawa to represent Alberta but wound up representing Ottawa to Alberta. Most oilmen saw themselves as good and decent builders, entrepreneurs, and environmentally conscious risk-takers helping to make a better world. Standing by them were a supportive press, the conservative business establishment, and the many thousands of Albertans reliant on the industry. That was just the way it was.

By mid-January 1971 OPEC nations were looking for even more revenue from the big oil companies through increased taxes and royalties. But this time the companies were not knuckling under. The standoff raised the

Oilman and publisher Carl Nickle. [*Nickle Galleries, University of Calgary*]

specter of OPEC cutting off supplies if a deal could not be reached, thus jeopardizing the economies of major importers such as Japan and western Europe.[14] These big consuming nations were firmly on the side of the big oil companies in this tussle with OPEC, but Canada, gaining handsomely from the higher prices, would not take sides. Greene observed, "As is so often in Canadian affairs, we are on both sides at the same time."[15]

The conflict soon ended with the signing of a five-year deal by six Middle East OPEC members and twenty-two international oil companies, providing for higher prices and taxes. Carl Nickle said that the deal would "scare the pants off politicians and I hope the public" in western countries and would make them realize there is no security of supply from overseas. He predicted that OPEC would continue to use its power to rake in as much cash from oil as it could. The deal—music to the ears of Alberta oilmen— was sure to stimulate new exploration and development activity.[16]

But the new riches also brought new concerns. In January the IPAC publication *Petroleum News* called its members' attention to the forthcoming report on foreign investment by Minister of Revenue Herb Gray and warned them to be prepared for increasing government incursions into their industry.[17]

Another threat posed by the federal government was the introduction of a bill establishing the Canada Development Corporation (CDC), which was to be a source of capital to create new enterprises and strengthen old ones and to reduce excessive foreign control of Canadian corporations.[18] Although the CDC had strong support from Canadian economic nationalists, the oilmen expected the worst from government involvement in any form. To calm the folks back home, Pat Mahoney—in a speech to the Exploration Geophysicists—called the CDC "Johnny Canuck's opportunity to become an investor," and that it was not "an arm of government policy but a commercial undertaking."[19]

One famous Calgary oilman who felt the impact of the federal government's interest in foreign ownership was Bobby Brown Jr. of Home Oil. Brown's oil entrepreneur father had hit it big in Turner Valley in the 1930s with Home becoming his flagship company. Brown Jr. took over the company in 1948, and turned it into one of Canada's largest independent oil companies. But by 1970 Brown and Home Oil owed a lot of money as a result of poor performing investments and declining stock values. With the banks banging at his door, he had to find a way to service Home Oil's debt of $93 million[20] so he began a quest to sell at least part of his empire. Deputy Minister of Energy Jack Austin[21] soon brought more stress Brown's bad heart didn't need, telling him that the government did not want Canadian-owned Home Oil to fall into foreign hands.

As Brown's health deteriorated through the fall of 1970, many interested large Canadian- and American-owned corporations poured over the company's books under the watchful eye of Greene and Austin. Brown received an offer from Ashland Oil of Kentucky that he found particularly enticing. Greene warned Brown that the government might introduce legislation to prevent Home Oil from falling into American hands just as it did the previous year in the Denison Mines case. Reporter Fred Kennedy reflected the attitudes of thousands of other Albertans: "Personally I don't give a hoot whether or not Bob Brown of Calgary sells his personal shares in the Home Oil Company to an American company, a Canadian syndicate or a cross eyed Korean."[22]

Brown had some significant political allies, including Senator Ernest Manning (who worked for a right-wing think tank Brown bankrolled), Premier Strom, and influential Liberal Harry Hays. Senator Hays had encouraged Brown privately and also stated publicly that continued "meddling" by the government in Canadian industry would lead to "mediocrity," and that "people should have the right to sell where they want to." Hays also warned the government "must be very careful not to kill the goose that laid the golden egg."[23] In any event, Ashland of Kentucky backed off after all federal political parties opposed the possibility of a US sale.

When Greene announced that the federal government had started negotiations with Brown to purchase a major interest in Home Oil,[24] IPAC quickly warned its members that this would pave the way for government to acquire companies as it wished. Alastair (Al) H. Ross,[25] incoming president of IPAC, said that there were sufficient controls to ensure Canadian jurisdiction over the petroleum industry and called fears of foreign control of Canadian resources premature, since less than 10 percent of Canada's potential reserves had been found to date.[26]

Hu Harries waded in, arguing that foreign investors should be pursuing only economically sterile investments such as municipal or provincial bonds, and leave more lucrative investments in Canadian control. Asked whether Canadians could afford to lose foreign investment, Harries made the analogy to a person questioning whether they could afford to go to a doctor. He said, "Don't say we can't afford to—we must change the system to make sure we can afford it." Harries' blunt views on foreign investment were certain to worry the oilmen.[27]

On April 22 Joe Greene announced that Consumers' Gas of Toronto—a company owned by 28,500 shareholders of whom 97 percent were Canadian residents—had bought controlling interest in Home Oil. Thus, not only was Brown spared from his creditors, the government had ensured his company would remain in Canadian hands.[28]

The Home Oil and earlier Denison Mines outcomes showed just how serious the federal government was about stopping foreign takeovers of Canadian corporations, even if unpopular in Alberta or among the oilmen. The timing of the Home Oil ownership control showdown was particularly unfortunate for Alberta Liberal fortunes because it neutralized the cascading good news about greater oil exports to the United States, continuing strong demand for Alberta oil, and the positive local impact of OPEC-driven higher prices.

In a mere eight months the legendary Brown, weakened by a life of excess and his recent stressful financial entanglements, would die from a heart attack.[29]

20

The Rough Sport of Politics

JULY 1970–MARCH 1971

EXPECTING A PROVINCIAL ELECTION within the year, political activity in Alberta shifted into high gear. Peter Lougheed and his Progressive Conservatives, flush with cash and optimism, were busy scouring the countryside for good candidates to contest all 75 legislative seats. By August they already had 42 nominated candidates with a good mix of backgrounds, including farmers, businessmen, professionals, and municipal politicians.[1] Alberta federal Tories were enthusiastic about Lougheed's chances and desperately wanted him to succeed. Since the Alberta election would be held before the federal election, a Lougheed victory would likely spur their own momentum in the province and give them a shot at winning back the four Alberta seats they lost in 1968.[2]

Social Credit, although it still formed the government and had all of the advantages of incumbency, faced some serious transition problems. Many of its 55 elected members had decided not to run and 10 new seats were up for grabs because of redistribution. It was now hunting for 15 to 30 new candidates to fill the vacancies.[3] Although the party was trying to modernize and attract new blood, Social Credit's annual gathering of their women's auxiliaries began with the party's 1935 campaign song, the hymn "O God Our Help in Ages Past." In the afternoon Premier Strom joined the ladies for a rendition of "Onward Christian Soldiers."[4]

The NDP, since 1968 under the inspired leadership of 32-year-old Grant Notley, was showing signs of life.[5] Born in Didsbury, north of Calgary, Notley grew up in the deeply conservative farming region west of town. After successfully completing his first year of law school, where we were fellow students, Notley left in 1961 to work for the newly formed NDP that had replaced its social democratic predecessor, the Co-operative Commonwealth Federation (CCF).[6] Although he had failed to win a seat in three contests up to 1971, he was now a much stronger politician.[7]

Recent Canadian provincial elections had brought changes of government in Manitoba, Quebec, Nova Scotia, and New Brunswick, and all the new premiers were younger than the 42-year-old Lougheed and a great deal younger than the 56-year-old Strom.[8] Riding nomination meetings for both the PCs and Socreds were noisy, well-attended affairs, drawing up to 1,500 persons. Membership sales were also brisk with the Socreds said to be at the 19,000 mark, followed closely by the Tories at 16,000.[9]

Lougheed was gathering momentum. In October he told 200 enthusiastic supporters in Camrose that the Strom government had done a "monstrous" job of handling federal–provincial relations and that despite having spent billions on education, the system was mediocre.[10] After attacking the government about the lack of industries in Alberta's smaller centres, the delegates at a Lethbridge party meeting resolved to support a $50 million rural industrialization program. Within days Strom reacted by announcing his own program to spur manufacturing.[11]

Members of the Strom government began to complain about media coverage. Minister of Mines Russell Patrick lashed out at the CBC, the *Edmonton Journal*, and "international in nature" conservation groups for intentionally causing public "hysteria" by falsely reporting pollution dangers of a recent oil spill in the Athabasca River.[12] Strom also accused a member of the media of leaking a government policy document to the

Tories, which he called an unethical violation of a confidence to "brazenly" help the Tories.[13]

Strom faced more problems. His government produced the largest deficit in Alberta's history. It tried to cope by raising taxes and license fees, but could not keep up with provincial spending, which had increased 44 percent over the previous five years, thus forcing it to borrow.[14] Strom faced rumblings within the ranks: ex-cabinet minister Alf Hooke said that the Alberta government was now "Social Credit in name only," and that some of Strom's policies contradicted what Social Credit stood for—such as eliminating the debt.[15] These were harsh words from a Social Credit stalwart with nine consecutive election victories. (Hooke had another reason to be unhappy. After he'd unsuccessfully run against Strom to replace Manning as leader in 1968, he was not invited to serve in Strom's first cabinet.)

The Alberta Liberal Party, leaderless, penniless, and divided, was still dogged by infighting. At the height of the October Crisis, with the nation's attention fixed on kidnappings and murder, leadership aspirant Bob Russell demanded the party president resign, accusing him of trying to keep rural party members from attending executive meetings. Russell's demand for a leadership convention continued to be met by stiff resistance[16] until mid-December when the party executive decided to ask the annual convention delegates if they wanted a leadership convention before the next election. Party spokesman Brian Stevenson said the party's financial difficulties had now resolved and it intended to contest some seats. He added, "certainly our major federal member of Parliament Agriculture Minister Bud Olson wants this to happen."[17]

The party was so weak it was hurting both federal and provincial Liberal organizations. Most Albertans did not distinguish between the two wings so if the provincial party appeared to be on death's door, this reflected on the federal party. And Lougheed—far and away the leader representing a new progressive force in the province—was already cultivating many provincial and federal Liberal voters.

Hu Harries declined an invitation to attend the Alberta party convention, saying that the provincial party had "nowhere to go and should therefore graciously bow from the scene." Harries acerbically noted that the Socreds and Tories now occupied the centre and right while the NDP occupied the left, and, "To the extent that provincial Liberals can be accused of having any understandable position, it is clear that we are, at best, a transparent plastic overlay."[18] Although Harries opposed Social Credit–Liberal ties one year earlier, he had now changed his tune. Edmonton lawyer Mike MacDonald, a candidate for the party presidency, publicly described Harries' position as "ludicrous."[19]

Pat Mahoney, chairman of the Alberta federal Liberal caucus, was quick to pile on, saying that as long as Albertans saw provincial Liberals as creatures of the federal party and the federal party continued to form government, the provincial party's chances of success were "very slim," and that liberalism in Alberta could be better expressed through parties other than the provincial. But, he added incongruously, as long as the Alberta worked at both federal and provincial politics, he would attend its conventions and work for it.[20] Mahoney told his constituency association it was obvious that many Alberta Liberals were becoming involved with other parties on the provincial scene. He said, "While I admit to no debt to the Party in Alberta for the success that met our effort in Calgary South or any other federal constituency I nevertheless regret that the Liberal Party does not present itself to all our federal supporters as a satisfactory vehicle for provincial political action." With his usual bluntness he said there would be no help, financial or otherwise, from the federal Liberals for the provincial Liberals if they decided to contest the campaign.[21]

Mahoney's new attack on the provincial Liberals showed astonishing political naïveté for someone who held such a lofty party position. He did not comprehend that Liberals who abandoned the provincial Liberals to support another party presented a great peril for him. If those Liberals leaving the provincial party supported the party with the momentum (i.e., Lougheed's Tories), the Tories could become their permanent home. Admitting "to no debt to the Party in Alberta" for his or the Party's success in Calgary South or elsewhere showed an ignorance of, and insensitivity to, the hundreds of committed Liberals, provincial and federal, who'd helped elect Alberta Liberal MPs. Many worked for both wings of the party and had done so for years. The other point that eluded him was that the single most important factor that had elected him and the other Liberals in the 1968 general election was the charismatic leadership of Pierre Trudeau. Trudeau had been elected leader by delegates who were party regulars from all provinces, including Alberta, while Mahoney, not yet a card-carrying Liberal member, had watched the convention on television in Calgary.[22]

But despite the blows from the most powerful federal Liberal forces in Alberta, the provincial party would not die. Days before its convention, the party released an impressive sixty-four-page draft election platform, prepared by party workhorse and policy chair David McDonald and his thirteen-person committee. Among its provisions, the visionary platform called for more powers for local governments, property tax relief, a natural resource export levy, poverty and literacy programs for Indigenous people, elimination of tuition fees at universities, improvements in the delivery of health services, legalization of marijuana, stronger pollution controls, better criminal rehabilitation programs, support for the refining and petrochemical industries, full disclosure of campaign fund sources, and limits on election spending.[23]

The Tory convention entitled "Breakthrough '71" got underway at Calgary's Palliser Hotel on January 22. In contrast to the federal Liberals, the federal PCs were out in force to promote their Alberta counterparts. All fifteen Alberta PC MPs were conspicuous, as were many prominent national PC party representatives from Ottawa, including federal party president Nathan Nurgitz.

While the Tory MPs spent the day bashing Trudeau, Nurgitz and his federal party colleagues heaped praise on Lougheed and his provincial party. Nurgitz predicted that a Lougheed victory would be "a national political event," and that Lougheed would "be a help and a guide for every Canadian, no matter what." He confirmed that the PC national organization was concerned with both federal and provincial affairs and that they were not mutually exclusive but complementary. He said, "Let us be equals. Let neither level of our organization or the people involved therein be condescending towards nor jealous of the other level."[24]

With 1,088 registered rural and urban delegates and 676 observers, the Tory convention was the largest political convention ever held in Alberta. A thirty-three-page opinion survey of delegates revealed that 90 percent believed that employees had a right to reasonable notice of job layoffs; a majority approved giving plebiscite voting rights to renters, and supported extension of daycare and pre-school education courses; 77 percent agreed that "large foreign-owned firms should be discouraged"; and 62 percent opposed operations of social services institutions such as hostels being turned over to the private sector.[25] Lougheed's Progressive Conservative Party was clearly leaning heavily on the "progressive" side of its name, and attracting precisely the constituency that Trudeau had succeeded bringing into his fold in 1968.

The following weekend the Alberta Liberals staggered into the same Palliser Hotel. Whereas Lougheed's convention opening had more than 800 happy and energized delegates cheering him on, the Grits opened to a pitiable 140 or so gloomy souls. A group supporting Bob Russell for leader immediately issued a statement castigating the executive of the party for shirking its responsibilities and warned "that any further delays [in having a leadership convention] will only place us in the political wilderness for another 20 years."[26]

Brian Stevenson, speaking for the executive about the leadership issue, reported that only Russell was available for the job, and described him as "an example of perseverance and dedication in the truest sense of the word 'Grit.'" He also reported that the Grits could not afford to pay their leader either a salary or expenses, a situation he described as "deplorable."[27]

On the second day with attendance having risen to close to 350, the delegates voted that a leadership convention be held before March 17 while Edmonton alderman and businessman B.C. (Ches) Tanner emerged the winner in the close race for the presidency. In his acceptance speech Tanner said it was impossible for the Liberals to support the Socreds in the next election, because they were "inept, inefficient, confused and as leaderless as we Liberals are," and called on the party to brace itself for hard work in the months ahead in an effort to advance a more "leftist" policy approach.[28]

Of the Alberta MPs, only Hu Harries was absent. Bud Olson told the delegates that there would be no financial help from the federal coffers because the money collected was earmarked by the donors for federal purposes. He said, "We have to level with the people we get the support from."[29] Pat Mahoney again confirmed Olson's stark tidings.[30] The treasurer's report revealed the Alberta Liberal Party had only $1,621 in the bank, with accounts payable standing at $4,769.[31]

Writing about the whole sorry mess, Fred Kennedy concluded, "Politics, when it reaches the professional level at any rate, is a pretty shoddy business at best. Some federal Liberals in high places see nothing wrong in their attempts to politically exterminate their provincial brothers. They have become so calloused and hardened in the quest to obtain and retain power that nothing else matters. So, if the provincial party gets in their way, to hell with them."[32]

One year after his resignation as party leader, Jack Lowery announced his intention to join the Social Credit Party, but remain intimately involved with the federal Liberal organization.[33]

Days before the March leadership convention, party president Ches Tanner confirmed that Don Peacock, the *Albertan*'s managing editor, who had also worked for both Hays and Trudeau, had been offered the job of party leader at an annual salary of $20,000 for four years. A group of influential party members made the offer doubtlessly with the full backing of Peacock's former boss, Senator Hays,[34] and the support of Olson and Mahoney.[35] Although Peacock rejected the offer, it showed that the federal power brokers were prepared to finance a leader of the provincial Liberals, as long as they selected him.

A surprising 324 voting delegates attended the Liberal leadership convention. Former party leader Senator J. Harper Prowse, who had spent much of his political career in provincial politics fighting Social Credit, gave the keynote address, passionately counselling the delegates to reject a merger with any other group. He said, "So long as there is one unsolved problem, one hungry family...there is a job for the Liberal Party."[36]

Russell handily won the contest on the first ballot, overwhelming three other opponents. In accepting the leadership, he promised the Alberta Liberals would be a party of "reform" and have a voice in Alberta politics. About the divisions within the party Russell said, "I think the fighting's over. There may be some wounds to heal, but I'll be getting around to do what I can about them." He said he did not expect the party to pay him a salary but neither was he going to give up his business interests if he won a seat in the legislature.[37] The provincial Liberal Party would face a long and arduous journey back to respectability.

21

Blissful Times and the Beginning of the End of Tax Reform

NOVEMBER 1970–JULY 1971

HEADING INTO 1971, the plight of the Alberta provincial Liberal Party did not concern Alberta federal Liberal MPs. Their chances of re-election looked much better with the national inflation rate beaten down to 3 percent and economists predicting a whopping 8.5 percent annual growth rate.[1] They also basked in the glory earned by their gutsy leader during the October Crisis; anti-government sniping had all but disappeared.

Another advantage to a continued Liberal presence in Alberta was its strong presence in the Prime Minister's Office. It was said around Ottawa that there were more people from southern Alberta working for Trudeau than from the whole of Quebec. They included policy advisor Ivan Head (from Calgary and the University of Alberta in Edmonton), press secretary Peter Roberts (who grew up in Lethbridge and attended the U of A), legislative assistant Joyce Fairbairn (Lethbridge and U of A alumnus), regional desk head Dave Thomson (U of A alumnus from Redcliff), and Vic Chapman (former Edmonton Eskimo football star), his travel secretary–advance man. Other influential native Albertans in the Trudeau halls of power were Deputy Minister of Energy Jack Austin (born and raised in

Calgary), and Blair Williams,[2] Bud Olson's young assistant (and a political scientist from Taber), who would be appointed Alberta campaign organizer for the Liberals for the 1972 election.

This happy state of affairs prompted Southam columnist Don Sellar to predict that the Alberta federal Tories would face "a hard-nosed political challenge" from the Liberals, particularly in and around the cities. He noted that Liberal fundraising was on the upswing and that the party was eyeing as ripe for the picking Edmonton Centre, where Bill Hawrelak had been the spoiler in 1968, and Calgary Centre, where Nick Taylor had lost a close one to Doug Harkness in 1968.[3]

But there were glitches. The success of the country's fight against inflation was now being blamed for significantly increasing unemployment. During 1970, Canada's unemployment rate[4] averaged more than 6 percent, the worst year in the last nine.[5] The winter peak was expected to put 750,000 Canadians out of work and adversely affect their families comprising two million others.[6]

In early December, these storm clouds prompted the scrapping of the wage and price guidelines,[7] and a new expansionary budget that included public works projects, corporate tax breaks, and extra government spending. Although the deficit would be about $600 million for 1971/72, Minister of Finance Benson predicted his budget would significantly reduce unemployment.[8] To help alleviate the pain of unemployment, Minister of Labour Bryce Mackasey introduced legislation extending unemployment insurance coverage to all workers not self-employed, and raising maximum weekly unemployment benefits.[9]

In March the 51-year-old Trudeau surprised the world by quietly marrying 22-year-old Vancouver beauty Margaret Sinclair.[10] This prompted the Canadian media to publicize every detail about the wedding, honeymoon, and happy couple.[11] Even curmudgeonly Fred Kennedy rhapsodized that the marriage would show Canadians "there is absolutely no reason why French Canadians and English-speaking Canadians should not be able to live in peace and happiness."[12] The fairy-tale wedding story would go on for a long time, leaving the opposition little to do but helplessly watch all the glorious publicity surrounding the prime minister.

But amid the bliss were signs of trouble ahead. In early April, Deputy Minister of Energy Jack Austin told the CPA that the government was developing a new national energy policy based on two principles: first, that the government fully understand all impacts of the energy industry, and second, that energy development must be of maximum economic benefit to Canada. Austin warned that although the government did not wish to get into the oil and gas business, if the private sector fell short, "there are those who will argue for state enterprise" to move into its place.[13]

There had also been a recent downturn in drilling activity in Alberta. Although many oilmen blamed it on a negative investment climate caused by fear of the forthcoming tax reform legislation, many also blamed the shifting of exploration attention from Alberta to the east coast and the Arctic.[14] Furthermore, the planned northern pipeline was not universally popular. Although Joe Greene predicted the project would employ 2,000 men, provide more income and other benefits for people of the north, and greatly expand mineral exploration[15] many Canadian economic nationalists disagreed, believing the $5 billion cost would increase the value of the Canadian dollar—and thereby harm Canadian exporters.[16]

President Nixon declared the oil situation in the United States so "urgent" in early June that it required an oil agreement within the year. His interior secretary said that any deal should give Canadian oil unrestricted access to the US market so long as it protected both countries from the oil shortages.[17] This was welcome news to the oilmen. Unlimited access to the US market would mean a big improvement to the industry's cash flow and a great boon for exploration and development.[18]

Meanwhile, demand for oil and gas galloped ahead. The US National Petroleum Council expected US demand for oil and gas to double between 1970 and 1985 while domestic supplies would only be able to service about half of that demand. Furthermore, US production of both oil and gas was expected to decline.[19]

But more ominous news of inflation continued. The increase of the consumer price index in the first quarter of 1971 was the biggest for that quarter in more than ten years.[20] In the spring Eric Kierans, a compassionate man with a great concern for the unemployed, resigned from cabinet because of differences over the government's economic policies. Trudeau commented, "[Kierans] could be minister of everything, he's a clever man," but described him as "an impatient man in terms of wanting to say here and now what's needed for the seventies."[21]

Trudeau again pushed sour tidings of unemployment and inflation and oil patch misgivings off the front pages when the newlyweds set off on the first official visit to the Soviet Union by a sitting Canadian prime minister.[22] The journey took them to Moscow, Leningrad, and several other cities within the Soviet bloc, with a fawning Canadian press covering all the tumultuous welcomes, receptions, speeches, and official meetings with the Soviet elites. A stylishly clad Margaret chatting with dour Soviet officials and their wives made the front pages of every Canadian newspaper.[23]

Trudeau and Russian premier Kosygin signed an agreement calling for regular consultations between their countries on economics, trade, and other common issues. In the course of an address, Trudeau advocated closer relations, noting that although Canada remained an ally of the United States, it was important to diversify relations "because of the overpowering presence of the U.S." and the "growing consciousness among Canadians of a danger to our national identity."[24] Marking the occasion was a huge reception organized by the Canadian government that columnist Charles Lynch called "one of the most glittering affairs we have ever put on anywhere in the world."[25]

The Russian adventure was a huge political success. Media reports were almost all positive, with even the popular American magazine *Life* featuring the Trudeaus swishing through Soviet high society.[26] This was Trudeau-the-statesman performing at the top of his game on the world stage.

On June 18 Benson finally introduced a new budget designed to lower unemployment, and at the same time, the long-awaited tax reform bill.[27] The white paper effort had been a noble exercise in participatory democracy, and the changes perhaps good ones, but the government had paid a heavy political price. It was hard to believe that nineteen months earlier, on the Monday following the white paper's release, the business community showed its enthusiastic approval with the biggest one-day stock price increase on record at the Toronto Stock Exchange. Moreover, if the process was intended to encourage the massive participation in the public debate on tax reform then it had failed miserably. The discussion reflected a small minority of the business community that had cared enough to make representations—usually recommendations to scrap the proposals or to change them beyond recognition. Nine million individual Canadian taxpayers were largely absent from the discussions.[28]

The main reform was the first capital gains tax in Canadian history, although Benson had watered it down, making it apply only to half the gain. The sale of a taxpayer's principal home was fully exempt from the tax, and there was a thousand-dollar exemption on the sale of personal property. The proposed legislation also provided for a 4 percent corporate tax reduction and a new low rate for small lower-income companies. Most white paper provisions criticized by the business community were scrapped and most reforms were to be implemented by January 1, 1972. One million taxpayers would not pay any income tax, 4.7 million (including all married taxpayers on salary) would pay lower taxes, 2 million would see no change, and 1.3 million would face a tax increase.[29]

In Alberta, Premier Strom, facing an imminent election, saw little benefit to agriculture or Alberta industry, but said he was pleased with measures to help low-income taxpayers. Mayor Rod Sykes called the budget "a business budget, a people's budget" and a "social development budget" because it met the existing economic circumstances and would help the needy.[30] Even oilman Carl Nickle said that the Benson package was better than expected.[31] However, there were many Canadians less than impressed, believing Benson sold out to the threats and forebodings of the business establishment during the white paper process.[32]

The uncertainty over, some oilmen believed it might bring more foreign investment. However, Al Ross, speaking for IPAC, called the write-off rates on exploration and development expenditures insufficient to attract more Canadian investment. He also complained that limitations on tax-free amalgamations would prevent small Canadian companies from getting larger and more competitive, and was critical of provisions that instituted a capital gain tax.[33]

None of Benson's new tax reforms drew more flak from the oilmen than the reduction of the depletion allowance (deductions from investment income earned from the exploitation of an exhaustible commodity—oil and gas—because the commodity was depleting). Many economists saw the depletion allowance as a give-away to an already well-heeled industry. The oilmen complained the reduction (effective in five years) would make the Canadian oil industry less competitive in attracting foreign investment.[34]

Press reaction to the tax reform proposed legislation and budget was positive. The *Financial Times of Canada* said that although Benson took too long with the legislation, the white paper process had shown the government could learn from informed public debate.[35] Columnist Charles Lynch raved that Benson was "one of the most competent finance ministers Canada has ever had," and that Trudeau's promise to Canadians of a just society had now been substantiated.[36]

The summer of 1971 saw the Alberta economy thriving. All of its main sectors—agriculture, manufacturing, construction, crude oil production, wholesale trade, and consumer spending—were improving. Wheat sales were up by 25 percent and building permits by almost 15 percent from the year before.[37] In June, for the third consecutive month, the unemployment rate shrank (to 3.7 percent, down from 4.2 percent the year before).[38]

Despite the nagging recurring issues of inflation and unemployment, Canadians were on a record-spending spree. In May department store sales were 11 percent higher than the year before and car sales were up 28 percent—both setting new records for the month.[39] Although still worried about jobs and their finances, according to a Maclean-Hunter poll, Canadians were more optimistic than at any time since the 1967 Centennial celebrations.[40] The results of a Gallup poll published in the last week of June had the Liberals at 44 percent, just a point behind what they received in the 1968 election. The Tories were at 26 percent (down 5.5 from 1968) and the NDP nipping at their heels at 24 percent.[41]

The Trudeau government's political luck that began in October 1970 was holding, despite the pasting taken in the white paper process and the pesky problems of unemployment and inflation. To get tax reform through Parliament, there were still more political hurdles, but for the federal Liberals the summer of 1971 was one to be enjoyed.

22

As Good as it Gets

JULY 1971

IN EARLY JULY Trudeau set out on a busy four-day political junket to Alberta, which included the honour of being Grand Marshal of the fifty-ninth annual Calgary Stampede parade. Trudeau spent the weekend before Stampede barnstorming southern Alberta, a region rarely visited by prime ministers. Given that it contained all of Olson's Medicine Hat riding and part of Sulatycky's Rocky Mountain riding, it was now significant Liberal real estate. An enthusiastic crowd of 500 led by Olson and Mayor Harry Veiner greeted the Trudeau party at Medicine Hat airport. Don Peacock for the *Albertan* called the greeting "a mild but unmistakable outbreak of Trudeaumania."[1] One of the purposes of Trudeau's visit was to help Olson regarding local ranchers' fears that his proposed new agriculture marketing boards might apply to beef cattle.[2]

The next day Mayor Veiner and a group from "the Hat," took Trudeau—in blue jeans, buckskin vest, and cowboy boots—on a trail ride before branding calves at the exhibition grounds.[3] The Trudeau party then boarded military helicopters for the 150-kilometre journey to Lethbridge, to be greeted by another friendly crowd of 700. The entourage then flew westward to the Standoff Blood Indian Reserve, near the Canada–US boundary, to meet an eclectic crowd of 2,000: chiefs and band elders from Alberta and Montana dressed in beaded buckskin and feathered headdresses; bearded Hutterites and their wives in traditional farmers' garb; as well as other residents of the region's small towns. Trudeau officially opened a manufacturing plant owned by the band, sipped tea in a teepee, received a painting by famous local artist Gerald Tailfeathers, and danced with hundreds of traditionally clothed band members.

The tour ended the day in the scenic Waterton Lakes National Park located in Sulatycky's riding. Arriving in the resort village a few kilometres from where Alberta, British Columbia, and Montana intersect, Trudeau was led by a piper through more crowds and attended an evening mass at the Catholic church before turning in at the chalet-style Prince of Wales Hotel amid the majestic peaks of the Waterton–Glacier International Peace Park.[4]

Sunday morning, Trudeau and his entourage once again boarded helicopters to travel north to Blairmore in the coal-mining region of Crowsnest Pass. Sulatycky had been involved in the planning and recalled that the PMO wanted a guaranteed good reception visiting the Alberta hinterland, unlike the 1969 Saskatchewan disaster during the wheat glut crisis.[5]

Trudeau's visit to the Crowsnest Pass was a first and only prime ministerial visit. Even ex-premier Manning had been a rare visitor, probably because of his long-time aversion to organized labour.[6] Three thousand people—half the total population of the Pass—came out to greet Trudeau. He rode in Barb-Wire Johnson's Crowsnest Pass Special (a brightly decorated bus that looked like a train) and watched a coal mine rescue drill. Trudeau and his party also played a softball game against a local girl's squad, to the delight of the cheering fans.[7]

Trudeau then attended a luncheon put together by a local women's committee of sixteen different ethnic groups that had settled in the villages since coal mining began there in 1895. Clad in various traditional costumes ranging from Dutch wooden shoes and Japanese kimonos, to the bright multi-coloured skirts and blouses of every country of central and eastern

Allen Sulatycky with Trudeau at a multicultural luncheon, Blairmore, Alberta, July 1971.
[*Vern Decoux Collection, Galt Museum and Archives*]

Europe, they proudly served special dishes from their families' homelands. Sulatycky believed that Trudeau, who had no idea of the hodgepodge of nationalities in the region, so enjoyed the event that it may have influenced the government's decision to introduce its multicultural policy later in the year. Until then, Sulatycky recalls, multicultural policy did not seem to be on anyone's agenda in Ottawa.[8] Three months after the Blairmore visit, Trudeau announced the "Implementation of Policy of Multiculturalism within a Bilingual Framework,"[9] which established meaningful federal assistance to ethnic organizations across the country so they could maintain and encourage their cultures.

Later the same day in Calgary, I observed a visibly tired Trudeau at a pre-scheduled press conference respond to questions about the timing of the next election ("We are closer to the next election than we are the last one") and the political significance of the trip ("The tour was designed mainly to boost my morale and it has done precisely that"). On the subject of proposed new farm-marketing legislation, which had been widely criticized by the agriculture community, he chided western Liberals for not explaining the government's case forcefully enough, and said that Alberta Liberals should try to explain the bill instead of listening to the opposition. He accused those trying to frighten Indians or cattlemen about his government's policies as being "false prophets" and that the policies were good, just not understood.[10]

Calgary Stampede parade day saw Trudeau in a big white cowboy hat perched on a silver saddle and clad in a brown western suit, silver brocade shirt, and cowboy boots astride a parade-proof Appaloosa named Sparky. He was the first prime minister in the parade's history ever to ride on horseback. An estimated 300,000 spectators lined the route to get a glimpse of the spectacle. Riding near Trudeau was Alberta's lieutenant-governor J.W. Grant MacEwan, a former leader of the Alberta Liberal Party, and Harry Strom, Bud Olson, and Peter Lougheed. The less daring of the special guests—including NHL legend Bobby Orr, Minister of Health John Munro, and Canadian impressionist Rich Little—were confined to horse drawn carriages or flashy convertibles.

One reporter wrote, "For 2.5 miles this morning Canada's prime minister was applauded, cheered, and whistled at in a show of admiration along the Stampede parade route." A lady among the spectators commented, "Isn't he be—ootiful on that horse." A few were heard telling him to get his hair cut (fashionably long in 1971 was perhaps too long for a prime minister visiting Calgary), while others shouted good-naturedly, "Pierre," "Fuddle-duddle,"[11] and "Yahoo!" Some observers from eastern Canada said the crowds gave him one of the warmest welcomes of his career.[12]

To raise money for Liberal Party coffers, a colleague and I organized a party barbecue at Heritage Park, a sprawling pioneer village of vintage buildings moved from Alberta towns and villages and rebuilt on the site. The four federal Liberal riding associations of the Calgary region sponsored the event with the plan for Trudeau to mingle and then address the crowd from the veranda of the Wainwright Hotel. One of the big question

> *Trudeau rides Sparky as Grand Marshal of the Calgary Stampede parade, July 12, 1971.*
[*Canadian Press/Ken Pole*]

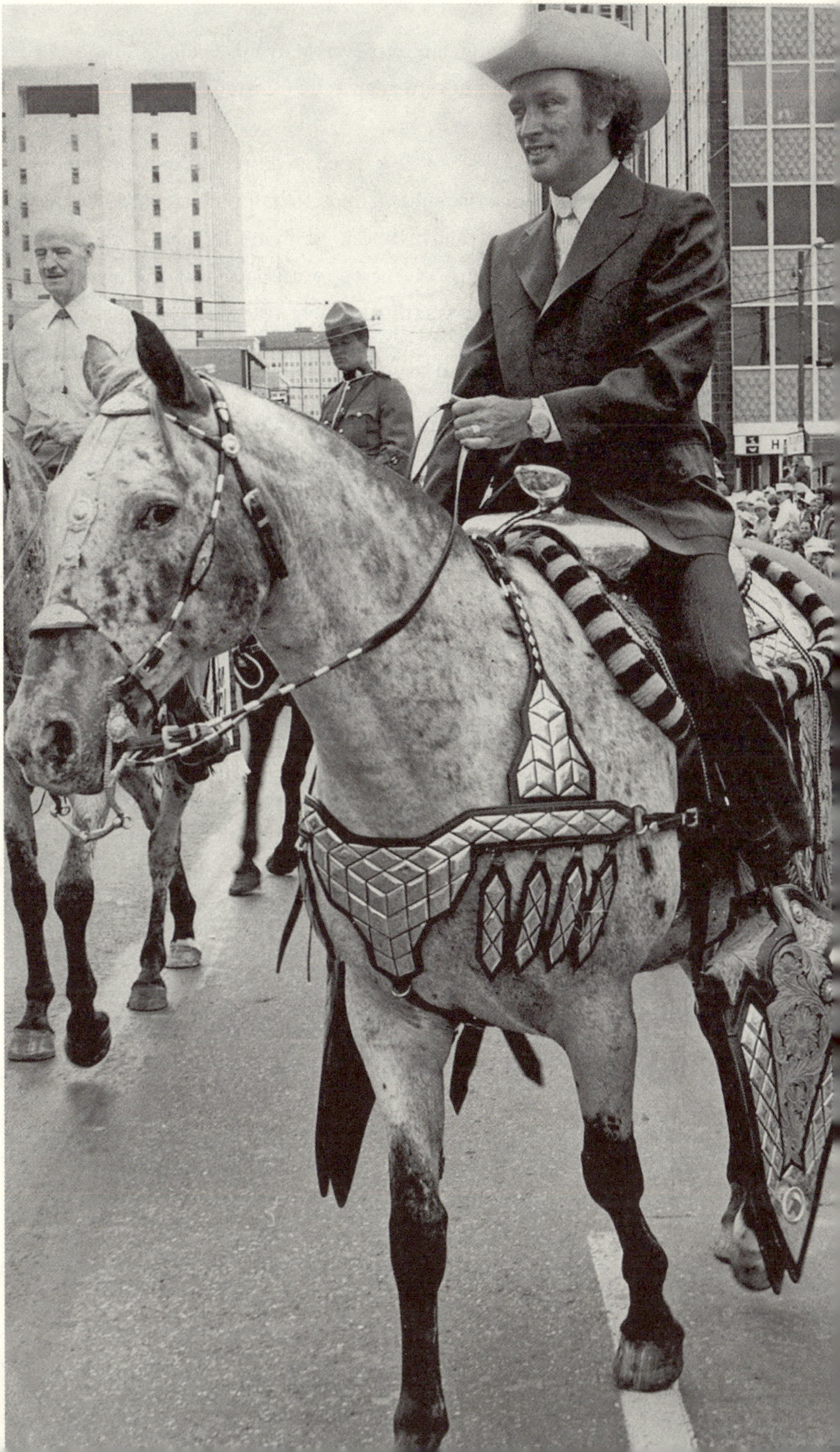

marks for the organizing committee was Margaret Trudeau. Since we had sold tickets advertising her attendance, we were relieved to get her confirmation the day before the event.

Ottawa comedian Rich Little warmed up the crowd from the hotel veranda with his John Diefenbaker impression (complete with stentorian tones and jowl shaking) and his uncanny imitation of the avuncular, lisping Lester Pearson. During his brief parody of the current PM, he invited the audience to pose questions as they might to Trudeau. To the question, "When will you call the next election?" Little perfectly imitated Trudeau's nonchalant, detached voice and shrug, "I don't know and could care less."

Meanwhile a few of us hustled out to greet Margaret and Pierre, Stampede officials and Mayor Sykes at the front gates. Trudeau looked vigorous and relaxed in his western outfit, and Margaret's maroon dress and white summer shoes complemented her flashing white teeth and auburn hair.[13] Spotting an excellent photo op, Trudeau boarded the park's antique steam locomotive, put on an engineer's cap and, with his wife and a qualified engineer by his side, took the controls for a ride through the park, with members of the press and crowd piled into the passenger cars. Then we began the slow process of taking the couple through the village's main street to meet the thousand or so attendees. The kisses, the handshakes, the well-wishers, the press, the picture takers (even Canadian rock and roller Bobby Curtola jumping around to position himself next to Margaret and Pierre for a publicity shot)—it was 1968 all over again.

Emceeing the event, I introduced Pat Mahoney, who introduced Trudeau. He told the crowd that he'd fulfilled a boyhood ambition riding in the Stampede parade that day. He then spoke of Canadians being privileged to have the freedom to make changes without resorting to violence, which drew loud applause, the October Crisis still obviously in everyone's

> *Top: Pierre and Margaret Trudeau enter Heritage Park. To the right of and behind Margaret are Calgary mayor Rod Sykes, the author, and Heritage Park Society chair Owen Funnell.* [Onions Collection, City of Calgary Archives, Cal A 2011-006-3813]

> *Bottom: Trudeau greets a crowd at Heritage Park while philanthropist oilman Eric Harvie looks on.* [Onions Collection, City of Calgary Archives, Cal A 2011-006-3830]

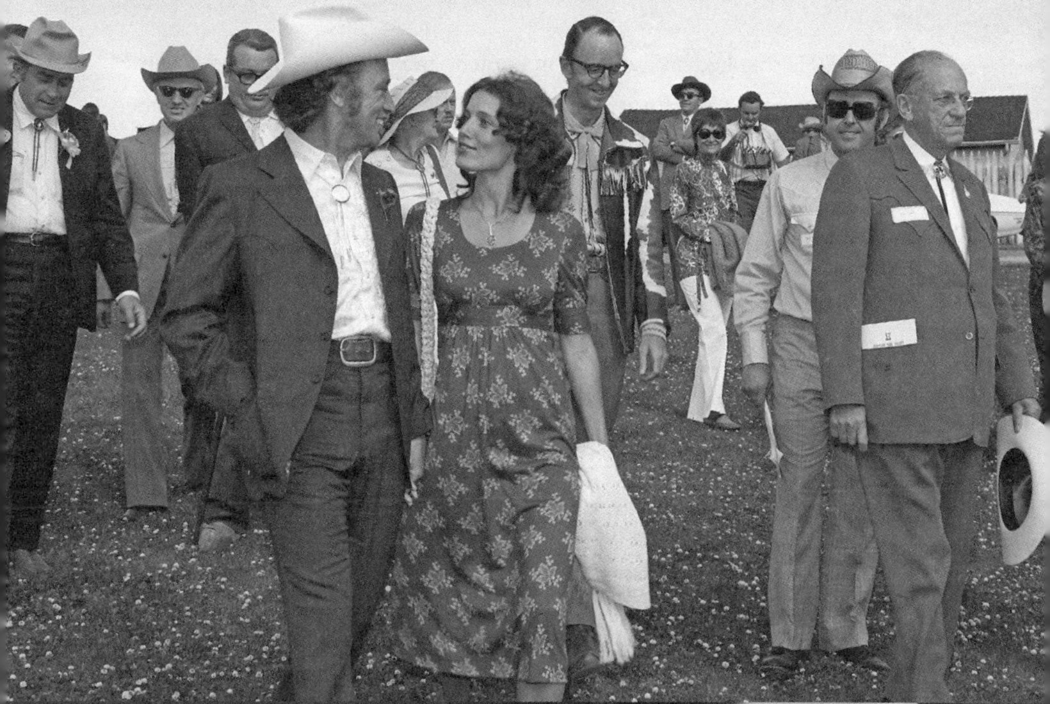

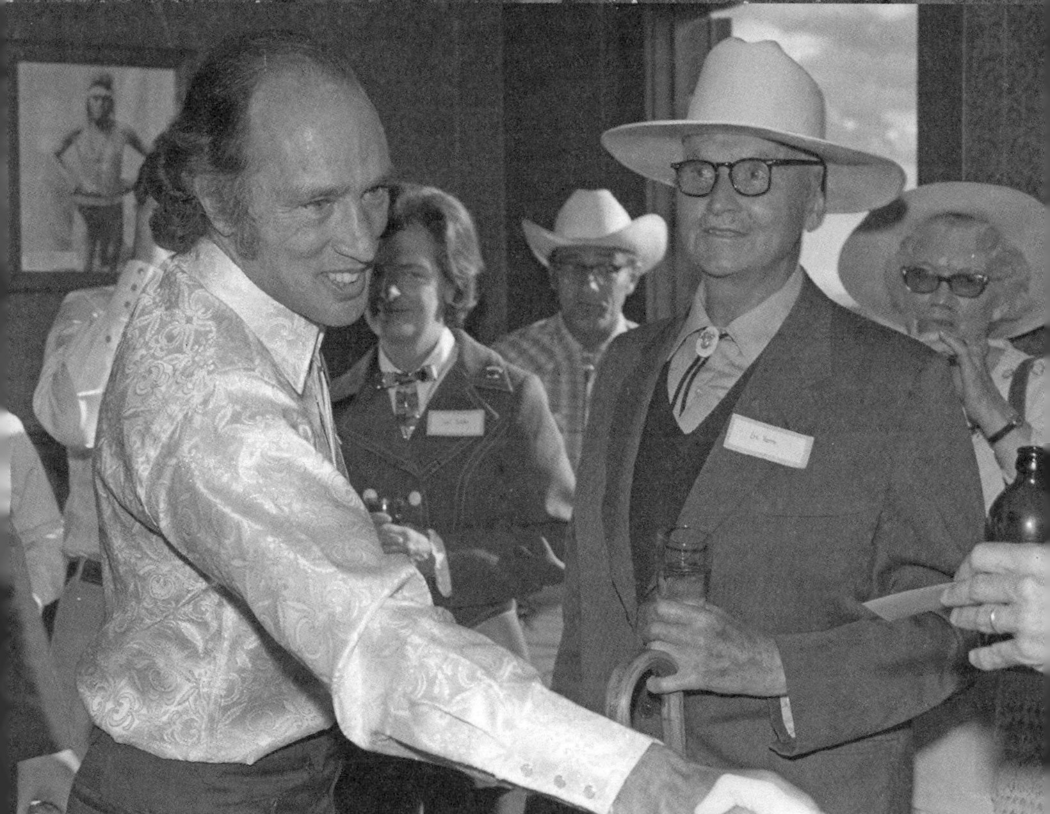

mind. He thanked his audience in French, Italian, Spanish, and German and received a warm ovation. The formalities concluded, he downed a beer while partaking in the usual Stampede fare of barbecued beef and beans before heading to the chuckwagon races and evening performance back at the Stampede grounds.[14]

The next day in a front-page story headlined "Pierre's Go-Round Gets a Big Lift from Margaret," *Herald* staff writer Jack Gorman described Trudeau's visit as a chapter that western writer Zane Grey could have written. "There was this trail hardened cowpoke named Pierre who rode hard all morning on a dusty parade route...By mid-afternoon, he arrives at a gentle little village known as Heritage Park nestled by an azure lake. The first thing you know he is embracing a vivacious young thing named Margaret and they walk hand-in-hand to where they are cooking up the grub and playing the music. And that is how it was for the prime minister Monday." Gorman said that Trudeau had conquered "the hearts of nearly 300,000 parade watchers" aboard Sparky and that at the grandstand during the evening performance "the crowd of 25,000 or more rose to its feet and applauded" when it was announced that the Trudeaus were in the audience."[15]

Trudeau's appearances in southern Alberta and the Calgary Stampede provided the high watermark of the federal Liberals' return to contention in Alberta in the election run-up. From the October Crisis on into the summer of 1971, his deft political skills and luck had taken his party back from the abyss. But the popularity he enjoyed in Alberta at that moment would never be achieved again.

The happy summer of 1971 was not yet over. Days later came another timely announcement that again threatened to push any bad stuff on to the back pages: Margaret was due to give birth in December. This would be the first time a prime minister had fathered a child in office since John A. Macdonald in 1869.[16]

VI

The Dawning of the Lougheed Era

23

Lougheed Comes to Power

FEBRUARY–SEPTEMBER 1971

ALBERTA'S FINAL LEGISLATIVE SESSION before the expected election found Lougheed scoring with attacks on the government for profligate spending and deficits, and for not doing enough about unemployment.[1] He demanded that Alberta labour be used on construction projects financed by public funds, chided the government for not updating its oil policy,[2] and called for tax relief for seniors and job creation programs.[3]

Discontent rumbled within the Social Credit ranks. When Edmonton Tory MLA Lou Hyndman proposed legislation to privatize some public services to create jobs, former Social Credit senior minister Alf Hooke and three other Social Credit MLAs supported the bill. Hooke said it was because the government had gone too far down the road toward socialism.[4]

Social Credit indicated it was not oblivious to changing times by introducing new age of majority provisions allowing people over the age of 18 to drink alcoholic beverages in taverns starting March 30, 1971.[5] But the Tories now demanded that the government allow beer and wine licenses at all restaurants.[6]

More trouble came for the Socreds when four hundred shouting civil servants invaded the legislature demanding the right to collective bargaining.[7] Municipalities joined in the attack when the government decided that it would be the only beneficiary of higher oil and gas revenues. Lougheed called the move a Social Credit scheme to destroy the effectiveness of local governments.[8]

Lougheed also made headlines fighting on behalf of a Fort Chipewyan trapper who had alleged that a new dam harmed Athabasca Delta residents. To discredit the trapper in the legislature, the minister of health disclosed that the trapper was on welfare. Lougheed attacked the minister for publicly disclosing personal confidential information and declared that individual rights would be a major election issue.[9]

In the spring of 1971 many Alberta Liberals—me among them—had to decide where to park our ballot in the next provincial election. About 11 percent of the Alberta electorate had voted Liberal in the 1967 provincial election, and 36 percent voted Liberal in the 1968 federal general election. With no credible provincial Liberal Party left, these voters were on the hunt for another provincial party to support.

Social Credit candidate Don Luzzi was contesting the inner city riding of Calgary–Buffalo. Since I had worked with Luzzi on various projects over the years, I had only momentary pangs of conscience when he asked me to manage his campaign. Why not? My party was not going anywhere. Thus began my brief and only flirtation with Social Credit.

A native of Connecticut, Luzzi had joined the Calgary Stampeders football team in 1958 following his US college career. He had achieved superstar status, winning awards and all-star selection many times.[10] Now a Canadian citizen and recently retired from football, his familiar large frame and many charitable activities, together with his celebrity status, had made him instantly recognizable around town—an excellent candidate. He had been encouraged to throw his hat into the ring by some business friends trying to revitalize Social Credit. But his tough Tory opponent was highly regarded young lawyer Ron Ghitter, an outstanding speaker with an experienced campaign team.

As the election neared, I threw a party for the Luzzi campaign team. Nearly all 150 or so attending were young urbanites of both sexes from the professions or business community who made themselves right at home with my well-stocked bar. Premier Strom himself arrived early in the evening. Cheerful and pleasant, he accepted a non-alcoholic drink and worked the room urging everyone to get out and work for his candidates. He soon took his leave, although he did not appear ill at ease with either the younger generation or the guzzling.[11]

Calling the election on August 30, Harry Strom reminded Albertans that his government had kept unemployment and taxes low, and fought against language rights being included in a Canadian constitution. Lougheed responded to the call saying that Tory success depended on his party's ability to communicate its platform and the strong qualities of his candidates. NDP leader Grant Notley said that his party was ready and boldly predicted a breakthrough. Liberal leader Bob Russell declared that jobs and quality of life were the main issues but warned that his responsibility was to win his own riding of St. Albert, where he would remain to campaign.[12]

The Tories were quick to capitalize on politically fortuitous events right from the start. A hailstorm that wiped out 70 percent of the crop in central Alberta brought a promise from Lougheed for increased hail insurance benefits and a simpler claim process.[13] The Tory candidate in Barrhead, Hugh Horner,[14] demanded help for flooded-out farmers in northwestern Alberta,[15] while Calgary–Foothills Tory candidate Len Werry attacked the Strom government for refusing to fund a student summer job program in Calgary, accusing Social Credit of bias toward Edmonton and southern Alberta.[16]

The Tories and the NDP also jumped on a government decision to allow the extraction of 200,000 tons of coal from a strip mine on the eastern slope of the iconic Mount Rundle near the Banff National Park boundary. Lougheed and Notley's NDP both attacked the government for not protecting sensitive lands and for charging an inadequate royalty of only ten cents per ton (which in this case would have yielded to the province a mere $20,000 for all of the coal extracted).[17] A lawsuit was commenced to shut down operations, naming the government of Alberta as a defendant.[18]

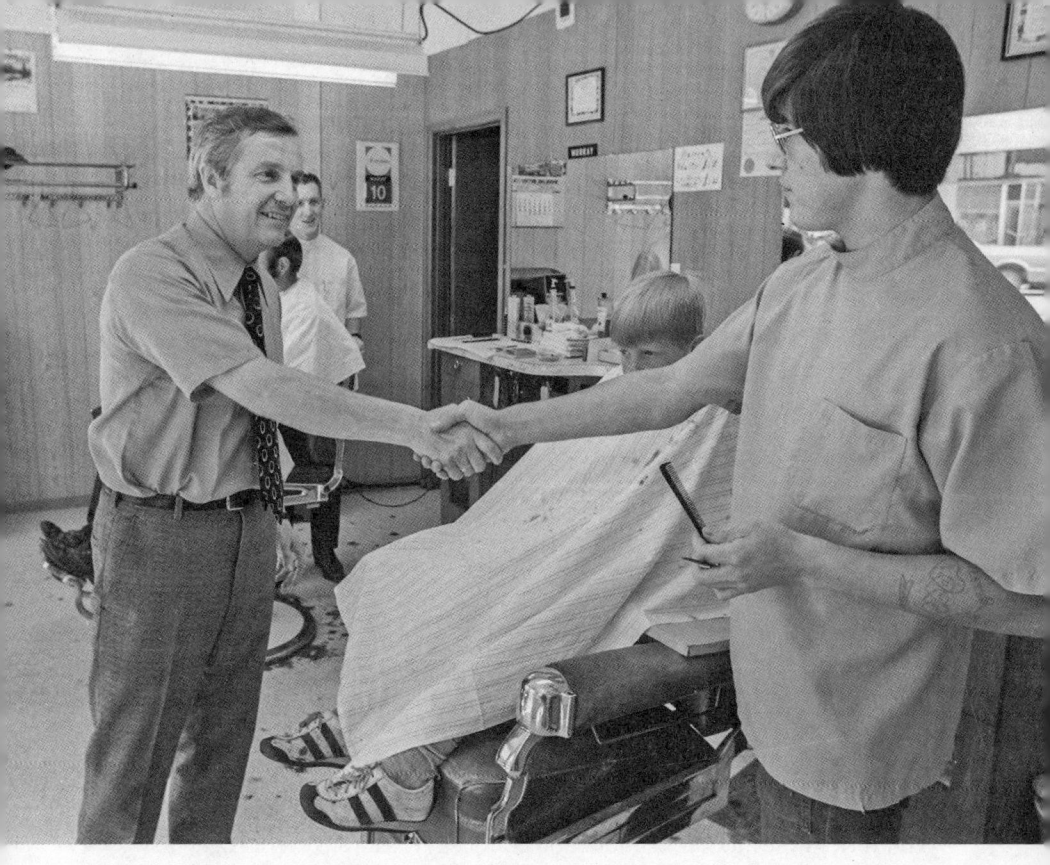

Peter Lougheed on the campaign trail, summer 1971.
[Edmonton Journal/*Provincial Archives of Alberta J 855.1*]

Lougheed's election platform promised reduced property taxes, more money for home mortgages, and more new housing starts. For labour, he promised better apprenticeship programs, reasonable notice of layoffs, more labour involvement in business decisions, and a commission to review the need for better workers' compensation pensions. For the businessman, he called for the provincial Treasury Branch to provide more capital for Alberta enterprises.[19]

During a three-day swing deep in the staunch Social Credit territory of southern Alberta, Lougheed campaigned from his campaign bus/office bearing signs that simply read "NOW!" while promising the large crowds new wilderness areas and the right balance between the protection of the environment and resource development. In shirtsleeves, he walked down the main streets of small towns shaking hands with the locals, talking to customers in shops, and distributing buttons. Albertans had seldom, if ever, witnessed this type of personal campaigning.[20]

Strom announced his platform in Edmonton on August 3. His main plank was a one-time-only $1,000 homebuyer grant to families that earned less than $15,000 a year. He also promised reduced medicare premiums, job creation programs, more daycare centres, better programs for the poor, improved urban transportation and rural roads, more support for the arts, and academic instruction in the languages and cultures of Alberta.[21] His homebuyer promise drew immediate and constant flak; the main complaint being that the government would use tax money of renters and existing owners as a subsidy to new homebuyers. Instead of helping the campaign, this program quickly became a liability.[22]

NDP leader Notley's platform called for a one-year moratorium of farmers' debts in hardship cases, programs to save the family farm, lower power bills and property taxes, higher corporate taxes, and higher royalties from oil companies.[23] All three parties' progressive platforms seemed to be trying to entice old Alberta Liberal Party or Trudeau Liberal votes.

The Liberals promised to lower unemployment, provide better social services, and clean up lakes and rivers, encourage foreign investment, create a new bank to meet farmers' credit needs, recognize women's rights, improve education and daycare, provide free medicare, and establish an Indigenous development agency.[24] But despite their imaginative platform the harsh truths remained: they had no organization, no money, and very few candidates.[25]

Shortly after the campaign got under way, Don Luzzi and I attended a Social Credit organization meeting in Edmonton with about 300 candidates, campaign managers, and others. The party's aging and portly perennial campaign manager was Orvis Kennedy who had religious and political ties to both Aberhart and Manning. Kennedy pranced about the stage introducing candidates, singing the campaign song, and urging everyone to get out and "Fight! Fight! Fight!" for Social Credit. It struck me that although Kennedy's revivalist style may have inspired many of the old guard, it would not have much stroke with the younger crowd in this new era of politics. Excepting a few candidates, most of the notables on stage did not represent the next generation of a more dynamic breed the Socreds were seeking.[26]

In mid-August Lougheed continued his progressive campaign, promising to appoint a public defender to ensure that citizens appearing before government boards had proper legal counsel. He also called for a simpler process to correct credit records, and a law prohibiting any disclosure of personal records without written consent.[27] In northern Alberta, large and enthusiastic crowds greeted Lougheed as he reached out to farm families, Indigenous and Metis communities, and small-town businessmen. He said confidently, "We are threatening the 36-year-old government for the first time because we offer a viable alternative."[28]

Strom continued to be confounded by unpredictable events. The Stoney Indians of the Morley reserve threatened to charge drivers using the Trans-Canada Highway a toll because of a land swap dispute with the provincial government.[29] In addition, the 500-strong correctional officers' union was threatening strike action for salary increases.[30]

Strom's torments continued with the publication of his ex-colleague Alf Hooke's memoir[31] criticizing Social Credit for abandoning its federal aspirations. Hooke also took a shot at Manning for accepting a directorship on a bank board[32] and an appointment to the Senate—institutions that Manning and his party had heavily criticized over the years. Hooke also attacked Manning for having accepted an appointment to the board of McIntyre Porcupine Mines Limited.[33]

On the closing day for nominations, a record 243 candidates were contesting a record 75 seats—more candidates than at any time since 1935. The Socreds and the PCs both had candidates running in all 75 ridings: only the third time in the province's history that an opposition party had a candidate in every riding. Notley's NDP came up with a respectable 70 candidates. The Liberals had only scraped up 20.[34]

Ten days before the election, Lougheed was getting large and enthusiastic crowds in the strong Social Credit country of central Alberta. He also had the most professionally produced television ads. Tory Barrhead candidate Hugh Horner forecast that the Tories would win 55 seats. The youthful Notley was predicting at least 4 seats for the NDP. The hapless Liberals were hopeless.[35]

The Socreds were stumbling. One week before election day, Strom spoke to a rally at the 750-seat Red Deer arena that was only half full. Days earlier, Peter Lougheed had filled the building.[36] Seemingly desperate, Strom warned his supporters that if they did not get out to vote, his party was in trouble. He also warned that the NDP wanted a Conservative government as "the first step in the takeover of Alberta by the socialists."[37]

The Luzzi campaign's mixed bag of a hundred volunteers—some modern and audaciously irreverent and some quaint and pious souls from the old Social Credit school—worked together in harmony. But those of us in the centre of that campaign believed we were in a close contest that could go either way.

Late in the campaign some 2,700 Social Credit supporters filled every seat in Edmonton's Jubilee Auditorium to hear their hero, Senator Manning, warn them that the election was no time to entertain "new experiments in government by untried and inexperienced men, no matter how nice they may look on television."[38] Strom attacked Southam Press, accusing its bosses in eastern Canada of telling local papers to support the Conservative Party. He asked the crowd, "Do Albertans want a change from a strong independent government to one that will be subservient to big eastern political and business interests?"[39]

In Edmonton the day after the Strom–Manning rally, it was Lougheed's turn to bring his Tory troops to the same Jubilee Auditorium for the last big Tory event of the campaign where he was greeted by 4,000 placard-waving, chanting, cheering supporters. Speaking without notes he reviewed his platform and closed by predicting victory for the first time: "It's going to be very, very close, but I've got that kind of feeling in here—and I think you have out there—that it's going our way."[40]

On August 30, Albertans elected 49 Tories, 25 Socreds, and one NDP. Lougheed's comfortable majority meant the Social Credit era was over

Peter Lougheed at the PC campaign rally in Edmonton's Jubilee Auditorium, August 1971. [Edmonton Journal/Provincial Archives of Alberta J 697.10]

after a thirty-six year run. In northern Alberta, Lougheed took 14 of 21 seats and in central Alberta (including Red Deer) he won 10 out of 14. Edmonton obviously loved him—he took all 16 seats. In hometown Calgary, he took 9 out of 13. The only region where the Tories failed to win a seat was south of Calgary. NDP leader Grant Notley took the northern Alberta riding of Spirit River–Fairview by a narrow 147 votes. The Liberals were wiped out. Voter turnout was exceptionally high (141,511 more voters than in 1967—a gain of 28%) as this statistical summary details:

- Tories received 296,934 votes—167,744 more than in 1967 (a gain of 130%) and captured 46.4% of the popular vote (a gain of 20.4%)
- Social Credit received 262,953 votes—40,683 more than in 1967 (a gain of 18%) and captured 41.1% of the popular vote (a loss of 3.5%)

Peter Lougheed and his new cabinet on the steps of the Alberta legislature, September 1971. [Edmonton Journal/*Provincial Archives of Alberta J 712.6*]

- NDP received 73,038 votes—5,572 votes less than in 1967 (a loss of 7.5%) and captured only 11.42% of the popular vote (a loss of 4.6%)
- Liberals received 6,475 votes—47,372 less than in 1967 (a loss of 88%) and captured only 1.01% of the popular vote (a loss of 9.8%)

While the number of Socred votes remained stable from 1967, the Tories' numbers shot sky-high. Although not scientifically analyzed, the results suggested that Lougheed's team captured the major share of the new voters. With his progressive policies, youth, energy, urbane image, and outstanding organization, he clearly took most of the Liberal vote—both provincial and federal (which would include most of the 35 percent of Alberta voters who'd voted for Trudeau in 1968).

The 10 percent drop for the provincial Liberals was an important number to both the Social Credit and the Tories. Given that the Tory popular vote was only 5.3 percent ahead of Social Credit when the votes were counted, Social Credit might have been better off had the provincial Liberals remained in the race with a viable leader and retained at least some of their 1967 vote. The Tory popular vote could then have been a few points lower and Social Credit could have been closer to, if not ahead of, the Tories. With the Liberals virtually out of the race and their vote going to Lougheed instead of Social Credit, the Liberal vote helped put Lougheed in power. The first half of the strategy promoted by the Alberta federal Liberal establishment—to sideline the provincial Liberal Party and thrust its supporters into the waiting arms of Social Credit—had not worked.

Unfortunately, my one experience working for a Social Credit candidate— I never became a member of the party—ended in failure. Tory Ron Ghitter came out on top beating Don Luzzi by a margin of 467 votes out of a total 12,307 cast.[41]

In September, Lougheed's new twenty-two-member cabinet was sworn into office, with seven ministers from Edmonton, and six including the premier from Calgary. The average age of the cabinet was fifteen years younger than the Strom cabinet. It had all of the appearances of a strong, young, and capable cabinet with experienced small-town and big-city professionals, businessmen, farmers and ranchers, municipal politicians, and the ten legislators who had served with Lougheed in opposition. The new minister of mines and minerals was Bill Dickie, who had been rejected by the federal Liberals in Calgary South in favour of Pat Mahoney only three years earlier. Lougheed's honeymoon with the people of Alberta had begun.

24

Tax Reform at Last

JULY—DECEMBER 1971

AS ALBERTANS WERE GETTING READY to go to the polls to elect Peter Lougheed, Trudeau's national popularity was showing signs of waning. Larger economic issues were eclipsing his October Crisis heroics. Stanfield's federal Tories were reminding the public that Canada now had the worst of both worlds—high unemployment and growing inflation—despite the government's claim to have had licked both, and many economic experts agreed.[1] These presented dangerous obstacles in the way of the Liberals' re-election hopes.

At a press conference on July 27, Trudeau admitted that his government was losing support as a result of high unemployment, and some of the public's dim view of his trips abroad. He said that as a result he planned to spend some time moving about the country to explain his economic policies to the people.[2]

The Trudeau government's economic headaches grew much worse in mid-August, when President Nixon announced his solutions to inflation and unemployment in the US. One measure—the imposition of a 10 percent temporary surcharge on all imports—immediately devalued the US dollar and made US-produced exports cheaper in other countries and US imports more expensive to Americans. Although good for the US economy, it was bad for almost all others.[3] The import surcharge was expected to adversely affect about a quarter of Canada's exports to the US—goods produced by the Canadian labour-intensive manufacturing sector.[4] The peril of massive layoffs loomed, with Canadian unemployment already unacceptably high.[5]

The Trudeau government's bill to provide financial help to industries hurt by the US import surcharge was attacked by Senator Manning because it only benefitted industries in Ontario, Quebec, and British Columbia. Manning claimed that, had Canada and the Canadian media worked as hard at cultivating US relationships as it did in fostering anti-American sentiment, the country would now be dealing with the United States from a position of strength.[6] Manning's opinion was shared by most of the oilmen and increasing numbers of Albertans.

Inflation and unemployment continued to mount. Canada suffered the largest midsummer increase in food prices in more than ten years and the consumer price index[7] stood at a record 135.[8] Despite Benson repeatedly stating that unemployment would fall, it had remained around 6.5 percent for most of 1971—little better than the 6.6 percent of September 1970.[9]

To add to the government's woes, the fight to implement tax reform was still not over. In late October Alberta's new premier, Peter Lougheed, said he would fight for a one-year delay: "We think the system is frankly loaded against Alberta and we're going to take a stand on it."[10]

Since June's introduction of the 707-page tax reform bill to largely positive reviews, by November there had been twenty-seven days of parliamentary debate dealing with only one-tenth of its 333 clauses—and the opposition was now making a last ditch effort to delay or derail it. It had now been before the public for more than two politically difficult years so the government was determined to pass the legislation by the year-end deadline in one single package.[11] It invoked a never-before-used procedural rule that limited debate to four more days. The opposition tossed papers and note pads as they howled in derision.[12]

Before the fight was over, Senator Manning again attacked the government, this time for not allowing time for the Senate to carry out its constitutional role and give serious study to the legislation. Nevertheless, he decided to support the government's timetable,[13] and on December 22 the struggle for tax reform ended with the Senate's final approval.[14] The ordeal over, the bill became law on January 1, 1972.

Pat Mahoney, who had done most of the painstaking work of guiding the bill through Parliament, admitted that the government had invited "flak" from the business community due to confusing and massive proposals, reports, and white papers. He sardonically observed that the business community was afraid members would lose control of their businesses to "some faceless, heartless and mindless bureaucrat and deprive his progeny of their inalienable right to inherit the fruits of his labour, tax free."[15]

Despite all the fears about the Nixon surcharge, its impact over three months had been minimal. Not only had there been no drop in Canadian exports to the US, there was a gain.[16] Figures released also showed that Canada's per capita income, the Gross National Product (GNP), and pre-tax corporate profits were up by about 10 percent in 1971, a very healthy sign.[17] After several weeks of negotiations, Trudeau's televised address to the nation explaining the surcharge, and even an inflationary mini-budget for new job creation programs to counteract the surcharge's impact, Trudeau and Nixon finally met to resolve their differences in early December. It was only the second meeting of the two leaders since either had taken office and the first in more than two and a half years. At a concluding press conference, Trudeau went out of his way to laud Nixon for his understanding of the problem created by the import surcharge, and said that he had received Nixon's assurance that the United States did not want to make Canada its economic colony—a statement, said Trudeau, that was "unequalled by any other president in speaking about Canada."[18] Trudeau said he now hoped that the surcharge on imports would be removed after December's Group of Ten[19] meeting in Washington.[20]

The Group of Ten agreed to raise the official price of gold from $35 to $38 an ounce, thereby devaluing the US dollar. Several other currencies (except Canada's) were revalued upwards, and the 10 percent surcharge on imports was lifted. Nixon called it "the most significant monetary agreement in the history of the world."[21] Stock markets soared. Edgar Benson predicted, "the Canadian economy would move forward with even greater vigour."[22]

25

Peter Lougheed Shows His Stuff

JULY 1971–MARCH 1972

JUST AS HARRY STROM was about to call his fateful 1971 election, the National Energy Board (NEB) began hearings to consider three applications to export Canadian natural gas to the US. The hydrocarbon spat this time pitted the gas-producing provinces and companies of Alberta and BC against the gas-consuming provinces (primarily Ontario and Quebec), their public utility companies, and consumers. Playing the role of referee and judge was the federal government's NEB. The three applications together sought to export 2.7 trillion cubic feet (TCF) of gas[1] over the next fifteen to twenty years.

The hearing in Ottawa was to be in two parts. The NEB would first hear both sides' experts on estimates of gas reserves and future Canadian requirements. If the NEB decided there was a surplus, the second part would then determine if the surplus was sufficient for the NEB to approve all or part of the applications.[2]

Western producers and exporters wanted to sell and export gas as quickly as possible after a gas discovery to generate immediate cash flow and to create competition between US and Canadian purchasers that would generate higher prices. The consuming provinces and their utility companies naturally wanted to reduce competition for the gas (by excluding US purchasers) so prices could remain low.[3]

The NEB formula for calculating a gas surplus took the estimated Canadian gas requirements four years from the time of the hearing (in this case 1975) and added twenty-five (the number of years to protect those Canadian requirements). Producers and producing provinces had to prove a surplus of gas to satisfy Canadian needs in the year 2000.[4] Any amount more constituted a surplus.[5]

The expert evidence from the Alberta government and the producers (the applicants) showed a significant surplus of gas for export. On the other side, Ontario gas utility companies submitted evidence that Alberta's supplies would be exhausted in just a few years if present trends continued, leaving no surplus gas. Counsel for the Alberta government countered that the Ontario gas utility companies' evidence was ridiculously conservative and discriminatory to the west.[6]

Since there had been two major discoveries of gas in the Arctic by the 45-percent federally owned Panarctic Oils, the applicants asked the NEB to conclude that more Arctic gas reserves would likely be found and therefore provide a sufficient surplus of gas for export. The future construction of an Arctic gas pipeline was obviously relevant to the proceedings. Alberta Gas Trunk Line CEO Robert (Bob) Blair,[7] testifying for one of the applicants, said construction of an Arctic pipeline could start as early as 1973.[8]

The consuming provinces and utilities companies argued that the remoteness of the Arctic gas discoveries made uncertain its delivery to southern markets. During the course of the hearings, one applicant company estimated Canadian gas surplus at 1.7 TCF while another applicant estimated 3.4 TCF—a 100 percent difference. The CPA supporting the applications estimated a whopping 7.6 TCF.[9] After nine days of testimony punctuated by acrimony and wide variance of reserve estimates, the NEB had to sort out the evidence, and how much of the 2.7 TCF of the applications—if any—could be approved.[10]

On November 19 (just as newly elected Premier Lougheed was starting to take charge) the western gas producers and the producing provinces were sent reeling by the NEB's decision to deny all three export applications on the grounds that the surplus gas was insufficient. The NEB also held that while gas had been discovered in the Canadian Arctic, not only did the size of the discoveries remain uncertain, the gas itself was too remote to be considered in the reserve calculations at that time.[11]

Carl Nickle, a director of Alberta and Southern Gas, one of the unsuccessful applicants, accused the NEB and the federal government of using western Canada's energy reserves "as chips in a gambling game" with Washington over Nixon's 10 percent import surcharge. Premier Lougheed wired Trudeau, requesting the NEB reconsider its finding and warned that the decision would depress the petroleum industry.[12]

For the oilmen, it was again east versus west and Ottawa versus Alberta.[13] The industry's public relations machines came alive, arguing that the decision would cost Canadians countless millions of dollars and jobs, further slow down the Alberta drilling business, already in a downturn, and stifle new construction of gas plants. They accused the federal government and the NEB of being in cahoots to apply pressure on Nixon to change his economic policy, and Ottawa-based NEB board members of being too close to eastern natural gas utility interests. They also warned that the unnecessarily large reserves required by the NEB to establish a sufficient surplus would result in lower returns to producers, thereby making it difficult to fund their operations.[14]

As the oilmen and their supporters waged their war of words, my wife and I were among the crowd watching the Grey Cup parade with Lougheed yahooing his way along the downtown Vancouver parade route. Riding a horse, brandishing a white Stetson, and flashing a Kennedy-esque smile, he looked every inch the strong provincial leader he was fast becoming. The next day the Calgary Stampeders edged the Toronto Argonauts 14–11 in a rain-soaked game at Vancouver's Empire Stadium. Lougheed's dynamic appearance followed by the first Grey Cup win for the Stampeders since

1948 symbolized the changes taking place in Alberta and within Canada. Alberta was a province becoming rich and important. It was a player.

Peter Lougheed's words and actions soon revealed that Alberta would be a far more nettlesome partner in Confederation than the gentle Harry Strom or the parochial Ernest Manning. While attending his inaugural first ministers' conference, Lougheed asked the federal government to disclose its economic plans, consult with the provinces regarding foreign investment policies, and provide observer status for Alberta at all Canada–US energy discussions. He also proposed that Alberta take control of all major federal–provincial shared-costs programs in return for an increase in income tax revenues, and called for a one-year delay in implementing Ottawa's tax reform changes.[15]

In December Lougheed asked Trudeau for assurances that energy issues would not be discussed when meeting with Washington officials without prior consultation with his government. At the same time, Minister of Intergovernmental Affairs Don Getty wrote acting Minister of Energy Otto Lang over concerns about the Trudeau government plan to sell Panarctic's northern gas reserves (on federal lands) into the US export market from which Alberta gas was restricted. He also complained that natural gas was being sold at unrealistically low prices in eastern Canada.[16] The new government's assertiveness was on display again when Don Getty described Alberta as an industrial and parkland province with sophisticated businesses, and as such, it was no longer appropriate to bunch Alberta in with Saskatchewan and Manitoba as the "Prairie Provinces."[17]

At the PC convention in Edmonton in January, Lougheed gave notice that his party organization would work for the federal Tories in all nineteen federal Alberta ridings in the next federal election[18]—ominous news for Alberta federal Grits.

The centrepiece of Lougheed's first throne speech was a new Alberta Bill of Rights, to "protect individual rights from the encroachment of the state." The speech disclosed the government's plans to strengthen anti-discrimination laws, guarantee the privacy of information, repeal the Sexual Sterilization Act,[19] improve mental health services, set up an arts foundation and review the existing natural gas and oil royalties system.[20] The speech declared, "Change will be viewed—not with fear and apprehension—but with optimism with a sense of challenge and of opportunities to be grasped."[21] As if to underline that Social Credit was now a movement of the distant (or Dickensian) past, in the Legislature former Socred Minister of Health Jim Henderson berated the government for their intention to repeal the Sexual Sterilization Act![22]

Lougheed's throne speech confirmed the progressive leadership he promised during the election campaign. Alberta not only had its very own Kennedy, but also its own 1968 Trudeau. Lougheed had received most of the collapsed provincial and federal Liberal vote, and if he carried out his intentions in his universally lauded throne speech,[23] he was likely to keep it.

VII

Stumbling toward
the Brink

26

The Grits Falter

SEPTEMBER 1971–MAY 1972

ALTHOUGH THE OILMEN were comfortable with the election of Lougheed and his government, they remained frustrated with Trudeau. Many of them believed that even though he neither understood nor cared about their industry, he was now plotting to control it.[1] With oil markets growing worldwide and Canada having the potential to be one of the big suppliers, they now had a great opportunity to cash in. But for that to happen they believed they needed better friends in Ottawa than they had now. Thus, many of them believed it was time to take the Liberals on, *mano a mano*. The place they would start would be in Pat Mahoney's riding of Calgary South.

In September 1971, 42-year-old Peter Bawden announced he would seek the PC nomination for Pat Mahoney's riding of Calgary South. Bawden, who had grown up in comfortable surroundings (his father former head of Dominion Securities), headed west from his Toronto home in 1948 to seek his own fortune. By 1952 he'd founded his own company, which became one of the world's largest privately owned drilling firms. Bawden also served on the board of directors of many major companies, including Air Canada,

Barclays Bank, Boeing, and Safeway.[2] He said he decided to run because of the Trudeau government's taxation policy, its intrusion into areas best served by private enterprise, and its failure to recognize western Canadian interests.[3]

Bawden's nomination meeting brought out an enthusiastic crowd of 2,500—one of the largest nomination meetings in the province's history. After presenting his program of oil and gas industry tax incentives, and calling for an end to low prices on oil and gas products from western Canada, Bawden romped to victory.[4] The oilmen were now fully engaged in federal politics, and except for the odd rebel, they were committed to the Progressive Conservatives.

With the election fast approaching Trudeau tried to boost the chances of two of his Alberta MPs by re-appointing Pat Mahoney parliamentary secretary to Minister of Finance Benson and appointing Allen Sulatycky as parliamentary secretary to Minister of Energy Joe Greene.[5] Mahoney's high profile role in Parliament, with his hard work on tax reform and his stout defence of government policies, had endeared him to Trudeau and his decision makers.[6] Sulatycky had proven himself to be a very astute and active politician who was managing his cumbersome riding very well.

In October Joe Greene's career[7] as a minister came to an abrupt end when he was felled by a stroke. This was a great loss for the government. Not only was he one of the Liberal Party's all-time great orators, with his quick wit and gregarious personality he had even charmed many oilmen who came to believe that he was an effective minister.

Trudeau had not abandoned the oil and gas industry. In Halifax in November he spoke glowingly about the bright future of the industry in Nova Scotia following a promising gas discovery on Sable Island. Trudeau's knowledge of industry facts and figures and his affirmation of a positive investment climate impressed sceptics and brought him rare praise from his usual detractors. Oil columnist Jim Armstrong wrote, "his words were sweet music to the industry."[8]

The Tories continued to nominate their candidates. After selecting Bawden to take on Mahoney in Calgary South, they nominated young engineering professor Harvie Andre to succeed retiring Douglas Harkness to contest Calgary Centre against Grit Nick Taylor.[9] The Tory nomination meetings attracted large boisterous crowds, a sure sign of trouble for the Alberta Grits. Also worrisome was an October national Gallup poll showing Tory support at 32 percent—up 9 percent since August, while the Liberals slipped 4 points to 38 percent and the NDP down a point to 23 percent. The Tories were now at their highest standing since the 1968 election.[10]

In November, High River native Joe Clark[11]—a long-time Tory apparatchik despite his tender 32 years—announced that he was seeking the Tory nomination in Sulatycky's federal riding of Rocky Mountain.[12] Clark had worked in Tory campaigns since his teens. In his twenties he had been secretary to Alberta provincial PC leader Cam Kirby, an assistant to Tory Minister of Justice Davie Fulton, president of the National PC Student Federation, an organizer and candidate for Peter Lougheed's Alberta PCs, and an executive assistant to national PC leader Robert Stanfield.[13]

In late 1971 Bill Davis' Tories won a majority victory in the Ontario provincial election, with the Liberals finishing a poor second and dropping 8 seats.[14] A week later, Premier Smallwood's Liberal grip on Newfoundland ended after twenty-two years when Frank Moores' Tories jumped from 3 seats to 21, winning one more seat than the Liberals. Although Smallwood would cling to power for a short time, in January Moores formed his own government.[15] Provincial Liberal parties now were in control of only three provincial governments: Quebec, Nova Scotia, and Prince Edward Island.

As both major federal parties got busier with eyes on the electoral calendar, so too did the hostility increase between them, and toward their critics. Saskatchewan MP Alvin Hamilton (who had been minister of agriculture under Diefenbaker) set about dashing the Liberal plans to co-opt Social Credit in Alberta by promising to talk with Harry Strom about running for the Tories against H.A. (Bud) Olson. Hamilton said, "If H.A.—that stands for horse's ass—Olson is left around much longer, there won't be any businessmen left, because he's getting rid of the farmers and once they're gone, the businessmen will disappear too."[16]

Addressing an Ontario Liberal meeting, Trudeau called BC Premier W.A.C. Bennett a "bigot," because Bennett had said there were too many French people in Ottawa. BC minister Phil Gaglardi counterattacked, saying it was Trudeau who was the bigot because he was trying "to stuff French down everybody's throat."[17] Neither was the *Calgary Herald* amused, saying that Trudeau's "recurring inability to curb his tongue is degrading Parliament and the entire Canadian political process."[18]

At year's end Trudeau proudly trumpeted his government accomplishments, while lamenting that Canadians were reluctant to express pride in them. He said that Canada's real GNP exceeded 6 percent annual growth for four consecutive quarters and that Canada's growth would likely be greater than every other major industrial country in the Western world including Japan. He admitted falling short on unemployment, but noted that was because Canada's labour force was expanding at a rate faster than in any other industrialized country.[19]

In a CTV interview, Trudeau said that his government had solved two great crises since 1968—the FLQ October Crisis and the crisis brought about by Nixon's 10 percent import surcharge—and it had governed in the meantime. He also pointed out that his government had increased trade to record levels, and had kept its word on establishing participatory democracy. In response to whether he would lead his party in the election he said, "I have no intention of not running, if God keeps me alive."[20] On the CBC television show *Weekend*, he also acknowledged that he would be an election issue, since it was becoming "more and more important to demolish the leader if you want to get rid of the government." As to whether he was arrogant he replied wryly, "It may be true that I'm arrogant. I hope it's not, but no man is without sin."[21]

Parliament Hill reporter Paul Jackson sized up the Alberta MPs, concluding that, with one exception, they were all well regarded and as active as any MPs. The exception was Hu Harries, who rarely appeared in the Commons. According to Jackson, one of Harries' fellow Alberta MPs said that when he did not get the cabinet appointment he expected,

Harries decided to work almost full time in his Edmonton riding. The MP also told Jackson that Harries' behaviour was a shame because he could have been a strong voice on behalf of western Canada. Harries was also growing his reputation as a loose cannon. He told the Calgary Chamber of Commerce that discriminatory freight rates had created a $2 billion trade deficit for western Canada with the east, and was responsible for the loss of 100,000 western Canadian jobs to Ontario and Quebec.[22] Public criticism of the government coming from one of his MPs did not appeal to the prime minister.[23]

The more loyal Mahoney said that although Liberals would have trouble getting support from western farmers, he saw Liberal strength in the western cities. He noted, "People in the urban West are more likely to identify with the problems of other cities than to identify themselves particularly with the agricultural difficulties of Estevan or Willow Bunch. We're conscious of our agricultural background but it isn't our immediate problem anymore." Mahoney said that he had moved to Ottawa after his election so that he did not have to return to Calgary to handle his political fence mending on weekends, which were days most people would rather not see him on business. Instead, he said, he spent two to five days a month in Calgary handling local issues, although he admitted hearing complaints about this from some members of his riding executive.[24]

Not being able to spend enough time back home for an MP to get his message out was a problem for MPs of all stripes who live far from Ottawa, because there were always duties in Ottawa. The problem is compounded when the MP's party's elected representation is so small that he has to convey the message throughout the province, not just his own riding. It is made overwhelming by the number of opposition MPs and a critical provincial government that are constantly on the attack.

Trudeau announced a major cabinet shuffle, moving Edgar Benson from finance to defence, John Turner from justice to finance, Donald Macdonald to energy replacing Joe Greene, and Otto Lang to the justice portfolio (though retaining the Wheat Board responsibility). In Alberta the big news was Pat Mahoney—the only new appointment in the shuffle—becoming minister of state (without portfolio).[25] Bud Olson stayed put in agriculture.[26]

Mahoney was an uncritical team player who seemed to have an unusual capacity for hard work and absorbing detail.[27] The appointment rewarded his plucky service in piloting the tax reform and Canadian Development Corporation bills through the Commons. He defended each bill through tedious clause-by-clause questioning by cranky opposition members, and held his own in detailed discussions on tax policy with top bureaucrats. His handling of these important pieces of legislation earned him respect on both sides of the house.[28] Not surprisingly Mahoney was acclaimed as Liberal candidate for Calgary South, nominated by IPAC president Al Ross. Despite the misgivings of the oilmen toward the Trudeau government, Ross was an old guard Liberal and one of the few leaders in the oil patch who would not abandon the Grits during this election or any other.[29]

Tory MP from Vegreville Don Mazankowski[30] predicted a big backlash in the west against the Liberals because of bilingualism and heavy spending policies. Mazankowski said he believed that western Liberal MPs had difficulty impressing on Trudeau how their voters felt about certain issues. Although he complimented Otto Lang for having tried the hardest to educate Trudeau on western issues, he said that Bud Olson had done the opposite and tried to explain Trudeau to the west.[31]

Manning continued to give the Trudeau government a bad time at most every opportunity. During a Senate debate on whether to extend federal government equalization payments to have-not provinces to bring services in line with the provinces of Ontario, Alberta, and BC, Manning urged federal authorities to listen to criticisms that Quebec, while one of the four richest resource-based provinces, was the only one of the four to receive equalization payments.[32]

Trudeau was attacked by his opponents in ever more graphic terms. Former national news anchor Peter Reilly, running for a Tory nomination in Ottawa, called Trudeau "a political disaster; a snide, smug, arrogant, contemptible liar; a foul-mouthed smirking, mincing, little mountebank who thumbs his nose from the back seat of his limousine."[33]

All of this took its toll. *Maclean's* magazine editor Peter C. Newman forecast that the Liberals would lose at least 10 of the 27 seats they held in the four western provinces and that the Tories were bound to win more than the meagre 17 Ontario seats they won in 1968. Newman also observed that all of this could have a salutary effect by helping to change Trudeau's "arrogant behaviour."[34]

A Gallup poll released on May 2 showed Liberal support at 39 percent, the Tories with 35 percent, the NDP at 19 percent, and others at 7 percent; with 27 percent of the voters undecided. This was a jump of five points for the Tories and a one-point drop for the Liberals since February. The Tories were now at their highest level of support since the June 1968 election and within striking distance.[35] Both Trudeau and the Grits were stumbling. And the election was just around the corner.

27

Chickens, Eggs, and Wheat Deals

JANUARY 1971–JUNE 1972

EVEN THOUGH there were still about 50,000 Alberta farmers working the land, tough times had forced many others to give up and move to the cities and towns. Despite improvements beginning in the last half of 1970, farmers had suffered for a long time and naturally remained angry. Neither were the western cattlemen in a good mood. In their minds the Canadian Wheat Board monopoly over feed grains harmed the beef business because it prevented establishing a price-setting mechanism for feed.[1]

Back in 1970 a prolonged series of disputes began as a result of Quebec's policy of protecting its egg producers against competition from other provinces. Soon other provinces retaliated with Ontario keeping Quebec chickens out of Ontario, Quebec keeping Ontario onions out of Quebec, Nova Scotia and New Brunswick threatening to stop bringing in Quebec chickens, and so forth, with all provinces soon involved in protectionist disputes over agriculture production.[2] This was the "chicken and egg war."

Minister of Agriculture Bud Olson tried to settle the war in the spring of 1971 by introducing a farm-marketing bill that would create marketing boards to distribute farm commodities in an orderly way. However, it was strongly opposed by both the Tories, who believed that it would interfere with the natural flow of products between provinces,[3] and western cattlemen, who wanted cattle and hogs excluded.[4]

The government was drawing heavy flak from the farmers on other issues, too. Proposed amendments to the Prairie Grain Advance Payments Act to replace the current system, prompted Tory MP Don Mazankowski to warn that they would "sink the western farmer into complete oblivion."[5]

The spring also marked the beginning of a prolonged scrap involving the new Grain Stabilization bill, which offered income protection during a farmer's low-income years from a new Grains Stabilization Fund (GSF) funded by contributions from the farmer and the government during good income years. The GSF bill was to replace the old act (Temporary Wheat Reserves Act of 1936), which paid farmers monthly for wheat delivered to board elevators and held in storage unsold. The new GSF bill also provided for a $100 million payment to farmers. Because the government anticipated an early passage of the GSF bill, it stopped monthly payments under the old act in August 1970.

Trouble with the new GSF bill began in early May 1971. The farmers opposed it because the payments were based on the average incomes of the previous five years, a time when farm prices were lower than normal. The other problem was that the government was $60 million in arrears to the farmers under the old act. Opposition MPs accused the government of holding western grain farmers hostage by tying the payment of the $100 million to the GSF bill passage, which they claimed would merely "stabilize poverty" on the Prairies.[6] Ged Baldwin (Tory MP, Peace River) accused the government of carrying out economic genocide against the small farmer, and Robert Thompson (Tory MP, Red Deer) said the bill would stabilize income at a level lower than costs of production.[7]

Summer recess came with the GSF bill still not passed and the farmers still not paid. When Parliament resumed, Baldwin called for the impeachment of Minister of Finance Benson, Minister of Wheat Board Otto Lang, and Minister of Justice John Turner, because of the non-payment.[8] Lang countered that he would gladly go to jail in the cause of the western farmer, and accused the Tory MPs of spreading despair and deceit.[9] The fight continued: Stanley Korchinski (Saskatchewan Tory MP) called Olson "a damn liar and a crook," while Erik Nielsen (Yukon Tory MP) called Trudeau "the most dangerous prime minister in Canada's history."[10]

On October 7, with the GSF bill before the House since April, the government issued an ultimatum: either the opposition abandon the debate by October 12 or the government would drop the bill.[11] The opposition stuck to its guns, the government withdrew the bill, and the arrears under the old act were paid.[12] But instead of the farmers receiving $100 million under a new GSF act, they received only the $60 million under the old act. It appeared as though the farmer had been hosed again. Like the wheat-marketing crisis of 1969/70, the GSF bill donnybrook damaged the Liberals in Prairie cities and towns. Hundreds of thousands of urban dwellers had roots on the farms and still had kinfolk there. Antipathy toward the federal government was bound to spill over into the urban areas.

A by-election in the largely rural Assiniboia riding in Saskatchewan set for November 8 (upon the recent death of the Liberal member) had as its major issue—who was taking care of the farmer? Was it the government? Or was it the opposition? All the federal parties threw what they had into the campaign, scouring every nook and cranny of the riding for votes. The residents of Assiniboia certainly had many farm issues to mull over: marketing boards; the GSF bill; the earlier wheat glut; the LIFT program; the task force on agriculture; and Benson's tax reform legislation (about to raise taxes on the riding's popular co-operatives).

In a tight three-way race, Assiniboia fell to the NDP candidate, Bill Knight, a teacher who at 24 became the youngest MP in the Commons. Less than 3,000 votes separated the top three candidates, with the Grit coming in third and the PC second. Premier Allan Blakeney called Knight's victory a repudiation of the farm policies of Trudeau and Otto Lang and said that the message to Ottawa was "that farmers do not want LIFT, they don't want a poverty stabilization bill and they don't want the task force on agriculture."[13] Senator Richard Stanbury, president of the Liberal Party of Canada, acknowledged that his party had a lot of work to do on the Prairies and speculated that Prairie farmers did not seem to accept the efforts of Lang and Olson.[14]

The farm-marketing bill fight that arose out of the chicken and egg war continued to rage after a brief Christmas break,[15] so the government decided to invoke closure as it had done with tax reform. This prompted an all-party compromise authorizing the creation of a national marketing board for poultry and eggs, and the creation of other national marketing boards for other farm products, provided provincial governments determined that a majority of producers wanted them. Cows and calves were exempted. After twenty-two months of debate and a seventeen-hour all-night sitting, the bill finally passed to the general approval of both farmers and cattlemen.[16]

Pressures on Ottawa over agriculture were now coming from a new direction. Alberta provincial Minister of Agriculture Hugh Horner sent an urgent complaint to Olson, Lang, and federal Minister of Transport Don Jamieson about the rail transportation logjams through BC mountains and on west coast loading docks that were hurting Alberta's agriculture economy.[17] Horner announced intentions to develop a pricing mechanism for feed grains, improve market opportunities and prices for Alberta farmers, and investigate grain transportation issues. Lang countered with plans to speed up transportation: he said his government would rise to the challenge of moving record volumes of grain.[18]

When Olson said that Alberta was ready to sign an agreement on a federal plan to give younger farmers opportunities to increase their farm holdings, and older, poorer farmers the chance to move into other occupations, Hugh Horner quickly responded that any such deal was premature because conditions had not been met, and warned Olson that could "end up killing negotiations."[19] Hugh Horner was becoming as much of a thorn in the government's side as his brother Jack back in Ottawa.

In March Olson unveiled an experimental program called Project 75, designed to simplify the agri-food business for the Canadian producer. The plan called for new technology in food production and better definition of market demand to avoid gluts and shortages. The cattlemen, clearly miffed at the implication that their operations were a fly-by-the-seat-of-your-pants industry, soon complained that Ottawa was meddling in its business.[20]

But relations between the federal government and the farmer were improving. In January 1972 Otto Lang announced a direct federal subsidy to increase the price of top-grade wheat sold in Canada to $3 a bushel, with the export price remaining at $1.95 a bushel. Thus, the Canadian farmers had their practical two-price policy for wheat—something they had long hoped for—and, as a result, an estimated extra $50 million annually in their pockets. Farm organizations reacted favourably.[21]

Lang, while accepting a salesman-of-the-year award in Saskatchewan in March, announced that grain sales were booming and next year's sales looking even better.[22] Lang also announced a huge new wheat sale to China. By the end of the crop year on July 31, Canada would ship a record number of 800 million bushels[23] to foreign countries— nice fat figures to run an election on.

In Winnipeg, Trudeau announced that his government was ready to buy 2,000 new hopper cars—to be manufactured in eastern Canada—to speed up grain deliveries. In the same city and to many of the same people whose ears were still ringing with the words, "Why should I sell your wheat?" Trudeau said, "There should be no doubt we have sold your wheat and we are delivering it."[24] The Liberals' luck with the farmers seemed to be taking a turn for the better at just the right time. But would it be enough?

28

Peter Lougheed Becomes a Star

DECEMBER 1971–JULY 1972

LOUGHEED BEGAN TO SPEAK MORE on national issues. At the Canadian Press annual dinner in Toronto, he called on the provinces and the federal government to develop an industrial strategy promoting potential growth areas and made a pitch for retaining the monarchy, which he said "plays a very vital and important role and gets us above the battle of political warfare."[1] He also joined the debate on the constitution, declaring that his government was no longer committed to the Victoria Charter,[2] which had almost been adopted but for Quebec's rejection the year before. Given that his objectives were to diversify the province's economy, balance growth between metro and rural areas, and create job opportunities for young people, he said those goals all required new constitutional relationships, specifically regarding government revenue sources and spending jurisdictions.[3]

Lougheed opened up another major natural gas issue when he told a farmers' convention that since prices for Alberta gas were too low, his government would now do everything it could to raise them. He noted that a price increase of one cent per thousand cubic feet (MCF)[4] of gas would mean $3 million to the provincial treasury.[5] To great acclaim from the oilmen,[6] he ordered the Alberta Energy Resources Conservation Board (ERCB) to hold a special hearing to review natural gas prices.[7]

Held in June 1972, the hearing's most important submission was a massive report commissioned by the CPA and IPAC and prepared by the Stanford Research Institute of California. The report concluded that a realistic market price for Alberta gas was at least 20 cents per MCF above prices then being paid to producers.[8] An expert witness predicted that new technologies and changing lifestyles would cause world energy demand to level off around 1990 because of declining population growth rates and "quality of life" factors such as switching from the use of cars to mass transit. He also forecast that it was possible that the world could reach zero economic growth and energy demand growth by the end of the century.[9]

Lougheed's next bright idea came in midsummer with his government's formation of Pan Alberta Gas (a wholly owned subsidiary of Alberta Gas Trunk Line Company) as the export marketing agency. It was to buy surplus gas from Alberta gas producers and then apply to the NEB to export it. Pan Alberta would pay double the price TransCanada Pipelines was paying to producers on behalf of its eastern Canadian customers.[10]

The National Petroleum Show opened in May 1972 in Calgary with Alberta Minister of Mines and Minerals Bill Dickie declaring 1971 a banner year for the oil and gas industry: Alberta was now the number one producer of minerals in Canada; its exports of oil and gas liquids to the US were up 13 percent over 1970; its natural gas sales were up by 11 percent with 45 percent of that production being exported to the US; its oil and gas had assured markets for many years into the future; and 370 billion barrels of recoverable reserves were still buried in the oil sands.[11]

But these rosy statistics did not tell the whole story. Drilling activity and oil reserves in Alberta were down dramatically due to disappointing exploration results, the lack of a big new Alberta oil play, and the diversion of exploration funds from Alberta to better opportunities elsewhere.[12] Many were concerned that this was the beginning of a long downward slide.[13]

As a result Peter Lougheed proposed a new tax on proven oil reserves that would raise about $70 million a year, which would be used to provide drilling incentives to attract exploration back to Alberta from other regions and help finance increased industrial activity in the province.[14] Public hearings on the new tax were held in Edmonton before all members of the legislature. Although the oilmen opposed the new tax, the government remained unmoved.[15]

This oil reserves tax was to go into effect January 1, 1973, and be in place for five years. Companies were given the option of entering into new royalty agreements, which raised provincial royalties from 16 to 21 percent, or alternatively pay the new tax until the existing royalty agreements expired, at which time they would enter into new and higher royalty agreements. The package also contained drilling incentives for new exploratory wells including a five-year royalty exemption and tax credits. Most companies took the new tax and royalty structure in stride, happy with the drilling incentives.[16]

The federal Income Tax Act allowed oil companies to deduct royalties paid to the province as a business expense. Ottawa now had to decide if it would allow Lougheed's higher royalties to be treated in the same way. This was the first Ottawa–Alberta tussle over the spoils of increased revenues in the era of rising oil prices. Ottawa decided to consider the tax-like provincial royalties as an eligible expense for purposes of calculating corporate income tax, expecting to lose $20 million a year in tax revenue.[17]

Lougheed activism again emerged during a major controversy involving Banff National Park. The federal government had invited proposals from investors to rejuvenate an area located at the intersection of the road to Lake Louise and the Trans-Canada Highway. The only proposal came from a consortium headed by Imperial Oil to establish a 3,500-bed recreational village and tourist facilities to accommodate 8,000 visitors and staff.[18] At that time Lake Louise had only about 200 full-time residents.

A public hearing on the proposal opened in Calgary in March 1972 to an overflowing crowd of 800 including dozens of newsmen from all over

Canada. As expected, the hearing was a battle between two fiercely opposed groups—one dominated by environmentalists determined to resist commercial expansion in the parks, and the other dominated by businesses and winter sports enthusiasts who wanted bigger and better resorts in the park.[19] Opponents were given only ten minutes each to speak against the 103-page brief; its promoters were not even present. Alberta Liberal leader Bob Russell called the hearing an "attempt to muzzle opposition,"[20] while Rod Sykes called it a "kangaroo court."[21]

In May the Lougheed government set out its position on the Lake Louise plan in a letter from Minister of Intergovernmental Affairs Don Getty to Minister of Northern Development Jean Chretien. It criticized the federal government for not consulting the province, but specified that before the province could support the project, there had to be an environmental impact study of the area, park zoning guidelines, and assurances that the project would provide new facilities for Canadian families of all income levels. He concluded on a positive note saying, "Painful progress of Village Lake Louise Limited has provided certain positive lessons and a base from which we can develop the best possible national parks policies for Alberta and Canada." It was a politically smart and effective contribution to the debate that zeroed in on real concerns and offered a workable process to resolve the issues raised by the project.[22]

Not yet one year in office, Peter Lougheed had already established himself as an imaginative leader, one of the federal government's most articulate critics, and a major political force in the country. His government's first session ended after a record three months while it guided popular legislation into the statute books over the objections of a weak and disorganized Social Credit opposition. Among the government's accomplishments were major energy initiatives, new benefits for seniors, and a provincial bill of rights. There was also now live radio and television coverage in the legislature and for the first time in the province's history, an official Hansard.[23]

Trudeau federal Liberals were facing a formidable opponent in Alberta. Lougheed had a clear road map of what he intended to accomplish and was not shy of confrontation. Furthermore, he had a team that shared his foresight, intellectual depth, and energy. Compared to the Lougheed government, the Social Credit administrations of Manning and Strom had been amateurish rivals. And the federal election was on the horizon.

On July 6 Premier Lougheed officially opened the Diamond Jubilee edition of the Calgary Stampede, recalling his time working on the grounds as a youngster: "I'm very pleased to be back home." Pat Mahoney and Mayor Sykes were also on hand for the official opening, but it was Lougheed's show. No longer a rising star, he was the star.[24]

29

The Eve of the Federal Election

APRIL—AUGUST 1972

IN EARLY 1972 much public attention focused on the northern pipeline—with its promise of oil and gas bounty for the economy, the oilmen, and government coffers. The Canadian government preferred a pipeline from the giant oil field in Alaska's Prudhoe Bay to proceed east into northern Canada and then south down the Mackenzie River Valley through Canada into the United States. The US favoured a pipeline out of Prudhoe Bay that did not enter Canada but went south to the Alaskan port of Valdez where the oil could be shipped via tanker to the US. Environmentalists were on the side of the Canadian proposal because of the fear of oil spills and other environmental disruption along the sensitive trans-Alaskan route both over land and sea. To the disappointment of the environmentalists and Canada, the US opted for the trans-Alaska route.[1]

Several major Canadian companies then combined forces to apply to Ottawa to build a gas pipeline along an all-Canadian route down the Mackenzie River Valley from the Arctic at a cost of between three and five billion dollars—up to then one of the most expensive projects ever undertaken by the private sector.[2]

Interest in oil sands development was also gathering steam. Several multinational oil companies were working on oil sands projects in various stages of planning, research, and development near Fort McMurray and Cold Lake. Syncrude Canada had received approval to produce 125,000 barrels a day and Great Canadian Oil Sands (since 1967 the only commercial producer) planned to increase its output.[3]

As the federal election approached, the oilmen were doing pretty well despite bumps along the road. By May 1972 the quota stood at 570,000 barrels a day—more than a twofold increase since 1967—with more increases expected.[4] Total Alberta oil production was now well over 50 percent more than in 1968, and as a result of the actions of OPEC prices were now—for the first time in almost twenty-five years—on the rise.

But public support for more Canadian control of the economy was also on the rise and the Trudeau government was listening. Minister of Revenue Herb Gray[5] presented to Parliament a draft bill proposing a new policy on foreign takeovers, necessary he said because foreign control of several industries had reached a point that further foreign acquisitions should concern both government and citizens.[6] Where foreign companies sought to take over an existing Canadian corporation with assets valued at more than $250,000 or having gross revenues exceeding $3 million, a proposed foreign buyer would have to demonstrate how the transaction would benefit Canada and among the criteria to be considered would be: the transaction's effect on Canadian economic activity, employment, and productivity; the degree of participation by Canadians in the resulting entity; and the compatibility of the acquisition with Canadian policies. The minister of industry, trade and commerce would recommend approval or non-approval to the cabinet.[7]

Businessmen quickly voiced concerns about more bureaucracy, excessive ministerial discretionary power, and the possibility that the policy could lead to the harassment of foreign investors and the intervention of lobbyists.[8] The NDP argued that the legislation did not go far enough, and the Tories argued that it did nothing to promote Canadian participation in Canadian business. NDP leader David Lewis said the report was like "using a popgun to hunt big game"[9] while Gray's ex-cabinet colleague Eric Kierans said it did not come to grips with the problem of "the magnitude of foreign ownership."[10] Oil industry spokesmen said that a lengthy approval process would discourage foreign and Canadian investment in the oil industry.[11]

Gray's bill received a nod of approval from Medicine Hat–born J.K. Jamieson, the chairman of Standard Oil Co. New Jersey (now Exxon), who said "that international business and positive nationalism can work together."[12] But the deputy general manager of the Bank of Nova Scotia thought otherwise, saying that it would not be a mild piece of legislation because it applied even to small companies: "In these days of inflation this would apply to a medium size car dealer."[13]

The maverick Liberal candidate in Edmonton West, Mel Hurtig, now co-chairman of the Committee for an Independent Canada, thought the bill too weak and attacked it at every opportunity. The issue of whether there should be more or less foreign ownership divided even Albertans, forcing Alberta Tories to scrutinize public reaction to Gray's proposals.[14]

In April, with the election now imminent, the Liberals seemed to be full of confidence. After columnist Charles Lynch attended a meeting of the western Liberal caucus, he reported that the Liberals believed they could now win more Prairie seats than in 1968 because of the big increases in grain exports, the popular new two-price system for wheat, and the farmers' new appreciation for the hard-working Otto Lang. Lynch marvelled at the nineteen trains of a hundred grain-filled box cars arriving in Thunder Bay every day and the eight grain-filled trains arriving in Vancouver daily, all carrying exports and putting plenty of new money into farmers' pockets.[15]

Also good for the Grits was John Turner's first budget, introduced in May. It provided tax cuts benefitting 2.7 million Canadians—roughly 10 percent of the population, tax incentives and cuts for business, tax cuts and pension increases for old age pensioners and veterans, and financial help for students. The budget could provide an excellent centrepiece to an election campaign.[16]

Although unemployment had dropped by 50,000 from March–April 1972, it remained a serious headache for the government. When Trudeau took office in June 1968 the unemployment rate was 5.1 percent with 395,000 Canadians out of work; in April 1972 the unemployment rate was 6.8 percent with 592,000 Canadians unemployed.[17]

Alberta's future was looking bright though: major pulp mills were being built and sawmills churning out the lumber; a new petrochemical industry was starting up; the $300 million tourism industry was growing rapidly; the construction industry was booming; agriculture was once again on its feet;[18] oil and gas production and exports were growing, and the development of the oil sands was about to take off.[19]

A late-April visit to test the affections of Alberta voters began for Trudeau in the town of Edson (in Sulatycky's riding of Rocky Mountain) in a gymnasium stuffed with an overflow crowd of more than 1,200 people. At the rally, the high school students' union president, speaking in both French and English, challenged Trudeau's recent statement that he could not interfere with a recent RCMP decision to change the lettering on its police cars from the traditional RCMP insignia to the simple POLICE. The student said that this seemed to be another concession to Quebec and would generate further hostility in western Canada. To everyone's surprise, Trudeau replied that since his government had discovered that western Canadians disliked the new signage, it would now halt the change. The audience roared its approval. He further explained that it had never been the government's intention to downgrade the reputation enjoyed by the RCMP; the only reason was to make the service more quickly identifiable.[20]

But that was the extent of Trudeau's pandering to the locals. He then went on to say that Ottawa had listened to the west about the RCMP signs, and now, the west would listen to him. He said, "You talk about Western alienation now because you say you are not loved in Ottawa. At least, we don't love you in your own language." He pointed out that seven out of ten Quebecers did not speak English and that there were simply not enough French Canadians in Ottawa to accommodate those from Quebec who spoke only French. Therefore, he said, "we're going to make the damn place bilingual."[21] He received a sustained and vigorous standing ovation.

The next day Trudeau moved on to Edmonton. At the Northern Alberta Jubilee Auditorium, he spoke to 3,000 high school students for an hour and a half and received a brief opposing the controversial Village Lake Louise redevelopment proposal. He responded to many questions on a host of issues including the sale of napalm to the US, foreign aid, and water policy. He again received loud and sustained applause.[22]

Later in the day he addressed another friendly crowd of about 3,000 in an arena where he spoke proudly of the legacy of the RCMP and announced the proposed construction of an all-weather highway stretching from the Alberta border to the Arctic Ocean, as a commitment to Alberta and the north. A further 2,000 people waited for more than two hours outside the arena hoping to meet him. As he left there were shouts of "Vive Trudeau" and Albertans singing "For He's a Jolly Good Fellow" in French. Southam News reporter Nick Hills wrote that the weather and the crowds had been perfect: "Sometimes, Pierre Trudeau still has the luck to have all the elements working for him; and when the luck and the political planning merge together, as they did here, he's unbeatable again. And in the West, that's really spooky."[23]

On July 7 Parliament finally shut down for a twelve-week summer break during which it was certain that an election would be called. Trudeau's first parliament—the twenty-eighth in Canadian history—had lasted longer than any since World War II.[24]

In mid-July Trudeau made a pitch for the hockey fans' votes by appealing to the NHL and Hockey Canada to allow the popular superstar Bobby "the Golden Jet" Hull to play in the Canada–Russia series that fall.[25] Hull had been blacklisted by the NHL brass because he'd been instrumental is starting up the rival World Hockey Association. In his telegram Trudeau urged the organizations "to keep the best interests of Canada in mind and to make sure that they are fully respected and served." Despite Trudeau's plea, the NHL did not allow Hull to play.[26]

The Trudeaus and their seven-month-old son Justin—marking his first visit to Alberta—stopped over in Calgary July 22 on their holiday west by train. Although the visit was brief and low-key, an attractive family photograph taken during the stopover occupied a quarter-page on the front page of the *Calgary Herald*—worth thousands of free political advertising.[27]

Mahoney, gearing up for the fight of his life, was now spending more time back home. Addressing a national Elks convention in July, he declared that national unity was no longer "hot politics," because the people had determined that the country would stay united after Trudeau's strong response to the October Crisis. As an example of some other Alberta attitudes of the day, Don Hartman, a usually affable and high profile, long-time city alderman and Tory (and mayor for a short time in 1989) told an Elks convention that "minority groups are trying to destroy what generations of us put together." He said club members should "try to salvage society. That's why I am in politics as an Elk."[28] His words sound impolitic today, but the sentiment behind those words ran strong in Alberta in those days.

In mid-August the Liberals released the fact sheets upon which their candidates could rely as they campaigned. Presented to put the government in the best possible light, they disclosed that since 1968 disposable income increased by $815 for every man, woman, and child in the country, industrial production had risen by 17.8 percent, manufacturing production had risen by 13.9 percent, and retail sales had risen by 25.6 percent. They also disclosed that exports were now at world records, Canada's job creation rate was one of the highest in the industrialized world, and that the GNP had grown by 20.4 percent.[29]

On the eve of the election call, opinion around the province ranged from bad[30] to good. A telephone survey conducted by the *Albertan* in Calgary ridings (excluding Palliser) looked pretty good for the Liberals. In Calgary South the poll gave Mahoney a ten-point lead over Bawden, and Liberal Nick Taylor ahead of his Tory opponent by twelve points in Calgary Centre.[31]

A real scrap was shaping up in Rocky Mountain. Due to the riding's size, Tory organizers held balloting meetings in ten different towns on different nights so that as many people as possible could vote. This cumbersome process created considerable acrimony among party members and magnified leftover hostility from the 1968 battle for the Tory nomination. Now in

1972 the same two Tories were at it again, this time battling for the nomination along with Joe Clark.[32] At one of the balloting meetings even Clark's mother, Grace, got into a spat about voting eligibility of some latecomers.[33] When all of the votes were counted, Joe Clark was selected to do battle against Sulatycky, and unlike 1968 he would not be splitting the vote with any other Tories on the ballot.[34]

On August 30 enough British Columbia voters turned against W.A.C. Bennett and his Social Credit party to give a majority government to the NDP headed by Dave Barrett. The end of Bennett's twenty-year reign brought the number of provincial government changes in the past four years to eight—British Columbia, Alberta, Saskatchewan, Manitoba, Quebec, Newfoundland, New Brunswick, and Nova Scotia. All these changes brought many new faces to provincial premierships and left Trudeau—at the ripe old age of 52—the oldest government party leader in Canada.

30

"The Land is Strong?"

SEPTEMBER–OCTOBER 1972

ON FRIDAY, SEPTEMBER 1, Trudeau called the general election for October 30. He saw the major issue was to ensure Canada remain united with room for the two major linguistic communities. Stanfield said that his party's task was to convince Canadians that the Tories could bring direction, openness, and competence to the administration of national affairs.[1]

In Alberta, the major obstacles to Liberal success were the oilmen, who still felt betrayed and abandoned by the Trudeau government over oil and gas export policy, foreign investment, and government incompetence. Furthermore, the popular Peter Lougheed, now undisputed champion of Alberta causes and a potent critic of many federal policies, was committed to helping the federal Tories. The issues of unemployment, inflation, farm policy, taxation, bilingualism, and Trudeau's apparent arrogance were further impediments to Grit gains.[2]

Alberta Liberal candidates had a big job ahead of them. The two sitting Liberal ministers—Olson and Mahoney—were in particularly tight spots, both having won their 1968 elections by narrow margins. Olson's tenure in Agriculture was fraught with problems and Mahoney was up against stiff competition in oilman Peter Bawden. Allen Sulatycky was now pitted against a unified Tory party in Rocky Mountain supporting a young energetic Joe Clark. Hu Harries' decision to opt out of the parliamentary process because of his bruised ego had weakened his candidacy in Edmonton–Strathcona.[3]

Many Alberta Liberal candidates would be worthy names on any ballot. The incumbents now had loads of experience, and in Mahoney's case, success in business, with an outstanding record as a parliamentary workhorse and team player. In Calgary Centre Nick Taylor was a successful oilman, had a large well-organized campaign team, and had come close to winning in 1968. In Edmonton Centre, energetic young lawyer Branny Schepanovich would contest for the Grits, who had narrowly lost the riding in 1968 because of vengeful ex-mayor Hawrelak. In Edmonton West Mel Hurtig, who in four years had shifted from drum-beating Trudeauphile party activist, to exuberant critic of the Alberta Liberal establishment to passionate economic nationalist, was bringing in droves of volunteer supporters. Although Harries had thus far botched his chance to make his mark as a Liberal MP for Edmonton–Strathcona, he was still an excellent communicator, an accomplished businessman, and an academic well versed on all economic issues. Veteran Liberal activist and city alderman Una Maclean Evans had the political experience to put up a good fight in Edmonton East. In Lethbridge the Liberals had famous author, guide, and naturalist Andy Russell as their candidate.[4]

Trudeau was expected to opt for a more low-key campaign than the 1968 Trudeaumania extravaganza. Instead of the charismatic swinger who drove sports cars, jackknifed off diving boards, and charmed women, this time Canadians would see him as a cerebral and serious, hard-working family man.[5] Stanfield was expected to concentrate on the twin issues unemployment and inflation, while David Lewis was expected to continue with his already successful "corporate welfare rip-off" attacks on the business establishment and their Liberal and Conservative cronies. Real Caouette, leader of a Social Credit rump confined to Quebec, was expected to dig deep into old Social Credit dogma and campaign on bread and butter economic issues.[6]

Trudeau told a reporter that "this time, they will listen to what I'm saying rather than be caught up in a kind of euphoria." He said the campaign would be "a catharsis, as a bath of fire in which you're purified," and "an indispensable exercise" required "because of the great centrifugal forces at work in modern societies."[7] Canadians had seldom, if ever, heard such highfalutin political discourse on the campaign trail. How would they relate to it? Would they understand it? Apparently Trudeau and his campaign strategists believed they would.

During the first week of the campaign the Liberals released a recording of their slow blues campaign song. The words of the first verse were

Take care, take time
The land is strong
With slow and careful love
The land stays young and free.[8]

Charles Lynch wrote, "This sounds like a song addressed to aging lovers, most of whom have no option but to take time, and to take it slow."[9] Together with the slogan "The Land is Strong," the song played on television ads over dramatic shots of the Canadian hinterland.

Trudeau's campaign literature had him conservatively attired, his hippie-like locks of hair shorn; he was described as "a pragmatic idealist" and "a believer in the kind of freedom that comes from a sense of balance and proportion." To some Liberal candidates in Toronto he said, "We're trying, in this period of two months, to meet intensively with the Canadian people all across the land…to discuss Canada with them…to see the future as they see it, as we believe it to be, according to our goals, according to a set of priorities which correspond to the feeling of the Canadian people."[10]

Would this cerebral droning lead Canadians to vote Liberal? On September 15 in Granby, Quebec, only 500 souls showed up for a Trudeau rally in an arena that could have held 4,000. Everybody, including the prime minister, reportedly lacked enthusiasm.[11] Trudeau's organizers had also violated one of the most hallowed rules of party politics: always rent a small hall for a big crowd because empty seats equals bad press and depressed party workers.

As Trudeau's bizarre campaign crawled forward, the Grits were once again greeted with bad unemployment numbers. August unemployment was up again to 6.7 percent compared to 6.3 percent for July.[12] Trudeau fought back, saying that the Canadian economy was regarded as one of the best managed in the world and that Canadians were earning, spending, and saving more than at any time in our history.[13] He also argued that the problem was not that Canadians were losing their jobs, but rather that many young Canadians new to the workforce could not find jobs. Statistics Canada confirmed this view. Of the 500,000 Canadians unemployed, more than half were between the ages of 14 and 24. The labour force had been growing at an annual rate of 3.1 percent, while new jobs at only 2.4 percent.[14] The Liberals' solution, Trudeau said, was in Turner's budget that would provide jobs. Besides, he argued, with the economy booming, many of the unemployed were being too choosy, collecting unemployment benefits while waiting for the right job. When attacked by Stanfield and Lewis for being callous toward the job seekers, he contended he was just telling the truth.[15]

The Conservatives demanded more income tax cuts for business so it would have sufficient funds to create new jobs. They also promised infrastructure projects such as new roads and bridges and to repeal the tax on building materials to help the construction industry employ more Canadians. The NDP wanted more money in the hands of consumers so they could buy more goods, which would create more jobs. It also called for personal income tax cuts, reduced interest rates, and investment into socially useful projects like housing and municipal public works.[16]

Tory leader Stanfield seemed to be doing pretty well in the early stages of the campaign. He had developed an engaging self-deprecating wit, and with both the media and the Canadian people showing some respect for him, the mood in his camp was upbeat.[17] Three weeks into the campaign with Ontario Premier Bill Davis by his side, Stanfield demanded an accounting of the unemployment insurance program costs because the public had not been informed.[18] Stanfield also hammered Trudeau for trying to reduce the concept of work to something that he said Trudeau would understand, "another four letter word." Stanfield's attacks were drawing blood.[19]

NDP leader David Lewis' assault on the "corporate welfare bums" was the most effective of all, even causing some CEOs of Canada's largest corporations to defend themselves publicly. Lewis shrewdly expanded his attack to corporate deferred taxes that effectively gave large corporations permanent interest-free loans at the expense of the average Canadian taxpayer.[20] Unlike Trudeau, Rhodes scholar Lewis was not trying to engage the public in any intellectual discourse; he was feeding people red-meat progressive politics and scoring points. At the University of Alberta he said that foreign ownership was a dead issue because Canadians were "terrified of what might happen to their jobs or standard of living should Canada regain control of its economy." Lewis also accused oil companies of exploiting Canada's natural resources while thinking only of profits rather than Canada's future,[21] and warned that the northern pipeline required massive foreign investment that would inflate the Canadian dollar and make Canada's manufactured products more expensive and thus lead to more unemployment.[22]

My Liberal riding association of Calgary North brought out the minister of transport, Newfoundland MP Don Jamieson, to speak at the last Liberal nomination before the election. Our candidate was Roland Lambert, a serious-minded psychology professor at the University of Calgary who had asked me to run his campaign. Like a lot of Liberal politicians running for the first time in Alberta, Lambert would find the experience a rough one. With Joe Greene in the Senate, Jamieson was now the undisputed Liberal oratorical champ, a title that he kept until he left the government in 1979.[23] Speaking to about 400 Liberals, he predicted Trudeau would be re-elected, pooh-poohed western alienation, and accused the Tories of asking westerners to put all of their eggs in one basket—"eggs that are getting old and starting to stink."[24] He also presented the city with a serious election goodie when he confirmed April 1973 as the start of the long-awaited new Calgary airport.[25]

With six weeks to go, the Tories nominated Canadian Cattlemen's Association president Bert Hargrave to oppose Bud Olson in Medicine Hat. Hargrave had nominated and voted for Olson in 1968 but since that time he and the cattlemen—who had never warmed up to the Liberal Party—had become miffed with many federal agriculture policies.[26]

Olson hoped to reel in Social Credit votes he had captured from 1957 to 1965 as a Socred MP. Since 1970, he and most of the Alberta federal Liberal caucus had tried to divert Liberal support to Social Credit. But Olson had only squeaked by in the 1968 election and since then had a rough four years as minister of agriculture. He was now taking a beating on the campaign trail over various farm issues. The Tories capitalized on his plight, describing farmers in their campaign materials as "the forgotten one-quarter" in an "increasingly desperate and shameful situation."[27]

When Trudeau and his entourage arrived at the Calgary airport September 26 after campaigning in Lethbridge and Medicine Hat,[28] Stan Cichon, a Saskatchewan-bred Liberal, and I were assigned the task of driving some of Trudeau's staff (Mahoney, Olson, their assistants and campaign staffers). At the Palliser Hotel the entourage disembarked (without the prime minister) for an early dinner and we accompanied them to their fancy suite, where the Ottawa notables took seats at the buffet table. Cichon and I sat next to each other on two chairs near the entrance, left to gaze upon the feast while watching and listening to the insiders guffawing at the day's events.[29]

At the Stampede Corral hockey arena—the site of his disastrous speech in April 1969 that so alienated the oilmen—Trudeau was greeted by an enthusiastic crowd of about 6,000 and parried easy questions posed by four local reporters in a "hot seat" forum format. After a half-hour or so, the public was given its chance, lining up twelve deep at the microphones to ask questions on a wide range of subjects and applauding every answer. Trudeau promised that taxpayers would not be carrying people who did not want to work, voiced his opposition to capital punishment and the legalization of

(L to R) Mel Hurtig, Allen Sulatycky, Pat Mahoney, John Borger, Trudeau, and Una Maclean Evans at a campaign event in 1972. [Courtesy of Allen Sulatycky]

marijuana, and suggested that Canadians should learn to have more respect for their bodies.

Since the event was the biggest Calgary turnout in memory for a political rally and no hecklers or protesters challenged him, organizers were happy. The press called the session "the biggest bore of the election campaign thus far"[30] and observed that the "once-potent Trudeaumania" was conspicuously absent. A singing group drew the only sustained applause when the crowd clapped to the rhythm of "Those Were the Days." One reporter commented, "But clearly those days are gone, if the Liberals were still counting on Pierre's patented 'charisma' to win any votes here."[31]

Meanwhile, David Lewis stepped up his attack on the proposed northern pipeline project, calling it "madness," because its multi-billion dollar cost would lead to the control by the US interests.[32] But during a campaign stopover in Calgary, Minister of Energy Donald Macdonald said the project would proceed and Canada would be in full control. Macdonald also kiboshed one of Lougheed's persistent demands by saying that Alberta would have no place at the table during any international energy negotiations because only the federal government could speak for all of Canada.[33]

The claim that unemployment insurance was too generous and too easy to obtain was gaining traction, along with the idea that hard-working taxpayers were financing benefits for "lazy" Canadians. The problem for the government was made worse by how unemployment benefits were funded. The June 1971 plan that increased benefits was financed by employer and employee contributions only up to an unemployment level of 4 percent. Any deficit was to be covered by the government's general revenues, which were now gushing into the fund.[34] Before a standing-room-only crowd of 3,000 at Edmonton's Jubilee Auditorium, Stanfield gave a half-hour speech (during which he was interrupted with applause thirty-six times) attacking the Trudeau government for its handling of both unemployment and the unemployment insurance fund that now had a deficit of $544 million.[35] Canadians soon learned that the unemployment insurance deficit for the year would be $800 million.[36]

With less than three weeks to go in the campaign, Statistics Canada figures showed the unemployment rate at 7.1 percent—the highest since September 1960 and the second highest in 20 years. Total numbers of unemployed stood at 459,000, or 25,000 higher than one year earlier. Trudeau promised more policies to deal with the problem while continuing to remind voters that Canada had a better record in job creation than any other industrial society.[37] In Alberta the economy was so strong in September 1972 that the unemployment rate was a paltry 3.3 percent.[38]

Inflation also remained a damaging issue for the government. By October the consumer price index had reached a new record of 141.8.[39] The rise in consumer prices between September 1971 and September 1972 was 5.3 percent—the largest gain for any one-year period in recent years. The food index had risen nearly 10 percent over the level of the previous year.[40]

On the energy front, ERCB statistics released in early October showed Alberta crude oil production booming, at about 1,255,000 barrels a day.

Total crude oil exports to the US in the first half of 1972 were 13.4 percent over the same period of 1971. Exports to the US still subject to quotas in the all-important market east of the Rockies now stood at 645,000 barrels a day. Since 1968, Canadian crude oil exports to the US quota zone had increased 230 percent (from 256,000 to 645,000 barrels a day).[41]

In Oakville, Ontario, with three weeks to go, Trudeau temporarily trashed his dull "The Land is Strong" pitch by calling his Tory and NDP critics "reactionaries," "poor-mouthers and bellyachers." Facing chants of "unemployment, unemployment," he grabbed the microphone with one hand and began stabbing his finger with the other, telling the unruly crowd that Canada was "the best country in the world," where "there are more new cars, more television sets, more refrigerators, more people who are traveling abroad, more leisure. You even see people who are lobbying for the 30-hour week."[42]

The NDP published a 118-page, fact-filled campaign paperback written by Lewis entitled *Louder Voices—The Corporate Welfare Bums*, which listed 115 major companies that Lewis said took more than their share of government money and power. The introduction was written by former Trudeau minister Eric Kierans, who accused Trudeau and Turner of misleading the public by saying their tax reform legislation had plugged many corporate tax loopholes. The companies Lewis fingered included many large oil and gas companies doing big business in Alberta—Imperial Oil, Shell Canada, and Alberta Gas Trunk Line Co, among them.[43]

Grit candidate Mel Hurtig continued beating the economic nationalism drum and heaping criticism on his own party, saying that Trudeau cabinets had been composed of old-fashioned politicians who did not have the vision necessary to maintain an independent Canada. Hurtig also promoted Canadian ownership of the Mackenzie Valley pipeline and the establishment of a western Canadian bank. His rebelliousness even prompted him to reject a campaign contribution from the Liberal Party itself because it did not disclose the source of the funds. Despite bashing his own Liberals with nearly as much vigour as he bashed the Tories, Hurtig's campaign was one of the best the Liberals had going in Alberta.

He had plenty of support from high school and university students in a riding where nearly half of the voters were on the voting rolls for the first time.[44]

The essence of Trudeau's "The Land is Strong" campaign was released in the latter part of the campaign in the form of a ten-page brief entitled "Together...The Land is Strong." Of importance to Alberta were pledges to reintroduce foreign takeover legislation, protect Canadian sovereignty, and improve federal–provincial relations. Other promises included new oceans and environmental policies, and new programs to protect farm incomes and to promote national sports and fitness. The document contained little detail and was broadly criticized as vague and too general.[45]

Many Liberals had come to believe that Trudeau was now hurting their campaign's cause. Mahoney's campaign strategists had little mention of Trudeau on their handout materials, and no mention in newspaper ads. Mahoney's opponent Peter Bawden was calling Trudeau a "fading playboy" while rapping him for "arrogance and obscene language" and not being "the type of man our children could admire."[46]

Stanfield called Trudeau's statements about a thriving Canadian economy lies, and said that four years of his government all added up to "four lost years in the course of nationhood." Charles Lynch wrote that Stanfield now had "a snap in his voice and a gleam in his eye" as he went on the attack. He also noted the "expert assistance" Stanfield was getting from Premier Bill Davis, who was now spending much time with him on the hustings.[47]

Lewis said that recent unemployment and inflation statistics showed that Trudeau was in trouble. He did acknowledge, however, that Trudeau's record on giving aid to Quebec and his efforts to promote the French language would allow the Liberals to stay in power after the election.[48] Lewis also received the endorsement of Eric Kierans, who in an open letter to Trudeau said that he remained a Liberal but had to vote for the NDP because he agreed with its stand against the government's economic policies. Kierans' living in Trudeau's riding of Mount Royal was icing on the cake for Lewis, who said that the NDP now had a realistic chance of forming the official opposition.[49]

But the news was not all bad for the Grits. Gallup poll results released in mid-October put the Liberals at 44 percent—just 2 points less than their support in 1968, with the Tories at 31 percent while the NDP had 21 percent; 11 percent of the voters were undecided.[50] And the Bank of Nova Scotia predicted that economic growth in Canada for 1972 would be higher than any time since the boom period of the mid-1960s, and that the GNP would surge by 10.5 percent—out of which 6.5 percent would be attributed to real growth in the economy.[51]

In Edmonton on a western swing on October 13, Trudeau urged Canadians to stay in shape like him to bring down health care costs. Asked about having Mel Hurtig in his caucus, he said Hurtig's Committee for an Independent Canada was "a good pressure group," but its "one-track minds" measured Canadian independence in merely economic terms. He said that Hurtig was "sometimes a thorn in my flesh" with "wilder statements" he didn't agree with, but guaranteed he would still listen to him in caucus.[52]

Public interest waned in the Mahoney–Bawden contest; attendances at forums dropped off dramatically. Bawden's attendance at these events also tapered off because he believed that his time was better spent meeting people at the doors.[53] The issue that seemed to attract the most interest and support from the people who attended the candidates' forums and parties was the reintroduction of capital punishment.[54] Charles Kelly, Mahoney's executive assistant, said this both astonished and disturbed him: "It was almost like a death cult. I can't tell you how many coffee parties I attended in upper middle class neighbourhoods in Calgary South and all they wanted to talk about was hanging! Go figure!" Although Mahoney had hundreds of volunteers doing the grunt work of door-to-door campaigning and Bawden was no match for Mahoney as a speechmaker, Bawden had one of the strongest constituency organizations and according to some of his works, had shaken hands with an estimated 15,000 people in the riding. Many of his workers wore cowboy hats and western vests on the campaign trail and frequently hauled out Peter Bawden Drilling's sponsored chuckwagon that had won five world championships in the Calgary Stampede.[55]

Lougheed's ministers and grassroots organizations throughout the province were working tirelessly for the Stanfield cause, although Lougheed personally—unlike Ontario Premier Bill Davis—had hardly participated.[56] But with less than nine days to go, Lougheed joined the campaign with a round of visits to Calgary and Edmonton Tory candidate headquarters accompanied by a five-car cavalcade, an oompah band, and plenty of press.[57]

Stanfield made his last major appearance in front of 4,000 placard-waving supporters in Calgary October 22 at the Jubilee Auditorium. Nine bands including a ninety-piece brass marching band welcomed Stanfield, premiers Peter Lougheed, Bill Davis, and Richard Hatfield, and eight southern Alberta Tory candidates. In his forty-minute address Stanfield accused the federal government of failing to develop Canada's resources, industry, and agriculture, and his solution was to coordinate policies between Ottawa and the provinces and abandon "the arbitrary imposition of policy," practiced by the Liberals. He assailed the government record on unemployment and spoke of his own platform—indexed federal pensions, tax cuts, temporary wage and price controls if required, and help to small business.[58]

With a week to go in the campaign, both Lewis and Trudeau made stops in Calgary—with Lewis generating by far the biggest crowd. Introduced by Alberta NDP leader Grant Notley to a wildly cheering crowd of 2,500 at the Calgary Kinsmen Centre, Lewis paid no deference to the powerful local oilmen. He said that Calgary had more "corporate welfare bums" than any other city in Canada and that the oil industry was teeming with "the princes of the corporate system" who had long exploited tax loopholes and subsidies all at the expense of the taxpayer. He named Gulf Oil Canada, Petrofina Canada, and TransCanada Pipelines as examples of corporations "living high off the hog" because of the unfair Canadian tax system created by both the Liberal and the PC parties. Lewis also defended the farmer about rising food prices, blaming food processors and chain supermarkets for the lion's share of the price increases.[59]

Trudeau's last Calgary appearances involved a province-wide question-and-answer telethon followed by a rally at the Stampede grounds that drew only about 700 supporters into the Victoria Pavilion. During the telethon he answered easy questions from true Grit believers, and was flattered and thanked by his admirers for having done a fine job in his four years as prime minister. He fielded questions about whether he was ever a communist (which he denied), whether his government would promote physical fitness (it would), and whether his government would legalize marijuana (it would not but there would be no prison sentences for mere possession). Later he said that the Official Languages Act had "laid the ghost of separatism to rest, if not forever, at least for a very long time." The crowd was in high spirits and gave him applause hearkening back to 1968 Trudeaumania.[60]

Despite the odd flash of excitement, the Liberal campaign was considered dull and "The Land is Strong" strategy a dud. Trudeau's pitch that the campaign would be a conversation with Canadians was widely regarded as an example of mindless arrogance or simply a joke. But at the same time, few believed Stanfield's message had engaged most voters, despite his well-run campaign and improvement as a campaigner. He remained slow and ponderous and did not seem to have much help from speechwriters. Most Canadians expected him to take another drubbing.[61]

The surprise of the campaign was David Lewis. His "Corporate Welfare Bums" routine generated big crowds and big headlines, and the message was timely, given Canada's unemployment and inflationary woes. Thus, the NDP was expected to make considerable gains. However, in Ontario, many forecast strategic voting by Liberals and Tories who would cast votes for each other's candidate in a close race, rather than see a seat fall to the NDP.[62]

The outcome was difficult to predict. With only days left the Tories released polls showing them running neck and neck with the Liberals.

However, the Liberals quickly released their own private polls showing that they had a nine-point lead over the Tories.[63]

Four days before the election the disintegration of the mighty Alberta Social Credit fortress took another step when ex-premier Harry Strom announced that he was quitting as leader and recommended that his successor be selected at the party's next annual meeting.[64]

The Trudeau campaign limped to the finish line. Even though the hugely popular Margaret joined Pierre in New Brunswick for a couple of rousing events, they failed to impress. Charles Lynch wrote that it was hard to tell if the Liberals saw her "as the icing on the cake or finger in the dike," and that if the listless approach to the campaign "turns out to be a mistake, it will have been a whopper" because Trudeau could have generated far more excitement had he cared to make the effort.[65]

The race had tightened up. A Gallup poll conducted on October 20 and 21 found that the Grits had dropped 5 points to 39 percent while the Conservatives gained 2 points to stand at 33 percent. The NDP stood constant at 21 percent, Social Credit and others at 7 percent and 17 percent were undecided. The poll had the Liberals well ahead in Quebec, but neck and neck with the Tories in Ontario. In the west, the Liberals were running third with the Tories and NDP in first and second place. In 1968 the Gallup had been remarkably close in its last-minute predictions. A CBC poll on the question of who would make the best prime minister had Trudeau with 38 percent followed by Stanfield at 20 percent and 10 percent for Lewis.[66]

And now it was time to count the ballots.

31

The Party's Over

OCTOBER–NOVEMBER 1972

IT WAS CLOSE. By midnight October 30 the Grits and Tories were tied with 107 seats each. The NDP had 30, Social Credit had 13—all from Quebec— and the others had 2, with just 5 seats undecided.[1]

Although who would form the next government still hung in the balance, the results in Alberta were clear. The Liberals had been decimated. Their promise of 1968 shattered, they had gone down to a resounding defeat in every riding. Trudeau's thorn, Mel Hurtig in Edmonton West, received the highest percentage of votes of all Alberta Liberal candidates: 36 percent. He was followed by Bud Olson in Medicine Hat with 34, Allen Sulatycky in Rocky Mountain with 32, and Nick Taylor in Calgary Centre, Hu Harries in Edmonton–Strathcona, and Pat Mahoney in Calgary South, each with 31 percent. Hurtig was also tops for the Grits in votes garnered with 21,040. He was followed by Mahoney with 18,437; Harries with 16,625; Taylor with 13,110; Roland Lambert with 12,647; and Una Maclean Evans with 11,997.[2]

In Athabasca, Tory Paul Yewchuk's margin over the second-place Liberal finisher increased from 1,200 votes in 1968 to over 8,000. In Calgary

Centre, despite Nick Taylor's tireless four-year campaign, newcomer Harvie Andre extended the Tory margin from 301 votes in 1968 to over 8,500 in 1972. Pat Mahoney's 1968 victory over his Tory opponent of 756 votes turned into a deficit of almost 16,500. In Edmonton–Strathcona, Hu Harries' edge of almost 6,000 votes in 1968 turned into a loss by almost 10,300 votes in 1972. In Edmonton Centre, the Tory margin increased from 251 to almost 10,300 over the second-place (Liberal) finisher. And so it went across the province.

In terms of the percentage of vote province-wide, the Liberals slipped from 35.7 percent in 1968 to 25 percent in 1972 (a loss of 10.7). The Tory vote increased from 51 percent to 57.6 percent in 1972 (a gain of 6.6). The NDP vote increased from 9.4 percent to 12.6 percent in 1972 (a gain of 3.2). The Social Credit vote actually increased from 1.9 percent to 4.5 percent in 1972 (a gain of 2.6). The Liberals finished second in 17 of the 19 ridings, with the NDP taking second place in two rural ridings: Peace River in the northwest and Battle River in central Alberta.

Just as the federal Liberal–Social Credit strategy had failed to help Social Credit in the Lougheed victory in 1971, the federal Liberals received little help from Social Credit in 1972. The federal Liberal strategy of sacrificing the provincial Liberal Party to the provincial Social Credit Party to further the interests of the federal Liberals was a bust.

Some of the Tory victors were less than magnanimous in victory. Palliser MP Stan Schumacher said that the people were disgusted with Trudeau's personality and predicted that John Turner would soon replace Trudeau as leader.[3] Eldon Woolliams said that Canadians had "repudiated a man today who was most arrogant" and who only thought of one part of Canada. Calgary Centre winner Harvie Andre said that the Liberals provided "government of the West by the East, but I am convinced things are going to look up for us here."[4] Peace River Tory MP Ged Baldwin cheerily predicted that the end of the Trudeau government was nigh and that the reins of power would soon shift to Stanfield, who would probably preside for a year or so before the next election.[5]

Liberals drowned their sorrows at various campaign wakes, muttering about their bad fortune and trying to figure out what hit them. For them, the most exciting event of the evening was when one of Roland Lambert's campaign workers drove through the headquarters' front window. Pat Mahoney took defeat gracefully, saying, "It appears we are headed for a minority government. If that's what the people want, that's what they'll get. That's the great thing about a democracy." He expressed solidarity with his victor saying, "Being a Member of Parliament is a very tough job, and Mr. Bawden will need the support of all of us."[6]

Trudeau emerged from a special cabinet meeting November 2 to say that he would disclose his intentions the next day. Reports had caucus divided over the next move, with some members fearing that if Trudeau appeared to cling to power it would further turn off the Canadian voter, while others urged him to keep power at all costs.[7]

David Lewis soon pledged the NDP support to keep a minority Liberal government in power, provided it brought in progressive legislation that would benefit individual Canadians. Watching Trudeau's press conference, he said he'd seldom seen a more chastened man. He described Stanfield's demand for tax cuts and other policies as "rubbishy," and said it was now essential that Parliament act fast to reduce unemployment, provide financial relief to pensioners, introduce tax policies that treated individual Canadians fairly, and hold back rising food costs and inflation. He warned that if Trudeau did not have the sense to act swiftly on these recommendations, "his government won't last a week."[8]

The numbers finally settled at 109 seats for the Liberals and 107 for the Tories. The NDP took 31 seats, Caouette's Quebec Social Credit won 15 Quebec seats, and Independent candidates won 2. Compared to the results in 1968, the Liberals lost 46 seats and 7 percent of the popular vote. Their losses came in Ontario where they lost 27 seats, in BC where they dropped 12, in Alberta where they lost 4, and Manitoba, where they lost 3. The Tories gained 35 seats and 3.65 percent of the popular vote. Their big gains were in Ontario where they picked up 23 seats, BC where they gained 8 seats, and

Pat Mahoney is interviewed on election night 1972 by Ralph Klein, then a television reporter in Calgary. [Glenbow Archives NA 2864-21982]

Alberta where they gained 4. The NDP gained 9 seats—5 in Ontario and 4 in BC—but only an additional 0.87 percent of the popular vote. The Social Credit Party gained one seat in Quebec and an additional 2.27 percent of the popular vote.

Mahoney, reflecting on his defeat, said that the outcome was "partly an anti-Trudeau vote and distinctly an anti-government vote." "Certainly," he said, "the Prime Minister and his personality was one factor." Mahoney was at a loss to explain the shift in vote in Alberta, but others claimed the intervention of the Lougheed team with ten days to go in the campaign had been a great help in the Tory win.[9]

Hu Harries was more voluble in his post-election comments. He said that given the government's poor showing, he and seven other defeated Liberals wanted an immediate party policy conference with a full accounting that would lead to "almost a social contract for action." He complained that he and other Alberta Liberal candidates were forced to recognize early in the campaign that Trudeau's image would be of little value. He also claimed that for four years he had been saying that Trudeau was receiving "bad information," and "listening to the wrong people," and now the time had come to get rid of them. Harries complained that Ivan Head, who he called Trudeau's chief advisor for Alberta, was completely out of touch with the province. He said "Many, many young people in this country thought the promise of 1968 could have been fulfilled," and that it would be "a tragedy if the needs and wishes of those young people are not considered."[10]

It was highly doubtful that Head was advising Trudeau on any meaningful Alberta matters as Harries suggested. From 1968 to 1970 Head assisted Trudeau on legal issues and in 1970 he was named a special assistant with responsibility for advice on foreign policy and foreign relations, which in light of Trudeau's interest in the subject must have been a full-time job. If Trudeau was getting any advice on Alberta, it was most likely from Harries' rival caucus colleagues, the most important of whom were Bud Olson, Pat Mahoney, Senator Harry Hays, and the western regional desk within the PMO itself. By virtue of his pique at being overlooked for cabinet and his subsequent abrasive behaviour, Harries was isolated from his Alberta caucus colleagues (with the exception of Allen Sulatycky).[11]

Some reasons for the Liberals' downfall in Alberta were the same in every part of Canada. The tough fight against increasing inflation, despite Trudeau's assurances that it was won, together with the intractable high unemployment rate it wrought, dragged the party down in most provinces, and Alberta was no exception. The firm government predictions that the unemployment rate would improve when Benson brought his tax reform package in June 1971, only to see the numbers go the other way, gave the government's opponents a huge political target. Things got worse during the election when the numbers continued in the wrong direction. Indeed, unemployment turned out to be the most effective weapon in the opposition's election arsenal. Even in Alberta, where the ravages of unemployment were modest compared to other parts of the country, joblessness was an issue in the campaign. Canada's anti-inflation policy that helped make economic growth rates and job creation in Canada the envy of most other developed countries made no difference to most voters.

Another problem for Liberals was the loss of much of Trudeau's Just Society and progressive cachet. David Lewis' effective "Corporate Welfare Bums" campaign, Stanfield's concerns for economic hardships faced by ordinary Canadians, Trudeau's battles with labour over inflation, and his critical comments against some of the unemployed took away from his 1968 progressive support and stuffed some of it into the pockets of the Tories and the NDP.

The white paper on taxation was a noble but disastrous experiment in participatory democracy. The effort left the government wide open to a two-year long siege by its political opponents before it culminated in tax reform legislation. That the white paper process was a way of getting better legislation was ignored, disbelieved, and drowned out by voices of those who wanted the government defeated.

Official bilingualism, a policy that did not sit well with most Canadian anglophones, hurt Liberals' chances in English Canada and particularly in the west. English-speaking Canadians generally seemed to tolerate bilingualism so long as it included being tough with Quebec or staring down the separatists. Bilingualism was generously supported only by francophones, and anglophones of good will—a group usually made up of "bleeding heart liberals," or worldly citizens, academics, or immigrants who knew the value of speaking another language. Otherwise, English Canada's attitude was, "Stop shoving French down our throats."

Negative perceptions of Trudeau's personality emerged shortly after the 1968 election. Careless and smug-sounding remarks, like "Why should I sell your wheat?" or "I like to disappoint some people sometimes," provided proof to his detractors that he was arrogant and uncaring. That view of him carried through the 1972 campaign and would stay in the minds of many. His highly publicized international travels inspired pride but, as time went on, were considered pompous extravaganzas rather than the good work of a government leader from a modest and self-deprecating democracy like Canada.

And finally, "The Land is Strong" theme, concocted by his egghead election strategists was far too intellectual and esoteric for most anglophone Canadians to embrace. Thus, instead of the coattails Trudeau offered in 1968 when his campaigning was an asset to all Liberal candidates, this time his presence was too often a disappointment. Descriptions of him as "a pragmatic idealist" and "a believer in the kind of freedom that comes from a sense of balance and proportion" left Canadians cold. "The Land is Strong" let the team down badly. Trudeau had been expected to sparkle on the campaign trail in 1972 as he did in 1968 but he did not live up to expectations and too often did not even seem to try. The 1972 Liberal campaign will stand as a landmark failure in the annals of Canadian political campaign history.

Greatly damaging to the Liberals throughout the west were the difficulties faced by the grain farmer, and the government's response to them. Trudeau's problems with agriculture began early—in December 1968, when he posed his explosive rhetorical question, "Well why should I sell the Canadian farmers' wheat?" That gaffe convinced many that he was callous and ignorant of farmers' needs, and lacked concern for the west. In the Prairie provinces, those perceptions of Trudeau grew exponentially during the first half of 1969 as the farm economy nosedived from collapsing international wheat markets, while the government's only apparent policy for many months was to wait it out.

The wheat economy remained a quagmire until February 1970 when Otto Lang finally came up with the LIFT program that in part—bizarrely, at least to the farmers—paid farmers not to grow wheat. The LIFT program provided some relief and soon grain export sales increased. But it had been a long and unpleasant run for the farmers, which they did not forget. The government's losing the bruising battle over the grain stabilization bill, confrontations with the cattlemen, getting behind in payments owed to the farmer, clumsily trying to solve the "chicken and egg war," encouraging some farmers to quit farming and move to the towns and cities—all contributed to the farmers' hostility toward the Trudeau government. The one bright spot in that depressing mélange was Otto Lang, minister in charge of the Wheat Board, who found solutions to the wheat glut for which he was rewarded with his 1972 re-election in Saskatoon–Humboldt when he increased his margin from less than 600 votes in 1968 to more than 8,000. Other Liberal candidates in farm areas fell all around him. Although there were no Liberal seats at risk in Alberta that relied exclusively on a farm economy, many urban Albertans were family members and friends of farmers who still worked the land; it is not an unlikely assumption that many of them (if not most) did not vote Liberal because of the farm issues. The same process was at work in all of the Prairie provinces. In 1972 the Liberals lost three seats in Manitoba, one in Saskatchewan, and four in Alberta. They were left with merely three seats on the Prairies—one in Saskatchewan and two in Manitoba.

Other major factors in the Liberal losses in Alberta were unique to Alberta: the constant opposition and demands of the oilmen and their allies; the coming to power of Peter Lougheed; and the collective naive actions of the Alberta federal Liberal caucus that tried to broker a marriage from hell between Alberta Liberals and Social Credit.

Most important among these factors was the opposition of the oilmen. Oil and gas was essentially an exclusive Alberta subject and *the* issue during the four preceding years. When ex-Tory MP and prominent oilman Carl Nickle not surprisingly endorsed Stanfield in 1968, it foreshadowed a rough road ahead for the federal Alberta Grits. Nickle's family's roots in the oil and gas business went back a couple of generations and his publication, the *Daily Oil Bulletin*, influenced most everyone in the oil patch.

Furthermore, Nickle had a cozy relationship with Southam Press, owner of the *Edmonton Journal*, *Calgary Herald*, *Medicine Hat News*, and interests in several Alberta radio, television, and other media properties, including the *Bulletin*.

Nickle and his allies had the power to do a lot of damage to the Alberta federal Liberals. He and his cohorts in the media, the important oilmen associations of IPAC and the CPA, and the oil company boardrooms, spread the message that the government was doing very little for their business and what little they were doing was inept and wrong. Trudeau himself got off on the wrong foot when in his early Calgary appearance in April 1969 he decided to talk about foreign policy instead of buttering up the industry by talking oil. That gaffe was a self-inflicted, almost mortal political blow in Alberta and set the stage for the confrontational relationship between the federal Liberals and the oilmen that continued with only temporary lulls through the 1972 election and far beyond.

According to the oilmen, between 1969 and 1972 the federal government never did its job. By 1972 most believed that the federal government did not protect them against the perils of competitive oil markets, that it stood in the way of selling Alberta oil into eastern Canadian markets, that it was not doing enough to promote more exports into the US, that it was not interested in seeking a continental oil policy with the US, that it scared off foreign investment with the white paper on taxation, that its tax reform legislation hurt the oil industry, that its actions on foreign takeovers was a flagrant intrusion into their business that also discouraged foreign investment, that it was competing unfairly with other oil companies with its stake in Panarctic, that it was imposing too many environmental restrictions on the industry, that its reliance on unsecure foreign oil supplies from Venezuela was hurting the advancement of their industry, that its National Energy Board was being unfair or ignorant in its calculations of surplus gas, that it was standing in the way of higher oil and gas prices: on and on went the unending litany of accusations, disappointments, and beefs.

Lost in the cacophony were many good things that had happened to the oil and gas industry between 1968 and 1972: Alberta oil production had doubled; exports to the United States had more than doubled; oil markets for Canadian oil soared in spite of the Alaskan Prudhoe Bay discovery; foreign investment in the Canadian oil and gas business picked up after tax reform; the gas industry was surging ahead; and oil sands development was really starting to roll.

In addition, many of the oilmen's complaints between 1968 and 1972 were rooted in problems over which the federal government had no influence. Canada had to wait to negotiate for more exports while Nixon conducted his study of the US domestic industry. Nixon was protective of the US oil industry. The NEB had a legitimate concern whether Canada had enough surplus gas for export because oil industry and utility companies' "expert" testimony differed dramatically. The NEB was right in not including gas from the high Arctic in calculations of surplus gas because no one knew how to transport it to markets economically.

But the oilmen, their spokesmen, Social Credit and PC provincial politicians, the 15 Tory MPs, and the Alberta premiers kept up their attacks on the federal government—in briefs, telegrams, editorials, executive presentations at corporate meetings, and speeches at professional or business conferences—throughout most of the Trudeau government's term.

And who was advancing the government position and the national interest in Alberta? Only the four lonely Alberta Liberal MPs, and probably the most capable one was absent from Ottawa too often because he was embittered at being overlooked for Trudeau's first cabinet. The other three did their best—two were ministers at the time of the election—but they were no match for their many vocal opponents, and they had little help from Ottawa.

In the end the oilmen—and hence the people of Alberta—convinced of the ineptitude, incompetence and general lack of interest in their industry on the part of the Trudeau government, decided to take back whatever power they had lost four years earlier—and they did, with the able assistance of the second-rate, dreary, national Liberal campaign.

The second Alberta factor leading to the rout of the Alberta federal Liberals was Peter Lougheed, a new, modern leader with a powerful public image, an activist approach to government, and a willingness to battle the federal government on behalf of his province. While Lougheed launched progressive policies on a host of issues, Trudeau was stuck with a fight against inflation and consequent unemployment. All this helped Lougheed glom onto the affections of disaffected or uncertain Liberals and turn them into Tories. Whereas Lougheed was visible everywhere and every day in Alberta, Trudeau was generally only seen from a distance and most of the time portrayed negatively as a foe of the province. Whereas Lougheed was set on improving the province's standing in the country economically and politically, Trudeau was perceived to be standing in his way.

Trudeau could have turned it around for the Liberals in Alberta when the October Crisis made him the most popular politician in the province and the country for several months. However, for honourable reasons, he passed up that rare chance to seize upon what might have been the great equalizer that may have even changed the course of Canada's history.

And finally, the third Alberta factor leading to the disappearance of the Alberta Liberal MPs were their own actions in abandoning and sabotaging the provincial party organization so that a deal could be struck for Social Credit support. In a high watermark of political naïveté, the Alberta federal party brass—completely ignoring Social Credit's vastly different history, culture, philosophy, leadership, and membership—nevertheless deep-sixed the provincial party and tried its best to merge all Alberta Liberals with a provincial arch-enemy that had been their foe for thirty-five years. The federal Liberals' refusal to assist and help finance the provincial party undermined its attractive and competent leader Jack Lowery and hastened his departure. When Lowery made his own effort to sustain some relevance for his party by working a deal with Social Credit—playing into the hands of the federal Liberals—his and his party's fates were sealed.

The federal party continued to starve the provincial party of funds, and discouraged the membership from picking a new provincial leader for over a year. So intent with their plans to seduce Social Credit, the federal Liberal brass did not stop with merely dismantling the provincial party; they even engineered a prestigious federal job offer for an aging highly conservative

Social Credit minister and set up the Senate appointment of Trudeau's most implacable public policy enemy, Ernest Manning. Although in later years Trudeau appointed a few politicians of other parties to the Senate, none were such vocal and constant critics of his defining policies as Manning. The wasted and damaging appointment gave Manning a comfortable seat among Ottawa power brokers, where he could ruminate and write about his favourite subject, political realignment, thus forming the philosophical basis for the Reform, Canadian Alliance, and Conservative parties of the future.

The effort to convince the party of Major Douglas, Aberhart, and Manning to join forces with the party of Laurier, Pearson, and Trudeau had failed miserably and thousands of provincial and federal Liberal voters then drifted into the waiting arms of Lougheed and the Alberta Progressive Conservative Party. The Liberal MPs in Alberta would probably have lost in 1972 regardless of the Social Credit caper. But had they understood politics better and encouraged and nurtured a provincial party and not tried to influence all Alberta Liberals to jump ship and support Social Credit in 1970–71, more Liberals might have remained to help the provincial party rebound and the federal party regroup.

Other aggravating issues hurt the Trudeau government in Alberta—the cable TV policy that seemed to discriminate against the west in terms of imported television programming and the slow federal approvals for the new Calgary airport—but these were trivial compared to the bigger real or imagined grievances of unemployment, inflation, bilingualism, oil and gas, and agriculture. The commanding presence of Lougheed, the dismal "The Land is Strong" campaign, and the clumsy demoralizing tactics of the federal party brass did the rest.

Epilogue

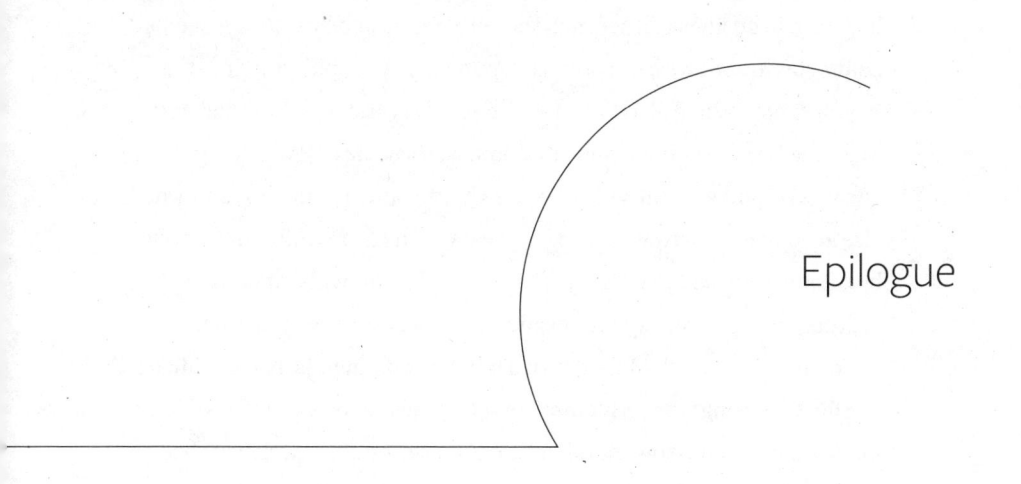

It is hard to fail, but it is worse never to have tried to succeed.[1]
—THEODORE ROOSEVELT

IN THE AFTERMATH OF THE ELECTION, most people expected Pat Mahoney to return to his hometown and his interrupted successful business career. Only 44 he had earned the extra cachet of political experience and connections across the country. He may have also had a chance to move back into public life.

But Mahoney was personally hurt and embittered with the way Calgary and his province had treated him despite his hard work. His last undertaking on behalf of the federal government was as a key organizer of the Western Economics Opportunities Conference (WEOC)[2] held in Calgary in October 1973.[3] Shortly afterward Mahoney began a new career as a judge of the Federal Court of Canada where he would serve on both the Trial and Appeal divisions until his retirement in 1994. Mahoney's acceptance of a judicial appointment was surprising, given his previous experience had been in business rather than the courtroom, and he'd always seemed comfortable both with the press and publicity. An appointment to the federal bench usually led to a career in relative obscurity. But that was Mahoney's choice; those who knew him well said he enjoyed being a judge, and was respected by all who appeared before him. He and his family had already moved to Ottawa during his years as an MP, and after his defeat, he seldom returned to Calgary.[4] When he did it was without fanfare.[5] His retirement years were spent in Vancouver; he passed away in 2012.[6]

As an MP, although Mahoney had his shortcomings, he had a brilliant intellect, a strong work ethic, and a genuine desire to make things better. But for the hostility toward Liberals in Alberta, he could well have had a long productive political career in many other places in Canada.

Mahoney's 1972 opponent Peter Bawden served as the Tory MP in Calgary South until 1979 after which two PC oil well drilling contractors succeeded him in successive elections in 1979 and 1984. In 1984, Barbara Jane (Bobbie) Sparrow, who ran Argus Drilling after the death of her husband, won the biggest plurality in Canadian federal election history up to that time by garnering 47,763 more votes than second-place finisher Liberal Harold Millican.[7] The oilmen had recaptured the riding of Calgary South.

Allen Sulatycky was arguably the best all-around MP of the four Alberta Liberals elected in 1968. He had maintained contact with his constituents and served as parliamentary secretary to two ministers. He believed that in 1972, although he ran a good campaign, widespread anti-French language resentment and a feeling that Trudeau cared only about Quebec did him in, thereby launching Joe Clark's career as an MP.

After the election Sulatycky, still only 34, returned to Alberta settling in Edmonton and later in Calgary, a partner of a major law firm. Although he had fully expected to run again after his defeat, he continued practicing law until 1982 when he was appointed to the Alberta Court of Queen's Bench. He served as a judge for the next thirty years (including stints on the Alberta Court of Appeal and as Associate Chief Justice of the Court of Queen's Bench). Throughout his long judicial career, he was an even-tempered and fair judge, popular among all his legal colleagues. He retired from the bench in 2013 at 75.

Fifty-year-old Hu Harries remained in Edmonton where he continued to work in his consulting firm while tending to his many business interests. He acted as a consultant to the World Bank and did projects on behalf of several provincial governments and many private companies. He owned a vineyard, and was in the ranching business in British Columbia and Alberta. He also participated in rodeo events well into his fifties. For a time in the 1970s Harries flirted with starting a new political party to be known as the National Party of Canada but the concept never got off the ground.

After Prime Minister Joe Clark's government was defeated in the Commons on its first budget, plunging the country into another election, Harries returned to federal politics as the Liberal candidate for Edmonton West. He once again fell short, losing to Tory Marcel Lambert by almost 9,000 votes. This ended Harries' political career and in 1986, he died suddenly at the age of 64.

Bud Olson had the longest political run of the four Liberal winners in 1968. As a senior member of the Trudeau cabinet, he had acquired some important political allies. He ran again as a Liberal in Medicine Hat in the 1974 election that produced another Liberal majority government. However, the Liberals were once again shut out of any Alberta seats with Olson losing, this time by over 6,000 votes.

Olson's political career, however, was far from over. To beef up Alberta Liberal representation in the Liberal caucus, Trudeau appointed Olson to the Senate in 1977, whereupon his political career sputtered back to life. During the short time that Trudeau was in opposition, he named Olson Senate opposition leader. After the February 1980 election, when Trudeau was again at the helm of a new majority government, he appointed Senator Olson minister of state for economic development and minister responsible for the Northern Pipeline Agency. Olson was now at the height of his political influence and once again the Liberal boss in Alberta.

In 1982 Olson was shuffled to the post of leader of the government in the Senate, a post he held until the Liberal defeat of 1984. In 1996 Prime

Minister Chretien, who Olson had supported in the party leadership contests in 1984 and 1990, appointed him Alberta's fourteenth lieutenant-governor. Olson completed his term in 2000 and passed away 2002 at the age of 76. It had been a long, and in the end successful, run for the ex-Social Crediter.

Senator Harry Hays continued to impress the Ottawa party brass with his fundraising skills. His role in government reached its apex during 1981 when he served as co-chairman with Quebec MP Serge Joyal of a special joint committee of the Commons and the Senate to hear public submissions on amendments to the constitution.[8] Hays' interesting life came to an abrupt end in 1972 when he suddenly died at the age of 72.

After running unsuccessfully in 1972, Mel Hurtig soon abandoned the Liberals, turning his attention to his book publishing business and promoting Canadian economic nationalism. He was a founding member of the Committee for an Independent Canada and later, founding chairman of the Council of Canadians. Hurtig returned to federal politics in 1992 to become leader of the new National Party of Canada whose purpose was to fight for Canada's economic and political independence. However, the new party won no seats and Hurtig himself was defeated in the riding of Edmonton Northwest by Anne McLellan in the first federal Liberal breakthrough in the province since 1968. Shortly thereafter the National Party was dissolved. A prolific writer, Hurtig received many awards for his accomplishments. Late in life he moved to Vancouver where he remained active writing and pursuing the cause of Canadian economic and political independence until his death at 84 in 2016.[9]

After the twin disasters of the 1971 provincial election and the 1972 federal election, the long-crippled Alberta Liberal Party might have totally succumbed but for the efforts of one man—Nick Taylor. In 1974 he stepped into the breach left by Bob Russell, who resigned the leadership after losing a 1973 provincial by-election. After soldiering on as leader over several elections, in 1986 Taylor's Liberals captured 4 seats and 12 percent of the vote—the party's best showing since 1963. Taylor himself won the northern Alberta riding of Westlock–Sturgeon. Ironically, Social Credit had disappeared by then. In 1996 Jean Chretien appointed Taylor to the Senate where he served for six years.

After the 1972 election, the oil and gas industry and Peter Lougheed continued to dominate the Alberta's political and economic life. Oil prices and profits continued to rise while the Lougheed government sought a larger share of the spoils and more power to develop Alberta resources. He left politics in 1985 for a successful career in the private sector.

The twelve remaining years of the Trudeau era would see continued fractious conflict between the federal government and Alberta. Ahead lay the oil price shocks of 1973 and 1979, more haggling over the spoils of oil, the National Energy Program, and the patriation of a new Canadian constitution.

History is a never-ending continuum, one event leading to another. But an examination of each segment has to end somewhere and this is where this present tale ends. The rest of the tumultuous Trudeau–Alberta story remains to be told.

Notes

Preface

1. The Crow Rate, established in 1897, gave the Canadian Pacific Railway (CPR) subsidies so that westerners could get preferential rates shipping their grain east and easterners, shipping their manufactured goods west. The subsidies also helped the CPR build a railway through the Pass to take advantage of resource development in the region. Westerners complained that the Crow Rate discriminated against them for almost the next hundred years.
2. The word "Tory" is a colloquial reference to members of the Progressive Conservative Party of Canada, and now, of the Conservative Party of Canada.
3. One unsuccessful candidate for the provincial party leadership in that convention was Peace River lawyer Wilbur Freeland. His granddaughter Chrystia Freeland, a Rhodes scholar and business journalist, would become a Liberal MP for Toronto Centre in November 2013 and later be appointed minister of International Trade by Prime Minister Justin Trudeau.
4. Sullivan, *Mandate '68*, 251.

1 The Great Race Begins

1. Peacock, *Journey to Power*, 174–81.
2. English, *Citizen of the World*, 456–58.
3. LeDuc et al., *Dynasties and Interludes*, 250.

4. The word "Grit" is a colloquial reference to members of the Liberal Party in English Canada.
5. Clark ran in Calgary–Elbow in the 1989 provincial election but lost a tight race to first-time Tory candidate, and later Alberta premier Ralph Klein. His son Greg Clark currently represents the riding and leads the Alberta Party.

2   The Coming of the Just Society

1. The modern Liberal Party of Canada comprises both a right (or business) wing and a left (or progressive) wing. The right wing is more business oriented while the left wing is more oriented to social issues. Clarkson and McCall, *Trudeau and Our Times*, 2:220–23.
2. Moshansky was later appointed to the Alberta Court of Queen's Bench.
3. The voting intentions of the Alberta delegates come from meticulous notes in the papers of Una Maclean Evans (Glenbow archives). She ran in four federal elections between 1957 and 1988, and served as president of the federal Liberals in Alberta. A three-term member of Edmonton city council, she later sat as a judge on the Edmonton Citizenship Court. She is the mother of CBC international radio and television journalist Margaret Evans.
4. W. Kenneth Moore was a close friend and early legal associate of Peter Lougheed. Moore later sat on the Alberta Queen's Bench and served as Chief Justice.
5. David C. McDonald was a Rhodes scholar, Edmonton lawyer and law professor, and active Liberal before his appointment to the Alberta Court of Queen's Bench. In 1977 he became head of the McDonald Commission, which investigated certain activities of the RCMP that gave rise to the Canadian Security Intelligence Service (CSIS) in 1984.
6. Sinclair was a long-time Liberal lawyer in Edmonton who later sat on the Alberta Queen's Bench and for a time served as Chief Justice of the Court and on the Alberta Court of Appeal.
7. Wachowich was a popular young Edmonton lawyer who went on to the Court of Queen's Bench of Alberta where he rose to Chief Justice.
8. Palmer came west from PEI to practice law and help found the law firm Burnet Duckworth Palmer.
9. O'Leary was a gold medalist in law from UBC who practiced in Calgary before being appointed to the Court of Queen's Bench and later to the Alberta Court of Appeal.
10. Stevenson grew up in Ottawa and rose to the position of Assistant Chief Judge at the Alberta Provincial Court. He also served as president of Lions Clubs International.
11. Sullivan, *Mandate '68*, 336.
12. A Liberal organizer and fundraiser, Kerans in 1970 became one of the youngest judges ever to be appointed to the Alberta District Court, later elevated to the Alberta Court of Appeal.

13. Dickie was a lawyer and car dealership owner who was one of only three Liberal MLAs in Alberta in 1968. He soon abandoned the Liberals to sit with Lougheed's Progressive Conservatives and would become Lougheed's first minister of mines and minerals.
14. Sullivan, *Mandate '68*, 337–38.
15. Pearson, *Mike*, 355–56.
16. Despite Winters' healthy appearance, he would die of a heart attack a year later at 59.
17. LaMarsh, a lawyer then in her early forties, was first elected in 1960 as Liberal MP for Niagara Falls and in 1963, became the second woman to serve as a federal cabinet minister.
18. Newman, *Distemper of Our Times*, 465.
19. Sullivan, *Mandate '68*, 347.
20. Peacock, *Journey to Power*, 293.
21. Peacock, *Journey to Power*, 293–94.
22. Newman, *Distemper of Our Times*, 466.
23. A. Alan Borovoy, "Going to Court with Ernst Zundel," *National Post*, February 21, 2014.
24. Newman, *Distemper of our Times*, 468.
25. Millican, a lifelong friend and confidant of Peter Lougheed, later served as an advisor and then deputy minister in the Lougheed government. However, he never gave up his Liberal credentials and ran and lost as a federal Liberal candidate in Calgary South in 1984.

3   Trudeaumania Goes West

1. For clarity the provincial Liberal Party arm of the Liberal Party in Alberta will be referred to as the Alberta Liberal Party, the provincial Liberal Party, the provincial party, or the provincial Liberals. The federal party arm will be referred to as the Alberta federal Liberal Party, the federal Liberal Party, the federal party, or the federal Liberals. All Alberta Liberals—federal and provincial—will be referred to as Alberta Liberals or Alberta Grits.
2. Wearing, *L-Shaped Party*, 1–15; Clarkson, *Big Red Machine*, 17–21.
3. Source for all federal election results is Elections Canada.
4. Gibbons, *Prairie Politics*, 173–86.
5. One early accuser that Trudeau was a communist was Ron Gostick, originally from Alberta. Gostick's mother was elected an Alberta Social Credit MLA in 1935. Gostick worked with the federal Social Credit party and became both a high-profile anti-communist and anti-Semite of the extreme right. Ron Csillag, "Ron Gostick, Far-Right Publisher 1918–2005," *Globe and Mail*, August 6, 2005.
6. The annual Hays Stampede Breakfast, a by-invitation-only Calgary Stampede institution, recently celebrated its sixty-fifth anniversary. Now held at Heritage Park, it

features marching bands, western entertainment, and speeches from prominent politicians, along with a hearty western breakfast. One popular ritual featured Hays in costume delivering a monologue while serving special guests a drink called syllabub. A cow was milked to provide the fresh milk mixed with vodka.

7. Interview with Charles Kelly, December 30, 2015.
8. "Mahoney Wears Many Hats in Cabinet," *Calgary Herald*, January 29, 1972.
9. Don Sellar, "Pat Mahoney Likes to Help People with Problems, *The Herald Magazine*, January 28, 1972.
10. In 1969 Dickie would cross the floor to sit with Peter Lougheed's Tories and in 1971, become minister of mines and minerals.
11. Taylor was also one of the best quipsters in the business. Years later when he was provincial Liberal leader and doing battle against the mighty Lougheed machine, he was asked what he would do if he woke up the day after the election and discovered he was premier. Taylor replied, "I'd demand an immediate recount."
12. Peacock, *Journey to Power*.
13. Obituary, "Donald Peacock," *Calgary Herald*, December 12, 2009.
14. As he explained to many voters who were having trouble pronouncing his name, "Sulatycky is pronounced like Salada-tea, except that the k is substituted for the t."
15. Interview with Allen Sulatycky, May 23, 2014.

4 The Battle for Edmonton Centre

1. Steumer, *Hawrelak*, 53–130.
2. Steumer, *Hawrelak*, 167.
3. Sinclair was the father of Margaret, who would become the wife of Pierre Trudeau.
4. Decore was the father of Laurence, later mayor of Edmonton and leader of the Alberta Liberal Party.
5. Mosychuk would be disbarred in May 1973. Levine, *Your Worship*, 45.
6. "Hawrelak Confirms Entry," *Edmonton Journal*, May 11, 1968.
7. Interview with Roger Kerans, September 22, 2006.
8. Guy Demarino, "Hawrelak Defies Liberal Leaders," *Edmonton Journal*, May 16, 1968; Steumer, *Hawrelak*, 183.
9. McLean, then a young Edmonton lawyer, later settled in Vancouver and served as chairman of CN Rail, and on boards of several Canadian corporations and volunteer organizations. McLean remained a loyal Liberal both federally and provincially and was a strong supporter of Jean Chretien.
10. Guy Demarino, "Hawrelak Defeated in Nomination Bid," *Edmonton Journal*, May 17, 1968.

11. Hawrelak's statement that he had been a Liberal all his life conflicts with his granddaughter's comment that he was an early supporter of Social Credit in the mid-thirties. Steumer, *Hawrelak*, 60.
12. Steumer, *Hawrelak*, 186–88.
13. Guy Demarino, "Hawrelak to Run as Independent," *Edmonton Journal*, May 31, 1968.

5   The Battle for Alberta

1. This did not change much until 2015, when Alberta had 34 seats. Justin Trudeau made several visits to the province, including at the beginning and end of the campaign at major rallies held in Calgary and Edmonton.
2. "Kissing Trudeau Woos West," *Globe and Mail*, May 13, 1968; Bruce Phillips, "Giant Love-In Engulfs Pierre," *Calgary Herald*, May 13, 1968; "Edmonton Goes Wild for Trudeau," *Albertan*, May 13, 1968; "Giggling Youngsters Mob PM," *Edmonton Journal*, May 13, 1968.
3. Shaw, *Saint Pierre*, 94.
4. Lynne Bell, "Poverty Main Threat—PM," *Edmonton Journal*, May 14, 1968.
5. Notions like *deux nations, special status*, and *distinct society* for Quebec have been poison to federal party leaders who have embraced them. Joe Clark's vision of a *community of communities* helped Trudeau ultimately prevail over him. Brian Mulroney's failed Meech Lake and Charlottetown Accords were major factors in his party's downfall. John Turner's Liberal leadership was further damaged when he embraced Mulroney's distinct society idea, incurring the wrath of the Trudeau faction of the party in the late 1980s. Paul Martin Jr.'s unsuccessful campaign against Jean Chretien for the Liberal leadership in 1990 was also hampered by his support of Mulroney's distinct society initiative.
6. Peacock, *Journey to Power*, 355–56.
7. "Crowd Welcomes PM in Northern Alberta," *Globe and Mail*, June 6, 1968.
8. "Gunman Fires at Red Deer Liberal," *Calgary Herald*, June 17, 1968.
9. "Nickle Criticizes Trudeau," *Calgary Herald*, June 14, 1968.
10. Sam Nickle Sr. (1889–1971) started out as a shoe salesman but switched to the oil business in Calgary in the 1930s. His companies achieved great success with holdings throughout North America, but he was parsimonious, particularly when it came to paying taxes and reasonable salaries to his staff. When he got wind that Canada might enact a capital gains tax, he sold his corporate holdings and then contributed much of his wealth to charitable foundations and the University of Calgary.
11. Interview with James Walasko, a geologist employed by Nickle's company who knew and worked with members of the family, January 15, 2012.
12. Don Sellar, "Politics in Alberta," *Calgary Herald*, June 15, 1968.
13. Marian Bruce, "4000 Mob Trudeau at Airport Whoop-Up," *Calgary Herald*, June 18, 1968.

14. Marian Bruce and Ken Hull, "'Peak Out on Quebec,'" *Calgary Herald*, June 18, 1968.
15. Advertisement, *Edmonton Journal*, June 24, 1968.
16. Art Robinson, "Hawrelak Support Claim Arouses Some Confusion," *Edmonton Journal*, June 20, 1968.
17. Don Sellar, "Politics in Alberta," *Calgary Herald*, June 22, 1968.
18. Bruce Phillips, "Angry Trudeau Stands Up to Bottle-Hurling Rioters," *Calgary Herald*, June 25, 1968.

6 Breakthrough

1. All voting statistics compiled and published by Elections Canada.
2. Gray was to disappear quickly from the political scene and return to motor vehicle sales.
3. Although Hawrelak stayed out of future federal politics, in 1974 he would once again be re-elected Edmonton mayor.
4. Don Sellar, "Politics in Alberta," *Calgary Herald*, June 26, 1968.
5. "Attitude Hurts Mahoney's Hopes," *Edmonton Journal*, June 26, 1968.
6. "Farm Spokesmen Feel Bud Olson Could Be the Natural Replacement for Joe Greene," *Edmonton Journal*, June 26, 1968.
7. "They're Cabinet Potential; Harries Could Wear Many Hats," *Edmonton Journal*, June 26, 1968.
8. Editorials, "The Election," *Calgary Herald*, June 26, 1968; "Trudeau Gets His Majority," *Edmonton Journal*, June 26, 1968.
9. Editorial, "The Cabinet," *Calgary Herald*, July 6, 1968.
10. Editorial, "New Faces Plus the Old Guard," *Edmonton Journal*, July 6, 1968.
11. Interview with Allen Sulatycky, March 31, 2012.
12. Mayor for twenty years the very athletic Veiner brought Medicine Hat lots of madcap publicity by challenging other mayors to physical competitions he would win, but despite his popularity and three respectable attempts, Veiner could never win a seat for the federal Grits against his Socred opponents.

7 The Honeymoon

1. "Alberta Liberals Plan Open Meet," *Calgary Herald*, September 9, 1968.
2. Don Sellar, "Alberta Liberal Leadership Sweepstake, on 6 May Run," *Calgary Herald*, November 1, 1968.
3. Bruce Phillips, "Income Tax Up 2 p.c. in Bid to End Deficits," *Calgary Herald*, October 23, 1968.
4. Editorial, "The Budget," *Calgary Herald*, October 23, 1968.
5. Trudeau and Stanbury believed at the time that the party bosses had all of the input in the party's policy-making process, while the grassroots had none. Under Stanbury's

leadership, the party established a two-year, multi-stage process for vetting grassroots policy resolutions through policy conferences and provincial conventions, before voting on them at a national policy convention. Clarkson, *Big Red Machine*, 21–27.
6. Don Sellar, "'New Politics' Swell Liberal Membership," *Calgary Herald*, November 2, 1968.
7. "Patronage Charge Laid against Grits," *Calgary Herald*, November 2, 1968.
8. Davey's career as a top Liberal organizer had begun in the late 1950s when he spearheaded the revival of the fortunes of both Lester Pearson and the federal Liberals, leading to their returning to power in 1963. Beginning in 1973 he went on to be a powerful political advisor to Pierre Trudeau.
9. Davey, *Rainmaker*, 131.
10. At this time, Lougheed was already leader of the Alberta provincial PC party and destined to win 6 seats in the next Alberta general election and become the official opposition.
11. The very gifted Cardinal would soon make his mark leading various Indian bands to reject a federal position white paper revamping the Indian Act. He would also become a lifelong Liberal, even running as a Liberal candidate in the 2000 federal election.
12. Don Sellar, "Liberals Stumble Over Sock-It-To-'Em Style," *Calgary Herald*, November 2, 1968.
13. Petrasuk's careers as politician and lawyer had an unhappy ending in 1981, when he was convicted of stealing millions from his clients and sentenced to ten years in prison.
14. Klein went on to become a television reporter, Calgary mayor, a PC cabinet minister, and premier of Alberta. From 1980 until 2007 he won eight consecutive municipal and provincial elections.
15. "Criticism over Biafra Shadowing Trudeau," *Calgary Herald*, October 26, 1968.
16. Fraser Perry, "IPAC Urges Policy to Cut Oil Imports," *Calgary Herald*, November 30, 1968.
17. Bob Hill, "'Instant Solutions' Don't Exist," *Calgary Herald*, November 22, 1968.
18. Interview with Allen Sulatycky, June 26, 2012.
19. Judy LaMarsh dubbed Woolliams "the Senator from Blow River" for his bellicose and florid oratory.
20. "Bud Olson Accusing Opposition of Seeking Publicity," *Calgary Herald*, November 28, 1968.
21. "Mahoney Lauds CYC Work, Suggests Budget Increase," *Calgary Herald*, November 7, 1968.
22. "Mahoney Pitches for Athletes," *Calgary Herald*, November 8, 1968.
23. Fraser Perry and Don Sellar, "3-Member Commission Named to Study North Petroleum," *Calgary Herald*, December 19, 1968.

24. Interviews with Roger Kerans, September 22, 2006, and Olson's Executive Assistant Blair Williams, January 12, 2016. Williams recalls Harries then as "full of himself and not a serious team player. However, he was fascinating to talk to when it came to home events that focused on his ideas, his past, and his potential for the future."

8 In Alberta, It's About the Oil, Stupid!

1. "Oil" and "crude oil" are used interchangeably in this book and refer to oil before it has been refined into another petroleum-based product such as gasoline.
2. According to the federal census, Calgary's population in 1941 was 88,904; in 1951 it was 129,060; in 1961 it was 249,641; and in 1971 it was 403,319.
3. "Oil Doubled Population of Province," *Calgary Herald*, April 10, 1968.
4. David Breen, "Calgary: The City and the Petroleum Industry since World War Two," *Urban History Review*, October 1977, 155–71.
5. Palmer and Palmer, *Alberta*, 307.
6. According to the federal census, Edmonton's population in 1941 was 93,924; in 1951 it was 158,012; in 1961 it was 276,018; and in 1971 it was 436,264.
7. MacGregor, *History of Alberta*, 292, 293.
8. "Canadian Petroleum Association Predicts Good Production Year," *Calgary Herald*, May 15, 1972.
9. "Development of Resources Industries Will Require $1 Billion in Ten Years," *Calgary Herald*, April 10, 1969.
10. Pat Carney, minister of energy in 1984, was refused entry into the main dining room of the Petroleum Club to meet with oil company officials so she invited them to meet her at the YWCA. In 1986, even after she had become an industry hero for scrapping the National Energy Program, the membership still voted to refuse women entry. (For an account of the evening, see *Ottawa Citizen*, "Petroleum Club Doors Still Shut to Women," November 18, 1986.) Only in 1989, after the issue was brought up in the House of Commons and big companies began to cancel their memberships, did the club allow women as full-fledged members.
11. Nielsen, *We Gambled Everything*, 209.
12. Alberta was by far the biggest producer of Canadian oil, with only a small proportion of oil being produced anywhere else in the country.
13. Editorial, "Canada First," *Calgary Herald*, February 7, 1969.
14. Editorial, "Spotlight on Oil," *Calgary Herald*, March 27, 1969.
15. Gray, *Great Canadian Oil Patch*, 413–31.
16. Anthony Westell, "Oil Quotas Springing Leaks," *Albertan*, May 14, 1969.
17. "U.S. Wants a Montreal Pipeline," *Albertan*, May 12, 1970.
18. Bob Hill, "Oil Pact Arouses West MPs," *Calgary Herald*, March 1, 1969.

19. Jim Armstrong, The Oil Patch, *Calgary Herald*, May 29, 1969.
20. "Better Resources Policy Urged by Alberta Senator," *Calgary Herald*, February 28, 1969.
21. Bob Hill, "Oil Pact Arouses West MPs," *Calgary Herald*, March 1, 1969.
22. Don Sellar, "Strom Taking Oil, Medicare to PM," *Calgary Herald*, March 6, 1969.
23. Lang is the father of senior CBC News correspondent Amanda Lang.
24. Fraser Perry, "No Special Treatment for Petroleum Industry," *Calgary Herald*, March 19, 1969.
25. Jim Armstrong, The Oil Patch, *Calgary Herald*, March 20, 1969.
26. "Oil Brief Arms Trudeau for U.S. Visit," *Calgary Herald*, March 21, 1969.
27. George Brimmell, "Warm Washington Welcome for Trudeau," *Calgary Herald*, March 24, 1969.
28. "Oil Export Talks Set for April 2," *Calgary Herald*, March 25, 1969.
29. Editorial, "A Good Start," *Calgary Herald*, March 26, 1969.
30. This is a parody of political strategist James Carville's famous message for the 1992 Bill Clinton presidential campaign: "It's about the economy, stupid." Clinton, *My Life*, 425.

9 Mr. Trudeau Lays an Egg

1. For more information, see Hamilton, *Children's Crusade*.
2. Suleman, *Name of Justice*, 1–18.
3. Suleman, *Name of Justice*, 71–74.
4. Suleman, *Name of Justice*, 82.
5. Gerry Deagle, "Chief Justice Blasts Press, Police-Baiting Demonstrators," *Calgary Herald*, April 8 1969; Jim Witte, "Chief Justice Lashes out at Sham Rights Demonstrators," *Albertan*, April 8, 1969.
6. Beneath his image of a kindly man of rectitude was also a man with a hair-trigger temper, at least after a few scotches and when he felt his dignity was under attack. At a gathering of lawyers and judges and their wives at the Jasper Park Lodge during an especially spirited party, a lawyer's young wife playfully squirted a water pistol at his face. In front of dozens, a very angry and flushed Milvain chased her, wrestled her to the floor and appeared to throttle her. She was released without harm through the intervention of some very startled young lawyers.
7. "Trudeau to Ski at Bugaboo," *Calgary Herald*, April 5, 1969.
8. Edythe Humphrey, "PM Invited to 'Bag' Meal, No Reply Yet," *Albertan*, April 12, 1969.
9. "Trudeau May Get Mixed Reception," *Calgary Herald*, April 12, 1969.
10. Jacques Hamilton, "PM Confrontation Termed Success," *Calgary Herald*, April 14, 1969; Graham Pike, "Mass Marchers Heckle Trudeau," *Albertan*, April 14, 1969.
11. During a private meeting before the dinner Trudeau's handlers argued about whether he should talk about NATO or oil. Ivan Head, an Albertan who was Trudeau's advisor on

    foreign affairs wanted Trudeau to talk about NATO, while one of Trudeau's senior staff members wanted him to talk about oil.
12. Sitting near the head table, a very inebriated realtor who was a close friend of one of the organizers, Peter Petrasuk, began heckling loudly. An embarrassed Petrasuk quickly arranged for a the heckler's hasty and permanent exit from the dinner and the Liberal Party of Canada.
13. Marian Bruce, "NATO Alliance Second to Foreign Policy—Trudeau," *Calgary Herald*, April 14, 1969.
14. Fairbairn was a young journalist from Lethbridge who I knew from the University of Alberta. In 1970 she was hired as Trudeau's legislative assistant, and for the next fourteen years prepared him for Question Period. Just before Trudeau's retirement, he appointed her senator and in 1993 she became the first woman government leader in the Senate.
15. Joyce Fairbairn, "'West Should Take Interest in Defence,'" *Albertan*, April 14, 1969.
16. Even though Peacock's Liberal connections in Ottawa had helped him secure employment, while *Albertan*'s managing editor and even after leaving the journalism business, he remained one of the Alberta Liberal Party's harshest critics.
17. Don Peacock, "The Dry Well from Trudeau: A Night that Never Was," *Albertan*, April 14, 1969.
18. Tom Kennedy, "Trudeau Admits Disappointing City Oilmen," *Albertan*, April 14, 1969.
19. Fred Kennedy, "Mr. Trudeau Lays an Egg," *Albertan*, April 15, 1969.
20. "Tomato Was Thrown at Press Trudeau Tells Calgary Mayor," *Calgary Herald*, April 22, 1969.
21. "Protests 'Successful, and Here to Stay,'" *Calgary Herald*, May 6, 1969.
22. "Pelletier Announces CYC Representatives," *Calgary Herald*, Sept 27, 1969.
23. It must be assumed that Trudeau did not enjoy the visit any more than the oilmen. It would take him more than ten years to attend another Liberal fundraising dinner in the province. In October 1979 in Calgary he attended his second and last similar event during Clark's brief reign while he was opposition leader and about to resign.

10 Oil, Economic Nationalism, and Mean Joe Greene

1. The phrase "oil patch" refers to the petroleum industry.
2. The National Energy Board is an independent federal agency established in 1959 to regulate various aspects of the energy industry including interprovincial and international pipelines, construction of international interprovincial power lines, the export and import of natural gas, oil and electricity, and frontier oil and gas activities.
3. Fraser Perry, "$75 Million Oil Loss Feared," *Calgary Herald*, April 29, 1969.
4. Editorial, "Oil Run-Around," *Calgary Herald*, May 1, 1969.

5. "Oil Sales to East Issue Termed Urgent," *Calgary Herald*, May 6, 1969.
6. Arthur Blakely, "Woolliams: US Punishing Canada," *Calgary Herald*, May 14, 1969.
7. Fraser Perry, "Oilmen Want Pipeline Now," *Calgary Herald*, June 16, 1969.
8. The foundation provided ideas to the Social Credit and federal Progressive Conservative parties during their leadership transitions and later evolved into a think tank promoting market capitalism and grassroots democracy.
9. Dome later had great success getting federal approval for massive income tax deductions for investment in northern exploration projects. By the mid-1980s its success would be cut short as a result of billions of burdensome debt and a prolonged period of low oil prices, causing the company to collapse and Gallagher's ouster as chairman and CEO.
10. Dabbs, *Preston Manning*, 64.
11. During the interview with Allen Sulatycky on June 26, 2012, he told me of the tour and provided me with a copy of the tour's briefing book.
12. During the 1979 election campaign, flanked by his local Liberal candidates (including me running in Calgary North), Trudeau spoke at the Calgary Petroleum Club packed to capacity with unfriendly oilmen. Adopting his gunslinger pose in front of a standing microphone with jacket open and thumbs stuck in his belt, he spoke quietly and without a note for forty-five minutes about energy issues and statistics to his sullen but respectful audience, who gave him restrained but genuine applause.
13. Bob Hill, "U.S. Oil Imports Expected to Rise," *Calgary Herald*, May 8, 1969.
14. "Ottawa Urges US to Drop Oil Quota," *Calgary Herald*, August 7, 1969.
15. Foster, *Blue-Eyed Sheiks*, 198.
16. "New Supply Patter" *Calgary Herald*, June 25, 1969.
17. Timothy Pritchard, "Long-Term Oil Demand Investors," *Calgary Herald*, October 2, 1969.
18. Jim Armstrong, "Ottawa's Silence Proves Frustrating," *Calgary Herald*, November 8, 1969.
19. Jim Armstrong, The Oil Patch, *Calgary Herald*, March 5, 1970, citing statistics provided by the CPA, the Canadian Oil Scouts Association, and government regulatory bodies.
20. "Crude Oil Production Increases," *Calgary Herald*, January 26, 1970, citing Alberta Oil and Gas Conservation Board statistics.
21. Don Sellar, "Strom Optimistic for Oil Boom," *Calgary Herald*, February 7, 1970. The report cited by Strom was prepared by Washington, DC, consultants Foster Associates.
22. George Brimmell, "Task Force Split on Oil Controls," *Calgary Herald*, February 21, 1970.
23. Editorial, "Outlook for Oil," *Calgary Herald*, February 21, 1970. These figures would turn out to be wildly off target.
24. Michael Cassidy, "Oil Exports Won't Drop," *Calgary Herald*, February 25, 1970.

25. "Trudeau On Resources: Why Not Sell Them," *Calgary Herald*, February 25, 1970.
26. Clarkson and McCall, *Trudeau and Our Times*, 2: 94–102.
27. William L. Ryan, "It's Not a Feud Today," *Calgary Herald*, November 26, 1971.
28. "Denison Sale Blockade May Force Closure," *Albertan*, March 21, 1970.
29. Fred Kennedy, "The Yanks Are Coming!" *Albertan*, March 11, 1970.
30. The dust finally cleared for Denison on Christmas Eve 1970 with the federal government agreeing to pay the company $30 million for buying and stockpiling uranium. All the miners kept their jobs.
31. Ben Tierney, "Foreign Ownership Limitations," *Calgary Herald*, March 24, 1970.
32. "Husky President Raps Buy-Back-Canada View," *Calgary Herald*, May 9, 1970.
33. "Living next to you [the US] is in some ways like sleeping with an elephant: no matter how friendly and even-tempered the beast, one is affected by every twitch and grunt." Speech to the National Press Club during March 1969 meetings with Nixon. Bothwell and Granatstein, *Pirouette*, 51.
34. Ben Tierney, "Energy Policy Tied to Oil Curbs," *Calgary Herald*, May 12, 1970.
35. Victor Mackie, "Opposition Attacks 'Belligerent' Greene," *Calgary Herald*, May 14, 1970.
36. Dalton Camp, "Joe Greene's Nationalism Baffles US Oil Tycoons," *Albertan*, May 22, 1970.
37. "Oilman Blasts Greene," *Calgary Herald*, May 27, 1970.
38. "Greene Slammed as Oil Industry Foe," *Albertan*, June 19, 1970.
39. "Lang Champions Resource Solidity," *Albertan*, June 8, 1970.
40. Richard Bronstein, "Western Liberals Support Greene," *Albertan*, June 9, 1970.
41. Tom Kennedy, "Greene Holds Tough Line," *Albertan*, June 23, 1970.
42. Don Sellar, "Ottawa Studying Oil Import Curves," *Calgary Herald*, August 8, 1970.
43. Bogdan Kipling, "NEB Gets Tough on Oil Imports," *Calgary Herald*, July 24, 1970.
44. Editorial, "Heavy Blow," *Calgary Herald*, August 5, 1970.
45. "Ruling Stuns Oil Industry, Action Expected," *Calgary Herald*, August 5, 1970.
46. Pat O'Callaghan, "Greene Plugs Oil Policy Gap," *Calgary Herald*, August 14, 1970.
47. Carl Mollins, "National Oil Policy Upheld," *Albertan*, September 18, 1970. Caloil's appeal to the Supreme Court of Canada was dismissed in November 1970.
48. Peter Calamai, "Assured Access to New Arctic Pipeline," *Calgary Herald*, August 14, 1970.
49. Jim Armstrong, "Sensible Move," *Calgary Herald*, August 22, 1970.
50. Jim Armstrong, "Many Implications from Gas Rulings," *Calgary Herald*, October 1, 1970.
51. "Western Liberal Attacks Gas Sale," *Calgary Herald*, October 2, 1970.
52. "Patrick Raps Ottawa's Natural Gas Decision," *Calgary Herald*, October 9, 1970.
53. Jim Armstrong, "Quota Decision Bans Inequities," *Calgary Herald*, October 3, 1970.

11 Hustle Grain!

1. Westell, *Paradox*, 67.
2. The IGA was an international agreement between wheat exporting and importing nations to provide price stability and security of supply after the disruptions caused by World War II. It included mandatory price ranges, and supply and purchase undertakings. "Grains Trade and Food Security Cooperation," International Grains Council, accessed July 2015, igc.int/en/aboutus/default.aspx
3. Bruce Phillips, "Damp Wheat Issue Causes House Uproar," *Calgary Herald*, November 28, 1968; Editorial, "Wheat Foul-Up," *Calgary Herald*, January 24, 1968.
4. The CWB at the time was a federal government vehicle that handled all aspects of grain marketing to protect the Canadian farmer from market disruptions. Its form had evolved since its World War I beginnings. "About us," Canadian Wheat Board, accessed May 2011, www.cwb.ca/public/en/about/history
5. Since the money due to each farmer could not be calculated until sales for the entire crop year were received, the CWB developed a two-payment system. Producers received an initial payment upon delivery, and a final payment when the value of all sales had been calculated. The initial payment was a floor price, guaranteed; if the farmer's final share calculation turned out to be less, the loss was to be assumed by the government.
6. Bob Hill, "10-Year Plan to Be Debated," *Calgary Herald*, March 22, 1969.
7. John Schmidt, "Don't Just Send Problem to U.S." *Calgary Herald*, March 26, 1969.
8. "Olson Slams Farm Groups," *Albertan*, April 14, 1969.
9. Bob Hill, "Farm Cash Program Unlikely," *Calgary Herald*, June 3, 1969.
10. John Schmidt, "Agricultural Alberta," *Calgary Herald*, June 11, 1969.
11. John Schmidt, "Agricultural Alberta," *Calgary Herald*, June 26, 1969.
12. Michael Cassidy, "Prairie Wheat Price Future in Balance As Talks Begin," *Calgary Herald*, July 10, 1969.
13. "Wheat Acreage Slashed," *Calgary Herald* on July 17, 1969.
14. "Westerners Feel Isolated—Olson," *Calgary Herald*, July 14, 1969.
15. Westell, *Paradox*, 68. A senior PMO staffer from that time also told me that Trudeau was not much interested in farm issues or indeed most economic matters, preferring to delegate to his ministers. While Trudeau was vitally interested in the distribution of wealth, he was mostly disinterested in the production of wealth.
16. "Too Much Wheat Trudeau Warns," *Calgary Herald*, July 15, 1969.
17. J.R. Walker, "Trudeau Given Rugged Time by Angry Farmers in Regina," *Calgary Herald*, July 17, 1969.
18. J.R. Walker, "PM Suggests Needy Farmers Receive Cash Advancement," *Calgary Herald*, July 17, 1969.
19. "Trudeau Warned of Farmer Crisis," *Calgary Herald*, July 18, 1969.

20. Patrick O'Callaghan, "The Battle Was Fierce but Trudeau Is Still Boss," *Calgary Herald*, July 28, 1969.
21. Editorial, "This Is the West?" *Calgary Herald*, July 18, 1969.
22. Mel Hurtig, "A Non-Political Visit to the West," *Calgary Herald*, July 30, 1969.
23. "Wheat Prices at Eight-Year Low," *Calgary Herald*, August 21, 1969.
24. "Farmers' Unions 'Not Too Excited,'" *Calgary Herald*, August 2, 1969.
25. Harold Greer, "Wheat Sale," *Calgary Herald*, September 2, 1969.
26. "Illegal Grain Sales Rising," *Calgary Herald*, February 23, 1970.
27. "Wheat Outlook Brightens," *Calgary Herald*, January 10, 1970.
28. "Lang Sees Price Boost," *Calgary Herald*, February 4, 1970.
29. Nick Hills, "$140 Million No-Wheat Policy," *Calgary Herald*, February 27, 1970.
30. "Agriculture Leaders Seem Happy," *Calgary Herald*, February 27, 1970.
31. Don Sellar, "Socreds, Tories Back Program," *Calgary Herald*, Feb 28, 1970.
32. "Runciman Hits Wheat Reduction," *Albertan*, March 12, 1970.
33. "Prairies Could Become Dust-Bowl," *Calgary Herald*, March 3, 1970.
34. "Wheat Scheme Angers MP," *Calgary Herald*, March 28, 1970.
35. "Wheat Program Claimed Doomed," *Calgary Herald*, March 25, 1970.
36. "Alberta May Enter Marketing Field," *Calgary Herald*, May 7, 1970.
37. Gordon Arnold, "Days of Decision for Alberta Farmer," *Calgary Herald*, May 2, 1970.
38. Nick Hills, "Wheat Nations Agree to Cut Crop Yield," *Calgary Herald*, May 6, 1970.
39. "Alberta Wheat Pool, Canadian Grain Exports Making Gains," *Albertan*, June 27, 1970.
40. "Farmers Taking the Pledge on Wheat," *Calgary Herald*, July 11, 1970.
41. Gayle K. Honey, "Stockpiles Face Farmers as Year Fades," *Albertan*, September 4, 1970.
42. "Grain Prospects 'Excellent'–Hays," *Albertan*, September 16, 1970.
43. Carl Mollins, "Record Grain Sales Ahead," *Albertan*, September 24, 1970.
44. Nick Hills, "Horner: The Tories' Rising Star," *Calgary Herald*, October 20, 1970.

12   The Infernal White Paper

1. Editorial, "Tax Hunger," *Calgary Herald*, January 13, 1969.
2. Don Sellar, "Tory MP Charges Trudeau Aiming for Dictatorship," *Calgary Herald*, January 13, 1969.
3. McQuaig, *Behind Closed Doors*, 123–53.
4. Editorial, "Nothing for the Pain," *Calgary Herald*, March 13, 1969.
5. Wearing, *L-Shaped Party*, 141–44.
6. "Main White Paper Proposals," *Calgary Herald*, November 8, 1969.
7. John Walker, "Tax Reforms to Help Poor," *Calgary Herald*, November 8, 1969.
8. Tom Kennedy, "Tax Ideas Wanted," *Albertan*, November 13, 1969.
9. Don Sellar, "Alberta Reaction Cautious," *Calgary Herald*, November 8, 1969.

10. "Woolliams Leads Tory Charge, Calls White Paper 'Fascist,'" *Calgary Herald*, December 2, 1969.
11. "Small Business Endangered," *Calgary Herald*, November 8, 1969.
12. Gillen was the husband of Alberta Senator Joyce Fairbairn.
13. Sykes served as mayor until 1977. He tried to revive the dying provincial Social Credit, and lead the party from 1980 to 1982. In 1984 Sykes ran as a Liberal in the riding of Calgary East but was soundly beaten; he later became an active supporter of the federal Reform and Canadian Alliance parties.
14. Don Sellar, "'Just Society' Not Cheap—Benson," *Calgary Herald*, November 13, 1969; "Liberals pepper Benson," *Albertan*, November 13, 1969.
15. Fraser Perry, "Tax Reform Proposals Worry IPAC Officers," *Calgary Herald*, November 15, 1969.
16. Nick Hills, "Prairie Crisis Warning Given," *Calgary Herald*, December 9, 1969.
17. "Ottawa Won't Abandon Goal of 'Just' Tax System-MP," *Calgary Herald*, December 9, 1969.
18. "Calgary MP to Assist Benson," *Calgary Herald*, October 2, 1970.
19. "Olson Raps Critics of Taxation Paper," *Calgary Herald*, January 23, 1970.
20. Jim Armstrong, The Oil Patch, *Calgary Herald*, January 27, 1970. When government pursued policies the oilmen did not like, they often threatened to move operations to the US. During the NEP days of the early 1980s, some companies did go south but met with little success, discovering that because of the steep decline in international oil prices, things there were even worse.
21. Carol Caney, "White Paper Would Raise Utility Rates," *Calgary Herald*, February 21, 1970.
22. Kevin Peterson, "Tax Changes Disastrous Lougheed Warns Alberta," *Calgary Herald*, February 24, 1970.
23. "White Paper Said Threat to National Unity," *Calgary Herald*, February 27, 1970.
24. "Tax Reform Plan 'Hysteria,'" *Albertan*, March 5, 1970.
25. Marcel Gauthier, "Lougheed Sounds Alarm on Oil Money," *Albertan*, March 25, 1970.
26. Asper was a right-wing Liberal who would later lead the Manitoba Liberals, and after politics he founded the CanWest Global Communications Group media empire. He was a supporter of John Turner's 1984 leadership bid.
27. Izzy Asper, "Your Taxes: The Heated Debate Is Under Way," *Albertan*, April 20, 1970.
28. "Oil Chief Sees Nationalism Aid in Tax Paper," *Albertan*, May 6, 1970; "'Managerial Class' Blamed for White Paper Opposition," *Calgary Herald*, May 6, 1970.
29. Don Peacock, "Income Tax Paper Favours Old Act," *Albertan*, June 6, 1970.
30. "$3 Billion Alta. Loss Predicted," *Albertan*, June 25, 1970.

31. Ben Tierney, "Benson to Ease Stand on Mining: Major Changes in White Paper," *Calgary Herald*, August 27, 1970.
32. "Aalborg Criticizes Tax Revisions," *Albertan*, September 3, 1970.
33. John R. Walker, "Senators Reject Benson Theses," *Calgary Herald*, October 3, 1970.
34. John R. Walker, "Senators Reject Benson Theses," *Calgary Herald*, October 3, 1970.
35. John R. Walker, "MPs Want Benson's Tax Reforms Diluted." *Calgary Herald*, October 6 1970.

13 Fighting Inflation and the Cunning Posties

1. Fraser Kelly and Peter Thomson, "Trudeau Looks around after a Year in Office," *Montreal Gazette*, April 26, 1969.
2. Editorial, "Don't Expect Relief," *Calgary Herald*, May 13, 1969.
3. Editorial, "More Taxes," *Calgary Herald*, May 22, 1969.
4. Vern Simaluk, "Budget Could Stifle City's Building Boom," *Calgary Herald*, June 4, 1969.
5. "West's Building Booms," *Calgary Herald*, June 30, 1969.
6. Editorial, "Mr. Benson's Credibility," *Calgary Herald*, September 23, 1969.
7. Dominion Bureau of Statistics.
8. Jane Becker, "Feeling the Pinch," *Calgary Herald*, September 3, 1969.
9. Editorial, "Fight Against Inflation," *Calgary Herald*, August 8, 1969.
10. Kevin Peterson, "In Calgary the Squeeze Is On," *Calgary Herald*, September 3, 1969.
11. "Canadians Face Pay, Price Freeze," *Calgary Herald*, August 7, 1969.
12. Charles Lynch, "Federal Spending Faces More Cuts," *Calgary Herald*, August 7, 1969.
13. "PM's Civil Service Freeze 'Unrealistic for Calgary,'" *Calgary Herald*, August 14, 1970.
14. Pat O'Callaghan, "Inflation Hurts Everyone," *Calgary Herald*, February 9, 1970.
15. "Interest Rates in Canada Beginning Downward Trend," *Calgary Herald*, February 25, 1970.
16. J.R. Walker, "Curbs on Credit: No New Taxes in the Budget," *Calgary Herald*, March 13, 1970.
17. "Commercial Building Curb Extended," *Calgary Herald*, March 13, 1970.
18. Tom Kennedy, "Fight against Inflation to Persist," *Albertan*, April 15, 1970.
19. Nick Hills, "Ottawa, Unions Heading for Wages Crunch," *Calgary Herald*, March 17, 1970.
20. Editorial, "Strike Folly," *Calgary Herald*, May 15, 1970.
21. "Kierans Won't Bow to Violence Threats in Postal Strike," *Albertan*, March 20, 1970.
22. "Slowdown Hits City Post Office," *Albertan*, May 19, 1970.
23. Nick Hills, "Mail Prospects Grim as Stoppages Spread," *Calgary Herald*, May 15, 1970.
24. "Posties Vote Strike Power," *Albertan*, May 21, 1970.
25. "Labour Backs Postal Battle," *Albertan*, June 12, 1970.

26. Editorial, "Exit Dr. Carrothers; Enter the Public," *Albertan*, June 4, 1970.
27. Editorial, "Strike Folly," *Calgary Herald*, May 15, 1970.
28. "Wage Ceiling till 'War Over,'" *Albertan*, June 12, 1970.
29. "Wage Control Next Step—Trudeau," *Albertan*, June 22, 1970.
30. Nick Hills, "One Postal Pact Signed, but Tough One Unsolved," *Calgary Herald*, July 17, 1970.
31. Nick Hills, "Angry Kierans Attacks Both Sides in Dispute," *Calgary Herald*, July 25, 1970.
32. Editorial, "Close It Down," *Calgary Herald*, July 25, 1970.
33. Bruce Little, "Price Stability Improving," *Calgary Herald*, July 14, 1970.
34. Judith Maxwell, "Experts Say Economy at Standstill," *Calgary Herald*, July 16, 1970.
35. "'Inflation Appears Checked,'" *Calgary Herald*, July 28, 1970.
36. "Work Opportunities Tight as Unemployment Rate Climbs," *Calgary Herald*, August 31, 1970.
37. Gary Park, "Building Slump Continues," *Calgary Herald*, August 31, 1970.
38. Editorial, "Settlement C.O.D.," *Albertan*, September 5, 1970.
39. Fred Kennedy, "Why the Posties Won," *Albertan*, September 5, 1970.

14 The Evolution of the Mighty Social Credit

1. Irving, *Social Credit Movement*, 4–32.
2. Irving, *Social Credit Movement*, 32–40.
3. Brennan, *Good Steward*, 1–7.
4. Brennan, *Good Steward*, 8–13.
5. Irving, *Social Credit Movement*, 44–47.
6. Brennan, *Good Steward*, 13–16.
7. Irving, *Social Credit Movement*, 102.
8. Irving, *Social Credit Movement*, 53–61.
9. Rennie, *Alberta Premiers*, 133.
10. Elections Alberta.
11. Brennan, *Good Steward*, 56–73.
12. MacGregor, *History of Alberta*, 287.
13. The "Protocols" is a notorious anti-Semitic essay describing how Jews were taking control of the world, first published in the Russian empire in 1903 and thereafter disseminated throughout the world.
14. Finkel, *Social Credit Phenomenon*, 104–07.
15. Brennan, *Good Steward*, 95.
16. Anti-Semitic views persisted within Social Credit: Jim Keegstra, later convicted of wilfully promoting hatred of Jews while teaching high school social studies in Eckville,

ran as a candidate in the federal elections of 1972, 1974, and 1984 in Red Deer. The party barely alive, the skeleton of Douglas' theories still rattled in the closet.
17. Groh, "Political Thought," 60–61.
18. Finkel, *Social Credit Phenomenon*, 106–07.
19. Brennan, *Good Steward*, 150–52.
20. Elections Canada.
21. "Another Role for Thompson," *Albertan*, February 4, 1972. During the war Thompson served as a flight lieutenant with the RCAF, after which he was a commander of the Ethiopian air force and an economic advisor to Emperor Haile Selassie.
22. Finkel, *Social Credit Phenomenon*, 159–61.
23. Many years later his concept of political realignment would form the basis of the federal Reform Party founded by his son Preston, and its later incarnations, the Canadian Alliance Party and then the Conservative Party of Canada.
24. Don Sellar, "Manning Resigns Convention Set," *Calgary Herald*, September 27, 1968.
25. Don Sellar, "Manning to Quit Seat after Leadership Meet," *Calgary Herald*, November 19, 1968.
26. Don Sellar, "Social Conservative Philosophy Described by Premier's Son," *Calgary Herald*, September 12, 1968.
27. Don Sellar, "Manning to Quit Seat after Leadership Meet," *Calgary Herald*, November 19, 1968.
28. I met Bobby Brown only once—at the bar of the Ranchmen's Club in Calgary following a Liberal fundraiser. The crowd had thinned out leaving myself and two other young lawyers swilling nightcaps with a diminutive, inebriated but friendly fellow. Brown then insisted that we join him at his nearby mansion, where we enjoyed a few single malts while he regaled us with stories of business deals, politicians, and his Gulfstream jet, as I fumbled away on his giant grand piano.
29. Brennan, *Good Steward*, 111–14.
30. In 1934 Pew was accused of being part of a plot of US industrialists to overthrow President Roosevelt. Archer, *White House*, 31, 160, 228.
31. "Manning Doubts Legality of New Languages Bill," *Calgary Herald*, November 9, 1968; Finkel, *Social Credit Phenomenon*, 149–51.
32. "Manning to Quit as MLA," *Calgary Herald*, December 30, 1968.
33. "Hon. E.C. Manning," *Calgary Herald*, February 18, 1969.
34. Fraser Perry, "Curb Foreign Interests Now, Manning Urges," *Calgary Herald*, May 7, 1969.
35. "PM No Good for West," *Calgary Herald*, June 13, 1969.
36. "Canada Headed for U.S. Union," *Calgary Herald*, September 9, 1969.

15 A Troublesome Relationship

1. Don Sellar, "Liberals Looking for Bigger Piece of Provincial Action," *Calgary Herald*, January 18, 1969.
2. Carstairs later ran unsuccessfully as a provincial Liberal in Calgary and served as Alberta party president before moving to Winnipeg where she became leader of the Manitoba Liberal Party. In the 1988 provincial election her Liberals won 20 out of 57 seats, which made her the first female opposition leader in a Canadian provincial legislature. Jean Chretien appointed his long-time loyalist to the Senate in 1994.
3. Manning is a town of about a thousand named after Ernest Manning in 1947.
4. Susan Jones, "Bob Russell Retiring, Not Retreating," *St. Albert Gazette*, February 8, 2012.
5. Branigan later moved to Whitehorse where he was elected mayor five times and ran three strong but unsuccessful federal campaigns. He continued practicing medicine. He also suggested using ultrasound to treat urban sewage and appeared on national television to perform "psychic surgery." "Deaths: Donald W. Branigan," *Canadian Medical Association Journal* 161, no. 8 (1999): 1087.
6. Don Sellar, "Liberals Pin Hopes on Lowery as Leader," *Calgary Herald*, April 28, 1969.
7. Don Sellar, "Grits Work Hard on Policy," *Calgary Herald*, April 26, 1969.
8. "'Grit Jinx' Broken at Edmonton?" *Calgary Herald*, April 28, 1969.
9. Sir James Lougheed was appointed to the Senate by John A. Macdonald and later knighted by King George V. He served in several ministerial capacities in the Borden government.
10. Wood, *Lougheed Legacy*, 1–44.
11. Wearing, *L-Shaped Party*, 173–80.
12. Sulatycky recalled that in 1968 the party president and treasurer told him he could only have $900 of party money for his federal campaign; most of the available party funds were earmarked for the campaigns of Mike Maccagno and Bud Olson, who were likely winners. Interview with Allen Sulatycky, June 26, 2012.
13. The William A. Switzer Provincial Park near Hinton now bears his name. He was a genuine war hero, possibly involved in an attack that wounded German Field Marshall Rommel in July 1944. RCAF Press Release 4958, January 4, 1945.
14. Editorial, "A Sick Scheme," *Calgary Herald*, February 12, 1969.
15. Don Sellar, "Medicare Entry Poses Problems: Salvage Difficult on Present Plan," *Calgary Herald*, March 21, 1969.
16. Editorial, "Is It Legal?" *Calgary Herald*, July 11, 1969.
17. Don Sellar, "Alberta a Friendly Oasis for PM," *Calgary Herald*, July 10, 1970.
18. Don Sellar, "Alberta a Friendly Oasis for PM," *Calgary Herald*, July 10, 1970.
19. Don Sellar, "Mahoney Says West's Grits Should Be United Force," *Calgary Herald*, December 8, 1969.

20. Interview with Allen Sulatycky, June 26, 2012. Speaker would go on to a political career with a host of Alberta right-wing movements and parties, and be a member of Stephen Harper's transition team in 2006. After Clark's Social Credit days were over in the 1990s, he became ethics commissioner for Ralph Klein's Tory government.
21. Before the negotiations became public Lowery consulted me, among several Alberta Liberals, about the idea of a cooperative deal with Social Credit. My advice (delivered then rather mildly I recall) was that it would be a very hard sell to Liberals because of the thirty-five-year-old antagonisms between the two parties.
22. "Gov't 'Developing Liberal Element,'" *Albertan*, February 24, 1970; Jim Stott, "Liberals, SCS Study Tie-In," *Calgary Herald*, December 30, 1969.
23. Jim Stott, "Liberals, SCS Study Tie-In," *Calgary Herald*, December 30, 1969.
24. "Coalition Proposal Spars Strong Provincial Reaction," *Calgary Herald*, December 30, 1969.
25. Interview with Allen Sulatycky, June 26, 2012.
26. Don Peacock, "Lowery Trying to Defossilize a Party of Lawyers," *Albertan*, January 2, 1970.
27. "Coalition Proposal Spars Strong Provincial Reaction," *Calgary Herald*, December 30, 1969.
28. Fred Kennedy, "Votes for Sale?" *Albertan*, January 2, 1970.
29. Don Sellar, "Liberals Spurned on Ridings Deal," *Calgary Herald*, January 7, 1970.
30. "Liberals Lowery Will Not Step Down," *Albertan*, January 5, 1970.
31. Don Sellar, "Olson to Hit Lowery Foes," January 21, 1970.
32. Peacock, *Barefoot on the Hill*, 9.
33. Interview with Nick Taylor, May 2011.
34. Interview with Allen Sulatycky, June 26, 2012.
35. Don Sellar, "Liberals Support Lowery," *Calgary Herald*, January 19, 1970; Interview with Allen Sulatycky, June 26, 2012.
36. Interview with Allen Sulatycky, June 26, 2012.
37. Pat O'Callaghan, "Party within a Party for West Liberals Get Less Than Unanimous Support," *Calgary Herald*, January 22, 1970.
38. Kevin Peterson, "Lowery Quits as Grit Leader," *Calgary Herald*, February 16, 1970.
39. David Mabell, "Liberal Convention 'A Waste,'" *Albertan*, February 17, 1970.
40. Fred Kennedy, "Little Men, What Now?" *Albertan*, February 18, 1970.
41. Horodezky's partner in the new project was Calgarian Sheldon Chumir, a brilliant scholar, lawyer, and entrepreneur, who would later be elected as a Calgary Liberal MLA.
42. Mike Hunter, "Aberhart's Office Now a Rock Club," *Albertan*, January 16, 1970.

16   The Making of a Senator

1. "Grit Meet to Go On as Planned," *Calgary Herald*, February 18, 1970.
2. "Two-Way Split Urged in Grit Organization," *Calgary Herald*, February 20, 1970.
3. Kevin Peterson, "Grit Gets Socred Post," *Calgary Herald*, January 7, 1970.
4. Kevin Peterson, "Bitter Debate on Grit–Socred Alliance Talks," *Calgary Herald*, February 17, 1970.
5. Don Peacock, "Gloom Reigns as Leaderless Liberals Meet," *Albertan*, February 28, 1970.
6. Don Peacock, "Two-Pronged Party Denied," *Albertan*, March 2, 1970.
7. Don Sellar, "Convention Fails to Propel Liberals Out of Wilderness," *Calgary Herald*, March 2, 1970.
8. Wearing, *L-Shaped Party*, 126.
9. Don Sellar, "Convention Fails to Propel Liberals Out of Wilderness," *Calgary Herald*, March 2, 1970.
10. Don Peacock, "Two-Pronged Party Denied," *Albertan*, March 2, 1970.
11. "Grits Oppose Any Coalitions," *Calgary Herald*, March 2, 1970.
12. Don Peacock, "Two-Pronged Party Denied," *Albertan*, March 2, 1970.
13. "PM's Deaf Ear on Farm Problems Has Socred Back-Bencher Riled," *Calgary Herald*, February 4, 1970.
14. "Tax Upheaval to Hurt Alta.—Lougheed," *Albertan*, February 24, 1970.
15. Don Sellar, "Tories, Socreds Rip White Paper," *Calgary Herald*, March 25, 1970.
16. Interview with Roger Kerans, October 6, 2006.
17. Interview with Charles Kelly, December 30, 2015.
18. According to Sulatycky, Olson's dislike for him stretched on for many years. In 1982 when Sulatycky expressed an interest in an Alberta judicial appointment, Olson, now a senator, a cabinet minister, and political minister for Alberta, opposed the appointment. However, Jean Chretien supported Sulatycky and prevailed on Olson to change his mind. Interview with Allen Sulatycky, June 26, 2012.
19. Don Sellar, "SCs Happy with Meeting," *Calgary Herald*, May 4, 1970; "Liberal Sizes Up Socreds," *Albertan*, May 2, 1970.
20. "16 Socreds Named as Key Albertans," *Calgary Herald* May 6, 1970. One was government policy advisor Jack Flaherty who actually became a Liberal MLA thirty-four years later, long after Social Credit had bitten the dust. Another was Don Hamilton, an executive assistant to Strom, who thirty years later would work as the PC government's ethics commissioner.
21. Interview with Allen Sulatycky, June 26, 2012; Marcel Gauthier, "Ottawa Love Affair Blooms," *Albertan*, May 1, 1970.
22. "Taylor Back in Highway Seat," *Calgary Herald*, May 7, 1970; Wayne MacDonald, "Taylor Concedes to Constituents," *Albertan*, May 7, 1970. After that Taylor did not come close

to supporting Liberals of any stripe. He was re-elected in 1971 and in 1973, once again sought unsuccessfully the leadership to replace Strom. He then sat as an Independent Social Credit member but supported the Lougheed Tories' legislative program. In 1979 he won the federal riding of Bow River as a right-wing PC.

23. John Mika, "Would You Believe, Senator Manning?" *Albertan*, May 20, 1970.
24. Don Sellar, "Manning Appointment Mirrors Thaw," *Calgary Herald*, October 7, 1970.

17 Western Alienation and the Rabble-rousers

1. Pratt and Stevenson, *Western Separatism*, 193–97.
2. Pratt and Stevenson, *Western Separatism*, 105–12.
3. Reich, *Origins of Terrorism*, 88.
4. Dunton et al., *Royal Commission*, 1:173.
5. Dunton et al., *Royal Commission*.
6. Pierre Elliott Trudeau, "Statement on the Introduction of the Official Languages Bill," speech, House of Commons, Ottawa, October 17, 1968. Accessed January 4, 2015. www.canadahistory.com/sections/documents/Primeministers/trudeau/docs-officiallanguagesact.htm
7. Frye, *Collected Works*, 12:46.
8. Bob Hill, "Language Discrimination Claimed by Ukrainians," *Calgary Herald*, December 15, 1968.
9. J.R. Walker, "One Country or None—PM," *Calgary Herald*, February 10, 1969.
10. Don Sellar, "Alberta Offers 'Deal,'" *Calgary Herald*, February 10, 1969.
11. "9000 Albertans Wire Protests," *Calgary Herald*, February 10, 1969.
12. J.R. Walker, "Bilingualism Progress Satisfactory—Trudeau," *Calgary Herald*, February 13, 1969.
13. Parker Kent, an ardent monarchist and conservative, was the father of Peter and Arthur Kent. Peter, who anchored CBC's *The National*, is currently Conservative MP for the Ontario riding of Thornhill. Younger brother Arthur was an NBC reporter and later ran unsuccessfully as a provincial PC candidate in Calgary in the 2008 Alberta general election.
14. Parker Kent, "Why Knock It?" *Calgary Herald*, February 17, 1969.
15. Parker Kent, "Languages Act," *Calgary Herald*, March 3, 1969.
16. Parker Kent, "It's Bad Law," *Calgary Herald*, June 2, 1969.
17. Editorial, "Slow Down," *Calgary Herald*, May 24, 1969.
18. "Western Premiers Hit for Language Opposition," *Calgary Herald*, March 25, 1969.
19. Letters to the Editor, *Calgary Herald*, June 5, 1969.
20. Editorial, "It's Dominion Day," *Calgary Herald*, July 3, 1969.
21. "Bilingual Class Likely by Fall," *Calgary Herald*, June 17, 1969.

22. "Language Bill Passes Parliament," *Calgary Herald*, July 8, 1969.
23. Charles Lynch, "The Nation," *Calgary Herald*, February 6, 1970.
24. Charles Lynch, "The Nation," *Calgary Herald*, February 6, 1970. Cameron, head of the Banff School of Fine Arts (1936–1969) was appointed Senator by St. Laurent in 1955.
25. Nick Hills, "Trudeau Sparks Row over West," *Calgary Herald*, February 10, 1970.
26. Harradence, who I knew and liked, had a flair for dramatic storytelling both in and out of the courtroom. In private profanity-laden conversations, he used a conspiratorial sotto voce, eyes darting about the room and head slightly crouched, as if making sure nobody else was listening. He was often amusingly imitated.
27. Harradence flew his own P-51 Mustang Vampire and F-86 Sabre jet in air shows across the continent, and World War II aircraft for dogfight scenes in the 1969 movie *The Battle of Britain*.
28. Gerry Deagle, "Calgarians Study Independent West," *Calgary Herald*, February 11, 1970.
29. Gerry Deagle, "Harries Declined Job with New West Group," *Calgary Herald*, February 12, 1970.
30. "Separatism No Option: Mahoney," *Albertan*, February 17, 1970.
31. "Big Business Backs Western Separatism," *Albertan*, February 17, 1970.
32. "Study on Separate West 'Could Result in Action,'" *Calgary Herald*, February 21, 1970.
33. Fred Kennedy, "A Wasted Effort," *Albertan*, February 24, 1970.
34. Charles Lynch, "The Nation," *Calgary Herald*, February 27, 1970.
35. Ben Tierney, "Alberta Seems to Be Centre of Separatism," *Calgary Herald*, March 9, 1970.
36. "Major Toronto Firm Consulted on Western 'Task Force' Plan," *Calgary Herald*, March 10, 1970. Stevenson later lost as a Liberal against Lougheed in 1971. Stevenson later related to me that he bumped into Lougheed after the election. Lougheed asked him if he planned on running against him again. Stevenson replied, "Definitely not. I ran against you the last time and you became premier. I'm afraid if I do it again you'll become Prime Minister." Lougheed later appointed Stevenson a Provincial Court Judge.
37. Carol Caney, "Case for West Separatism," *Albertan*, March 19, 1970.
38. "PM Pleads with West," *Calgary Herald*, March 21, 1970.
39. Richard Bronstein, "Call for Independent West," *Albertan*, April 10, 1970.
40. "Demand Soars for New Offices" *Albertan*, March 12, 1970.
41. "Where Is Canada Going? Asks Jack Horner, PC," *Albertan*, May 21, 1970.
42. Jack Horner was first elected as a Tory by the central Alberta riding of Acadia (later Crowfoot) in 1958 and was re-elected six more times as a Tory by huge majorities. He was a strident critic of both Trudeau and his government. In 1976, when he ran for the Tory leadership, he lost out to fellow Albertan Joe Clark. In April 1977, after several squabbles with Clark, Horner was enticed to join the Liberals with the offer of a senior

cabinet portfolio. However, as a Liberal Horner suffered back-to-back losses to his Tory opponent in 1979 and 1980, thus bringing his political career to a close.

Several months after Horner's defection, who should present himself to buy a membership and register for the Liberal convention but his cousin Harradence. After I expressed my surprise, he replied in his conspiratorial near-whisper, eyes darting about the room, "Son of a bitch, Raymaker. Jesus Christ! Just sell me a goddamn membership!" Chuckling, I took his ten bucks. Several months later, Minister of Justice Marc Lalonde appointed Harradence to the Alberta Court of Appeal. I had sold Harradence his lucky ticket.

18   The October Crisis

1. "U.K. Official Kidnapped in Montreal," *Calgary Herald*, October 5, 1970.
2. John Gray, "Pierre Elliott Trudeau: 1919–2000, How Trudeau Halted the Reign of Terror," *Globe and Mail*, September 30, 2000.
3. "Police Watching Separatist Moves," *Calgary Herald*, October 6, 1970.
4. "Kidnappers Give Another Deadline," *Calgary Herald*, October 7, 1970.
5. "Fate of Diplomat Remains Mystery," *Calgary Herald*, October 8, 1970.
6. "Kidnapping Break—Two Sides Talk, Quebec Cabinet Meets," *Calgary Herald*, October 13, 1970.
7. "Kidnapping Break—Two Sides Talk, Troops On Guard in Ottawa," *Calgary Herald*, October 13, 1970.
8. English, *Just Watch Me*, 82–84.
9. "War Measures Act Proclaimed, Terrorist FLQ. Now Outlawed, Police Hit Separatists," *Calgary Herald*, October 16, 1970.
10. "War Measures Act Proclaimed, Terrorist FLQ. Now Outlawed, Police Hit Separatists," *Calgary Herald*, October 16, 1970.
11. Nick Hills, "'Violence Forced My Hand,'" *Calgary Herald*, October 16, 1970.
12. "Stanfield, Douglas Attack Liberals' Actions," *Calgary Herald*, October 16, 1970.
13. "Trudeau—Right or Wrong? Commons Debates Issues," *Calgary Herald*, October 17, 1970.
14. Editorials *Calgary Herald*: "Don't Blame Quebec," October 6, 1970; "Only Course," October 8, 1970; "Dire Necessity," October 16, 1970; "Care Needed," October 17, 1970.
15. "Mixed Feelings Greet Measure," *Calgary Herald*, October 16, 1970.
16. "Lougheed Lauds Government Move," *Calgary Herald*, October 17, 1970.
17. "Veiner Withdraws Ransom Offer," *Calgary Herald*, October 17, 1970.
18. "Police Find FLQ Hideout," *Calgary Herald*, October 19, 1970.
19. "Canada—Call for Unity Resounds," *Calgary Herald*, October 19, 1970.
20. "Calgary—86 P.C. Back Proclamation," *Calgary Herald*, October 19, 1970.

21. "Canada—Call for Unity Resounds," *Calgary Herald,* October 19, 1970.
22. "FLQ Action Discussed in Schools," *Calgary Herald,* October 19, 1970.
23. "Liberal MP Sees More FLQ Trouble," *Calgary Herald,* October 21, 1970.
24. Tom Kennedy, "Manning Points a Firm Finger at Ottawa Policies," *Albertan,* November 6, 1970.
25. "Terrorism Hasn't Ended, PM Warns," *Calgary, Herald,* November 6, 1970.
26. "Anti-Kidnap Security Cut," *Calgary Herald,* November 10, 1970.
27. Leon Levinson, "Sedition Charges Laid Against 10," *Calgary Herald,* November 6, 1970.
28. "Laporte Case Suspect Held," *Calgary Herald,* November 7, 1970.
29. "PM Wins Phone Poll Approval," *Albertan,* November 16, 1970.
30. "'Attack Violence at Root'—Manning," *Calgary Herald,* November 19, 1970.
31. Susan Becker, "Manning Backs War Act Move," *Albertan,* November 19, 1970.
32. "Quebec Stand by Tories Hit," *Calgary Herald,* December 16, 1979.
33. Editorial, "The Only Way," *Calgary Herald,* December 5, 1970.
34. Charles King, "Ottawa's Stand Had Strom's Support," *Calgary Herald,* December 14, 1970.

19 The Splendours of OPEC and the Saga of Home Oil

1. "Crude Oil Output Up," *Calgary Herald,* October 30, 1970.
2. Fraser Perry, "Greene Says Oil Sales to U.S. Will Increase," *Calgary Herald,* November 17, 1970.
3. Nielsen, *We Gambled Everything,* 143–44.
4. "U.S. to Drop Quotas on Oil," *Albertan,* November 25, 1970.
5. Tom Kennedy, "Oilmen React Cautiously," *Albertan,* November 26, 1970.
6. "U.S. Price Hikes 'To Be Felt Here,'" *Calgary Herald,* November 17, 1970.
7. OPEC, an organization of oil exporting nations, was founded in 1960 by Iran, Iraq, Kuwait, Saudi Arabia, and Venezuela to set and stabilize international oil prices to ensure steady streams of oil income to its member nations. By 1970, its members included the original six nations plus Qatar, Indonesia, Libya, the United Arab Emirates, Algeria, Nigeria, Ecuador, and Gabon.
8. Jim Armstrong, "Suddenly, Ours Is the 'Cheap Oil,'" *Calgary Herald,* December 11, 1970.
9. "More Firms Lift Crude Oil Price," *Calgary Herald,* December 16, 1970.
10. Jim Armstrong, "Critics of Hike Away Off Base," *Calgary Herald,* December 19, 1970.
11. Jim Armstrong, The Oil Patch, *Calgary Herald,* January 7, 1970, citing year-end estimates for 1970 compiled by *The Daily Oil Bulletin.*
12. Jim Armstrong, The Oil Patch, *Calgary Herald,* January 12, 1971, citing the Toronto Dominion Bank's 1971 *Canadian Petroleum Industry: Achievements and Prospects.*
13. "Oilmen Warned; Public Skeptical," *Calgary Herald,* January 21, 1971.

14. "Oil Countries Stand Pat on Revenue Demands," *Calgary Herald*, January 17, 1971.
15. "Canada Won't Get Involved in World Oil Price Fight," *Calgary Herald*, January 21, 1971.
16. "Pact Boosts Activity Here," *Albertan*, February 16, 1971.
17. Ben Tierney, "Oil Group Says Controls Likely," *Calgary Herald*, January 25, 1971.
18. Maurice Western, "We're All Going to Invest in CDC," *Albertan*, February 1, 1971.
19. Tom Kennedy, "CDC—Chance for J. Canuck," *Albertan* February 10, 1971.
20. Smith, *Treasure Seekers*, 254–96.
21. Austin, born and raised in Calgary, was a Vancouver corporate lawyer and mining entrepreneur before becoming Greene's deputy minister. He later helped establish Petro-Canada, and did a stint as Trudeau's chief of staff before moving on to the Senate in 1975, where he served as minister of state for social development and leader of the government.
22. Fred Kennedy, "Dry Those Oily Tears," *Albertan*, February 23, 1971.
23. Smith, *Treasure Seekers*, 278.
24. "Gov't Bid for Home Control" *Albertan*, March 12, 1971.
25. Al Ross, a Calgary oil company executive, was also a lifelong Liberal even though he was often at odds with the party's policies. In October 1980, when Minister of Energy Marc Lalonde asked for some influential locals to brief about the nascent national energy policy, I invited Ross, two other oil executives, and three party executives. Ross courageously took the lead pleading with Lalonde to reject interventionist policies that could very well break up the country. To which an exasperated Lalonde replied, "If the country can break up that easily, maybe it's not worth saving." The National Energy Program was passed, thus giving Alberta and the Tories a club with which to beat the heads of Alberta Liberals for the next thirty-plus years.
26. Tom Kennedy, "IPAC Urges Caution in Home Takeover," *Albertan*, March 16, 1971.
27. David May, "Harries Suggests Limitations on Foreign Investing," *Albertan*, March 18, 1971.
28. Smith, *Treasure Seekers*, 284.
29. "R.A. Brown, Jr., Dies at 57; Headed Home Oil Since 1952," *Calgary Herald*, January 4, 1972.

20 The Rough Sport of Politics

1. Don Sellar, "Lougheed Mustering Tory Might," *Calgary Herald*, July 11, 1970.
2. "PCs Have High Hopes in Alberta," *Calgary Herald*, August 10, 1970.
3. Don Sellar, "Strom Holding Fire on Pre-Election Cabinet Shuffle," *Calgary Herald*, October 1, 1970.
4. Don Sellar, "Province to Use Ottawa Facilities," *Calgary Herald*, November 20, 1970.
5. "Record Slate Trying for Legislature Seats," *Calgary Herald*, January 5, 1971.

6. Craig Baird, "Grant Notley: An Alberta Legend Gone Too Soon," *High River Times*, December 8, 2010.
7. Finally elected in 1971 in the riding of Spirit River–Fairview, Notley was re-elected three times and became leader of the opposition, but sadly died in a plane crash in 1984. In 1961, while Notley and I were in our first year of law school, he invited me to a CCF meeting on campus to hear soon-to-be leader Neil Reimer. When the meeting ended and the party regulars joined hands and started singing "Solidarity Forever," I quickly made my exit. His daughter, Edmonton MLA Rachel Notley, became leader of the Alberta NDP in 2014 and premier of Alberta in 2015 when her party routed the PCS after forty-four consecutive years in office.
8. Patrick O'Callaghan, "The Big Test Awaits Strom," *Calgary Herald*, November 14, 1970.
9. Don Sellar, "Election Still Months Away but Parties Already Plotting," *Calgary Herald*, November 3, 1970.
10. "Spending Crisis 'Socreds Fault,'" *Calgary Herald*, October 5, 1970.
11. Don Sellar, "Program Counters Tory Criticism," *Calgary Herald*, November 9, 1970.
12. "Patrick Charges CBC 'Hysterical,'" *Calgary Herald*, November 18, 1970.
13. Don Sellar, "Media Accused of Skullduggery," *Calgary Herald*, November 21, 1970.
14. Don Sellar, "Election-Year Budget Strom's Next Hurdle," *Calgary Herald*, December 28, 1970.
15. "Hooke Slams Socreds," *Calgary Herald*, February 9, 1971.
16. "Petrasuk Refuses to Resign," *Calgary Herald*, October 19, 1970.
17. Don Sellar, "Liberals Looking for New Leader," *Calgary Herald*, December 15, 1970.
18. "Bow from Scene MP Tells Grits," *Calgary Herald*, January 6, 1971.
19. Don Sellar, "Lawyer to Seek Alberta Grit Presidency," *Calgary Herald*, January 7, 1971.
20. Don Sellar, "Lawyer to Seek Alberta Grit Presidency," *Calgary Herald*, January 7, 1971.
21. "Independence Urged for Provincial Grits," *Calgary Herald*, January 19, 1971.
22. Don Sellar, "Pat Mahoney Likes to Help People with Problems," *The Herald Magazine*, January 28, 1972.
23. Don Sellar, "Liberals Draft Election Line," *Calgary Herald*, January 23, 1971.
24. Don Sellar, "Six Out of Ten Provinces Tory in '71," *Calgary Herald*, January 23, 1971.
25. Don Sellar, Kevin Peterson, "Tories Show They're Set for Battle," *Calgary Herald*, January 25, 1971.
26. "Political Wilderness Ahead, Unless Grits Pick Leader Now," *Calgary Herald*, January 27, 1971.
27. "Liberals Still Grappling with Leadership Issues," *Calgary Herald*, January 30, 1971.
28. Richard Bronstein, "Alberta Liberals Take Move to Left," *Albertan*, February 1, 1971.

29. Olson's statement strained credulity. In my extensive experience in political fund-raising, I do not recall a donor insisting that their contribution be earmarked, except on the rare occasion when it was for a specific candidate.
30. "Grits Net No Money," *Albertan,* February 1, 1971.
31. Don Sellar, "Liberals Vote to Choose New Leader," *Calgary Herald*, February 1, 1971.
32. Fred Kennedy, "The 'Poor' Liberals," *Albertan,* February 1, 1971.
33. Don Sellar, "Ex-Grit Leader Lowery Wants to Join Socreds," *Calgary Herald*, February 4, 1971.
34. In 1986 Peacock wrote a highly complimentary biography about Hays entitled *Barefoot on the Hill.*
35. "Liberals' Candidate Tally Is Four," *Albertan*, March 12, 1971.
36. "Grits Warned of Merger," *Albertan,* March 17, 1971.
37. Don Sellar, "Russell Captures Grit Leadership," *Calgary Herald*, March 15, 1971.

21 Blissful Times and the Beginning of the End of Tax Reform

1. Gordon Pape, "Lowest Inflation Seen for Canada," *Calgary Herald*, January 11, 1971.
2. Williams would later serve as national director of the Liberal Party of Canada.
3. Don Sellar, "Grits Gain Ground While Stanfield's Tory Opponents Lie Low," *Calgary Herald*, January 21, 1971.
4. Unless stated otherwise, unemployment rates quoted are Canadian "seasonally adjusted" unemployment rates as published by Statistics Canada. This rate was the actual unemployment rate adjusted by a mathematical formula that took into account the effect on unemployment excluding all seasonal variations. Alberta unemployment rates were real rates, not seasonally adjusted.
5. "Current Year's Unemployment Worst Average in Nine Years," *Calgary Herald*, December 12, 1970.
6. Michael Barkway, "Two Possibilities Open to Benson," *Calgary Herald*, December 2, 1970.
7. Pat O'Callaghan, "Voluntary Wage-Price Guidelines Cancelled," *Calgary Herald*, December 2, 1970.
8. "300 Million Set to Help Jobless," *Calgary Herald*, December 4, 1970.
9. "Unemployed Get Pay Raise," *Albertan*, March 11, 1971.
10. "Trudeau Marries," *Albertan,* March 5, 1971.
11. "Trudeau Stuns Nation—Weds," *Calgary Herald,* March 5, 1971; "PM Honeymoons in Snow and Mist," *Albertan,* March 6, 1971.
12. Fred Kennedy, "For Pierre, the Summit," *Albertan*, March 6, 1971.
13. Jack Gorman, "Short-Term Sale of Surplus Energy Advocated," *Calgary Herald*, April 7, 1971.

14. Jack Gorman, "Cloudy Economy its Oil Drillers," *Calgary Herald*, May 7, 1971.
15. "Oil Pipeline Means 2000 New Jobs," *Calgary Herald*, April 1, 1971.
16. John R. Walker, "Oil Pipeline an Economic Disaster," *Calgary Herald*, April 1, 1971.
17. Tim Traynor, "Nixon Seeks New Oil Pact," *Albertan*, June 5, 1971.
18. Paul Jackson, "Oilmen Remain Cautious," *Albertan*, June 4, 1971.
19. Peter Buckley, "Report Predicts Shortage of Natural Gas Within US," *Albertan*, July 16, 1971.
20. Nick Hills, "Consumer Prices Rise Again; New Inflation Bout Indicated," *Calgary Herald*, April 13, 1971, citing statistics from the Dominion Bureau of Statistics.
21. Nick Hills, "Kierans: Tough and Honest Politician," *Calgary Herald*, May 3, 1971.
22. "Trudeau Met by Kosygin in Moscow," *Calgary Herald*, May 15, 1971.
23. "Nervous Margaret Trudeau Meets Russian Society," *Calgary Herald*, May 19, 1971.
24. "Canada Joins Call to Reduce Troops," *Calgary Herald*, May 28, 1971.
25. Charles Lynch, "Canada, Soviet Pact May Spark New Era in Nations' Relations," *Calgary Herald*, May 20, 1971.
26. "Trudeau Takes His Bride to Moscow," *Life*, June 4, 1971, 32–34.
27. J.R. Walker, "Tax Break for Everyone," *Calgary Herald*, June 18, 1971.
28. Carl Mollins, "PM's Participatory Democracy Put to Test in New Tax Laws," *Calgary Herald*, June 17, 1971.
29. J.R. Walker, "Tax Break for Everyone," *Calgary Herald*, June 18, 1971.
30. "Even Budget's Opponents Are Only Mildly Unhappy," *Calgary Herald*, June 19, 1971.
31. Jack Gorman, "Oil Industry Budget Reaction Cautious," *Calgary Herald*, June 19, 1971.
32. Clarkson and McCall, *Trudeau and Our Times*, 2: 93.
33. Jack Gorman, "IPAC Says Tax Change to Hurt Oil Exploration," *Calgary Herald*, June 23, 1971.
34. Jack Gorman, "IPAC Says Tax Change to Hurt Oil Exploration," *Calgary Herald*, June 23, 1971.
35. Michael Barkway, "Tax Reforms Show Public Debate Effective," *Financial Times of Canada*, June 21, 1971.
36. Charles Lynch, "The Nation," *Calgary Herald*, June 19, 1971.
37. "Alberta Economy Had Gains in All Sectors," *Calgary Herald*, July 21, 1971.
38. "Building Doubles, Farms Oil Strong," *Albertan*, August 20, 1971.
39. Judith Maxwell, "Production Up; 'Recession Ending,'" *Calgary Herald*, July 5, 1971.
40. Judith Maxwell, "Economy Gets Spending Lift," *Calgary Herald*, August 4, 1971.
41. Ben Tierney, "Poll Shows NDP Gaining on Tories," *Calgary Herald*, July 5, 1971.

22 As Good as It Gets

1. Don Peacock, "Yes, Trudeaumania!" *Albertan*," July 10, 1971.
2. Ben Tierney, "PM Wows 'Em—But Where's Margaret?" *Calgary Herald*, July 10, 1971.
3. Don Peacock, "Reflections on Trail Riding with Trudeau," *Albertan*, July 12, 1971.
4. Don Peacock, "Bloods Have Lessons for Canadians—Trudeau," *Albertan*, July 12, 1971.
5. In both 1968 and 1972 general elections, Sulatycky carried that area of his riding for the Liberals. Interview with Allen Sulatycky, June 26, 2012.
6. Finkel, *Social Credit Phenomenon*, 112.
7. Carol Hogg, "Trudeau Finds a New Mood During a Western Weekend," *Calgary Herald*, July 12, 1971.
8. Interview with Allen Sulatycky, June 26, 2012.
9. In 1982 multiculturalism was affirmed in section 27 of the Canadian Charter of Rights and Freedoms.
10. "Trudeau Here for Fun, Not Votes," *Calgary Herald*, July 12, 1971.
11. During a Commons skirmish, opposition members accused Trudeau of having mouthed "fuck off" in their direction. Trudeau denied those words, but admitted moving his lips. Asked, "What were you thinking when you moved your lips?" he replied, "What is the nature of your thoughts, gentlemen, when you say 'fuddle-duddle' or something like that?" English, *Just Watch Me*, 106.
12. Al Scarth, "Crowds Were Friendly Except for the Odd 'Die, Die, Die,'" *Albertan*, July 13, 1971.
13. Don Peacock, "Mrs. Trudeau Was Scene Stealer," *Albertan*, July 13, 1970.
14. "Trudeaus Get Souvenirs," *Calgary Herald*, July 13, 1971.
15. Jack Gorman, "Pierre's Go-Round Gets a Big Lift from Margaret," *Calgary Herald*, July 13, 1971.
16. "Big Day in December for Margaret and Pierre," *Calgary Herald*, July 24, 1971.

23 Lougheed Comes to Power

1. Richard Bronstein, "Verbal War Over Jobless," *Albertan*, February 18, 1971.
2. Richard Bronstein, "Full Use of Albertan Labor Force Urged," *Albertan*, March 12, 1971.
3. Richard Bronstein, "Lougheed Urges Broad Tax Changes," *Albertan*, March 17, 1971.
4. Richard Bronstein, "Ranks Split Over Free Enterprise Call," *Albertan*, March 5, 1971.
5. David May, "Law Catches Taverns on the Wrong Foot," *Albertan*, April 1, 1971. It was only in 1958 that the government first allowed alcohol to be served in dining rooms and lounges; and only since 1967 that men and women in Alberta were allowed to drink beer together in the same beverage room without restrictions.
6. "Legislature Told Liquor Law Outdated," *Calgary Herald*, April 6, 1971.

7. Richard Bronstein, "Civil Servants Storm Legislature for Union Rights," *Albertan*, April 10, 1971.
8. "Socreds 'Destroy' Local Gov't," *Albertan*, April 24, 1971.
9. Richard Bronstein, "Strom Avoids Election Call," *Albertan*, April 28, 1971.
10. Obituary, "Donato Antonio Luzzi Jr.," *Calgary Herald*, November 3, 2005.
11. During the party, the wife of one of Luzzi's campaigners, cheerfully numbed by the evening's refreshments, stumbled and fell on my front steps while walking to her car. We led her back into the house and I called a doctor friend to come over and examine her. After he pronounced her fine, he then stayed on until the wee hours with the remaining partiers. For that evening at least, even the party's theme song could have changed from the hymn "Oh God, Our Help in Ages Past, Our Hope for Years to Come" to "Show Me the Way to Go Home." Like the province, Social Credit was now making a valiant attempt to change.
12. Don Sellar, "Strom Names the Day: Alberta Votes Aug. 30, Election Includes Plebiscite on DST," *Calgary Herald*, July 22, 1971.
13. "Lougheed Hits 'Inadequate' Hail Insurance," *Calgary Herald*, July 27, 1971.
14. Hugh Horner was the brother of MP Jack Horner and the father of former Tory MLA Doug Horner, who served in the Alberta legislature from 2001 to 2015.
15. "$50 Million Urged in Rural Area Aid," *Calgary Herald*, July 28, 1971.
16. "Werry Sees Bias in Job Fund Refusal," *Calgary Herald*, July 28, 1971.
17. Peter Vogan, "Strip Mine at Canmore Becomes Election Issue," *Albertan*, August 4, 1971.
18. "Suit Fights Mt. Rundle Strip Mine," *Albertan*, August 10, 1971.
19. Peter Vogan, "PCs Will Cut Property Tax," *Albertan*, August 4, 1971.
20. Kevin Peterson, "Wilderness in Foothills Promised by Lougheed," *Calgary Herald*, August 5, 1971.
21. Don Sellar, "Strom Offers Home Grants," *Calgary Herald*, August 4, 1971.
22. Editorial, "Housing Policy," *Calgary Herald*, August 6, 1971.
23. "Notley Promises Help to Farmers," *Albertan*, August 5, 1971.
24. "Liberals Pledge Jobs and a Bank," *Calgary Herald*, August 4, 1971.
25. "Grits Seek Candidates," *Calgary Herald*, August 5, 1971.
26. Don Sellar, "Socred Workers Warned: Don't Be Complacent," *Calgary Herald*, August 4, 1971.
27. Al Scarth, "Citizen Integrity," *Albertan*, August 11, 1971.
28. Al Scarth, "PCs Guarantee Citizen Integrity," *Albertan*, August 14, 1971.
29. Don Peacock, "Stoneys Toll Threat Branded 'Political,'" *Albertan*, August 12, 1971.
30. "Jailers Threaten Strike Aug. 25," *Albertan*, August 14, 1971.
31. Hooke, *30 +5: I Know, I Was There*.
32. Announcement, Business Section, "E.C. Manning," *Calgary Herald*, February 18, 1969.

33. The mine in Grand Cache required the construction of the Alberta Resources Railway, which the Manning government had financed to the tune of several million dollars. Hooke was upset with Manning for taking his seat on the Railway board even before trains started moving the coal.
34. Walter Krevenchuk, "Record 243 Race for 75 seats, as SCs and PCs Contest All," *Albertan*, August 17, 1971.
35. W. Krevench, "Notley Foresees at Least Four New Democrat MLAs," *Albertan*, August 20, 1971.
36. "Strom Attacks Media, Opposition," *Calgary Herald*, August 24, 1971.
37. "Strom Attacks Media, Opposition," *Calgary Herald*, August 24, 1971.
38. Don Sellar, "No Time to Change—Manning," *Calgary Herald*, August 26, 1971.
39. "Strom Says Herald Told to Back Tories," *Calgary Herald*, August 26, 1971.
40. Don Sellar, "Lougheed Has 'That Feeling'" Tories Headed for Victory," *Calgary Herald*, August 27, 1971.
41. Elections Alberta.

24 Tax Reform at Last

1. "Canadian Imperial Claims Economy Improving," *Calgary Herald*, July 22, 1971; "...But Bank of Nova Scotia Less Optimistic," *Calgary Herald*, July 22, 1971.
2. Nick Hills, "Curtailing Travel Abroad," *Calgary Herald*, July 28, 1971.
3. "Nixon Freezes U.S. Prices, Invites Devaluation of Dollar," *Albertan*, August 16, 1971.
4. "Canada Asks for Exemption," *Calgary Herald*, August 17, 1971.
5. "Canadian Jobs in Jeopardy," *Albertan*, August 21, 1971.
6. Susan Becker, "Manning Criticizes Favouritism," *Albertan*, October 1, 1971.
7. The consumer price index figures were based on 1961 prices equalling 100.
8. "Food Forces Index Up," *Calgary Herald*, September 16, 1971.
9. Editorial, "Dark Clouds," *Calgary Herald*, September 17, 1971.
10. "Lougheed to Seek Tax Bill Delay," *Calgary Herald*, October 29, 1971.
11. "Tax Bill Hits Snag in House," *Calgary Herald*, November 10, 1971.
12. Nick Hills "Door Closed in Tax Debate," *Calgary Herald*, December 2, 1971.
13. "Manning: No Option Left," *Calgary Herald*, December 20, 1971.
14. Ben Tierney, "Tax Reform Bill Passed by Senate," *Calgary Herald*, December 22, 1971.
15. Paul Jackson, "No Surprise Business Annoyed with Tax Bill," *Albertan*, December 16, 1971.
16. Arthur Blakely, "Job Outlook Getting Better," *Calgary Herald*, November 27, 1971.
17. James Nelson, "National Income Rises 10%, GNP Rate at $93.7 Billion," *Calgary Herald*, December 1, 1971.

18. Duart Farquharson, "Nixon 'Respects' Our Economic Goals," *Calgary Herald*, December 7, 1971.
19. In 1971 the Group of Ten included eleven: Belgium, Canada, France, Germany, Italy, Japan, Netherlands, Sweden, Switzerland, United Kingdom, and the United States.
20. After Trudeau left the meeting, Nixon called him "an asshole" and a "pompous egghead," and said to Henry Kissinger, "What in the Christ is he talking about?" and to his chief of staff, "That Trudeau, he's a clever son of a bitch," all recorded on the infamous Nixon tapes. Years later when asked to comment Trudeau said, "I've been called worse things by better people." Lee-Anne Goodman, "Nixon Tapes Include Testy Trudeau Chat," *Toronto Star*, December 8, 2008.
21. "World Money Back in Shape," *Calgary Herald*, December 20, 1971.
22. "Benson Sees More Buoyant Economy," *Calgary Herald*, December 21, 1971.

25 Peter Lougheed Shows His Stuff

1. Trillion cubic feet (TCF) is a measurement commonly used by the oil and gas industry to describe volumes of natural gas. US natural gas production peaked in 1973 at 22.6 TCF. In 1973 the US consumed approximately 26.03 TCF.
2. "Conflicting Evidence on Gas Needs," *Calgary Herald*, July 14, 1971.
3. Jim Armstrong The Oil Patch, *Calgary Herald*, July 22, 1971.
4. The formula used by the Energy Resources Conservation Board to determine necessary surpluses was based on contracted requirements for the coming year, plus thirty years.
5. "Conflicting Evidence on Gas Needs," *Calgary Herald*, July 14, 1971.
6. Gary Fairbairn, "Alberta Calls for Open Gas Export Market," *Albertan*, July 16, 1971.
7. Blair, an engineer and later CEO of Nova Corporation (formerly the Alberta Gas Trunk Line), Alberta's biggest natural gas pipeline company, was a rarity in the oil patch—a strong economic nationalist who got along well with both the federal and provincial governments. Since his views isolated him from the oilmen's mainstream he was seldom seen in the posh Calgary Petroleum Club. After his retirement he ran unsuccessfully as a Liberal in the 1993 federal election, and later attended Liberal, NDP, and Progressive Conservative party conventions, always supporting economic nationalist policies and candidates. "Former Nova Corp. Boss Leaves a Lasting Legacy," *Alberta Oil*, August, 2009.
8. "Pipeline Start Possible in '73: Blair," *Calgary Herald*, July 19, 1971. An Arctic gas pipeline has yet to be built. The NEB finally approved it in December 2010 but with 264 conditions and a cost then estimated at $16.2 billion. Given low gas prices and major new North American gas discoveries, many now predict that it will never be built. To this day no appreciable amount of gas has ever been produced and transported commercially from Panarctic's discoveries in the high Arctic.

9. "First Phase of Gas Hearing Over," *Calgary Herald*, July 26, 1971.
10. "First Phase of Gas Hearing Over," *Calgary Herald*, July 26, 1971.
11. John Gorman, "$1 Billion Sale to U.S. Rejected," *Calgary Herald*, November 20, 1971.
12. "Lougheed Urges Gas Ruling Review," *Calgary Herald*, November 22, 1971.
13. Editorial, "Energy Policy," *Calgary Herald*, November 23, 1971.
14. Jim Armstrong, The Oil Patch, *Calgary Herald*, November 23, 1971.
15. "Lougheed Chides Ottawa," *Calgary Herald*, November 13, 1971.
16. "Alberta Tells PM: Don't Talk Oil," *Calgary Herald*, December 2, 1971.
17. Editorial, "The False 'Prairie' Label," *Calgary Herald*, January 20, 1972.
18. "Stanfield Promised Lougheed's Backing," *Calgary Herald*, January 28, 1972.
19. Between 1929 when Alberta was introduced to the Sexual Sterilization Act until 1972, almost 3,000 Albertans (mostly women, teens, and Aboriginal people) were sexually sterilized upon Eugenics Board approval. British Columbia was the only other province to enact comparable legislation. The procedures required the consent of the individual unless classified as "mentally defective." Involuntary sterilizations continued in Alberta long after they were abandoned in other North American jurisdictions. Jane Grekul, Arvey Krahn, and Dave Odynak, "Sterilizing the 'Feeble-Minded': Eugenics in Alberta, Canada, 1929–1972," *Journal of Historical Sociology* 17, no. 4 (2004), 358–84.

    More information about eugenics in Canada can be found at eugenicsarchive.ca. The site outlines the grounds for sterilization: "were typically that a person's undesirable mental or physical disabilities were thought to be heritable."
20. Kevin Peterson, "Tories Put Stress on Human Rights, Throne Speech Outlines Bills," *Calgary Herald*, March 2, 1972.
21. Don Whiteley, "Moderation Will Be Session Tone," *Calgary Herald*, March 2, 1972.
22. Don Whiteley, "Socreds, NDP Not Impressed," *Calgary Herald*, March 3, 1972.
23. Editorial, "Lougheed Succeeds," *Calgary Herald*, March 3, 1972.

26 The Grits Falter

1. Charles Kelly, executive assistant to Mahoney in the fall of 1971, said that the impression he got from speaking to oilmen is that they believed that Canada was being run by a "bunch of idiots." Interview with Charles Kelly, December 30, 2015.
2. "Peter C. Bawden (1929–1991)," *Canadian Petroleum Hall of Fame*. Accessed September 12, 2011. http://canadianpetroleumhalloffame.ca/peter-bawden.html
3. "Oilwell Drilling Contractor Seeks South Tory Nomination," *Calgary Herald*, September 8, 1971.
4. Don Sellar, "Bawden Wins Tory Race in a Walk," *Calgary Herald*, September 24, 1971.
5. Victor Mackie, "Albertans Named to House Posts," *Albertan*, October 1, 1971.
6. "Mahoney Defends Competition Act," *Albertan*, December 6, 1971.

7. Greene was soon appointed to the Senate where he served until he passed away in 1978 at age 58.
8. Jim Armstrong, The Oil Patch, *Calgary Herald,* November 16, 1971.
9. "U of C Prof Andre Succeeds Harkness as Tory Candidate," *Albertan,* October 1, 1971.
10. Nick Hills, "Tories 'Gallup-ing' Ahead," *Calgary Herald,* October 20, 1971.
11. I attended university in the late 1950s with Clark, and was well acquainted with him. One afternoon at the Zeta Psi fraternity house, a group of friends and I, with little on our minds besides Saturday night social activities, noticed students outside carrying placards and chanting "Go Joe Go!" It was Clark, out shaking hands and seeking support for the university model parliament election. Surely, we scoffed, a young man pursuing such infantile goals would never amount to anything! Joe Clark would be leader of the national PCs by 1976 and PM by 1979.
12. "Former Aide to Stanfield Seeks PC Nod," *Calgary Herald,* November 5, 1971.
13. Humphreys, *Joe Clark,* 5–67.
14. Elections Ontario.
15. Elections Newfoundland and Labrador.
16. Egon Frech, "PC Lobby Wants Strom to Switch," *Albertan,* December 7, 1971.
17. "P.M. Calls Bennett a Bigot," *Albertan,* February 14, 1972.
18. Editorial, "Trudeau's Big Mouth," *Calgary Herald,* March 1, 1972.
19. "The Country's in Good Shape, Says PM," *Calgary Herald,* December 24, 1971. The article cites a speech Trudeau gave to the Canadian and Italian Business and Professional Men's Association.
20. "Trudeau Claims Success in Solving Major Crises," *Calgary Herald,* December 29, 1971.
21. "Trudeau Sees Industrial Policy as Key Federal Election Issue," *Calgary Herald,* January 10, 1972.
22. Editorial, "Keep the Freight Rates Issue on the Track," *Albertan,* February 9, 1972.
23. Interview with Charles Kelly, December 30, 2015.
24. Don Sellar, "Pat Mahoney Likes to Help People with Problems, *The Herald Magazine,* January 28, 1972.
25. Charles Kelly recalls being in Mahoney's Toronto hotel room for his own job interview when Mahoney received Trudeau's telephone call about the cabinet appointment. Mahoney quickly hauled out a bottle of scotch to celebrate with him. On Kelly's first day on the job, Mahoney instructed him on how he wanted his martinis prepared and handed Kelly a travelling liquor case, with the responsibility of keeping it full on the road. Interview with Charles Kelly, December 30, 2015.
26. Paul Jackson, "Re-Election Deck Gets PET Shuffle," *Albertan,* January 29, 1972.
27. Interview with Charles Kelly, December 30, 2015.

28. Interview with Charles Kelly, December 30, 2015. "Work is Mahoney Lifestyle," *Albertan*, January 29, 1972.
29. "Mahoney Renominated, Raps Tories' Appeal to Bigotry," *Calgary Herald*, March 4, 1972.
30. Mazankowski, a 32-year-old car dealer when first elected in 1968, became a highly respected parliamentarian who went on to a long career serving the Clark, Mulroney, and Campbell administrations, as minister of transport, and of finance as well as deputy PM.
31. Paul Jackson, "Small Western Communities Also Bitter against Federal Government's Policies," *Albertan*, March 11, 1972.
32. "Manning Criticizes Payments to Quebec," *Albertan*, March 23, 1972.
33. Victor Mackie, "'Snide, Smug, Foul-Mouthed' PM Said Reason Newsman Joins Tories," *Albertan*, March 21, 1972.
34. "Sobering Election Predicted for PM," *Calgary Herald*, April 26, 1972.
35. Ben Tierney, "Tories Take Big Leap Forward," *Calgary Herald*, May 3, 1972.

27 Chickens, Eggs, and Wheat Deals

1. Gayle K. Honey, "Official Urges Cattlemen to Compromise on System," *Albertan*, February 5, 1971.
2. Ken Hull, "Canada's Farmers' Backs Are Up," *Calgary Herald*, January 9, 1971.
3. Nick Hills, "Court to End Chicken–Egg War," *Calgary Herald*, May 1, 1971.
4. "Ranchers Lead Markets Fight," *Calgary Herald*, May 5, 1971.
5. "Western Farmers' Oblivion One Step Nearer, says Tory," *Calgary Herald*, May 6, 1971.
6. "Commons Battle Continues Over Grain Payments to the Prairies," *Calgary Herald*, May 8, 1971.
7. "Farm 'Genocide' Next," *Calgary Herald*, May 15, 1971.
8. Nick Hills, "Impeachment Suggested for Three Cabinet Ministers," *Calgary Herald*, September 16, 1971.
9. Nick Hills, "Wheat Payments Spark Angry Debate," *Calgary Herald*, September 17, 1971.
10. "Fight to the Finish Vowed on Grains Bill," *Calgary Herald*, September 24, 1971.
11. "Liberals Ready to Drop Grain Bill," *Albertan*, October 8, 1971.
12. "Grain Bill Torpedoed by Pact Failure," *Albertan*, October 13, 1971.
13. "Farmer's Victory Says NDP Winner, Protest against Liberal Policies," *Calgary Herald*, November 9, 1971.
14. "Grits Have Much to Do—Stanbury," *Calgary Herald*, November 9, 1971.
15. "East West Lines Drawn for Battle," *Calgary Herald*, December 29, 1971.
16. "Farm Market Bill Passed," *Calgary Herald*, December 31, 1971.
17. Rick Kennedy, "Alberta Asks Grain Action," *Albertan*, March 11, 1972.
18. Rick Kennedy, "New Grain Body Formed," *Albertan*, March 16, 1972.

19. "Horner Contests Olson Statement," *Calgary Herald*, May 17, 1972.
20. John Schmidt, "Agricultural Alberta," *Calgary Herald*, May 30, 1972.
21. "Farmers Welcome New Wheat Price," *Calgary Herald*, January 24, 1972.
22. "Record Sales Year Predicted by Lang," *Calgary Herald*, March 3, 1972.
23. "New China Grain Deal Sets up Record Shipments," *Calgary Herald*, June 2, 1972.
24. Nick Hills, "Grain Trade Gets a Boost," *Calgary Herald*, May 27, 1972.

28 Peter Lougheed Becomes a Star

1. Bob Cohen, "Separate West Myth: Premier," *Calgary Herald*, April 20, 1972.
2. The Victoria Charter was a set of amendments to the Canadian Constitution proposed in 1971, which included a bill of rights and an amending formula.
3. Kevin Peterson, "Alberta's Constitutional Role," *Calgary Herald*, April 8, 1972.
4. 1 MCF is the volume of 1,000 cubic feet (CF) of natural gas, which equals 1 million British Thermal Units (BTU). 1 BTU is the heat required to raise the temperature of 1 pound of water by 1 degree Fahrenheit.
5. "Lougheed Promises Action to Increase Oil and Gas Prices," *Albertan*, December 13, 1971.
6. "Oilmen Support Gas Price Review," *Calgary Herald*, January 18, 1972.
7. Don Sellar, "Premier Orders Review of Natural Gas Pricing," *Calgary Herald*, January 13, 1972.
8. Jim Stott, "Brief Supports Hike in Natural Gas Price," *Calgary Herald*, June 8, 1972.
9. Jim Stott, "30-year Gas Reserves Too Much, Says Witness," *Calgary Herald*, June 21, 1972. These predictions turned out to be nonsense. In the last three decades of the twentieth century, global energy consumption doubled, with fossil fuels providing nearly 90 percent of that consumption. From 2007 to 2035, energy consumption was expected to rise a further 49 percent. *US Energy Outlook 2010*, US Energy Information Administration.
10. Editorial, "Natural Gas Export Plan," *Calgary Herald*, August 11, 1972.
11. Bill Dickie, "Alberta Boom Keyed to Oil," *Calgary Herald* May 15, 1972.
12. Jim Armstrong, The Oil Patch, *Calgary Herald*, April 25, 1972.
13. Jim Armstrong, The Oil Patch, *Calgary Herald*, March 23, 1972.
14. Kevin Peterson, "Tax Sought on Oil Reserves; New Incentives to Industry," *Calgary Herald*, April 25, 1972.
15. Kevin Peterson, "Tax Would Send Oil Rigs on Way," *Calgary Herald*, May 24, 1972.
16. Editorial, "A Fair Plan: More Oil Revenues," *Calgary Herald*, July 31, 1971.
17. Don Sellar, "Oil Reserve Tax Plan Causes Ottawa Concern," *Calgary Herald*, June 29, 1972.

18. Erickson/Massey Architects and Planners, "Village Lake Louise Development Plan," Vancouver, December, 1971.
19. Peter Walls, "Lake Louise: What the Shouting Is About; Many Were Turned Away," *Calgary Herald*, March 10, 1972.
20. "Russell Says Louise Village for American Jet Set," *Albertan*, March 10, 1972.
21. Ron Nowell, "Kangaroo Court Charged," *Calgary Herald*, March 10, 1972.
22. Don Getty, "Lake Louise Project, Rejected," *Calgary Herald*, June 1, 1972. Even though Trudeau, a winter sports enthusiast, favoured the proposal, in June 1972 Minister of Northern Development Jean Chretien decided to scrap it because of the many environmental concerns. The implications were enormous. It led to far more winter sports development elsewhere in western Canada and particularly in Whistler, BC. Interview with Allen Sulatycky, June 26, 2012.
23. "The Session Ends," *Calgary Herald*, June 3, 1972.
24. "'Old Boy' Opens Stampede," *Calgary Herald*, July 7, 1972.

29 The Eve of the Federal Election

1. C. Robert Zelnick, "Best Bet: Mackenzie Valley Pipeline," *Calgary Herald*, May 15, 1972. The sea hazards came starkly home in 1989 when the tanker *Exxon Valdez* full with Alaskan oil and bound for California struck a reef causing a spill estimated at 750,000 barrels of crude oil. It was one of the most devastating environmental catastrophes in history with damages reaching into the billions. Joanna Walters, "Exxon Valdez—25 Years after the Alaska Oil Spill, the Court Battle Continues," *The Telegraph*, March 23, 2014.
2. Editorial, "Major Step to Market," *Calgary Herald*, June 15, 1972.
3. "U.S. Interest in Oil Sands Increasing Rapidly," *Calgary Herald*, July 18, 1972.
4. "Nixon Moves to Boost US Oil Imports," *Calgary Herald*, May 12, 1972.
5. The first Jewish federal cabinet minister, Gray was first elected in 1962 and re-elected twelve successive times in the Windsor riding of Essex West, the longest continuously serving MP in Canadian history. He served in the Pearson, Trudeau, Turner, and Chretien governments in several capacities, including deputy prime minister. "Former Deputy PM Herb Gray Dies at 82," *Toronto Star*, April 21, 2014.
6. Gray pointed out that US interests owned 80 percent of all foreign-controlled business assets in Canada. Foreign owners controlled 58 percent of Canadian manufacturing assets, almost all of the oil industry, 90 percent of the rubber, chemical, and transport industries, and 100 percent of the automobile industry.
7. Ben Tierney, "Cabinet Stops Short of Hard-Line Approach," *Calgary Herald*, May 3, 1972; "The Foreign Ownership Report," *Calgary Herald*, May 3, 1972.
8. "Proposals under Heavy Fire from Opposition Spokesmen," *Calgary Herald*, May 3, 1972.

9. "Foreign Investment Bill 'Like Using a Popgun to Hunt Big Game,'" *Calgary Herald*, June 5, 1972.
10. "Kierans Attacks Foreign Takeovers Bill," *Calgary Herald*, June 6, 1972.
11. "Ottawa Take-Over Bill Would 'Hamper' Oil Men," *Calgary Herald*, June 16, 1972.
12. "Oil Spending Expected to Top $400 Million," *Calgary Herald*, June 5, 1972.
13. "Takeover Review 'Not Mild,'" *Calgary Herald*, June 6, 1972.
14. Charles Lynch, "The Nation," *Calgary Herald*, June 3, 1972. Even though the election took place before Gray's proposals were passed, they set the stage for the Foreign Investment Review Agency (FIRA) that would be passed in 1973 to review foreign takeovers.
15. Charles Lynch, "Liberals' Hopes for Western Seats High," *Calgary Herald*, April 24, 1972.
16. Ben Tierney and Don Sellar, "Manufacturers Big Gainers in Budget," *Calgary Herald*, May 9, 1972.
17. Guy Demarino, "Election Based on Jobless Drop May be Cancelled by Labour Unrest," *Calgary Herald*, May 17, 1972.
18. Peter Lougheed, "People, Environment Keys to New Industrial Philosophy," *Calgary Herald*, May 25, 1972.
19. Bill Dickie, "Alberta's Mineral Production Worth $16 Billon," *Calgary Herald*, May 25, 1972.
20. Nick Hills, "Trudeau Calls a Halt to RCMP Name Shift," *Calgary Herald*, April 28, 1972. The changeover to the "POLICE" signage was to comply with an international agreement to make police signs more universally recognizable to world travellers. The Tories quickly raised fears the Trudeau government was intentionally eroding the English language and the monarchy—an accusation widely believed in western Canada.
21. Nick Hills, "The PM's Spooky Alberta Visit," *Calgary Herald*, May 5, 1972.
22. Bunny Wright, "Students Run the Gamut in Questions to PM," *Calgary Herald*, April 29, 1972.
23. Nick Hills, "The PM's Spooky Alberta Visit," *Calgary Herald*, May 5, 1972.
24. "MPs Leave Poor Legislative Record," *Calgary Herald*, July 8, 1972.
25. Arthur Blakely, "PM Says: 'Let Hull Play,'" *Calgary Herald*, July 15, 1972.
26. I had a few opportunities to meet Hull when he visited Calgary. He was an engaging fellow and an amusing speaker who had high praise for Trudeau. Whether Trudeau's appeals to the NHL had anything to do with Hull's political affections, I never thought to ask.
27. "Trudeau's Plan Week at Resort," *Calgary Herald*, July 24, 1972.
28. "National Unity No Longer 'Hot Politics'—Mahoney," *Calgary Herald*, July 24, 1972.
29. Stewart MacLeod, "Statistics Likely 'Bullets' in Next Election Campaign," *Calgary Herald*, August 15, 1972.
30. Rick Kennedy, "Liberal Future Dim in City?" *Albertan*, August 16, 1972.

31. Rick Kennedy, "Incumbent MPs Safe," *Albertan,* August 17, 1972.
32. Ralph Willsey, "Politics in a Riding that Takes a Lot of Riding," *Calgary Herald*, March 8, 1972.
33. Stephani Keer, "Rift Develops Over Ballots," *Albertan*, March 9, 1972.
34. Stephani Keer, "Clark Wins PC Backing," *Albertan*, March 20, 1972.

30 "The Land is Strong?"

1. Victor Mackie, "PM Calls Vote—October 30," *Albertan*, September 2, 1972.
2. Fred Kennedy, "An Election Free-For-All," *Albertan*, September 5, 1972.
3. Paul Jackson, "Tough Fight Expected," *Albertan*, September 8, 1972.
4. Shortly after the election was called, while on holiday at sea, I received an "urgent" radio message from Alberto Romano, friend and president of the Calgary North federal Liberal riding association, pleading with me to stand for the nomination in the riding. If successful, I would be pitted against the great soapbox rhetorician Eldon Woolliams. Although I declined that invitation, in 1979 I chose otherwise and went down to a crushing defeat.
5. Arthur Blakely, "PM's Swinging Image Toned Down," *Calgary Herald*, September 13, 1972.
6. Tom Mitchell, "Trudeau Depicted as Solid Leader," *Albertan*, September 2, 1972.
7. Peter Desbarats, "For Whom the Bells Toll; It Tolls for Thee," *Brandon Sun*, September 11, 1972.
8. "Take Care; Take Time Is Liberal Answer," *Calgary Herald*, September 12, 1972.
9. Charles Lynch, "The Nation," *Calgary Herald*, September 13, 1972.
10. Ben Tierney, "PM Charts Strange Course," *Calgary Herald*, September 15, 1972.
11. Ben Tierney, "PM's Fledgling Campaign 'Flat,'" *Calgary Herald*, September 16, 1972.
12. "Jobless Rate Above Last Year," *Albertan*, September 13, 1972.
13. "Trudeau Defends Economic Policy," *Albertan*, September 14, 1972. Alberta's economy was humming with an unemployment rate of only 3.6 percent. "Jobless Rate Above Last Year," *Albertan*, September 14, 1972.
14. Bruce Little, "Unemployed Rate Continues to Rise," *Calgary Herald*, September 12, 1972.
15. Don Sellar, "PM Denies Hard Stand on Welfare Recipients," *Calgary Herald,* September 22, 1972.
16. "The Issues: Huge Unemployment Poses Huge Problems," *Calgary Herald*, September 26, 1972.
17. Peter Calamai, "Mood Buoyant in Stanfield Camp," *Calgary Herald*, September 19, 1972.
18. "Job Insurance Cost 'Scandal'—Stanfield" *Calgary Herald*, September 22, 1972.
19. Don Sellar, "Tory Chief Renews His Attack on Jobless Insurance 'Scandal,'" *Calgary Herald*, September 30, 1972.

20. "'Welfare Bums' Rapped by Lewis," *Albertan*, September 11, 1972.
21. Guy Demarino, "Foreign Ownership Is a Dead Issue—Lewis," *Calgary Herald*, September 13, 1972.
22. "Pipeline Route Said Disastrous," *Albertan*, September 13, 1972. Forty-one years later NDP leader Thomas Mulcair would echo Lewis' concerns about the money required for the large oil sands developments, which he said would lead to the "Dutch disease."
23. One of the most entertaining speeches I have ever heard was from ex-broadcaster Jamieson at an Ottawa banquet in January 1979. Speaking without notes he regaled his Liberal audience for an hour with hilarious anecdotes about the Trudeau era. The crowd demanded more, so he continued for forty-five minutes before a rousing and lengthy standing ovation.
24. "Lambert Named in Rousing Style," *Calgary Herald*, September 21, 1972.
25. "Jamieson Confirms '73 Start on New Terminal for Airport," *Calgary Herald*, September 21, 1972.
26. "Rancher Faces Olson in Medicine Hat," *Calgary Herald*, September 18, 1972.
27. Don Sellar, "Farm Issues Hurt Trudeau Despite Expensive Effort," *Calgary Herald*, September 25, 1972.
28. "Trudeau Tours Workshop," *Albertan*, September 27, 1972. Blair Williams, as 1972 Alberta federal campaign chairman, accompanied Trudeau and Olson to Taber, where Williams was raised, to meet and hear from farmers. Trudeau said little and left Olson to discuss initiatives that could help the farmer. In Lethbridge, however, Trudeau treated the travelling journalists to an exhibition of his diving skills at the hotel pool. Interview with Blair Williams, January 12, 2016.
29. After a few minutes we left the suite and went to a nearby second-rate eatery at our own expense. Nevertheless, we returned to the hotel to fulfill our obligations. To this day, every time Cichon and I sit down and talk about the old days over a good lunch accompanied by a fine vintage, we still grumble (and guffaw) about that maltreatment.
30. Rick Kennedy, "Trudeau Finds 'Hot Seat' a Little Too Cool for Comfort," *Albertan*, September 27, 1972.
31. Dave Mabell, "PM All Business at Calgary Rally: Trudeaumania Seemed All Gone," *Albertan*, September 27, 1972.
32. Bob Cohen, "Lewis Warns Pipeline Costly Exploitation," *Calgary Herald*, October 3, 1972.
33. Gordon Jaremko, "MacDonald Belittles Lewis Pipeline Charge," *Calgary Herald*, October 4, 1972.
34. Richard Anco, "Job Fund Dispute a Campaign Key," *Calgary Herald*, October 10, 1972.
35. Kevin Peterson, "Stanfield Presses Job Fund Attack," *Calgary Herald*, October 5, 1972.
36. "UIC Deficit May Go over $800 Million," *Calgary Herald*, October 7, 1972.

37. "Jobless Score Bad News Again," *Calgary Herald*, October 10, 1972.
38. "Alberta Rate Highest in Years," *Calgary Herald*, October 10, 1972.
39. Based on 1961 prices equalling 100.
40. Don Sellar, "Price Index Up Half a Point as September Trend Reverses," *Calgary Herald*, October 11, 1972.
41. Jim Armstrong, The Oil Patch, *Calgary Herald*, October 10, 1972.
42. Peter Calamai, "Trudeau Gets into Top Gear as He Flails 'Belly-Achers,'" *Calgary, Herald*, October 10, 1972.
43. "NDP Book Names Names of 'Bums' with Loudest Voices for Ottawa Aid"; "…And Here Are the 'Bums,'" *Calgary Herald*, October 11, 1972.
44. "Economic Nationalism Emerges as Key Issue in Edmonton West," *Calgary Herald*, October 10, 1972.
45. Don Sellar, "Liberal Election Promises Leak," *Calgary Herald*, October 11, 2011.
46. "Economy Gets Worked Over by Calgary South Candidates," *Calgary Herald*, October 12, 1972.
47. Charles Lynch, "The Nation," *Calgary Herald*, October 13, 1972.
48. Ben Tierney, "Lewis Says Trudeau in Trouble," *Calgary Herald*, October 12, 1972.
49. Ben Tierney, "PM Loses Kierans' Vote in Own Riding," *Calgary Herald*, October 17, 1972.
50. Don Sellar, "NDP Gains Indicated," *Calgary Herald*, October 14, 1972.
51. Gordon Pape, "Bank of Nova Scotia Predicts Impressive Economic Growth," *Calgary Herald*, October 13, 1972.
52. Peter Calamai, "Get Fit and Save Canada Cash: PM," *Calgary Herald*, October 14, 1972.
53. Kevin Peterson, "A Cool Campaign Grows Cooler," *Calgary Herald*, October 16, 1972.
54. Interview with Charles Kelly, December 30, 2015.
55. Kevin Peterson, "Calgary South: Five Candidates Set for Tough Battle," *Calgary Herald*, October 18, 1972.
56. Kevin Peterson, "The Province," *Calgary Herald*, October 16, 1972.
57. "City Tories Get Lougheed Aid," *Calgary Herald*, October 21, 1972.
58. Peter Walls, "New Deal Offered Provinces," *Calgary Herald*, October 23, 1972.
59. Peter Walls, "Calgary First on 'Bum' List," *Calgary Herald*, October 24, 1972.
60. Kevin Peterson, "'Separatism Ghost' Laid to Rest—PM," *Calgary Herald*, October 24, 1972.
61. Ben Tierney, "Stanfield Had Better Pull Out All Stops—'Or Else,'" *Calgary Herald*, October 24, 1972.
62. Harold Greer, "Conservatives' Ontario Picture Believed Not Too Rosy with Liberals Seen Losing a Few, NDP Advancing," *Calgary Herald*, October 24, 1972.
63. Bob Cohen, "Liberals Are Well Ahead in a Neck-And-Neck Race," *Calgary Herald*, October 24, 1972.

64. Kevin Peterson, "Strom Quitting as SC leader," *Calgary Herald*, October 26, 1972.
65. Charles Lynch, "The Nation," *Calgary Herald*, October 27, 1972.
66. In 1968 Gallup had forecast 47% support for the Liberals, 29% for the Tories, and 18% for the NDP with 6% for others. The actual vote was 46%, 32%, 16%, and 6%, respectively. Guy Demarino, "Election Could Go Either Way," *Calgary Herald*, October 28, 1972.

31 The Party's Over

1. "Party Standing Across Canada: Vote by Provinces at Midnight MST," *Albertan*, October 31, 1972.
2. All voting statistics from Elections Canada—some rounded to the nearest tenth or whole number.
3. Jim Dau and Lynn Baldwin, "Schumacher Wins, Credits Trudeau," *Albertan*, October 31, 1972.
4. David Mabell, "Calgary Conservatives Jubilant," *Albertan*, October 31, 1972.
5. Paul Jackson, "Claims Trudeau Gov't Won't Survive," *Albertan*, November 4, 1972.
6. Michael McNinch and Peter Crosby, "Defeat Conceded Early by Mahoney," *Albertan*, October 31, 1972.
7. Victor Mackie, "PM's Decision Likely Today," *Albertan*, November 2, 1972.
8. Paul Jackson, "Lewis' Party Offers Support," *Albertan*, November 3, 1972.
9. "Mahoney Qualifies Defeat," *Albertan*, November 3, 1972.
10. "Defeated MP Says Trudeau Listened to Wrong People," *Albertan*, November 3, 1972.
11. Olson's executive assistant and the 1972 Alberta Liberal campaign chairman Blair Williams said that Harries was "full of himself and not a serious team player," although "he was fascinating to talk to and he was a great party host when it came to home events that focused on his ideas, his past, and his potential for the future." Interview with Blair Williams, January 12, 2016.

Epilogue

1. Theodore Roosevelt, *The Strenuous Life*. Speech, Hamilton Club, Chicago, April 10, 1899, accessed February 23, 2015. www.bartleby.com/58/1.html
2. Its proceedings nationally televised, WEOC was chaired by Trudeau, and attended by the premiers of British Columbia, Alberta, Saskatchewan, and Manitoba, together with cabinet representatives and officials. While Trudeau wanted to emphasize his government's policies of assistance to the west, the western premiers also aggressively advanced their own concerns and agendas. Despite a lot of press coverage, WEOC yielded no new policy directions and was the first and last of its kind.

3. Robert Roach, *An (In)Auspicious Gathering: The Western Economic Opportunities Conference of 1973*, Building the New West Project Report #20, Canada West Foundation, October 2003.
4. Unfortunately, nine days before our scheduled interview for this book, Mahoney passed away.
5. Interview with Charles Kelly, December 30, 2015.
6. Obituary, "Patrick Morgan Mahoney," *Ottawa Citizen*, June 13, 2012.
7. Elections Canada.
8. Hays was an amusing if somewhat quaint chairman. After listening to some critical comments from a women's group, he thanked "the girls" and then speculated that if all their positions were accepted, "No one would be home to look after the babies." Sheppard and Valpy, *National Deal*, 139.
9. Ameya Charnalia, "Edmonton-born Publisher, 'Passionate Canadian' Mel Hurtig Dead at 84," *Edmonton Journal*, August 3, 2016.

Bibliography

Andrew, J.V. *Bilingual Today, French Tomorrow.* Richmond Hill: BMG Publishing, 1977.

Archer, Jules. *The Plot to Seize the White House.* New York: Hawthorn Books, 2007.

Asper, Israel H. *The Benson Iceberg: A Critical Analysis of the White Paper on Tax Reform in Canada.* Toronto: Clarke, Irwin, 1970.

Axworthy, Thomas S., and Pierre Elliott Trudeau, eds. *Towards a Just Society: The Trudeau Years.* Toronto: Viking, 1990.

Bashevkin, Sylvia B, ed. *Canadian Political Behaviour: Introductory Readings.* Toronto: Methuen, 1985.

Bliss, Michael. *Right Honourable Men: The Descent of Canadian Politics from Macdonald to Mulroney.* Toronto: Harper Collins, 1994.

Bom, Philip C. *Trudeau's Canada: Truth and Consequences.* St. Catharines: Guardian Publishing, 1977.

Bothwell, Robert, and J.L. Granatstein. *Pirouette: Pierre Trudeau and Canadian Foreign Policy.* Toronto: University of Toronto Press, 1990.

Brennan, Brian. *The Good Steward: The Ernest Manning Story.* Calgary: Fifth House Publishers, 2008.

Butler, Rick, and Jean Guy Carrier, eds. *The Trudeau Decade.* Toronto: Doubleday Canada, 1979.

Cahill, Jack. *John Turner: The Long Run.* Toronto: McClelland & Stewart, 1981.

Camp, Dalton. *Points of Departure.* Toronto: Deneau and Greenberg Publishers, 1979.

Cardinal, Harold. *The Unjust Society: The Tragedy of Canada's Indians*. Edmonton: Hurtig Publishers, 1969.

Carstairs, Sharon. *Not One of the Boys: A Woman, a Fighter, a Liberal with a Cause*. Toronto: Macmillan, 1993.

Chretien, Jean. *Straight from the Heart*. Toronto: Key Porter Books, 1985.

Clarkson, Stephen. *The Big Red Machine: How the Liberal Party Dominates Canadian Politics*. Vancouver: University of British Columbia Press, 2005.

Clarkson, Stephen, and Christina McCall. *Trudeau and Our Times, Volume 1: The Magnificent Obsession*. Toronto: McClelland & Stewart, 1990.

———. *Trudeau and our Times, Volume 2: The Heroic Delusion*. Toronto: McClelland & Stewart, 1994.

Clinton, Bill. *My Life*. New York: Alfred A. Knopf, 2004.

Cohen, Andrew, and Jack Granatstein, eds. *Trudeau's Shadow: The Life and Legacy of Pierre Elliott Trudeau*. Toronto: Vintage, 1999.

Dabbs, Frank. *Preston Manning: The Roots of Reform*. Vancouver: Greystone Books, 1997.

———. *Ralph Klein: A Maverick Life*. Vancouver: Greystone Books, 1995.

Davey, Keith. *The Rainmaker: A Passion for Politics*. Toronto: Stoddart Publishing, 1986.

Dobbin, Murray. *Preston Manning and the Reform Party*. Toronto: James Lorimer, 1991.

Doern, G. Bruce, and Glen Toner. *The Politics of Energy: The Development and Implementation of the NEP*. Toronto: Methuen, 1985.

Dunton, A. Davidson, André Laurendeau, Jean Louis Gagnon, et al. *Report on the Royal Commission on Bilingualism and Biculturalism*, 6 vols. Ottawa: Queen's Printer, 1967–1970.

Elliott, David R., ed. *Aberhart: Outpourings and Replies*. Calgary: Historical Society of Alberta, 1991.

English, John. *Citizen of the World: The Life of Pierre Elliott Trudeau, Volume 1: 1919–1968*. Toronto: Alfred A. Knopf, 2006.

———. *Just Watch Me: The Life of Pierre Elliott Trudeau, Volume 2: 1968–2000*. Toronto: Vintage, 2009.

Evans, C.D. *Milt Harradence: The Western Flair*. Calgary: Durance Vile, 2001.

Finkel, Alvin. *The Social Credit Phenomenon in Alberta*. Toronto: University of Toronto Press, 1989.

Foster, Peter. *The Blue-Eyed Sheiks: The Canadian Oil Establishment*. Toronto: Collins Publishers, 1979.

———. *Other People's Money: The Banks, the Government, and Dome*. Don Mills: Totem Books, 1984.

———. *The Sorcerer's Apprentices: Canada's Super Bureaucrats and the Energy Mess*. Toronto: Collins Publishers, 1982.

Fotheringham, Allan. *Malice in Blunderland: or How the Grits Stole Christmas.* Toronto: Key Porter Books, 1982.

Fraser, Graham. *PQ: René Lévesque and the Parti Québécois in Power.* Toronto: Macmillan, 1984.

Frye, Northrop, *Collected Works of Northrop Frye,* vol. 12, *Northrop Frye on Canada,* eds. Jean O'Grady and David Staines. Toronto: University of Toronto Press, 2003.

Gibbons, Roger. *Prairie Politics and Society: Regionalism in Decline.* Toronto: Butterworth's, 1980.

Gordon, Walter. *A Political Memoir.* Toronto: McClelland & Stewart, 1977.

Gray, Earle. *The Great Canadian Oil Patch: The Petroleum Era from Birth to Peak.* Toronto: Maclean-Hunter, 1970.

Groh, Dennis. "The Political Thought of Ernest Manning." MA thesis, University of Calgary, 1970.

Gwyn, Richard. *The Northern Magus.* Toronto: McClelland & Stewart, 1980.

Hamilton, Ian. *The Children's Crusade: The Story of the Company of Young Canadians.* Toronto: Peter Martin, 1970.

Harbron, John D. *This Is Trudeau.* Don Mills: Longman's, 1968.

Hilborn, James D., ed. *Dusters and Gushers: The Canadian Oil and Gas Industry.* Toronto: Pitt Publishing, 1968.

Hockin, Thomas A. *Apex of Power: The Prime Minister and Political Leadership in Canada.* Scarborough: Prentice-Hall, 1971.

Hooke, Alf. *30 + 5: I Know, I Was There.* Edmonton: Institute of Applied Art, 1971.

Horner, Jack. *My Own Brand.* Edmonton: Hurtig Publishers, 1980.

Humphreys, David L. *Joe Clark: A Portrait.* Toronto: Deneau and Greenberg Publishers, 1978.

Hustak, Allan. *Peter Lougheed.* Toronto: McClelland & Stewart: 1979.

Irving, John A. *The Social Credit Movement in Alberta.* Toronto: University of Toronto Press, 1959.

Kierans, Eric. *Challenge of Confidence: Kierans on Canada.* Toronto/Montreal: McClelland & Stewart, 1967.

LaMarsh, Judy. *Memoirs of a Bird in a Gilded Cage.* Toronto: McClelland & Stewart, 1969.

Laschinger, John, and Geoffrey Stevens. *Leaders and Lesser Mortals: Backroom Politics in Canada.* Toronto: Key Porter Books, 1992.

LeDuc, Lawrence, Judith I. McKenzie, Jon H. Pammett, and André Turcotte. *Dynasties and Interludes: Past and Present in Canadian Electoral Politics.* Toronto: Dundurn, 2010.

Le Riche, Timothy. *Alberta's Oil Patch: The People, Politics and Companies.* Edmonton: Folklore Publishing, 2006.

Lévesque, René. *Memoirs.* Translated by Philip Stratford. Toronto: McClelland & Stewart, 1986.

Levine, Allan G. *Your Worship: The Lives of Eight of Canada's Most Unforgettable Mayors*. Toronto: James Lorimer, 1989.

Lyon, Jim. Dome: *The Rise and Fall of the House that Jack Built*. Scarborough: Avon, 1983.

MacEwan, J.W. Grant. *A Short History of Western Canada*. Toronto: McGraw Hill-Ryerson, 1968.

MacGregor, James G. *A History of Alberta*. Edmonton: Hurtig Publishers, 1972.

Machiavelli, Niccolo. *The Prince*. Edited by Lloyd C. Crocker. New York: Washington Square Press, 1963.

Mackey, Lloyd. *Like Father, Like Son: Ernest Manning and Preston Manning*. Toronto: ECW Press: 1997.

Macpherson, C.B. *Democracy in Alberta: Social Credit and the Party System*. Toronto: University of Toronto Press, 1962.

Mann, William E. *Sect, Cult, and Church in Alberta*. Toronto: University of Toronto Press, 1955.

Manning, E.C. *Political Realignment: Challenge to Thoughtful Canadians*. Toronto: McClelland & Stewart, 1967.

Martin, Lawrence. *The Presidents and the Prime Ministers*. Toronto: Doubleday, 1982.

Martin, Paul. *Canada and the Quest for Peace*. Toronto: Copp Clark, 1967.

———. *A Very Public Life, Volume II: So Many Worlds*. Toronto: Deneau, 1985.

McCall-Newman, Christina. *Grits: An Intimate Portrait of the Liberal Party*. Toronto: Macmillan, 1982.

McDonald, Jack, and Jim McDonald. *The Canadian Voter's Guidebook*. Toronto: Fitzhenry and Whiteside, 1972.

McQuaig, Linda. *Behind Closed Doors*. Markham: Penguin Books, 1987.

Newman, Peter C. *The Canadian Establishment: Volume 1*. Toronto: McClelland & Stewart, 1975.

———. *The Distemper of Our Times*. Toronto: McClelland & Stewart, 1968.

———. *Home Country: People, Places, and Power Politics*. Toronto: McClelland & Stewart, 1973.

———. *Renegade in Power: The Diefenbaker Years*. Toronto: McClelland & Stewart, 1963.

Nielsen, Arne. *We Gambled Everything: The Life and Times of an Oilman*. Edmonton: University of Alberta Press, 2012.

Palmer, Howard. *Patterns of Prejudice: A History of Nativism in Alberta*: Toronto: McClelland & Stewart, 1982.

Palmer, Howard, and Tamara Palmer. *Alberta: A New History*. Edmonton: Hurtig Publishers, 1990.

———, eds. *Peoples of Alberta: Portraits of Cultural Diversity*. Saskatoon: Western Producer Prairie Books, 1985.

Peacock, Donald. *Barefoot on the Hill*. Vancouver: Douglas & McIntyre, 1986.

———. *Journey to Power*. Toronto: Ryerson Press, 1968.

Pearson, Lester B. *Mike: The Memoirs of the Right Honourable Lester B. Pearson, Volume 3*. Toronto: University of Toronto Press, 1975.

Pickersgill, J.W. *The Liberal Party*. Toronto: McClelland & Stewart, 1962.

Pratt, Larry. *The Tar Sands: Syncrude and the Politics of Oil*. Edmonton: Hurtig Publishers, 1976.

Pratt, Larry, and Garth Stevenson, eds. *Western Separatism: The Myths, Realities, and Dangers*. Edmonton: Hurtig Publishers, 1981.

Radwanski, George. *Trudeau*. Toronto: Macmillan, 1978.

Reich, Walter. *Origins of Terrorism*. Washington, DC: Woodrow Wilson Center Press, 1998.

Rennie, Bradford J., ed. *Alberta Premiers of the Twentieth Century*. Regina: Canadian Plains Research Center, 2004.

Ricci, Nino. *Pierre Elliott Trudeau*. Toronto: Penguin, 2009.

Sawatsky, John. *The Insiders: Government, Business, and the Lobbyists*. Toronto: McClelland & Stewart, 1987.

Sharp, Mitchell. *Which Reminds Me...: A Memoir*. Toronto: University of Toronto Press, 1994.

Sharpe, Sydney, and Don Braid. *Storming Babylon: Preston Manning and the Rise of the Reform Party*. Toronto: Key Porter Books, 1992.

Shaw, Brian. *The Gospel According to Saint Pierre*. Richmond Hill: Simon and Schuster, 1969.

Sheppard, Robert, and Michael Valpy. *The National Deal: The Fight for a Canadian Constitution*. Toronto: Fleet Books, 1982.

Simpson, Jeffrey. *Discipline of Power: The Conservative Interlude and the Liberal Restoration*. Toronto: Personal Library, 1980.

———. *Spoils of Power: The Politics of Patronage*. Toronto: Collins Publishers, 1988.

Smith, David E. *The Regional Decline of a National Party: Liberals on the Prairies*. Toronto: University of Toronto Press, 1981.

Smith, Philip. *The Treasure Seekers: The Men Who Built Home Oil*. Toronto: Macmillan, 1978.

Steubling, Douglas, John Marshall, and Gary Oakes. *Trudeau: A Man for Tomorrow*. Toronto: Clark, Irwin, 1968.

Stewart, Walter. *Divide and Con: Canadian Politics at Work*. Don Mills: New Press, 1973.

———. *Shrug: Trudeau in Power*. Don Mills: New Press, 1971.

Stuemer, Diane King. *Hawrelak: The Story*. Calgary: Script, the Writers' Group, 1992.

Suleman, Azmina. *In the Name of Justice: Portrait of a Cowboy Judge*. Calgary: Legal Archives Society of Alberta, 1990.

Sullivan, Martin. *Mandate '68: The Year of Pierre Elliott Trudeau*. Toronto: Doubleday, 1968.

Thomas, L.G. *The Liberal Party in Alberta: A History of Politics in the Province of Alberta, 1905–1921*. Toronto: University of Toronto Press, 1959.

Troyer, Warner. *200 Days: Joe Clark in Power*. Toronto: Personal Library, 1980.

Trudeau, Margaret. *Beyond Reason*. New York: Paddington Press, 1979.

———. *Consequences*. Toronto: McClelland & Stewart, 1982.

Trudeau, Pierre Elliott. *Conversations with Canadians*. Toronto: University of Toronto Press, 1972.

———. *Essential Trudeau*. Edited by Ron Graham. Toronto: McClelland & Stewart, 1998.

———. *Federalism and the French Canadians*. Toronto: Macmillan, 1968.

———. *Memoirs*. Toronto: McClelland & Stewart, 1993.

Turner, John N. *Politics of Purpose*. Toronto: McClelland & Stewart, 1968.

Van Herk, Aritha. *Mavericks: An Incorrigible History of Alberta*. Toronto: Penguin, 2001.

Wearing, Joseph, *The L-Shaped Party: The Liberal Party of Canada 1950–1980*. Toronto: McGraw Hill-Ryerson, 1981.

Westell, Anthony. *Paradox: Trudeau as Prime Minister*. Scarborough: Prentice-Hall, 1972.

White, Theodore H. *The Making of the President, 1960*. New York: Atheneum Publishers, 1961.

Wood, David G. *The Lougheed Legacy*. Toronto: Key Porter Books, 1985.

Yergin, Daniel. *The Prize: The Epic Quest for Oil, Money, and Power*. New York: Simon and Schuster, 1991.

Zink, Lubor J. *Viva Chairman Pierre*. Toronto: Griffin Press, 1977.

Zolf, Larry. *Dance of the Dialectic*. Toronto: James Lewis & Samuel, 1973.

———. *Survival of the Fattest: An Irreverent View of the Senate*. Toronto: Key Porter Books, 1984.

Index

Photographs indicated by page numbers in italics

Aalborg, Anders, 108
Aberhart, William, 72, 119–21
agricultural policy
    Assiniboia by-election and, 237
    beef industry and, 92, 195, 235
    farm-marketing legislation problems, 197–98, 235–36, 238
    Grain Stabilization Fund conflict, 236–37
    Olson–Horner conflict, 59
    opposition to Trudeau government on, 59–60
    Prairie Grain Advance Payments Act conflict, 236
    Project 75 conflict, 238–39
    Tory promises in 1971 Alberta election, 207
    transportation concerns, 92–93, 238, 239
    Trudeau government problems with, 235, 237–38, 275–76
    Trudeau's lack of interest in, 299n15
    See also wheat industry
Aird, John, 57
Alberta
    economic downturn, 115
    economic growth, 157–58, 192, 250, 326n13
    on hippies, 71, 73
    impact of oil and gas industry on, 65–66, 294n12
    maturation in federal politics, 54, 221–22
    medicare and, 132–33

watershed federal elections in, 37
See also Alberta Liberal Party; western alienation; *Alberta general elections*
Alberta general election (1935), 22, 72–73, 120–21
Alberta general election (1963), 154
Alberta general election (1967), xviii–xix, 122, 206
Alberta general election (1971)
  candidates, 210
  Liberal campaign, 183, 207, 209
  Liberal voter dilemma, 206
  Luzzi campaign, 206–07, 211, 214, 317n11
  NDP campaign, 180, 207, 209
  projected results, 210–11
  results, 211–14
  Social Credit campaign, 179–80, 207, 209–10, 211
  Tory campaign, 179, 180, 207–09, 210, 211
Alberta Liberal Party
  1968 convention, 56, 58–59
  1970 convention, 140–41
  1971 convention, 184–85
  author's decision to join, xviii
  crisis over proposed split of federal and provincial wings, 133–38, 139–41
  fundraising dinner with Trudeau, 73–77
  fundraising event with Trudeau at Stampede, 198, 200, 202
  fundraising overview, 130–32
  Maccagno's career in, 145
  organization, 21
  support for Trudeau, 142
  terminology, 289n1

See also Alberta Liberal Party (federal wing); Alberta Liberal Party (provincial wing); Hurtig, Mel; Petrasuk, Peter; Taylor, Nick
Alberta Liberal Party (federal wing)
  1968 candidates and nomination meetings, 25–30, 34–36
  1968 election campaign, 37–38, 41–42, 43, 44, 305n12
  1968 election impact on, 55–56
  1968 election results, 45–46, 48, 206
  1972 candidates, 256
  1972 election campaign, 252, 259–60, 263–64, 265–66
  1972 election challenges faced by, 255–56, 276–80
  1972 election reaction to results, 271, 272–73
  disconnect with provincial wing, 134–35, 137, 142, 182–83, 187, 279–80
  electoral results history, 21–22
  fundraising, 130
  Trudeaumania and, 24, 26
  See also Alberta Liberal Party; Harries, Hu; Hays, Harry; Mahoney, Patrick (Pat); Olson, H.A. (Bud); Sulatycky, Allen
Alberta Liberal Party (provincial wing)
  1967 election, xviii–xix
  1969 leadership convention, 127–29
  1971 election campaign, 181, 183, 207, 209, 210
  1971 election results, 211–14
  1971 election voter dilemma, 206
  1971 leadership convention, 185–86
  disconnect with federal Liberal establishment, 57–58

disconnect with federal wing, 134–35, 137, 142, 182–83, 187, 279–80
electoral results history, 22–23, 132
fundraising challenges, 130, 131–32
policy resolutions, 128, 183
post-1972, 284
proposed alliance with Social Credit, 133, 135–37, 279, 306n21
See also Alberta Liberal Party; Lowery, Jack; Russell, Bob

Albertan, 252
Alberta Party, 288n5
Alberta Resources Railway, 318n33
alcohol policy, 128, 205, 316n5
alienation, *see* western alienation
Andre, Harvie, 229, 270
anti-Semitism, 121–22, 303n13, 303n16
Argue, Hazen, 98, 153
Armstrong, Jim, 70, 83–84, 105–06, 228
Asper, Izzy, 106–07, 301n26
Assiniboia by-election, 237–38
Athabasca (federal riding), 29, 44, 48, 269
Athabaska (federal riding), 22
Austin, Jack, 175, 176, 187–88, 189, 312n21
Axworthy, Lloyd, 77
Ayer, John, 48

Baldwin, G.W. (Ged), 156, 236, 270
Ballard, Ray, 24, 45
B and B Commission (Royal Commission on Bilingualism and Biculturalism), 14, 150, 156. *See also* bilingualism
Banff National Park, 243–44, 324n22
Barnsley, Greg, 69
Barrett, Dave, 253
Basford, Ron, 92
Battle River (federal riding), 29, 48, 270

Bawden, Peter, 227–28, 256, 264, 265–66, 282
Beattie, Alan, xx
beef industry, 92, 195, 235
Beguin, Rene, 30
Bennett, W.A.C., 230, 253
Benson, Edgar
   1968 budget, 56
   1969 budget, 103, 111–12
   1970 budget, 188
   1971 budget, 190–91
   on Canadian economy, 218
   Grain Stabilization Fund conflict, 236
   tax reform white paper, 102, 104, 108, 109
   in Trudeau cabinet, 50, 231
   on unemployment, 216
Bentley, James, 49–50
Berry, Adrian, 145
Biafra, 59
bilingualism
   Anglophone opposition to, 124–25, 133, 151–53, 156, 274
   Anglophone support for, 152, 153
   Manning on, 124–25
   Official Languages Act, 150–51, 153
   Royal Commission on, 14, 150
   Strom on, 151, 167
   Trudeau's defence of, xx, 250, 267
Blair, Robert (Bob), 220, 319n7
Blakeney, Allan, 237
Boras, John, 28, 48
Borger, John, 261
Bourassa, Robert, 166
Branigan, Don, 30, 127, 128, 305n5
Brennan, Brian, 124
British Columbia, 253, 320n19

Brown, R.A. (Bobby), Jr., 82, 124, 175–77, 304n28
budgets, *see* financial policies

cable TV policy, 280
Cadieux, Leo, 50
Calgary
  bilingual schools, 153
  economic growth, 157–58
  impact of oil and gas industry on, 65
  Liberal federal seats won in, 22
  Liberal fundraising dinner with Trudeau, 73, 75–76, 77
  NOW encounter with Trudeau, 73–74, 76–77
  population, 294n2
  Trudeau campaign events, 8, 42–43, 260–61
Calgary–Buffalo (provincial riding), 206–07
Calgary Centre (federal riding)
  1968 election, 26–27, 41–42, 46
  1972 election, 188, 229, 252, 256, 269
  acrimony over Social Credit alliance proposal, 139–40
Calgary Herald
  on 1968 federal election, 50
  on bilingualism, 152, 153
  on federal spending cuts, 111
  on medicare, 133
  on October Crisis, 166
  on oil quotas, 80
  on postal strike, 115
  on Trudeau, 44, 95, 230, 252
  on Trudeau cabinet, 51
Calgary North (federal riding), 29, 46, 48, 128, 259–60, 326n4

Calgary North (provincial riding), 23
Calgary Petroleum Club, 66, 294n10, 297n12, 319n7
Calgary Prophetic Bible Institute, 119–20, 138
Calgary South (federal riding)
  1963 election, 22, 24
  1968 election, 25–26, 42, 45–46
  1972 election, 227, 228, 232, 252, 265–66, 269
  1984 election, 289n25
  history of, 24–25, 282
  Nickle as MP for, 42
Calgary Stampede, 25, 195, 198–202, 199, 201, 245, 289n6
Calgary Stampeders, 60, 206, 221
Caloil, 89, 298n47
Cameron, Donald, 153, 309n24
Camp, Dalton, 88
Canada Development Corporation (CDC), 175, 232
Canada federal election (1957), 31–33
Canada federal election (1968)
  Alberta Liberal campaign, 37–38, 41–42, 44, 305n12
  Alberta Liberal candidates and nomination meetings, 25–30, 34–36
  Alberta Liberal results, 45–46, 48, 206
  calling of, 24
  Hawrelak in Edmonton Centre, 43
  impact on Alberta Liberals, 55
  national results, 49
  national unity issue, 40–41
  projected results, 329n66
  Stanfield's public image, 39–40
  St. Jean Baptiste Day riot, 44

Trudeau campaign events in Calgary, 42–43
Trudeau campaign events in Edmonton, 38–39, 39
Trudeaumania and, 24
Canada federal election (1972)
  Alberta Liberal candidates, 256
  Alberta Liberal challenges, 255–56, 276–80
  Alberta Liberal reaction to results, 271, 272–73
  Alberta Tory reaction to results, 270
  calling of, 255
  "corporate welfare bums" issue, 259, 263, 266
  hostility in lead up to, 229–30, 232–33
  Hurtig campaign, 263–64, 265
  Jamieson event in Calgary, 259–60
  Liberal campaign, 256, 257–58, 263, 264, 265, 267, 268, 327n28–29
  Liberal challenges, 255, 262, 273–76
  Liberal confidence, 249
  Mahoney-Bawden contest, 252, 265–66
  NDP campaign, 256, 258, 259, 261, 263, 264–65, 266–67
  Olson campaign, 260
  pipeline issue, 261–62
  projected results, 232, 233, 252, 265, 267–68
  results, 269–70, 271–72
  Social Credit campaign, 256–57
  Tory campaign, 256, 258–59, 262, 264, 266
  Tory candidates, 227–28, 228–29, 252–53
  Trudeau campaign events in Alberta, 260–61, 261, 265, 267, 327n28
  Trudeau government preparation, 230, 250–52
  unemployment issue, 258–59, 262
Canadian Alliance Party, 280, 304n23
Canadian Bar Association, xix–xx, 3
Canadian Pacific Railway (CPR), 287n1
Canadian Petroleum Association (CPA), 69, 81–82, 172, 220, 242
Canadian Security Intelligence Service (CSIS), 288n5
Canadian Wheat Board (CWB), 92, 299nn4–5
Caouette, Real, 123, 166, 256–57
capital cost allowance deferrals, 112, 113
capital gains tax, 101, 102, 103, 104, 105, 108, 191
capital punishment, 166, 260, 265
Cardinal, Harold, 58, 293n11
Carney, Pat, 294n10
Carstairs, Sharon, 128, 141, 305n2
Carter Commission, 42, 102
Carville, James, 295n30
cattle industry, 92, 195, 235
CDC (Canada Development Corporation), 175, 232
Chalifoux, Paul, 30
Chapman, Vic, 187
Charlottetown Accord, 291n5
chicken and egg war, 235–36, 238, 276
Chretien, Jean
  at 1968 Liberal leadership convention, 10
  Carstairs and, 305n2
  as Indian Affairs minister, 58
  on Lake Louise resort proposal, 324n22
  Olson and, 284
  pipeline announcement, 89

Sharp and, 6
   Sulatycky and, 307n18
   in Trudeau cabinet, 50
Chumir, Sheldon, 306n41
Cichon, Stan, 260, 327n29
Clark, Bob, 135, 306n20
Clark, Gilbert (Gib), 7, 288n5
Clark, Greg, 288n5
Clark, Joe, 229, 253, 256, 282, 291n5, 309n42, 321n11
coal mining, xvii, 207
Cohen, Harry, 8
Committee for an Independent Canada, 265, 284
community of communities policy, 291n5
Company of Young Canadians (CYC), 60, 71, 77, 104. *See also* NOW (No Other Way)
Conservative Party of Canada, 304n23
constitutional reform, xx, 3, 151, 241, 284, 285, 323n2
consumer price index, 190, 216, 262, 318n7
Council of Canadians, 284
CPA (Canadian Petroleum Association), 69, 81–82, 172, 220, 242
Cross, James, 161, 166
Crowfoot (federal riding), 29, 48, 309n42
Crow Rate, xvii, 287n1
Crowsnest Pass, xvii–xviii, 196–97, 316n5
CSIS (Canadian Security Intelligence Service), 288n5
Curtola, Bobby, 200
CWB (Canadian Wheat Board), 92, 299nn4–5
CYC (Company of Young Canadians), 60, 71, 77, 104. *See also* NOW (No Other Way)

Dantzer, Vince, 33, 38
Davey, Jim, 8, 293n8
Davey, Keith, 11, 18, 57
Davis, Bill, 229, 259, 264
Davis, Jack, 106
death penalty, 166, 260, 265
Decore, John, 32, 290n4
Decore, Laurence, 11, 13, 290n4
defence policy, 75
Denison Mines, 85, 298n30
Dent, Ivor, 164
depletion allowance, 105, 192
deux nations policy, 40, 291n5
Dickie, Bill
   at 1968 Liberal leadership convention, 13
   on Alberta Liberals crisis, 136
   failed Calgary South Liberal nomination, 25–26
   floor crossed to Tories, 132, 290n10
   in Lougheed cabinet, 214
   on oil and gas industry, 242
   political career, 289n13
Diefenbaker, John, 4, 13–14, 33, 60, 67, 123, 154
distinct society policy, 40, 291n5
divorce laws, 3
Dome Petroleum, 82, 297n9
Douglas, C.H., 120, 122
Douglas, Tommy, 163, 166
Drapeau, Jean, 44
Drury, Charles (Bud), 50
Dzenick, Russell, 35

economic issues
   foreign ownership, 85–88, 175–77, 248–49, 263, 324n6, 325n14

impact on Alberta, 115
postal worker strikes, 113–15, 115–16
as problem for Trudeau government, 116, 215
Trudeau defence of policy, 230
US import surcharge issue, 215–16, 217–18
See also financial policies; inflation; tax reform; unemployment
economic nationalism, *see* foreign ownership
Edmonton, 22, 38–39, 39, 65–66, 294n6
Edmonton Centre (federal riding), 33–36, 43, 46, 188, 256, 270
Edmonton East (federal riding), 30, 32–33, 48, 256
Edmonton Journal, 35, 43, 50, 51, 180
Edmonton-Strathcona (federal riding), 28, 45, 51, 52, 256, 269, 270
Edmonton West (federal riding), 28, 32, 48, 256, 269, 283
Edson, 250
elections, see *Alberta general elections*; *Canada federal elections*
energy industry, *see* oil and gas industry
Energy Resources Conservation Board (ERCB), 242, 262, 319n4
eugenics, 222–23, 320n19
Evans, Margaret, 288n3
Ewasew, John, 43
Expo 67, xix, 155
Exxon Valdez, 324n1

Fairbairn, Joyce, 75, 187, 296n14, 301n12
Faribault, Marcel, 40, 50
farm-marketing legislation, 197–98, 235–36, 238

federalism, 4, 40, 43
financial policies
1968 budget, 56
1969 budget, 111–12
1970 budget, 188
1971 budget, 190–92
1972 budget, 249, 258
See also economic issues; foreign ownership; inflation; tax reform
Financial Times, 83, 93
Financial Times of Canada, 192
FIRA (Foreign Investment Review Agency), 325n14
first minister's conference (1969), 151–52
Fisher, Douglas, 50
Flaherty, Jack, 307n20
FLQ (Front de libération du Québec), 150, 161–62, 163. *See also* October Crisis
Foreign Investment Review Agency (FIRA), 325n14
foreign ownership, 85–88, 175–77, 248–49, 263, 324n6, 325n14
Francophone Canadians, 150
Freeland, Chrystia, 287n3
Freeland, Wilbur, 287n3
Front de libération du Québec (FLQ), 150, 161–62, 163. *See also* October Crisis
Fulton, Davie, 229
fundraising, 130–32, 314n29
Funnell, Owen, 201

Gaglardi, Phil, 230
Gagnon, Louis, 159
Gallagher, Jack, 82, 297n9
Gerhart, Edgar, 164
Getty, Don, 222, 244
Ghitter, Ron, 206, 214

Gibson, Kelly, 171
Gillen, Michael, 104, 301n12
Globe and Mail, 115
Gordon, Sonny, 8
Gorman, Jack, 202
Gostick, Ron, 289n5
Govier, George, 82, 83
grain industry, *see* wheat industry
Grain Stabilization Fund (GSF), 236–37
Gray, Don, 35, 36, 46, 292n2
Gray, Herb, 86, 175, 248, 324nn5–6
Great Canadian Oil Sands, 248
Great Depression, 120
Greene, Joe
    in 1968 Liberal leadership race, 6, 15, 18
    background, 6
    end of political career, 228
    foreign ownership and, 86–88
    health problems, 69, 228
    Home Oil sale and, 176, 177
    oil and gas industry and, 59, 84, 89, 171–72, 189
    Peacock and, 27
    photograph of, 87
    in Senate, 259, 321n7
    in Trudeau government, 50, 231
Grey Cup, 60, 221–22
Grit, use of term, 288n4
Group of Ten, 217–18, 319n19
GSF (Grain Stabilization Fund), 236–37

Hamilton, Alvin, 229
Hamilton, Don, 307n20
Hansen, Eric, 66
Hargrave, Bert, 260
Harkness, Douglas, 46, 107, 188, 229

Harradence, Milt, 153–55, 156, 157, 159, 165, 309nn26–27, 309n42
Harries, Hu
    1968 federal election, 28, 45, 47, 51, 53
    1971 Alberta Liberal convention, 185
    1972 federal election, 256, 269, 270
    on 1972 federal election results, 273
    background, 51
    cabinet speculation about, 49, 50
    disconnect from Alberta Liberals, 107, 137, 142, 182, 273
    exclusion from cabinet, 51–52
    experience as MP, 60–61, 230–31, 273, 278
    on foreign investment, 176–77
    Mahoney and, 135
    on New West Task Force, 155
    post-MP career, 283
    on proposed Alberta Liberal alliance with Social Credit, 135
    on western Liberal caucus proposal, 137
    on wheat industry, 92–93
    Williams on, 294n24, 329n11
Hartman, Don, 252
Harvie, Eric, 201
Hastings, Earl, 17, 18, 34–35, 144
Hawrelak, Bill
    1957 federal election, 31–33, 32
    1968 Edmonton Centre nomination race, 33–36
    background, 31
    campaign as independent Liberal, 43, 46
    as Edmonton mayor, 31, 33, 292n3
    political affiliations, 291n11
    real estate scandals, 33

Hays, Dan, 11
Hays, Harry
　1963 federal election, 22
　1968 Liberal leadership convention, 11
　Alberta Liberal leadership and, 185
　biography by Peacock, 314n34
　Brown and, 176
　on constitutional reform committee, 284, 330n8
　fundraising role, 25, 57, 130–31
　Hays Stampede Breakfast, 25, 289n6
　Mahoney and, 49, 60
　Olson and, 49
　Peacock and, 27
　political career, 24–25, 284
　provincial wing of Alberta Liberals and, 57
　Social Credit and, 137
　on splitting Alberta Liberal Party, 134
　Sykes and, 105
　Trudeau and, 273
　on wheat industry, 99
Hays Stampede Breakfast, 25, 289n6
Head, Ivan, 187, 273, 295n11
Hellyer, Paul, 5, 10, 11, 13, 15, 17, 18, 50
Henderson, Jim, 223
Henderson, Lloyd, 17
Hill, Bob, 59
Hills, Nick, 251
hippies, 71, 73. *See also* Company of Young Canadians
Holowach, Ambrose, 33
Home Oil, 82, 175–77
homosexual conduct, 3
Hooke, Alf, 181, 205, 210, 318n33
Horner, Doug, 317n14
Horner, Hugh, 207, 211, 238, 317n14

Horner, Jack
　1968 federal election, 29, 48
　attack on Liberals, 158–59
　cousin to Harradence, 154
　on farmer reaction to agricultural policy, 99
　floor crossed to Liberals, 159, 309n42
　opposition to agricultural policy, 59, 98
　photograph of, 158
　political career, 309n42
　Sulatycky and, 142
Horodezky, Dave, 138, 306n41
Hull, Bobby, 251, 325n26
Hunter, Dave, 13
Hurtig, Mel
　at 1968 Liberal leadership convention, 11
　at 1970 Alberta Liberal convention, 140
　1972 federal election, 256, 261, 263–64, 269
　as Alberta Liberal policy chair, 127, 128
　attack on Liberals, 95–96
　on bilingualism, 152
　on foreign ownership, 88, 249
　idealism of, 96
　on natural gas exports, 90
　on New West Task Force, 155
　photograph, 96
　photographs, 261
　political popularity, 129
　post-1972 career, 284
　on proposed Alberta Liberal alliance with Social Credit, 135–36
　Trudeau on, 265
Hutton, John, 139
Hyndman, Lou, 205

IGA (International Grains Agreement), 91, 299n2
import surcharge, US, 215–16, 217–18, 230
Independent Petroleum Association of Canada (IPAC), 59, 81–82, 89, 105, 172, 176, 192, 242
Indigenous policy, 58, 293n11
industrialization policy, 180, 241
inflation
    anti-inflation measures, 111–12, 115
    impact of, 112
    postal workers strike and, 112–13
    problems for Trudeau government from, 190, 262, 273
    unemployment blamed on, 188
    US import surcharge and, 215–16, 217–18
International Grains Agreement (IGA), 91, 299n2
IPAC (Independent Petroleum Association of Canada), 59, 81–82, 89, 105, 172, 176, 192, 242
Irwin, Doug, 30, 42

Jackson, Paul, 230
Jamieson, Don, 238, 259–60, 327n23
Jamieson, J.K., 249
Jaques, Norman, 122
Johnson, Daniel, 4, 40, 44
Johnson, Lyndon, 10

Keegstra, Jim, 303n16
Kelly, Charles, 265, 320n1, 321n25
Kennedy, Fred
    on 1967 Alberta election, 138
    on 1971 Alberta Liberal convention, 185
    on Denison Mines decision, 85
    on Home Oil sale, 176
    on New West Task Force, 155–56
    on postal workers strike, 116
    on proposed Alberta Liberal alliance with Social Credit, 136
    on Trudeau marriage, 188
    on Trudeau speech at fundraising dinner, 76
Kennedy, John F., xviii
Kennedy, Orvis, 209
Kennedy, Tom, 76
Kent, Arthur, 308n13
Kent, Parker, 152, 308n13
Kent, Peter, 308n13
Kerans, Roger, 13, 34, 142, 288n12
Kierans, Eric
    in 1968 Liberal leadership race, 7, 9, 15–16, 17, 18
    background, 7
    on foreign ownership, 249
    on postal workers strike, 115
    resignation from Trudeau government, 190
    support for NDP in 1972 federal election, 263, 264–65
    in Trudeau government, 50
King, Jack, 139–40
King, Martin King, Jr., 14, 16
Kirby, Cam, 229
Klein, Ralph, 59, 272, 288n5, 293n14
Knaut, Rod, 29
Knight, Bill, 237
Knights, Bill, 156
Korchinski, Stanley, 237

Laing, Arthur, 88
Lake Louise, 243–44, 324n22

Lalonde, Marc, 309n42, 312n25
LaMarsh, Judy, 15, 18, 289n17, 293n19
Lambert, Marcel, 28, 48, 283
Lambert, Roland, 259, 269, 271
Lang, Amanda, 295n23
Lang, Otto
- 1972 federal election, 276
- agricultural issues and, 97–98, 99, 236–37, 238, 239, 249, 275
- on Assiniboia by-election, 237
- background, 69
- father to Amanda Lang, 295n23
- Mazankowski on, 232
- oil and gas industry and, 69–70, 82, 222
- photograph, 69
- in Trudeau government, 50, 51, 231

Laporte, Pierre, 162, 164
Leavitt, Lee, xviii–xix
Lee, Bill, 11
Leger, Ed, 33
Lemieux, Leo, 13, 34
Leslie, Jack, 77, 104, 112
Lethbridge (federal riding), 27–28, 48, 75, 195, 256
Lévesque, René, 4, 7
Lewis, David, 248–49, 256, 259, 261, 263, 264–65, 266–67, 271, 274. *See also* New Democratic Party (federal)
Liberal Party (federal)
- disconnect from Alberta, 57–58
- organization, 21, 288n1
- overtures to Social Credit, 143
- participatory democracy approach, 56, 57, 95–96
- patronage and, 56–57
- Pearson government, 13–14
- provincial fortunes, 229
- seats in Alberta, 21–22, 38, 291n1
- *See also* Alberta Liberal Party; Liberal Party, 1968 leadership race; Quebec Liberal Party; Trudeau, Pierre; *Canada federal elections*

Liberal Party, 1968 leadership race
- atmosphere at convention, 10
- author as delegate to, 4–5, 9, 12, 17, 18, 20
- candidates, 5–8, 11, 13
- election of Trudeau, 20
- farewell to Pearson, 13, 14
- Sharp's withdrawal from, 10
- speeches by candidates, 14–17
- support for Trudeau, 3–4, 11
- Trudeau at convention, 10–11, 13, 16, 19
- Trudeau campaign in Calgary, 8
- Trudeau's appeal, 4, 9
- voting, 17–18, 20
- world events in background, 10, 14

LIFT (Lower Inventories for Tomorrow) program, 97–98, 275–76
linguistic rights, xx, 13. *See also* bilingualism
liquor policy, 128, 205, 316n5
Little, Rich, 198, 200
Lougheed, James, 130, 305n9
Lougheed, Peter
- 1967 Alberta election, 293n10
- 1971 Alberta election, 207, 208, 208–09, 210, 211, 212
- as advocate for oil industry, 89
- on anti-inflation measures, 113
- attacks on Social Credit, 180, 205, 206
- background, 130
- at Calgary Stampede, 198, 245
- on constitutional reform, 241
- federal Liberals' familiarity with, 57–58

on industrialization, 241
on LIFT wheat program, 98
on Lowery's resignation as Liberal
   leader, 138
on Manning's appointment to Senate,
   144–45
on natural gas, 221, 241–42
on October Crisis measures, 164
on oil policy, 68–69, 70, 243
post-1972 career, 285
as problem for Liberals, 278–79
public image, 221
Stevenson and, 309n36
support for federal PCs, 222, 255, 266
on tax reform, 103, 106, 216
See also Lougheed government;
   Progressive Conservative
   Association of Alberta
Lougheed government
   on Alberta's federal role, 52, 222
   Banff National Park issue, 243–44
   dominance of, 285
   first cabinet, 213, 214
   first throne speech, 222–23
   popularity, 223
   successful first session, 244–45
   See also Lougheed, Peter
Lowery, Jack
   1970 Alberta Liberal convention, 140
   background, 127–28
   departure as Alberta Liberal leader, 138,
      279
   election as leader, 128
   fundraising concerns, 130
   photograph, 129
   political career after resignation, 185
   proposed Alberta Liberal alliance with
      Social Credit, 133, 135–36, 306n21
   at Strom's thinker's conference, 143
Luzzi, Don, 206–07, 209, 211, 214, 317n11
Lynch, Charles
   at 1968 Liberal leadership convention,
      14
   on 1972 federal election, 249, 257, 264,
      268
   on tax reform, 192
   on Trudeau trip to Soviet Union, 190
   on western separatists, 156

Maccagno, Mike, 11, 29, 44, 48, 55–56, 145,
   305n12
Macdonald, Donald S., 19, 50–51, 231,
   261–62
MacDonald, Mike, 140, 182
MacEachen, Allan J., 6, 15, 18
MacEwan, J.W. Grant, 22–23, 198
Mackasey, Bryce, 50, 188
Maclean Evans, Una, 11, 141, 256, 261, 269,
   288n3
Mahoney, Patrick (Pat)
   1968 federal election, 25–26, 42, 45–46
   at 1971 Alberta Liberal convention, 185
   1972 federal election, 231, 232, 252,
      255–56, 261, 264, 265, 269, 270, 271
   on 1972 federal election, 272–73
   Alberta Liberal leadership and, 185
   on bilingualism, 152
   cabinet speculations about, 49
   at Calgary Stampede, 200, 202, 245
   on Canada Development Corporation,
      175
   on Company of Young Canadians, 77
   death, 330n4

disconnect from Alberta Liberals, 142,
    182–83
at Glencoe Club fundraising dinner,
    104, 105
Harries and, 135
on Manning's appointment to Senate,
    145
martini preferences, 321n25
on New West Task Force, 155
NOW encounter with Trudeau and, 74
on October Crisis measures, 164
on oil and gas industry, 173
photographs, 27, 83, 272
political strengths, 232, 282
post-MP career, 281–82
proposal to split Alberta Liberals,
    133–34, 140, 182
Social Credit and, 137
on tax reform, 101, 105, 217
Tory takeover of riding, 227, 228
Trudeau and, 273
in Trudeau government, 60, 228, 232,
    321n25
on Trudeau's fundraising dinner
    speech, 76
western Liberal caucus proposal, 137
Manning (AB), 305n3
Manning, Ernest
    on 1971 Alberta election, 211
    in Alberta Social Credit government,
        121, 122, 124
    against anti-Semitism, 122
    appointment to CIBC, 125
    appointment to Senate, 143–45, 280
    attacks on Trudeau government, 125,
        133, 165, 232
    background, 119–20
    on bilingualism, 124–25
    Crowsnest Pass and, 196
    federal Social Credit and, 123
    Hooke on, 210, 318n33
    on import surcharge issue, 216
    on medicare, 133
    National Public Affairs Research
        Foundation, 82, 124
    on October Crisis, 166
    on oil and gas industry, 122
    Olson and, 53
    photograph, 144
    political realignment philosophy,
        123–24, 304n23
    relationships with oilmen, 124, 176
    on tax reform, 217
    See also Social Credit Party (Alberta)
Manning, Preston, 82, 124, 143, 304n23
Marchand, Jean, 7, 159
marijuana policy, 128, 183, 260–61, 267
Martin, Paul, Jr., 291n5
Martin, Paul, Sr., 5, 11, 12, 14, 17–18
Mazankowski, Don, 232, 236, 322n30
McClary, Gordon, 35
McDonald, David, 13, 183, 288n5
McDonald Commission, 288n5
McIntyre Porcupine Mines Limited, 210,
    318n33
McKinnon, F.A., 171
McLean, Dave, 11, 35, 290n9
media, 180–81
medicare, 6, 42, 104, 111, 122, 128, 132–33
Medicine Hat (federal riding)
    1962 election, 123
    1965 election, 123
    1968 election, 29, 45, 46, 123
    1972 election, 260, 269

Index   349

1974 election, 283
   Liberal history in, 52
   Trudeau tour through, 195
Meech Lake Accord, 291n5
members of parliament (MPS), 231
Michener, Roland, 24, 25
Miller, Abe, 28
Miller, Tevie, 28, 48
Millican, Harold, 20, 282, 289n25
Milvain, J.V.H. (Val), 71–72, 72, 295n6
monarchy, 241, 325n20
Moore, W. Kenneth (Ken), 11, 26, 288n4
Moores, Frank, 229
Mosely, Oswald, 120
Moshansky, Virgil, 11, 288n2
Mosychuk, Nick, 33, 290n5
Motut, Roger, 164
Mowers, Cleo, 20
MPS (members of parliament), 231
Mulcair, Thomas, 327n22
Muller, Carl, 141
Mulroney, Brian, 291n5
multiculturalism, 197, 316n9
Munro, John, 198

National Advisory Committee on
   Petroleum (NACOP), 171–72
National Energy Board (NEB)
   introduction to, 296n2
   Arctic gas pipeline, 319n8
   Caloil scandal and, 89
   natural gas exports to US, 90, 219–21, 278
   oilmen opposition to, 277
   US-Canada quota agreement and, 80, 82

National Energy Program (NEP), 285, 294n10, 312n25
National Farmers' Union (NFU), 92
National Hockey League (NHL), 251
National Party of Canada, 284
National Petroleum Show, 242
National Public Affairs Research
   Foundation, 82, 124, 297n8
natural gas industry
   Albertan growth, 83
   Arctic pipeline, 220, 319n8
   exports to US, 90, 219–21, 278
   Lougheed government on prices, 241–42
   measurements in, 319n1, 323n4
   Pan Alberta Gas, 242
   See also oil and gas industry
NEB, *see* National Energy Board
NEP, *see* National Energy Program
New Democratic Party (Alberta), 136, 180, 207, 209, 210, 211–13
New Democratic Party (BC), 253
New Democratic Party (federal), 1972
   election, 256, 258, 259, 261, 263, 264–65, 266–67, 270, 271, 274. *See also* Lewis, David
Newfoundland, 229
Newman, Peter C., 233
New West Task Force, 154–56, 157, 159, 165
NHL (National Hockey League), 251
Nichol, John, 20
Nickle, Carl, 42, 82, 172, 174, 175, 191, 221, 276–77
Nickle, Sam, Sr., 291n10
Nielsen, Arne, 172
Nielsen, Erik, 237
Nigeria, 59

Nixon, Richard, 70, 189, 215–16, 217, 218, 278, 319n20
Notley, Grant, 180, 207, 211, 266, 313n7. *See also* New Democratic Party (Alberta)
Notley, Rachel, 313n7
Nova Scotia, 228, 229
NOW (No Other Way), 73–74, 76–77. *See also* Company of Young Canadians
Nowlan, Patrick, 50
Nurgitz, Nathan, 183–84

October Crisis
    Alberta support for Trudeau during, 164–65, 166–67
    decline of election opportunity, 165, 279
    ending of, 165–66
    kidnapping and death of Laporte, 162, 164
    kidnapping of Cross, 161
    Manning and, 165, 166
    public support for action against, 166
    Trudeau response to FLQ, 162
    Trudeau response to press, 162–63, 163–64
    Trudeau self-promotion on, 230
    War Emergencies Measures Act invoked, 163, 164
Official Languages Act, 14, 124–25, 133, 150–51, 153, 267. *See also* bilingualism
oil and gas industry
    access to eastern Canada issue, 59, 67, 80, 89
    Caloil scandal, 89, 298n47
    Canada Development Corporation and, 175
    consumption forecasts, 84, 242, 297n23, 323n9
    continental oil policy proposal, 59, 68–69
    discovery of oil in Leduc, 121
    economic and political clout of, 79–80, 285
    exports to US, 88–89, 189
    foreign ownership issues, 85–86, 175–77, 249
    growth in Alberta, 84, 171, 172–73, 242, 248, 262–63, 277–78
    Home Oil sale, 175–77
    impact on Alberta, 65–66
    Lewis on, 266–67
    Lougheed as advocate, 89
    Mahoney on, 173
    as male dominated, 66
    National Advisory Committee on Petroleum, 171–72
    in Nova Scotia, 228
    oil sands, 66, 68, 108, 124, 242, 248, 327n22
    oil stocks, 83
    OPEC crisis, 173–75
    opposition to Trudeau government, 80–82, 83–84, 221, 227, 255, 276–77, 278, 320n1
    pipelines, 89, 189, 220, 247, 259, 261–62, 319n8
    positive relations with Trudeau government, 60, 84, 89–90, 171–72
    problems facing, 66, 189, 242
    quota issue with US, 67–68, 80–81, 82, 86, 90, 172
    revenue beneficiaries, 206
    self-perception, 173

Social Credit and, 122
support for Tories, 42, 228
surplus formula, 319n4
tax on oil reserves, 243
on tax reform, 105–06
threat to move to US, 301n20
Trudeau educational tour, 82, 83
Trudeau government policy, 69–70, 189
Trudeau lack of mention of at
    fundraising dinner, 75–76, 277,
    295n11, 296n12
Trudeau's knowledge about, 82, 228,
    297n12
use of "oil" term, 294n1
US task force on, 84
See also natural gas industry
oil sands, 66, 68, 108, 124, 242, 248, 327n22
oil stocks, 83
O'Leary, Willis, 13, 288n9
Olson, H.A. (Bud)
    1968 federal election, 29, 45, 46, 305n12
    at 1968 Liberal leadership convention,
        17
    at 1970 Alberta Liberal convention, 140
    at 1971 Alberta Liberal convention, 185
    1972 federal election, 255–56, 260, 269
    agricultural policy and, 59–60, 235–36,
        237, 238
    Alberta Liberals and, 142, 181, 185
    background, 52–53
    cabinet speculations about, 49–50
    at Calgary Stampede with Trudeau, 198
    Hamilton on, 229
    Horner on, 159
    Mazankowski on, 232
    photograph, 53
    political career, 29, 53–54, 123
    post-MP career, 283–84
    on splitting Alberta Liberal Party,
        134–35, 137, 140
    Sulatycky and, 307n18
    tax reform and, 105
    Trudeau and, 273
    in Trudeau government, 51, 232
    Trudeau's southern Alberta
        barnstorming and, 195
    wheat crisis and, 92, 93, 97–98
Olympic team, 60
Ontario, 229
OPEC (Organization of Petroleum
    Exporting Countries), 172, 173–75,
    248, 311n7
Orr, Bobby, 198

Palliser (federal riding), 48
Palmer, Jim, 13, 26, 288n8
Pan Alberta Gas, 242
Panarctic Oils, 220, 222, 277, 319n8
Paproski, Steve, 36, 46, 68
participatory democracy, 56, 95–96, 102,
    106–07, 191, 230, 274, 292n5
Parti Québécois, 7
Patrick, A. Russell, 89, 90, 180
patronage, 56–57
Peace River (federal riding), 30, 48, 128,
    270
Peacock, Don, 27–28, 75, 136, 185, 195,
    296n16, 314n34
Peacock, Fred, 112
Pearson, Lester, 3, 4, 13–14, 24–25, 27
Pelletier, Gerard, 7, 159
Pembina (federal riding), 30
Pepin, Jean-Luc, 50, 60, 89, 97
Petrasuk, Peter

1968 federal election, 29, 46
    at 1968 Liberal leadership convention, 11
    at 1969 Alberta Liberal fundraising dinner, 129, 296n12
    at 1970 Alberta Liberal convention, 140
    as Alberta Liberal president, 58, 139, 141
    on Calgary city council, 55
    end of political career, 293n13
Petroleum News, 175
Petroleum Tax Society, 173
Pew, John Howard, 124
Pickersgill, Jack, 31
Pierce, Jack, 80, 88
postal workers, 113–15, 115–16
Prairie Grain Advance Payments Act, 236
Prince Edward Island, 229
Pringle, Bill, 8
Progressive Conservative Association of Alberta
    1971 convention, 183–84
    by-election win in Manning's old seat, 152
    Harradence as leader, 154
    as official opposition to Social Credit, 122, 132
    support from federal Tories, 183–84
    See also Lougheed, Peter; Lougheed government; *Alberta general elections*
Progressive Conservative Party (federal)
    attack on Trudeau government, 215
    Diefenbaker victories, 37, 123
    Manning on, 124
    oilmen support for, 42, 228
    See also Stanfield, Robert; *Canada federal elections*

Progressive Conservative Party (Ontario), 229
Project 75, 238–39
prosperity certificates ("funny money"), 121
"Protocols of the Learned Elders of Zion," 122, 303n13
Prowse, J. Harper, 11, 22, 68, 185–86
Prudham, George, 11, 32
Prudhoe Bay (Alaska), 66, 89, 247

Quebec
    alienation in, 150
    in chicken and egg war, 235
    deux nations policy, 40, 291n5
    English Canada on, 4, 40–41
Quebec Liberal Party, 7, 229
Queens Park (provincial riding), xviii–xix

Ralfe, Tim, 162–63
Ralliement créditiste du Québec, 49, 123
Ranchmen's Club, 66
Raymaker, Darryl
    1967 Alberta election, xviii–xix
    1968 Liberal leadership race and, 4–5, 7, 9, 12, 17, 18, 20
    1979 federal election, 326n4
    at Calgary Stampede with Trudeau, *xix*, 201
    decision to join Liberals, xviii
    first impressions of Trudeau, xx
    Social Credit and, 206
Raymaker, Pat, xix, *xix*, 4–5, 9, 17, 20, 75, 221
RCMP (Royal Canadian Mounted Police), 250, 288n5, 325n20
Red Deer (federal riding), 30, 42, 123, 303n16

Index   353

Reform Party, 304n23
Reilly, Peter, 232–33
Reimer, Neil, 313n7
Richardson, James, 50, 51
Roark, Gene, 88
Robarts, John, 166
Roberts, Peter, 187
Robinson, John, 136
Rocky Mountain (federal riding)
    1968 election, 28–29, 44, 45, 46
    1972 election, 229, 252–53, 269
    Trudeau tour through, 195
Roebuck, Arthur, 15
Roman, Stephen, 85
Romano, Alberto, 326n4
Roosevelt, Theodore, 281
Ross, Alastair (Al) H., 171, 176, 192, 232, 312n25
Royal Canadian Mounted Police (RCMP), 250, 288n5, 325n20
Royal Commission on Bilingualism and Biculturalism (B and B Commission), 14, 150, 156. *See also* bilingualism
Russell, Andy, 256
Russell, Bob
    1968 federal election, 35
    at 1968 Liberal leadership convention, 11
    in 1969 Alberta Liberal leadership race, 127, 128
    1971 Alberta election, 207
    Alberta Liberal crisis and, 136, 141, 181, 184
    as Alberta Liberal leader, 186, 284
    background, 128
    on Banff consultations, 244

Russia, *see* Soviet Union
Saltsman, Max, 108
Schepanovich, Branny, 256
Schreyer, Ed, 105
Schumacher, Stan, 101, 270
Sellar, Don, 42, 44, 49, 133, 188
Senate, 143, 283
separatism, *see* western alienation
Sexual Sterilization Act, 222–23, 320n19
Sharp, Mitchell, 6, 10, 56
Sharp, Noel, 29, 48
Sherring, Frank, 28
Shewchuk, Pat, 30, 48
Sinclair, James, 32, 290n3
Sinclair, Margaret, *see* Trudeau, Margaret
Sinclair, William, 13, 28, 288n6
Skoreyko, Bill, 48
Smallwood, Joey, 229
Social Credit Party (Alberta)
    introduction to, 119
    1935 election into government, 72–73, 120–21
    1967 election, xviii–xix, 122
    1971 election, 179–80, 209–10, 211–14
    Alberta Liberal proposed alliance with, 133, 135–37
    anti-Semitism and, 121–22, 303n16
    author's involvement with, 206
    demise of, 122, 123, 138, 284–85
    federal Liberal overtures to, 143
    as governing party, 121, 122
    ideological basis, 120, 122, 141
    Lougheed attacks on, 205, 206
    oil and gas industry and, 122
    Olson and, 53
    opposition to Trudeau government, 141–42

problems facing government, 180–81,
    205–06, 209–10
Strom as leader, 125, 268
Strom-Trudeau relationship, 132–33
thinker's conference, 142–43
women's auxiliaries gathering, 179–80
See also Manning, Ernest; Strom, Harry
Social Credit Party (BC), 253
Social Credit Party (federal), 37, 123,
    256–57, 270
Southam News, 42, 82, 211, 277
Soviet Union, 190
Sparrow, Barbara Jane (Bobbie), 282
Speaker, Ray, 135, 306n20
special status policy, 40, 291n5
Stanbury, Richard (Dick), 56, 237–38, 292n5
Standoff Blood Indian Reserve, 196
Stanfield, Robert (Bob)
    1968 federal election, 39–40, 50
    1972 federal election, 255, 256, 258–59,
        262, 264, 266, 274
    background, 39–40
    Joe Clark and, 229
    October Crisis and, 163, 166
    photograph, 81
    public image, 4, 39–40, 161
    on unemployment insurance, 262
    See also Progressive Conservative Party
        (federal)
Stevenson, Brian, 13, 157, 181, 184, 288n10,
    309n36
St. Jean Baptiste Day riot, 44
St. Laurent, Louis, 31, 32
Stoney Nation, Morley reserve, 210
Strom, Harry
    1971 Alberta election, 207, 209, 211
    agricultural policy and, 98

attack on media, 180–81
on bilingualism, 151–52, 167
at Calgary Stampede with Trudeau, 198
on capital cost allowance deferrals, 112
on industrialization policy, 180
on October Crisis, 164, 166–67
oil and gas industry and, 70, 84, 89
photograph, 58
problems facing government of, 180–81
on proposed Alberta Liberal alliance
    with Social Credit, 135
resignation as Social Credit leader, 268
selection as Social Credit leader, 125
at Social Credit women's auxiliaries
    gathering, 180
on tax reform, 102, 191
thinker's conference, 142–43
Trudeau and, 132–33
See also Social Credit Party (Alberta)
Sulatycky, Allen
    1968 federal election, 28–29, 44, 45, 46,
        53, 305n12
    1972 federal election, 229, 253, 256, 261,
        269, 282
    background, 28
    Crowsnest Pass and, 316n5
    disconnect from Alberta Liberals, 142
    Harries and, 51–52, 142, 273
    Olson and, 59, 142, 307n18
    political strengths, 282
    post-MP career, 282–83
    pronunciation of name, 290n14
    on splitting Alberta Liberal Party, 134,
        137, 140
    in Trudeau government, 228
    Trudeau's southern Alberta
        barnstorming and, 196–97, 197

Index   355

Sullivan, Martin, xx
Suncor Energy, 124
Sun Oil, 124
Switzer, Bill, 11, 132, 305n13
Sykes, Rod
   on 1971 budget, 191
   on Banff consultations, 244
   at Calgary Stampede, 200, 201, 245
   political career, 104, 301n13
   on proposed Alberta Liberal alliance with Social Credit, 136
   on tax reform, 104–05
   on western separatism, 156–57
Syncrude Canada, 66, 108, 248

Tailfeathers, Gerald, 196
Tanner, B.C. (Ches), 184–85
tax reform
   announcement of, 101, 102
   defence of, 102–03, 105, 106, 107
   discussion at Glencoe Club fundraiser, 104–05
   failure of white paper process, 191, 274
   impact on Trudeau government, 109
   implementation of, 191, 216–17
   oil royalties and, 243
   opposition to, 101, 104–06, 108, 141, 153, 191–92
   positive press reaction, 192
   Senate and Commons recommendations, 108–09
   white paper process, 106–07
Taylor, Gordon, 143, 229, 307n22
Taylor, Nick
   1968 federal election, 26–27, 41, 41–42, 46
   1972 federal election, 252, 256, 269
   Alberta Liberal crisis and, 139–40
   as Alberta Liberal leader, 284
   background, 108
   in Senate, 285
   on tax reform, 107
   wit of, 290n11
Temporary Wheat Reserves Act, 236
Thatcher, Ross, 105, 106
Thompson, Robert, 123, 156, 236, 304n21
Thomson, Dave, 93, 187
Tomyn, William, 141
Toronto Stock Exchange Oil Index, 83
Tory, use of term, 287n2
trillion cubic feet (TCF), 319n1
Trudeau, Justin, 251, 291n1
Trudeau, Margaret, 188–89, 190, 198, 200, 201, 202, 268, 290n3
Trudeau, Pierre
   1967 speech on constitutional reform, xx, 3
   appeal to English Canadians, 4, 23, 44
   author's first impressions of, xx
   background, 7–8
   at Calgary Stampede, *xix*, 195, 198, 199, 200, 201, 202
   federalism debate, 4
   as Justice minister, 3
   lack of interest in production of wealth, 299n15
   marriage to Margaret Sinclair, 188–89
   Nixon on, 319n20
   on participatory democracy, 292n5
   public image problems, 275, 316n11
   sceptics on, 24
   Trudeaumania, 8, 10–11, 23–24, 26, 50
   on US, 298n33

See also Trudeau, Pierre, 1968 federal
    election; Trudeau, Pierre, 1968
    Liberal leadership race; Trudeau,
    Pierre, 1972 federal election;
    Trudeau government
Trudeau, Pierre, 1968 federal election
    calling of, 24
    campaign events in Calgary, 42–43
    campaign events in Edmonton, 38–39,
        39, 53
    national unity issue, 40–41
    St. Jean Baptiste Day riot, 44
    Trudeau as focus, 37–38, 44
    See also Canada federal election (1968)
Trudeau, Pierre, 1968 Liberal leadership
    race
    appeal to English Canada, 4, 9
    campaign in Calgary, 8
    at convention, 10–11, 16, 19
    election as leader, 20
    on policy, 13
    qualifications, 7–8
    support for, 3–4, 9, 11
    votes for, 17, 18, 20
    See also Liberal Party, 1968 leadership
        race
Trudeau, Pierre, 1972 federal election
    Alberta campaign events, 267, 327n28
    calling of, 255
    campaign difficulties, 257–58, 263, 264,
        268
    campaign message and style, 256, 257,
        264
    factors for defeat, 273–76
    pre-election trips to Alberta, 250–51,
        251–52
    See also Canada federal election (1972)

Trudeau government
    1969 first minister's conference, 151–52
    Albertan members, 187–88, 230–31, 273
    Albertan support for, 50, 202
    cabinet, 49–52, 231–32
    honeymoon period, 61
    poor Albertan representation, 278
    post-1972, 285
    southern Alberta barnstorming, 195–
        98, 197
    Soviet Union trip, 190
    See also agricultural policy; economic
        issues; financial policies; foreign
        ownership; inflation; October
        Crisis; oil and gas industry; tax
        reform; Trudeau, Pierre, 1972
        federal election; unemployment;
        wheat industry
Trudeaumania, 8, 10–11, 23–24, 26, 50
Turner, John
    in 1968 Liberal leadership race, 5–6, 13,
        17–18, 20
    1972 budget, 249
    1984 Liberal leadership bid, 301n26
    background, 5–6
    distinct society policy and, 291n5
    Grains Stabilization Fund conflict and,
        236
    in Trudeau government, 50, 231

Ukrainian Canadian committee, 151
unemployment
    as 1972 election problem for Liberals,
        215, 216, 230, 249–50, 258, 259, 262,
        273–74
    in Alberta, 115, 192, 262, 326n13

Index   357

anti-inflation measures and, 113, 115, 188
explanation of rates, 314n4
in Great Depression, 120
legislation to help, 188, 190
in Quebec, 164
Union Nationale, 7
United Farmers of Alberta, 22
United States of America
import surcharge, 215–16, 217–18
natural gas exports to, 90, 219–21, 278
oil exports to, 88–89, 189
oil quota issue, 67–68, 80–81, 82, 86, 90, 172
task force on oil policy, 84
Trudeau on, 298n33
See also Nixon, Richard
University of Alberta, 38–39
uranium industry, 85, 298n30

Van Brabant, Jules, 30
Vegreville (federal riding), 30
Veiner, Harry, 52, 164, 195, 292n12
Victoria Charter, 241, 323n2

Wachowich, Allan, 13, 288n7
Walsh, Tom, 7
War Emergencies Measures Act, 163. *See also* October Crisis
Waterton Lakes National Park, 196
WEOC (Western Economics Opportunities Conference), 281, 329n2
Werry, Len, 207
western alienation
introduction to, 149
agricultural issues and, 93, 153
Crow Rate, xvii, 287n1
growing sense of, 156

Horner's attacks on Liberals, 158–59
hostility towards Pearson, 13–14
Liberal Party blamed for, 149–50
Official Languages Act and, 151, 152–53
separatism discussions, 154–57, 159
Trudeau's response to, 157
Western Economics Opportunities Conference (WEOC), 281, 329n2
Wetaskiwin (federal riding), 30
wheat industry
Canadian Wheat Board, 92, 299nn4–5
demonstrations against Trudeau, 93–95
federal response to crisis, 92, 97–98, 239, 275–76
good news from, 98–99, 249
Grain Stabilization Fund conflict, 236–37
impact of crisis on Liberals, 99
International Grains Agreement, 299n2
LIFT program, 97–98, 275–76
rural depopulation from crisis, 98
surplus production problem, 91–92, 93, 97
transportation concerns, 92–93, 238, 239
Trudeau's relationship with, 51, 91, 93, 94, 95
See also agricultural policy
white paper process, 106–07, 274
Whitford, Jim, 35
Williams, Blair, 188, 294n24, 314n2, 327n28, 329n11
Winters, Robert
in 1968 Liberal leadership race, 5, 10, 11, 12, 14–15, 17, 18, 20

    background, 5
    death, 289n16
Woolliams, Eldon
    1968 federal election, 46
    on 1972 federal election, 270
    on foreign ownership policy, 87–88
    LaMarsh on, 293n19
    on oil and gas policy, 68
    proposal for author to run against, 326n4
    on tax reform, 104
    on US–Canada relations, 80–81, *81*
    on western separatism, 156
    on wheat crisis, 60

Yewchuk, Paul, 48, 269
Young, Bob, 7
Young, John, 112, 115
Yurko, Bill, 132

Zundel, Ernst, 17

a PROUD PARTNER in

Campus Alberta

A book in the Campus Alberta Collection, a collaboration of Athabasca University Press, the University of Alberta Press and the University of Calgary Press.

AU PRESS
Athabasca University

Athabasca University Press | aupress.ca

Public Deliberation on Climate Change
Lessons from Alberta Climate Dialogue
Edited by Lorelei L. Hanson
978-1-77199-215-2 (paperback)

Visiting with the Ancestors
Blackfoot Shirts in Museum Spaces
Laura Peers and Alison K. Brown
978-1-77199-037-0 (paperback)

Alberta Oil and the Decline of Democracy in Canada
Edited by Meenal Shrivastava and Lorna Stefanick
978-1-77199-029-5 (paperback)

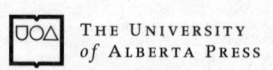

THE UNIVERSITY of ALBERTA PRESS

University of Alberta Press | uap.ualberta.ca

Trudeau's Tango
Alberta Meets Pierre Elliott Trudeau, 1968–1972
Darryl Raymaker
978-1-77212-265-7 (paperback)

Seeking Order in Anarchy
Multilateralism as State Strategy
Robert W. Murray, Editor
978-1-77212-139-1 (paperback)

Upgrading Oilsands Bitumen and Heavy Oil
Murray R. Gray
978-1-77212-035-6 (hardcover)

UNIVERSITY OF CALGARY Press

University of Calgary Press | ucalgary.ca/ucpress

Writing Alberta
Building on a Literary Identity
Edited by George Melnyk and Donna Coates
978-1-55238-890-7 (paperback)

The Frontier of Patriotism
Alberta and the First World War
Edited by Adriana A. Davies and Jeff Keshen
978-1-55238-834-1 (paperback)

So Far and Yet So Close
Frontier Cattle Ranching in Western Prairie Canada and the Northern Territory of Australia
Warren M. Elofson
978-1-55238-794-8 (paperback)